The Age of Oprah

Cultural Icon for the Neoliberal Era

Janice Peck

Paradigm Publishers

Boulder • London

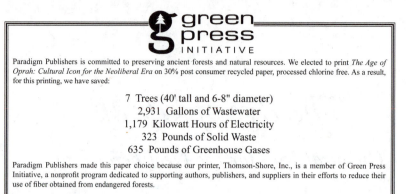

Copyright © 2008 Paradigm Publishers

Published in the United States by Paradigm Publishers, 3360 Mitchell Lane, Suite E, Boulder, CO 80301 USA.

Paradigm Publishers is the trade name of Birkenkamp & Company, LLC, Dean Birkenkamp, President and Publisher.

Library of Congress Cataloging-in-Publication Data

Peck, Janice.
    The age of Oprah : cultural icon for the neoliberal era / Janice Peck.
        p. cm.
    Includes bibliographical references and index.
    ISBN-13: 978-1-59451-468-5 (hardcover : alk. paper)
    1. Winfrey, Oprah—Criticism and interpretation.   2. Oprah Winfrey show.
I. Title.
    PN1992.4.W56P43 2008
    791.4502'8092—dc22

                                                                                    2007046103

Printed and bound in the United States of America on acid-free paper that meets the standards of the American National Standard for Permanence of Paper for Printed Library Materials.

Designed and typeset by Straight Creek Bookmakers

12 11 10 09 08   1 2 3 4 5

Contents

Preface

In April 2006, Oprah Winfrey introduced an episode of her talk show thus: "Today, a topic so taboo, so controversial, my producers had a hard time getting people to even talk about this" (*Oprah Winfrey Show,* April 21, 2006). Given the genre's reputation for sensationalism, we might assume the program was poised to reveal bizarre neuroses or sexual obsessions, were it not that the very ubiquity of TV talk shows has rendered such matters utterly mundane. Instead, the topic "so taboo" no one wanted to touch it was "class in America."

Apparently inspired by a *New York Times* series from 2005 titled "Class Matters,"[1] the show's opening segment suggested a serious treatment of issues of class inequality: clips of experts citing the growing gap between rich and poor, shots of Hurricane Katrina victims crying for help, and Winfrey's own statement that "nearly 40 percent of all the country's wealth is being held by the richest 1 percent." The fact that one of the guests was Robert Reich, U.S. secretary of labor under Bill Clinton, underscored the solemn tone as he spoke of declining manufacturing jobs, a shrinking middle class, mounting economic anxiety, and millions of Americans who are "working very hard" but still "not making it" (ibid.) in what some are now calling the "new gilded age" (Uchitelle 2007).

But even as Reich called into question the viability of the "American dream," Winfrey reaffirmed it. She referred to a *New York Times* poll where "80 percent" of those surveyed said they "believe you can go from rags to riches in America"; followed it up with a video clip of a young woman convinced she would acquire "the big house, fantasy engagement ring, and nice cars" because "if you work hard, you can achieve anything"; and finally declared herself not only "a believer in the American dream of rags to riches" but living proof of its veracity. Although Reich dutifully decreed his host "a great model for America," he pressed on with his argument that success and failure are not simply matters of individual effort. "Part of it is luck," he said, "part of it is connection, part of it is education." Winfrey replied tersely, "I don't believe in luck, Bob.... I think luck is preparation meeting the moment of opportunity.... I don't consider myself lucky at all." Nor, she added, did she consider Bill Gates lucky, even though Gates had told her he considers himself a fortunate man.

That a woman now worth $1.5 billion and ranked number 242 on the Forbes 400 list would be a cheerleader for the "American dream" is not terribly surprising (Goldman and Blakely 2007; "Forbes" 2004). That a member of the 1 percent of the population that possesses 40 percent of the nation's wealth and that, thanks to George W. Bush's tax cuts, pays income, Medicare, and Social Security taxes at the same rate as people making $50,000 to $75,000 a year can say she does "not believe in luck" is unsettling (Herbert 2005d). That millions of people in that $50,000–$75,000 bracket and below it agree with and strive to emulate her is what moved me to write this book.

Based on 2003 demographic data for Winfrey's talk show and magazine audiences, I fall squarely within her target market (Mediamark 2003). I am female, like 77 percent of *Oprah Winfrey Show* viewers, and white, like 81 percent of them. Along with Winfrey and roughly 30 percent of her show's audience, I am a child of the baby boom. I am college educated. So is Winfrey, and 50 percent of her viewers and a whopping 78 percent of her magazine readers have attended and/or graduated college. Like nearly half of her talk show audience, I am employed, and like 61 percent, I am married. Along with nearly a quarter of the show's viewers and a third of the magazine readership, my household income is in the $75,000–$149,000 range. I own a home (as do 78 percent of Winfrey's viewers) valued at $150,000–$499,000 (similar to 34 percent of them).[2] By such measures, I could easily be among the legions who regularly tune in to *The Oprah Winfrey Show* and its cable companion, *After the Show*; who read *O: The Oprah Magazine, O at Home,* and Oprah's Book Club selections; who log on to Oprah.com, line up for tickets at Winfrey's Personal Growth Summits, purchase her recommended "favorite things," and subscribe to her philosophy that we are "responsible for our lives."

Yet I am not a fan of Winfrey and never have been. I have, however, spent a great deal of time immersed in studying her wide-ranging enterprise and the vast domain of popular and scholarly treatments of her public persona, her media empire, and the "Oprah brand." Employing what Douglas Kellner terms a "diagnostic critique," which situates media texts and institutions within a social and historical context with an eye toward comprehending "the defining characteristics, novelties, and conflicts of the contemporary era" (Kellner 2003, 27), my goal in writing this book is to understand why and how Oprah Winfrey has become an icon for millions, and what that says about the times in which we live. In the process of tracing the history of her ascent from mere talk show host to cultural icon, and situating that journey in relation to the rise and triumph of neoliberalism, I hope also to contribute some knowledge to the vexed subject of "class in America."

I would like to acknowledge a number of people who have helped sustain me over the course of this project. A series of graduate students assisted me in gathering and organizing the mountains of data: my thanks to Scott Webber, Helga Tawil Souri, Dinah Zeiger, Mark Finney, Kyle Kontour, and especially Madeleine Shufeldt-Esch, whose organizational skill and careful eye made the final stages of manuscript preparation much less painful. Several colleagues and friends provided support of varying kinds: engaging in discussions about theoretical issues that extend beyond but also inform this study; reading and critiquing portions of this research; offering practical advice about the publication process; and generally encouraging me to see the project through, even as it seemed to grow ever bigger and more complicated. My thanks and appreciation to Andrew Calabrese, Mark Andrejevic, Trysh Travis, Dan Schiller, Bob McChesney, Monica Emerich, and, especially, Rick Angell, whose knowledge of history never ceases to amaze me and whose careful reading encouraged me to dig deeper in my historical comprehension of mind cure. I am grateful to the University of Colorado, which supported the research with a sabbatical leave, a fellowship in the Center for the Humanities and the Arts, where I developed my early work on Oprah's Book Club, and an individual faculty growth grant. Parts of this research have been presented at meetings of the Euricomm Colloquium, the International Communication Association, and the Association for Education in Journalism and Mass Communication. My thanks to the various respondents and anonymous reviewers who have helped me identify weaknesses and thereby strengthen my work. I am particularly appreciative of the detailed and helpful comments provided by the anonymous reader of this manuscript. Jennifer Knerr, my editor at Paradigm, and David Paletz, editor of the Media and Power series, have been immensely supportive of this project and equally patient as I grappled with bringing it to a close. Finally, I wish to thank Bill Riordan, whose notion of redemption has always been materially and collectively based, for reminding me always to look for the "dialectical intelligibility" of any phenomenon. This book is for him.

CHAPTER

⸻ I ⸻

The Age of Oprah

Culture and Politics in the Neoliberal Era

In the weeks following the September 11, 2001, attacks on the World Trade Center and Pentagon, Oprah Winfrey jettisoned the regular fare of her top-rated talk show and devoted numerous episodes to what had been reduced in media speak to "Attack on America." In addition to a lineup of victims, survivors, and heroes, the episodes included appearances by Henry Kissinger, Rudy Giuliani, Jean Kirkpatrick, Joseph Biden, Jesse Jackson, and Madeleine Albright. That a slate of political heavyweights agreed to appear on a daytime TV talk show during a time of intense national turmoil—and even thanked the host for the opportunity—testifies to Winfrey's peculiar prominence in U.S. culture. Indeed, former Secretary of State Albright told Winfrey it was up to "our leaders, both in the government and people such as you [Oprah], to keep people's attention focused on dealing with long-term problems" ("What Really Matters Now?" *Oprah Winfrey Show*, Sept. 26, 2001). The identification of Winfrey with public leadership was underscored when Giuliani invited her to host the "Prayer for America" ceremony at Yankee Stadium in New York City twelve days after the attacks (Anderson 2001). The nationally televised event featured invocations from religious figures, speeches by politicians, and patriotic and spiritual music. During the three-hour spectacle, Winfrey was joined onstage by Giuliani, former president Bill Clinton, Senators Hillary Rodham Clinton and Ted Kennedy, and Governor George Pataki—a rather unusual cohort for a TV talk show host. Four days later, Giuliani visited Winfrey's show and thanked her for hosting the ceremony, saying "people felt comforted" by her presence ("Americans Take Action," *Oprah Winfrey Show*, Sept. 27, 2001).

A decade earlier, this same woman was being chastised for harming the public, thanks to her part in the phenomenon of "trash TV," or what *Washington Post* writer Tom Shales labeled "talk rot." As talk shows proliferated in the late 1980s and early 1990s and grew increasingly outrageous in their competition for viewers, denunciations of the genre were rampant. Ralph Nader pointedly named Winfrey in his charge that talk shows appeared to "get all their ideas from the *National Enquirer*" (quoted in Mair 1994/1998, 211). Shales decried talk shows as a "daily parade [of] wackos, loonies, stars, celebrities, freaks, geeks and gurus." Referring to *The Oprah Winfrey Show*, he noted "on one of her few serious, outer-directed shows, Winfrey dealt with declining literacy among the young and the escalating crisis in American education. In promos she looked into the camera and asked, 'How dumb are we?' There's every possibility that talk rot is making us dumber'" (214). An early *McCalls* magazine feature on Winfrey described her program thus:

> What the *Oprah Winfrey Show* does best is "get-'em-in-the-gut" show topics: sexual disorders, battered wives, self-mutilation, people who hate overweight people, people who hate their bosses, how to find a man, men who pay for sex. Nothing is taboo. (Rubinstein 1987, 138)

By the end of the decade, media treatment of Winfrey had undergone a dramatic turnaround. *Time* elected her one of the 100 most influential Americans of the twentieth century. *Newsweek* christened her a "Woman of the New Century" and deemed ours the "Age of Oprah" (Clemetson 2001). A *Los Angeles Times* story on Winfrey's Personal Growth Summit tour opened as follows:

> A prophet walks among us and her name is Oprah. You know her as a television talk show host, one of the most popular, successful and recognizable women of our time. But make no mistake, she also is a teacher, sent to Earth to spread the word. Perhaps it is only fitting that a 21st century wise man is a woman and that her chief medium is electronic. Buddha might have taken to the airwaves, had they been available. Gifted with profound moral insight and exceptional rapport with her followers, Oprah Winfrey has grown from a masterful communicator into an inspirational phenomenon. (Avins 2000)

Winfrey's political cache has followed a similar trajectory. Vice President Al Gore and Governor George W. Bush jumped at the chance to appear on her show in their run for the White House (Mitchell 2000; Skinner 2000a, 2000b; Millman 2000b).[1] A wing of Ross Perot's Reform Party even floated the idea of making her its presidential candidate that year ("President Oprah" 1999). In 2003 a writer for *American Prospect* suggested that Winfrey seek an Illinois senate seat, and the following year filmmaker Michael Moore created a "Draft Oprah for President" petition on his web page, arguing that she "represents the interests of the American people" (Jones 2003; Moore 2004; Jicha 2004). Winfrey has thus far declined such invitations. As she stated in a 1995 interview, "I think I could have a great influence in politics, and I think I could get elected.... But I think that what I do every day has far more impact" (Adler 1997, 246; also "Oprah for president?" 2003). She has since decided to put that influence to the test by endorsing Senator Barack Obama's (D-IL) presidential bid. Initially deeming her endorsement more valuable than a financial contribution, Winfrey subsequently hosted an extravagant fundraiser for Obama at her vast California estate (Bellandi 2007; Sweet 2007). In December 2007 she took the unprecedented step of joining Obama and his wife Michelle for campaign rallies in Iowa and South Carolina, as the media speculated whether Winfrey's "magic touch" would "extend to the realm of presidential politics" (Jones, 2007; Gillette and Neyfakh 2007; Goodman and Blakeley 2007; Halperin 2007; Marks 2007; Mastony 2007; Noveck 2007; Seelye 2007; Zeleny 2007).

Winfrey's clout is not confined to the United States. A 2002 *Fortune* article revealed that the talk show star's perennial fiancé, Stedman Graham, had encouraged her to "partner" with the United Nations so as "to distribute her message all over the world." And although she had not spoken to anyone at the UN, Winfrey informed the reporter that when the article appeared, "they're going to be calling me" (Sellers 2002). Such hubris is not without foundation. Besides being one of the richest and most powerful figures in show business, Oprah Winfrey resides in an exclusive club of celebrities recognized worldwide by first name only. Indeed, her name has entered popular parlance as a verb and a process noun. According to *Jet* magazine, to "Oprah" someone is "to engage in persistent, intimate questioning with the intention of obtaining a confession" (Lowe 1998, 3; Mair 1994/1998, 267). In 1997 the *Wall Street Journal* lamented that political discourse had succumbed to "Oprahfication," or "public confession as a form of therapy" ("Queen Oprah" 1997). The *National Review* retorted that "Oprahfication" referred to "nothing less than the wholesale makeover of the nation, and then of the world" (Steyn 1998, 30).

Hyperbole notwithstanding, Winfrey's success and public prominence are undeniable. Reaching 46 million U.S. viewers a week and airing in 134 countries, *The Oprah Winfrey Show* has commanded the top-rated talk show spot for each of its twenty-one seasons ("Oprah Winfrey's biography" 2007). Thanks to Oprah's Book Club, which made every selection a bestseller, Winfrey has been credited with resuscitating the publishing industry, remaking the landscape of American fiction, and even saving the written word (Max 1999). Less than a year after its inaugural issue, *O, The Oprah Magazine* was selling 2.5 million copies a month and was widely considered one of the most successful magazine launches in publishing history (Wilson 2001). Winfrey's web site, Oprah.com, averages 64 million page views and more than three million unique visitors per month; 12,000–15,000 e-mails pour in every week (Oprah.com "Facts" 2006). Founder and head of Harpo, Inc., the first multimedia corporation (television, film, radio, print, and online) owned by an African American, Winfrey enjoyed a net worth in 2007 of $1.5 billion (Ulrich 2006, 190; Goldman and Blakely 2007). As *USA Today* has put it, "everything she touches turns to gold" (Wilson 2001). Or, as Winfrey herself once observed, "Money just *falls* off me. I mean it *falls* off!" (Adler 1997, 242).

George Mair predicted in his 1994 biography that Winfrey's "enormous popularity as a television talk show host will fade in the next several years" because the genre had exhausted its possibilities. Even so, he noted, she had already accomplished her mission: "She is the ultimate American success story. That a tiny, illegitimate black girl from dirt-poor Mississippi can transform herself into the richest and most powerful black woman in the world is a triumph of the human spirit and the American dream. It is a message of hope that uplifts us all" (1994/1998, 349). Mair's prediction about the show's decline was wrong, of course. Nor are we done with being uplifted by Oprah Winfrey. *The Oprah Winfrey Show* is scheduled to continue until at least the 2010–2011 season, when it will celebrate its twenty-fifth anniversary in syndication ("Oprah Winfrey signs" 2004). How are we to understand this transformation of a figure once known chiefly for her dubious distinction as "queen of television talk" (Rubinstein 1987, 137–138) into a spiritual guru, cultural heroine, and public leader whose program is a sought-after venue among presidential candidates? And what might the process of this transformation tell us about the politics and culture of our age?

A key moment in Winfrey's metamorphosis occurred the same year that Mair predicted her exit from talk TV. In January 1994—a few weeks before her fortieth birthday—Winfrey opened her show by telling viewers she intended to stop "talking about how bad things are" and start working to "bring more peace to the world" (*Oprah Winfrey Show*, Jan. 14, 1994). The occasion of this announcement was an appearance by Marianne Williamson—former nightclub singer, self-described "spiritual psychologist," occasional adviser to Hillary Clinton, "spiritual guide" for Hollywood stars, and a major inspiration behind Winfrey's own cosmology. A devotee of *A Course in Miracles* (a set of books representing "an integration of psychology and spirituality" claimed to have been "scribed by Jesus" and channeled through two New York psychologists in the 1960s [Wapnick 1989, 17]), Williamson first appeared on *The Oprah Winfrey Show* in 1992 to promote her book, *A Return to Love: Reflections on the Principles of a Course in Miracles* (1992). Thanks to Winfrey's endorsement, the book enjoyed a 34-week run on the *New York Times* best-seller list. Williamson became a recurring fixture on *The Oprah Winfrey Show* and was later recruited to write a column for *O, The Oprah Magazine* and host a program on Winfrey's satellite radio channel, *Oprah and Friends.*

Williamson's January 1994 appearance—"What is going on with the world?"— opened with television news footage as Winfrey announced that the day's topic was "how to end the violence around us." During the hour, the two women identified various social problems (crime, drug addiction, TV violence, war, child abuse, prejudice) as "the price we pay for ignoring our souls." Born of "denial," this collective neglect of soul had produced a "diseased" and "dysfunctional" society. The antidote, Williamson proposed, was a "shift in paradigm on the planet" to activate "an amazing healing force"—the "spirit of divine consciousness which is within our souls." While she prescribed various steps toward planetary "healing," from praying to participating in support groups, all were predicated on replacing "negative thoughts" with positive ones, because "our thoughts determine the experiences of our lives." Williamson pointedly accused the media of contributing to this "negativity" by imposing "societal thought forms" on "individual thought forms." An exception, she noted, was Winfrey, whose "position of power as someone who touches millions" might counter this sorry state of affairs. Winfrey enthusiastically accepted the mantle, vowing that her program would thereafter emphasize positive ideas because "our thoughts are the most powerful thing on earth." She then joined Williamson in a "prayer for the nation"—one of the earliest but by no means last times that prayer would be featured on *The Oprah Winfrey Show* ("Moral Dilemmas," *Oprah Winfrey Show*, Jan. 14, 1994).

Given that her program was then the top-rated talk show in the United States—a position it had enjoyed since its national premiere in 1986—Winfrey's decision to shift course may seem surprising. But in addition to the mounting criticism of "talk rot," there were signs Winfrey's domination of the genre was eroding. Her overall audience share was slipping as the number of talk shows proliferated. Especially troubling was competition from the likes of *Ricki Lake* and *Jerry Springer*, which was loosening Winfrey's grip on the coveted 18-to-49-year-old female market (Rosenthal 1994). In light of these industry pressures, her decision to redirect the program could be read as a business strategy to differentiate her product. Winfrey pursued the shift to more upbeat content over the objections of her executive producer, Debra DiMaio, who resigned abruptly in June 1994. Although Winfrey's ratings declined further, she justified her decision in an interview later that year, reminding the reporter that her show remained number one:

> We've made a concerted effort to move on from dysfunction to 'Let's celebrate what you feel is of value in the world'.... What we're really doing is trying to disassociate ourselves from the 'Trash Pack.' There's a whole genre of television talk shows I'm not proud to be part of and don't appreciate being lumped in with. (Lorando 1994)

The timing of the switch to "Oprah light" was fortuitous (ibid.). It exempted Winfrey from the extensively covered scandals involving the *Jenny Jones* and *Jerry Springer* shows in 1995. It spared her from the concerted assault on talk shows spearheaded that year by former Secretary of Education William Bennett and Senators Joseph Lieberman and Sam Nunn with their "Empower America" campaign. And it was the basis for a wholesale revamping of *The Oprah Winfrey Show* in 1996, which included modifying the genre's topical focus in the direction of a magazine format, adding more celebrity features, and launching Oprah's Book Club, her phenomenally successful "initiative to promote reading." Winfrey's pursuit of things upbeat continued with Oprah's Angel Network, introduced in 1997, which solicited spare change from viewers to create college scholarships and contribute to Habitat for Humanity. She unveiled "Change Your Life TV" a year later, declaring in the season premiere, "I am more dedicated than ever to try to do television that inspires us to make positive changes in our lives" ("Season Premiere," *Oprah Winfrey Show*, September 8, 1998). April 2000 brought the inaugural issue of *O, The Oprah Magazine*, described on Winfrey's web site as "another medium through which Oprah can connect with her viewers and provide possibilities for transforming their lives" (Oprah.com "Facts" 2006). Promoted as "a woman's personal growth guide for the 21st century," the magazine has been called Winfrey's "talk show in print, an Oprah bible for her millions of fans" (Kuczynski 2000b).

The use of religious terminology in connection with Winfrey has become commonplace. Fran Lebowitz in 1996 ordained Winfrey "probably the greatest media influence on the adult population. She is almost a religion." A *Los Angeles Times* article on her Personal Growth Summit was titled "Flocking to the Church of Oprah" (Avins 2000). Writing in *The Christian Century*, Marcia Nelson described Winfrey as "both pastor and best friend," her program as "an hour-long ritual," and her audience as a "congregation" (Nelson 2002; also Garrett 1998; Taylor 2002; Lofton 2006). Given Winfrey's universal name recognition and identification with popular spirituality, it is no wonder that she was recruited to host the post–September 11 "Prayer for America." That Winfrey relishes this cultural power is clear, as is evident in the official biography posted on her web site in 2001: "Oprah's legacy has established her as one of the most important figures in popular culture. Her contributions can be felt beyond the world of television and into areas such as publishing, music, film, philanthropy, education, health and fitness, and social awareness" ("Oprah Winfrey's biography" 2006).

In *Oprah Winfrey and the Glamour of Misery* (2003), Eva Illouz describes Winfrey's enterprise as a "criss-crossing of expert knowledge, multiple media technologies, and orality intertwined with multiple forms of literacy, overlapping media industries, cyberspace, support groups, and traditional charismatic authority" (5). Winfrey's appeal, she argues, "works at the interface of moral leadership, entertainment, psychology, capitalist entrepreneurship, spiritual quest, comic performance, and literature" (ibid., 212). For Illouz, this "tentacular structure" of Winfrey's multiple activities makes it "difficult to hold on to a single political or moral point of view to approach her text" (ibid., 5, 212). While I agree that Winfrey's enterprise is complex, I propose it is possible to grasp it as a unity if we keep sight of what it strives to achieve. Winfrey's rise to prominence cannot be explained solely by reference to her personal qualities or talents. That her multifaceted enterprise has resonated across an entire culture is a testament to the powerful historical roots of its appeal. Winfrey's journey from talk show queen to "one of the most important figures in popular culture" must therefore be situated in relation to other developments of which it is an integral part.

Those developments include the dramatic "growth of therapy as an institution and industry in American culture" over the past century (Epstein and Steinberg 1998,

84), particularly the explosion in the 1980s of the "recovery movement"—an amalgam of therapeutic practices, self-help groups, publications, mental health policies, and treatment programs that Elayne Rapping calls "one of the most important and telling phenomena of our day" (Rapping 1996, 8); a revived emphasis in U.S. religious sensibilities on "personal meaning" and individualized "spiritual growth" that is rooted in nineteenth century religious movements (Roof 1999, 7); the irruption in the 1980s of a national obsession with "the family" (its "values," its "dysfunction," its purported "crisis," etc.), which is increasingly held responsible for everything from the state of the economy to children's performance on math tests (B. Williams 1999, 66); and the waning of the second-wave women's movement in the face of a multifront assault in the 1980s and its subsumption by "postfeminism," which Judith Stacey characterizes as "the simultaneous incorporation, revision and depoliticization of many of the goals of second-wave feminism" (Stacey 1990b, 339).

Conditioning all of these developments is the rise in the 1980s and triumph in the 1990s of "neoliberalism"—an interlocking economic, political, and ideological project to establish a new set of rules for governing the functioning of capitalism. An "updated, and more extreme" variant of the classical liberal economic theory of Smith and Ricardo (Kotz 2003, 15), neoliberalism "begins with the premises of private property and self-interest" (Lebowitz 2004, 14) and the assumption that capitalism is an expression of both human nature and natural economic laws. Emerging in the 1980s with the elections of Ronald Reagan in the United States and Margaret Thatcher in the United Kingdom, neoliberalism was organized from the start around the goal of "transforming the role of the state in the economy" (Kotz 2003, 15). As David Kotz notes, "neoliberal restructuring" over the past two-plus decades has "entailed renouncing the use of government spending and taxing to moderate the ups and downs of the business cycle; loosening or eliminating government regulation of corporate behavior in both the domestic and international spheres; privatization of government enterprises and public responsibilities; and large cutbacks in social programs" (ibid.).

Neoliberalism is more than an economic theory, however. It comprises economic practices organized around "an imperative to remould the world to conform to an imagined ideal of perfectly working markets spread as wide and deep as possible" (Fine 2001, 8), political practices devoted to "the valorisation of free market transactions of commodities as the best way of ordering society" (Dovey 2000, 175), and ideological practices that legitimize a specific system of social relations and the forms of subjectivity amenable to it. Whether in its "monetarist" guise under Ronald Reagan or its "New Liberal" incarnation under Bill Clinton, the interconnected economic, political, and ideological practices of neoliberalism have produced a transformation of the role of government; a marked upward redistribution of wealth and decline in economic security; and a reconfiguration of class alliances to support, maintain, and legitimize a social environment of deepening inequality. In this respect, as economist

Jeff Madrick argues, neoliberal restructuring can be understood as a "social revolution" (Madrick 2002; also Hacker 2006; Uchitelle 2006).

The fact that Oprah Winfrey's road to fame and fortune has paralleled the political-economic revolution of neoliberalism is no coincidence, as this book seeks to demonstrate. Taking seriously *Newsweek*'s claim that we inhabit "The Age of Oprah," the book explores the relationship between Winfrey's ascent to a position of singular cultural authority and the larger sociohistorical and political-economic processes that have made her popular canonization possible. Rather than seeing her enterprise either as "cause" or "effect" of those processes, and hence external to them, I treat their relationship as mutually constitutive. Here I share Raymond Williams's view that cultural analysis should seek to discern "the indissoluble connections between material production, political and cultural institutions and activity, and consciousness" (Williams 1977, 80). This goal of synthesis determined the scope, objects, and method of my study, which examines Winfrey's entire enterprise (her talk show, book club, magazine, web site, personal growth tours, philanthropic activities, etc.) from the mid-1980s to the present, as well as the enormous popular and scholarly literatures on Winfrey and her media empire, and situates both in relation to major currents in American political, economic, cultural, and religious history. Starting from the position that Oprah Winfrey's appeal cannot be understood apart from the concrete historical conditions within which she has metamorphosed from "queen of talk TV" to cultural icon and public leader, the analysis employs what Douglas Kellner terms "diagnostic critique," in that it tacks back and forth between text and context with the aim of providing "critical readings of media texts" that simultaneously "illuminate the contemporary era" (Kellner 2003, 33). Combining a political analysis of Winfrey's media empire and public persona with a historical analysis of the political, economic, and ideological practices of neoliberalism that have produced and sustain "The Age of Oprah," the book proposes that tracing the history of Winfrey's enterprise since her emergence on the national scene in the 1980s provides a means by which to critically examine the intersection of American politics and culture over the past quarter-century.

The Plan of This Work

In his critical study of the history of psychotherapy, Philip Cushman (1995) writes: "Every era has a particular configuration of self, illness, healer, technology; they are a kind of cultural package. They are interrelated, intertwined, interpenetrating. So when we study a particular illness, we are also studying the conditions that shape and define that illness, and the sociopolitical impact of those who are responsible for healing it" (7). Winfrey's identification as a spiritual healer, her diagnosis of what ails us, and her prescribed cure are rooted historically in the therapeutic enterprise that emerged in the nineteenth century and was fully institutionalized in the United States by the mid-twentieth century. Debbie Epstein and Deborah Steinberg suggest that the "centrality of therapeutic discourse to the framing of the *Oprah Winfrey Show*" issues from "the increasing ubiquity of therapy as language of self and interpersonal relationships, and even as a way of life" (Epstein and Steinberg 1998, 84). Winfrey's media enterprise draws heavily on a "self-help" model of therapy with its peculiarly American belief in the individual's power to "initiate a renaissance of self, of nation, of Other" (ibid.). This promise of individual efficacy and liberation is the ground upon which Winfrey stakes her claim to "empower" her followers. It is also the basis of observers' claims that she is an "inspirational phenomenon," a public leader, and "almost a religion."

In Chapter 2, "The Therapeutic Enterprise and the Quest for Women's Hearts and Minds," I interrogate such assertions through a historical examination of the larger therapeutic enterprise—the conditions of its emergence, the process by which it acquired legitimacy and power, the problems and populations to which it has been applied, and the social and political implications of the triumph of what Ellen Herman terms "the psychological worldview" (Herman 1995, 1). I explore connections between the rise of neoliberalism, the explosion of the "recovery movement," and the proliferation of the "therapy talk show" in the 1980s by grounding these developments in the history of the therapeutic enterprise, including the fusion of psychology and spirituality in the nineteenth–century New Thought or "mind-cure" movement and its special appeal for white middle-class women. This chapter also considers the extension of a psycho-spiritual worldview into the talk show genre and the particular resonance of this cultural form for women, who comprise the majority of the talk show audience, the clientele for therapeutic services and products, and the adherents of contemporary mind-cure cosmologies. Tracing the complicated history of women's relationship to the therapeutic enterprise, I question the propensity to equate "healing" and "empowerment" and conflate paying attention to women's lives with forwarding a feminist political agenda, whether in therapeutic practices or in TV talk shows. Here I engage critically with scholars who suggest that Winfrey's program and other media productions are "empowering" and/or feminist in some way.

While Winfrey's project from the beginning has been thoroughly inflected by a therapeutic mode of making sense of the world, the configuration of self, illness, healer, and technology that drive her mission of "empowerment" has not remained static. I argue in Chapters 3 and 4 that from its national premiere in 1986 through the early 1990s, Winfrey's program was organized around the "dysfunctional self" associated with the "recovery movement," which in the mid-1980s became "a near-universal way of thinking about human troubles in the larger society" (Rapping 1996, 77). Neither the recovery movement nor the therapy talk show can be understood in isolation from the historical conditions and political-economic context in which both have flourished. Chapter 3, "Backlash Politics, the Dysfunctional Self, and the

Recovery Cure," situates *The Oprah Winfrey Show* in relation to the "Reagan Revolution"—conceived here as an economic project devoted to redistributing wealth and a political-ideological project that sought to legitimize that redistribution by reconfiguring class alliances and forging a backlash politics aimed at women, minorities, and the poor. This political backlash was orchestrated through the specter of a "crisis in the family," whereby all manner of social problems could be blamed on a purported deterioration of "family values." Increases in homelessness, poverty, female single-parent households, crime, spousal and child abuse, and so on were deemed the result of eroding personal values, which were in turn presented as fallout from a crisis of the traditional family. This diagnosis lent itself handily to notions of pathology and wellness associated with the recovery movement, which similarly conceives individual suffering largely in terms of the "dysfunctional family."

I argue in Chapter 4, "Recovery and Reaganism: The Psychologization of the Political and the Politics of Pathology," that *The Oprah Winfrey Show*'s appropriation of a recovery framework of intelligibility served to depoliticize women's struggles by translating them into individual psychological defects. This psychologization process was also extended to the show's treatment of explicitly political-economic issues, such as poverty, homelessness, welfare, and unemployment. By reducing the social to the personal and the political to the psychological, Winfrey's program echoed and helped legitimize Reaganism's backlash political agenda and its "blame the victim" ideology. Affiliating with the recovery paradigm's conception of the dysfunctional self—and its parallel in Reaganism's deficient self—Winfrey's show in the 1980s and early 1990s became a serial display of an endless supply of damaged psyches. This made her vulnerable to mounting criticism that her program deserved Tom Shales's condemnation as a "parade of wackos, loonies [and] freaks" (quoted in Mair 1994/1998, 214).

While Winfrey's decision in the mid-1990s to accentuate the positive was motivated in part by a desire to separate her program from the talk show "trash pack," the particular contours of her public makeover were decisively shaped by Marianne Williamson's brand of "psychospirituality" and Bill Clinton's therapeutically inflected "politics of meaning." These mutually reinforcing influences are the focus of Chapter 5, "Mind Cure, the Enchanted Self, and the New Liberal Covenant." In contrast to the diseased self of recovery and the immoral self assailed by Reaganism, Williamson's cosmology proclaimed the existence of an innately perfect self. This "enchanted self," whose origins lie in late-nineteenth-century American religious/spiritual movements, required neither a lifetime of "recovery" nor a lengthy regimen of discipline to become "empowered." It needed only to rediscover and esteem itself. Williamson's message of empowerment through positive thinking provided Winfrey with a new technology of healing that shielded her from the renewed assault on TV talk shows that erupted in the mid-1990s with the Jenny Jones murder scandal. Indeed, through strategic efforts at self-reformulation, Winfrey emerged from the "talk show wars" of 1995 with a reputation as the *exception* to the general debasement of the genre.

As Williamson was proselytizing for a new spiritual paradigm to activate the "healing force" of "divine consciousness," Bill Clinton was stumping for his "New Covenant"—an ensemble of policies that promised to "heal America" by igniting citizens' inner sense of responsibility (Clinton and Gore 1992, 229). Clinton's self-image as a "healer," his calculated use of spiritual and therapeutic language, and his appropriation of a communitarian "rhetoric of responsibility" (Reed 1999a, 2) meshed with Williamson's mind-cure technology of healing and provided a fertile political climate for Winfrey's public metamorphosis in the mid- through late 1990s. Chapter 5 explores Winfrey's shift to a new configuration of self, healer, and technology and its relationship to Clinton's New Democrat brand of neoliberalism. I examine the emergence and rise of New Liberalism, which, under the direction of the Democratic Leadership Council and its pre- miere presidential candidate, sought to move the Democratic Party to the right by appropriating the economic, political, and ideological practices of Reaganism. The chapter traces the common ground between Clinton's New Liberal "values politics" and Winfrey's revamped "empowerment" mission, including their parallel image makeovers in 1994–1995, when Winfrey elevated herself above the talk show "trash pack" by vowing to be "a light to the world" and Clinton ascended from the ashes of the 1994 Republican landslide to resurrect himself and the New Liberal political agenda.

Both Oprah Winfrey and Bill Clinton are portrayed as figures unusually adept at bridging the racial divide in American society. Winfrey is routinely exalted for her ability to traverse race and class lines and cultivate a majority white following by embodying what *People* magazine has called "a comfortable and unthreatening bridge between the white and black cultures" (Richman 1987, 56). Clinton's popularity among African Americans is legendary. Indeed, he has been given the somewhat startling moniker of "America's first black president" (Gray 2004, 96). Overwhelming support from blacks during the Monica Lewinsky scandal was credited with helping Clinton "weather the impeachment process" (Kim 2002, 78), and in 2004 he was inducted into the Arkansas Black Hall of Fame—the only white among sixty-two inductees (Gray 2004, 96, 97).

Chapter 6, "'Transcending Race': The Racial Politics of Oprah Winfrey and New Liberalism," explores Winfrey's and Clinton's reputed ability to "transcend race," focusing especially on their treatment of welfare and the latter's "Initiative on Race." I propose that the pair's handling of these issues is driven by the same underclass ideology that animated Reaganism, as well as by what Claire Kim calls an "emerg- ing consensus" between conservatives and New Liberals in the 1990s regarding the "problem of race" (Kim 2000, 175). As racial inequality was recast as the consequence of inadequate "personal responsibility," the "cure" revolved around changing individual attitudes and behavior rather than addressing structural political inequities. Winfrey's rise to the status of "public leader" and the New Liberal "reinvention" of the Democratic Party are implicated in, as well as expressions of, this fundamental redefinition of "the American race problem" (Kim 2000, 175). I argue that the "transcendence of race" in both cases involves a combination of downplaying the social significance of race, positing racism as a problem of the past, courting white support, and "placating blacks with largely symbolic gestures" (Kim 2002, 57).

If Winfrey's purported transcendence of race is one key to her phenomenal success, her transcendence of the "low culture" ghetto of talk TV has been equally important in her popular beatification. Central to her migration from the "trashy" to "classy" pole of the cultural hierarchy was the creation in 1996 of Oprah's Book Club. In Chapter 7, "The Oprah Brand and the Enterprising Self," I argue that Winfrey's "initiative to promote reading"—which elicited near universal praise from the print media establishment—played a pivotal role in transforming her place in the American cultural landscape. Drawing its power and prestige from the powerful ideology of literacy that equates reading with citizenship, Oprah's Book Club amplified Winfrey's proclaimed mission to "uplift, educate and empower." As Illouz notes, the "reverence for literacy" that underpins Winfrey's book club "resonates deeply with a society that makes the written word paramount not only in the ways knowledge is transmitted but also in defining moral competence" (Illouz 2003, 199).

Oprah's Book Club not only helped Winfrey distinguish herself from the talk show "trash pack," it demonstrated her appeal to an upscale "literate" market beyond the traditional TV talk show base. Accordingly, Chapter 7 also treats the book club as a key moment in the strategic creation of the "Oprah brand" in the late 1990s—the beginning of what Trysh Travis calls "an ambitious program of 'soul-branding'" organized around generating "an aura of positive feeling and receptivity" (Travis 2005, 13). Buoyed by the extraordinary success of the book club—and the legitimacy it bestowed on its namesake—Harpo, Inc. in the late 1990s became "a juggernaut of 'brand extension'" (ibid., 16). Oprah's Angel Network, Change Your Life TV, Oprah. com, Oxygen Network, Lifestyle Makeover, and the Personal Growth Summit were all part of a soul-branding strategy based on producing "new varieties of the same experience and marketing it in different media" (ibid.).

Having mastered broadcast TV, cable, movies, the Internet, and the fiction business, it was only a matter of time before the Oprah brand set its sights on the magazine industry. As David Usborne has commented, "If ever there was a brand waiting to be turned into glossy print, Oprah must be it" (Usborne 2000). Thus was born *O, The Oprah Magazine*—a joint venture with Hearst Magazines. Launched in May 2000 and described as a "bible" for "those who bow at the altar of Oprah" (Keeler 2000), an "extension of her therapeutic television show" ("Uh O!" 2000), and "a soft form of religion" (Brook 2000), the magazine delivered the affluent, professional audience with its stamp of respectability that had once eluded the "talk show queen." I propose that the creation of *The Oprah Magazine* signaled the completion of Winfrey's ascent to "cultural icon of mainstream America" (Brown 2002, 242)—at which point she was beyond reproach in the establishment media, political figures and A-list celebrities scrambled for association with her program, and her mind-cure message found its most receptive constituency among professional middle-class women.

The final chapter—"The Anxieties of the Enterprising Self and the Limits of Mind Cure in the Age of Oprah"—is a critical assessment of Winfrey's ascent to cultural icon and media tycoon and the relationship of that journey to the political and economic priorities of the neoliberal era. I consider the links between the enchanted self-inherited from nineteenth-century mind-cure movements and the "enterprising self" (Rose 1998) through which neoliberalism seeks to govern, the appeal of both configurations of self for the professional managerial sector of the middle class, and the determinate social problems to which Winfrey's technology of healing is necessarily a provisional fix.

CHAPTER

~ 2 ~

The Therapeutic Enterprise and the Quest
for Women's Hearts and Minds

The time has come for this genre of talk shows to move on from dysfunctional whining and complaining and blaming. I've had enough of people's dysfunction. I don't want to spend an hour listening to somebody blaming their mother.... I'm tired of it. I think it's completely unnecessary. We're all aware that we do have some problems and we need to work on them. What are you willing to do about it? And that's what our shows are going to be about.
—Oprah Winfrey, 1994; quoted in Adler 1997, 76

It is ironic that Oprah Winfrey's "makeover" in the 1990s from "queen of gab" to "inspirational phenomenon" would be predicated on rejecting the very thing upon which her success had been built: the outpouring of pain and trouble that constituted the primary subject matter and appeal of daytime TV talk shows. Early in her career, in fact, Winfrey countered criticisms of the genre by defending the value of making public the private miseries of women, who comprise the majority of viewers:

Many of the shows that people like Phil [Donahue] and myself get criticized for, shows like 'Women Whose Husbands Leave Them,' are female-oriented. These shows may sound sleazy, but they're not. I know because I sit there and I look at the pain these people experience every day of their lives. I also get the letters, sometimes four thousand a week, that show me that these shows are touching people. (Winfrey quoted in Mair 1994/1998, 214)[1]

Two decades before the debut of *The Oprah Winfrey Show,* Phil Donahue had pioneered the issue-oriented, audience-participation TV talk show. In 1967, when Donahue moved his Dayton, Ohio, radio call-in show to local TV, the country was undergoing political upheaval. President Lyndon Johnson had recently declined to seek reelection because of opposition to U.S. involvement in Vietnam, and many African Americans, women, and young people were calling for sweeping social changes. In contrast to celebrity-based talk shows, such as *Mike Douglas* and *Merv Griffin*, Donahue made political and social issues the focus of his program. Bringing the studio and home audience into the discussion, he laid the foundation for a new genre of talk TV that violated convention by tackling political topics with a primarily female audience when it was widely assumed in the television industry that women had no interest in politics. As he later recounted, "At the time, the male-dominated media thought there was nothing dumber than a dumb housewife. But we had women in the audience talking about politics and the Vietnam war.... We also talked about unnecessary surgery for women, homosexuality, and other topics that hadn't been discussed much on the air" (Hall 1996a). In 1973 Donahue moved to Chicago and went national. Blending his passion for politics, his focus on female viewers' concerns, and his instincts as an entertainer, he won a large, loyal audience and a reputation for being sympathetic to feminism. Said Gloria Steinem, who appeared on the show seventeen times over the years, Donahue "showed a view of the world in which women mattered" (Span 1996).

When Winfrey was hired in 1984 to host *A.M. Chicago*, a half-hour program airing opposite Donahue's show, he was the undisputed ruler of daytime talk TV. Although Winfrey was initially nervous about competing head-to-head with the "titan of talk," her fears were quickly dispelled as she proceeded to beat Donahue in the Chicago market within three months. A year later, when her program was expanded to an hour and renamed *The Oprah Winfrey Show*, Donahue moved to New York and left Winfrey to rule Chicago. In 1986 her program went into national syndication and rapidly earned the top-rated talk show spot it has maintained ever since. That same year she established Harpo Productions, Inc. and acquired ownership of *The Oprah Winfrey Show*, demonstrating early on her business acumen.

Winfrey consciously modeled her show on Donahue's. In 1987, upon receiving the first of what would become many Emmy awards, she credited him with demonstrating that "women have an interest in things that affect their lives, and not just how to stuff cabbage." Without his example, she said, "my show wouldn't be possible" (Adler 1997, 52). From the beginning, however, Winfrey differentiated herself from Donahue. In contrast to his more intellectual, journalistic, issues-oriented approach, she emphasized emotional intimacy, self-revelation, and her ability to identify with her female viewers' experiences. Indeed, Donahue attributed Winfrey's popularity to the fact that "she can dish with women better than I can; she can talk about weight and clothes and men and the real-life drama of a single woman in a more personal way than I can" (Robertson 1988).

If Donahue was the architect of the fusion of public issues and private problems that came to define the genre, it was Winfrey who moved it fully into therapeutic territory. Her skill at evoking and engaging in emotional display, coupled with on-air confessions of her personal struggles, laid the foundation for her legendary bond with her audience. *Time* magazine characterized the difference between the two hosts early on:

Few would have bet on Oprah Winfrey's swift rise to host of the most popular talk show on TV. In a field dominated by white males, she is a black woman of ample bulk. As interviewers go, she is no match for, say, Phil Donahue.... What she lacks in journalistic toughness, however, she makes up in plainspoken curiosity, robust humor and, above all, empathy. Guests with sad stories to tell are apt to rouse a tear in Oprah's eye.... They, in turn, often find themselves revealing things they would not imagine telling anyone, much less a national TV audience. It is the talk show as group-therapy session. (Quoted in Mair 1994/1998, 81)

That talk shows mine broader therapeutic currents in American culture has been widely acknowledged in popular press and academic accounts of the genre and has elicited critical attention from the psychology profession (Heaton and Wilson 1995; McKee 1995; Lamb 1989).[2] In the "therapy talk show," topics are cast in psychological terms, the majority of guest experts hail from some sector of the mental health industry, and solutions are framed within a self-help ethos grounded in "a belief in the individual's active cognition of his or her problems" (Shattuc 1997, 115). As George Mair argues,

The great attraction of ... the therapy talk show, such as the *Oprah Winfrey Show*, is that the host is going to save you, make you well, make you happy, make the hurt go away, do things for you that you can't do for yourself. Americans are obsessed with self-improvement, self-help, self-everything. It is a national fixation. No nation in the world has so many improvement courses, videocassettes, audiotapes, consultants, counselors, books, seminars, and regimes. (Mair 1994/1998, 66)

By endorsing the individual's ability to recognize and overcome her problems, talk shows have incorporated the Enlightenment equation of knowledge and power and extended it to the therapeutic equation of self-knowledge and individual "empowerment." Winfrey explicitly subscribes to that equation when she proclaims her show's mission to "enlighten" and "empower" her viewers—a view echoed in scholarly examinations of the genre. Paolo Carpignano and his colleagues argue that talk shows have contributed to the transformation of "the nature of the political" by publicizing what was previously seen as the merely "private" concerns of women (1991, 51). Corinne Squire credits *The Oprah Winfrey Show* with popularizing "aspects of black feminist thought" (1994, 76). Gloria-Jean Masciarotte (1991) suggests that talk shows "afford women the political gesture of overcoming their alienation through talking about their particular experience as women in society" (90). Such "cultural work," she argues, "is *best defined* by Oprah Winfrey" (ibid., 101), whose program provides "a reinterpretation of the marginal object into the powerful subject" (ibid., 103). Debbie Epstein and Deborah Steinberg (1998) contend that Winfrey's show "is often explicitly informed by a feminist sensibility that challenges the split between public and private, aims toward a kind of egalitarianism, and can be said to embody and generate a version of Black (liberal) feminism" (78).

In Jane Shattuc's (1997) estimation, talk shows derive their "moral power" from their aim "to build up women's self-esteem, confidence, and identity" (122). Indeed, she has argued that by representing "women's subordination in a 'man's world,'" talk shows constitute "popular TV at its most feminist" (136). Religious studies scholar Judith Martin also views Winfrey's program through a feminist lens: "I really think of Oprah as caring. If you compare her with somebody like Geraldo [Rivera], she has wealth and influence, but she uses it to empower others—and that's a big feminist thing" (quoted in Nelson 2002). Eva Illouz contends that "one of the chief contributions of Oprah Winfrey to American culture has been to draw our attention to the category of 'psychological abuse'" (Illouz 2003, 230). By mobilizing a "therapeutic narrative of suffering," Winfrey "has taken on the function of a healer ... offering a narrative of self-help and techniques of self-change" (ibid., 172, 231).

But these analyses also reveal tensions within the shows' practice. Squire comments that while "a narrative of empowerment structures each episode" of *The Oprah Winfrey Show,* the program's "repeated accounts of victimization often seem to overwhelm" that narrative as descriptions of male power "collapse in a fruitless reiteration of stories of personal suffering" (Squire 1994, 102). This recurring display of victimization is evident as well in Masciarotte's characterization of *The Oprah Winfrey Show*'s "own construction of its object: the psychosocial problems of modern living, that is, women who love too much; married cross-dressers; victims of incest, of child abuse, of spousal abuse, of substance abuse, of racial prejudice, of 'bad relationships,' of distant fathers, of overbearing mothers, of sibling order, of too much or too little sexual desire, and so on" (Masciarotte 1991, 98). Shattuc (1997) concedes that although talk shows solicit the female audience with a "veiled feminism and a consciousness of the inequalities of power" the programs ultimately "are not feminist" because they "do not espouse a clearly laid out political position for the empowerment of women" (122, 130). Epstein and Steinberg (1998) note that the "radical potential" of *The Oprah Winfrey Show* is typically undercut by "the show's problematic adherence to an 'American Dream'" (78). As Illouz (2003) observes, Winfrey's "recycling of pain into a victorious narrative of self-transformation" ultimately reflects a "failure to provide an acceptable account of 'our condition'" (233).

Talk shows are not alone in incorporating a therapeutic orientation. Therapeutic discourse can be found across an array of televisual forms, from religious programming to home shopping channels to prime-time entertainment. Public issues are increasingly framed in therapeutic terms, as is the press's treatment of those issues (Reeves and Campbell 1994). So firmly has this orientation implanted itself in American culture, according to James Nolan, that in the past fifteen years it has become institutionalized within the operation of the state. Based on an examination of civil case law, criminal justice, education and welfare policies, and political rhetoric, Nolan (1998) contends that "the state has adopted elements of the thera-peutic impulse as a new form of legitimation" (308).[3] The ubiquity of psychological explanations across broad swaths of contemporary life attests to what Philip Rieff (1966) nearly four decades ago termed "the triumph of the therapeutic" as the dominant cultural frame of understanding in American society. Joel Kovel claims "the modern era is the age of psychology" (Kovel 1980, 125) while Ellen Herman proposes that "psychological insight is the creed of our time" (Herman 1995, 1), and Epstein and Steinberg suggest that therapy, as a "language of self and interpersonal relationships, and even as a way of life," had become so pervasive in late-twentieth-century American culture "that it is virtually impossible to live in the United States without being interpellated into the therapeutic experience in some way" (Epstein and Steinberg 1998, 84).

Defining psychology not as a delimited discipline or profession but as "an em-phasis on analyzing mental processes, interpersonal relationships, introspection and behavior as a way of explaining both individual and social realities," Herman traces the historical process by which a "psychological worldview" achieved such centrality that we now take for granted that psychology "possesses worthwhile answers to our most difficult personal questions and practical solutions for our most intractable social problems" (Herman 1995, 1, 5). Philip Cushman makes similar arguments in his study of the history of psychotherapy, which, he says, has become "an unquestioned part of our world" by "develop[ing] functions in the society that are so integral to the culture that they are indispensable, unacknowledged, and finally invisible" (Cush-man 1995, 1). In the same vein, Nikolas Rose claims that psychology "has played a rather fundamental part in making up the kinds of persons we take ourselves to be" (Rose 1998, 10).

If, as Russell Jacoby claims, psychology "is deeply entangled in the social reality" (Jacoby 1975, xvii), it is important to consider the implications of that entanglement for social relations and individual experience before turning to an examination of the therapy talk show. Even as the psychological worldview promises freedom from personal suffering and all manner of social problems, it has generally refrained from examining its own role in both. Critics of the therapeutic enterprise suggest that behind its promise of liberation reside well-honed strategies of social control (i.e., "normalization"). This is the basis, for example, of Michel Foucault's criticism of the means by which medicine, the mental health professions, the penal system, and the educational apparatus have produced the "normalized" subject (Foucault 1977; 1965/1988). Drawing on Foucault, Nikolas Rose argues that since the late nineteenth century, the "intellectual and practical technologies" of what he calls the "psy disciplines" have been bound up with "transformations in the exercise of political power," in conjunction with "transformations in forms of personhood." The psychological disciplines, he contends, have "played a constitutive role in the practices of subjectification" (Rose 1998, 11, 13).

Understanding the appeal of the "therapy talk show"—and thus of the particular therapeutic project of *The Oprah Winfrey Show*—involves making visible the indispensable functions of the psychological worldview from which this cultural form draws much of its social power. The therapeutic ethos is not a monolithic concept under which all manner of concrete social phenomena can be subsumed, but a complex set of historical practices directed at ameliorating various forms of human suffering and related societal problems. That history is fraught with internal tensions and contradictions that have been conserved in Winfrey's contemporary quest to "heal" and "empower" her viewers. It is therefore necessary to take a detour through the history of the therapeutic enterprise before returning to consider Winfrey's place within it, and her relation to the intersection of psychology and government that informs the neoliberal revolution.

The Rise of the Therapeutic

The historical seeds of the "therapeutic ethos" (and the disciplines of psychology, psychiatry, psychoanalysis, and psychotherapy) were planted during the nineteenth-century rise of the corporate monopoly form of industrial capitalism—which, in conjunction with accelerated immigration and urban growth, the "managerial revolution" (Chandler 1977) with its intensified division of labor in the factory production system and resulting labor struggles and unrest, and sweeping technological innovations in production, transportation, and communications—brought dramatic changes in social relations and individual existence. The fledgling disciplines of sociology and psychology sought to establish their scientific validity and practical utility by fashioning explanations for these changes and formulating responses to public and private problems resulting therefrom.[4]

Formulated within an Enlightenment notion of progress based on the application of scientific rationality to practical problems and infused with liberal political philosophy's privileging of the individual as the building block of society, the new psychological disciplines sought to apply scientific knowledge to the treatment of individual problems in service to social order and progress. The history of the psychological disciplines is thus marked by repeated attempts to articulate the nature of the relationship between the individual and societal order. That relationship has chiefly been formulated as a linear causality, either by positing the existence of some abstract, autonomous process (e.g., "modernization," "civilization," "rationalization," etc.) to which individuals are subjected and must ultimately adapt, or by understanding the social as the sum of individual dispositions and behaviors. Societal problems are therefore seen to originate in individuals—either because people have failed to properly adjust to natural and/or inevitable historical processes independent of them, or because their aggregated personal psychological deficiencies spill over into the social realm and thwart historical progress. Therapeutic theories and practices have tended to focus on influencing individuals' emotions and behavior on the assumption that this will ameliorate social problems. Indeed, the legitimacy of the therapeutic disciplines and professions has depended on their ability to demonstrate the public relevance of their diagnosis and treatment of private problems.

One problem on which the psychological sciences trained their sights in the late nineteenth century, according to Jackson Lears, was the "collective nervous crisis" that appeared to be afflicting the "civilized world" on both sides of the Atlantic (Lears 1981, 50). Although the myriad symptoms of this modern malaise—"fatigue, incapacity, headache, insomnia, fits, convulsions, depression, dyspepsia, hypersensitivity, sexual disinterest or impotence, and obsessive, fixed ideas" (Cushman 1995, 134)—seemed to plague the U.S. and European middle classes equally, the diagnosis of its cause differed on the two continents. In the United States, physician George Beard coined the term *neurasthenia* to describe this new pathology, which he attributed to a depletion of individuals' "nervous energy" brought on by the accelerating pace and demands of a modernizing society. As Beard wrote in *American Nervousness, Its Causes and Consequences,*

> . The causes of American nervousness are complicated, but are not beyond analysis: First of all modern civilization.... The modern differ from the ancient civilizations mainly in these five elements—steam power, the periodical press, the telegraph, the sciences, and the mental activity of women. When civilization, plus these five factors, invades any nation, it must carry nervousness and nervous diseases along with it. (Beard 1881, 96)

The result was "nervous exhaustion" or "paralysis of the will" (Lears 1981, 50) that hindered a person's ability to be productive. In Europe, Sigmund Freud interpreted the same symptoms as the irruption of repressed conflict between human drives and societal norms, which surfaced as neurosis or, in extreme cases, as psychosis. For both men, the proliferation of individual psychological difficulties was detrimental to society. In Beard's case the epidemic of nervousness would hamper people's ability to perform their duties and contribute productively to the national good, while for Freud, an upswing of neurosis would lead to increased acts of violence or sexual perversity that threatened civilization.

As their diagnoses differed, so did their prescriptions. By medicalizing his patients' symptoms and locating their cause in the physical organ of the brain, Beard could construct a curative regimen that relied primarily on physiological intervention: electrotherapy, rest, mild exercise, dietary changes, medication, and "chats" based on medical education and personal encouragement (Cushman 1995, 135). Freud, in contrast, saw his patients' symptoms as veiled information about intra-psychic conflict of which they were not consciously aware. His treatment was the "talking cure," in which the patient might come to recognize the raging struggle between his/her drives and the social strictures that had driven them underground to create the unconscious (ibid., 115). For Freud, it was only through the development of insight that the patient could reconcile and rationally manage that conflict and then redirect it into nondestructive activities. In both cases, curing the ills of individuals was necessary to a well-functioning social order. Beard's neurasthenics needed to be replenished with psychic energy so as to participate effectively in the expansion of the American economic system. Freud's neurotics needed to learn how to direct their impulses in constructive ways to advance civilization. Both figures, then, constructed technologies of healing based on the adaptation of the individual to the requirements of the existing social order, and in this respect they fashioned therapies of normalization for purposes of social control. At the same time, Beard and Freud subscribed to science's ability to yield knowledge and contribute to social progress, and therefore envisioned their theories and practices as freeing their patients from ignorance and suffering.

While this tension between therapy as a means of control and therapy as individual liberation was shared by Freud and Beard—and indeed, has continued to haunt the therapeutic enterprise into the twenty-first century—their conceptions of self and technologies of healing differed in important ways. Beard considered psychological problems to be purely biological in origin: individuals were born with a specific physical capacity to store nervous energy. If society placed high demands on people's energy reserves, medical science could intervene and show them how to conserve and replenish that resource. In this model, the patient is conceived as an object of scientific knowledge and practice—a biological specimen who, through the intervention of medical expertise and techniques, could find relief from illness.

Although biology played a key role in Freud's theory, which considered sexual and aggressive drives to be inherent in human nature, Freud did not reduce mind and its pathologies to the physical properties of the brain. Rather, he believed "it was the psychological, and not the physiological, world of his patients that caused their emotional distress" (ibid., 114). Freud thus conceived mind "as a kind of interior battleground for the three modern forces of the human condition: instincts, rationality, and culture." In this diagnosis, Cushman argues, "life is a constant contest, a struggle to determine which aspect of the mind would dominate and which suffer from the consequences of submission" (ibid., 115). Freud identified these three forces within the human psyche as the id (the body's instinctual drives of sex and aggression), the superego (the internalized norms and mandates of culture/society), and the ego (reason and common sense). While he thought it necessary for the instinctive drives to be harnessed and repressed to some extent by social norms, he also believed too much repression resulted in neurosis or psychosis, which was damaging to individuals and, if widespread, to society as well. Freud's solution was to facilitate awareness of the struggle between id and superego by means of the psychoanalytic dialogue, in which patients were to apply reason to their problems and achieve insight into the hidden causes of their illness. Freudian theory thus conceived patients as subjects capable of a degree of self-knowledge, rather than objects to be manipulated by medical science. However, to the extent that Freud believed civilization "could not survive without the harnessing of the impulses" (ibid., 116), the psychoanalytical process was also directed toward this larger social goal. As Cushman notes, psychoanalysis was intended to help the individual "to know, and thus to better manage and utilize the drives through rational self-domination and creative sublimation" (ibid., 115).

The Contradictions of the Therapeutic Enterprise

Comparing the theories of Beard and Freud reveals core tensions that have characterized the therapeutic enterprise from the beginning, driving its efforts to diagnose and ameliorate individual and collective ills. Cushman characterizes the difference between Freud and Beard as issuing from the different historical contexts within which they operated:

> Where Freud saw dangerous, dark secrets and sexual or aggressive wishes, Beard saw lethargy and exhaustion; an absence of energy, enthusiasm and resolve; an incapacity to enact the proper bourgeois role. Where Freud saw the necessity of restraining and controlling the self (albeit in the least harmful and most rational and conscious manner), Beard saw the need to energize and invigorate the self, to liberate and expand it, to set the self free to work. (Cushman 1995, 137)

In Cushman's view, Freud's solution of rational self-domination was more compatible with nineteenth-century European society, where "one of the main tasks of the state was to *control* the modern populace, to ensure order and the continuity of the modern state and the capitalist economy in an area of limited resources" (ibid., 138). In the United States, in contrast, the state was more concerned with how to *mobilize* citizens "to work, take risks, settle the frontier . . . in order to ensure growth and the ongoing health of the capitalist economy." If it was to accomplish such historic tasks, the American self needed to be "repaired, expanded, and especially replenished." This was the goal of the techniques of "self-liberation" associated with Beard's therapeutic model (ibid.).

A further tension within the therapeutic enterprise involves the extent to which people's emotional disturbances and troubling behaviors are understood as physiological in origin. Beard conceived neurasthenia as a disease or malfunction of the brain that could be treated with somatic procedures. This biological model was the basis of psychiatry, which developed in the nineteenth century in conjunction with the insane asylum (Scull 1989), and of the mental hygiene movement that emerged in the United States in the early twentieth century.[5] Ironically, the hygiene movement, launched in 1908 by a former psychiatric hospital inmate, grew out of efforts to reform the inhumane treatment and gruesome conditions typical of the public asylum. Quickly commandeered by prominent physicians and psychologists, who procured federal funding for mental hospital reform and preventative education for the general public, the mental hygiene movement succeeded in defining the parameters of psychic "health" and "illness" and "normal" versus "abnormal" mental functioning. According to Cushman, "At this time, mental and emotional difficulties and disruptive public behavior became forever located in the purview of medical science" (Cushman 1995, 152). Adopting a stimulus/response model of human functioning, mental hygienists conceived psychic problems as the result of "pathogenic interactions" that could be corrected by exposure to "healthy" interactions. In this view, because deviant social behavior was the result of illness, it could be eliminated through medical treatment. Joel Kovel (1980) contends that because mental hygiene reified the mind as a repository of "healthy" or "pathological" material (80, 81), therapeutic practice involved "dredging" the brain of psychological "dirt" so as to produce a "sanitized unconscious" (Cushman 1995, 152).

This mechanistic conception of mind, which "conceived of emotional problems as being in the same category as physical illness" (ibid., 153), more readily appropriated the mantle of medical science than did the Freudian view of mind as a site of struggle between instincts, culture, and reason. In proposing that mental health could be quantified and measured, the hygienist movement also won the endorsement of the state. During World War I, the U.S. government funded psychological research, expanded university training programs in psychology and psychiatry, and initiated public education campaigns based on the hygienist model of mental health. The growth of experimental psychology after the war, with its quest to discover the "natural laws" governing the human psyche, further strengthened this mechanistic, biology-based conception of mind, which continues to be a powerful strand of the contemporary therapeutic enterprise.

A final tension in the history of the therapeutic enterprise is the extent to which society itself is called into question in theorizing the sources of individuals' emotional distress and the means by which their suffering might be allayed. The contrast of Beard and Freud is instructive. Although Beard saw the depletion of energy that led to nervous exhaustion as due in part to societal demands associated with "modernization," he considered these changed social conditions as given—a natural consequence of historical progress to which individuals would of necessity adapt. Psychiatry and the mental hygiene movement shared Beard's acceptance of existing social arrangements and sought to help patients reintegrate as functional units of that order. Beard imagined that scientific/medical knowledge could devise techniques of healing to bring individuals into harmony with the requirements of society. In his therapeutic model, neither society nor the individual are marked by internal division or conflict; to the extent that they are temporarily out of sync, it is simply a matter of undertaking the necessary physiological and behavioral adjustments. Further, he assumed that individuals would welcome such adjustments insofar as they were rational beings who acted in their own interest, and the sum of such rational beings constituted a well-ordered society.

Freud similarly viewed "civilization" as necessary, but he was more cognizant of its costs. Despite his belief that unfettered human instincts were a threat to social order, he was critical of societal norms that were unduly repressive of the individual psyche. He publicly criticized Victorian sexual morality on these grounds, for example, and even famously commented in *The Future of an Illusion* that "a civilization which leaves so large a number of its participants unsatisfied and drives them into revolt neither has nor deserves the prospect of a lasting existence" (Freud 1964, 15–16). Although Freud ultimately came down on the side of civilization at the expense of the individual, his theory undermined two of the most cherished premises of liberal ideology: the notion of the "'independent,' free, rational individual" and the assumption that society reflects the activities of the aggregate of such individuals. Against this "illusion of self-determination," Richard Lichtman argues, Freud posited "the necessary warfare of each with all, the inherent destructiveness of social existence, and the unalterable opposition between the irrational individual and the repressive social order" (Lichtman 1982, 110). By demonstrating through his clinical practice "how this individual-social antagonism is reproduced *within the individual* and reproduced throughout social life," Freud revealed "a reality that operated 'behind the backs' of unsuspecting individuals" (ibid.).

But if Freud's psychoanalytic theory destabilized powerful assumptions about both the individual and society—in particular, exposing the fallacy of individual autonomy—it suffered from inherent limitations as social critique because it posited as eternal and universal what are actually historical phenomena. Freud's assumption of a fundamental conflict between individual and society "led him to reify his insights and to attribute either to biology, physics, or universal anthropology what was, in fact, the precipitate of bourgeois social relations" (ibid., 131). That is, he "lacked a theory of the social construction of the individual unconscious" and therefore imagined that he had discovered the eternal essence of the individual psyche (ibid., 263). Because Freud believed that the individual/society opposition emanated from "the fixed nature of individuals" and conceived civilization as *essentially antagonistic and repressive*," it followed that "no particular social or political transformation can do more than modify the most extreme instances of its pathology" (ibid., 110). Psychoanalysis thus ended up legitimizing existing social arrangements insofar as it seeks to "bring to consciousness what had previously been repressed" so as to "reconstitute the rebellious inclination by introducing it into the fabric of normal, acceptable relationships" (ibid., 170).

The Marriage of Psychology and Mind Cure

To the extent that Freud's vision of the individual/society antagonism gave the lie to the idea of the self-determining individual—and to the notion that society is the realm for the indefinite expansion of individual freedom—his theory would prove troubling when it crossed the Atlantic. Psychoanalysis's successful migration to the United States involved purging its tragic undertones and refashioning it into what Shattuc calls "the self-determination model of American psychology" (Shattuc 1997, 115). The American reformulation of Freud was conditioned by the encounter between psychology and an ensemble of therapeutic/religious movements that developed during a period of religious turmoil in the late nineteenth century. Variously labeled "mind cure," "New Thought," positive thinking, or "abundance therapy," all, according to William Leach, renounced "negative thinking" and evinced "the American conviction that people could shape their own destinies and find true happiness" (Leach 1993, 227). A key figure in the historical emergence of mind cure was Phineas Quimby, who proposed that emotional and physical disease were the result of incorrect ideas originating outside the self. Treatment involved "correcting the patient's 'mistaken' ideas" so as to release the universal, spiritual truth that resided within (Cushman 1995, 124). Central to Quimby's teaching was that "the single most common cause of illness was the mistaken belief that the material conditions of the world controlled individual lives and that the opinions of others, such as the moral standards of a community or the rules of a religion, should determine or even influence individual behavior" (ibid.). By renouncing the power of external conditions, believers would gain access to the "wisdom and well-being of the supreme force" dwelling within them (ibid., 124–125).

After Quimby's death in 1866, his teachings were taken up first by Christian Science founder Mary Baker Eddy, and then by the New Thought or positive thinking movement. The proliferation of these new spiritual/therapeutic movements, according to Philip Rieff, heralded the birth of the "therapeutic ethos" that made the quest for an "intensely private sense of well-being" an end in itself "rather than a by-product of striving after some superior communal end" (Rieff 1966, 261). In *No Place of Grace* (1981), Jackson Lears argues that as the quest for well-being turned inward under the influence of these spiritual therapies, it narrowed in scope and focused increasingly on the individual's "immediate emotional requirements" (55). In so far as all varieties of mind cure preached that wellness "was to be found in *liberation* of one's interior," they were predicated on an understanding of the inner self as "inherently good, potentially saturated in spirituality, and capable of controlling the external world" (Cushman 1995, 118). Believing that emancipating this already perfect interior would lead to personal and societal well-being, the new mind-cure therapies denied any resistance on the part of material reality to individual desire. Thus, Cushman argues, mind cure's founding doctrine of "self-contained individualism" and its "extreme belief in

... the powers of the mind over personal circumstances" led it to ignore "sociopolitical causes of personal suffering" (ibid., 67–68).

As the various strands of mind cure proliferated in the late nineteenth and early twentieth centuries, taking root especially among white middle-class women in urban areas, they attracted the attention of William James. In *The Varieties of Religious Experience* (1902), James suggested that these emerging religious movements, being more attuned than traditional religion to contemporary developments in U.S. society, constituted America's "only original contribution to the systematic philosophy of life" (quoted in Cushman 1995, 137–139; James 1902, 284). The contemporary appeal of mind-cure principles—whether on *The Oprah Winfrey Show* or elsewhere—owes much to the encounter between New Thought and psychology in the early twentieth century. Characterizing both as "discourses of the self," Beryl Satter argues that distinctions between them "began to blur" as New Thought writers increasingly adopted psychological terminology (Satter 1999, 239). Rather than conceiving psychology as a modern, scientific surpassing of New Thought's outmoded metaphysics, it is more accurate to say "the two evolved somewhat in tandem, with a constant mutual influence. Indeed, the meaning of psychology for Americans cannot be fully understood without the background of New Thought" (ibid., 240; see also Caplan 1998, 150–152).

Thanks to this intertwined history, portrayals of psychology and psychoanalysis in popular media have borne traces of New Thought principles from the beginning. If the discipline of psychology has "forgotten or written out" of its official history this early relationship with New Thought in order to "be seen as a science and not associated with religion," the appropriation of elements of psychology stamped New Thought with a seal of scientific credibility, historical relevance, and cultural resonance in a self-consciously "modern" world. (Manning 2000). As we will see in subsequent chapters, this fusion of psychology and mind cure has proven remarkably resilient and has provided the foundation of Winfrey's empowerment mission in the late twentieth century. In fact, Kathryn Lofton suggests, "Had Winfrey emerged in the mid-nineteenth century, she most certainly would have been incorporated into William James' roster of spiritual heroes in *The Varieties of Religious Experience*" (Lofton 2006, 601).

The Institutionalization of the Psychological Worldview

Less than a decade after Freud's inaugural visit to the United States in 1909, according to Kovel, "psychoanalysis in America had been near-totally accommodated to the categories of mental hygiene" and the American Psychoanalytic Association had become "a medically-dominated field" (Kovel 1980, 90–91).[6] Counter to Freud's view that the struggle between id and superego was interminable, the fledgling field of American psychoanalysis envisioned bringing the shadowy unconscious fully into the light where it could be sanitized and thoroughly sublimated into socially productive pursuits. Kovel notes the compatibility of this hybridized "hygienic psychoanalysis" with the concomitant rise of scientific management, as well as its further accommodation to the corporate order in the 1920s "with the discovery that the new psychology could be used as a key instrument for the shaping of desire in the age of consumerism" (ibid., 91). Thus, in the "Americanized version of psychoanalysis, Freud's breathtaking insights into the psychological depths became instantaneously banalized" (ibid., 90).

The Americanization of psychoanalysis continued with the development of "ego psychology" by Heinz Hartmann, Anna Freud, and others in the 1940s and 1950s. Described by Cushman as "the most conservative mid-century adaptation of Freudian drive theory" (1995, 186), ego psychology reformulated Freud's id/superego/ego triad by privileging the ego and making it relatively independent of the instincts and culture. In contrast to Freud, who exposed the ego's physiological and social foundations and thus "unearthed the objective roots of the private subject" (Jacoby 1975, 26), ego psychology rejected the very idea of such determinate foundations by equating the ego with the "self" and carving out a "conflict-free" zone in which the ego operated free of pressure from the irrational id and unyielding superego. The goal of therapy was to strengthen and expand the ego's terrain of mastery so as to facilitate the individual's smooth assimilation into society. As Hartmann wrote, ego psychology sought "to help men achieve a better functioning synthesis and relation to the environment" (1958, 81).

In Cushman's view, ego psychology's conservatism issues from its rejection of conflict and its emphasis on individual adjustment: "The theory proceeded by assuming that it is proper to adapt and conform to social norms and social expectations. Because the social world was considered apolitical, and its demands and requirements universal, ego psychology was free, under the banner of objective science, to develop a rationale for social conformity and political compliance" (1995, 186–187). Ego psychology's institutional success and public popularity stemmed from its fit with the cultural and political climate of the United States in the 1940s and 1950s. By eschewing Freud's emphasis on conflict and antagonism and turning the ego into a "thing" that could be made the object of scientific study and intervention, ego psychologists solidified their professional legitimacy: "They had an improved, medicalized language to describe and justify their work, and they had a way to discuss not only neurosis but also 'normal' mental functioning, and thus a justification for their profession's involvement in many aspects of everyday life, such as human development, family relations, schools, and the workplace" (ibid., 190–191).

In the immediate post–World War II period "the mental health industry began its great boom" (Kovel 1980, 93). By the 1950s, according to Ellen Herman, the psychological worldview was thoroughly institutionalized. The alliance of the state and the mental health professions that began during World War I was cemented during the second world war as the crisis nature of wartime "offered psychologists unprecedented opportunities to demonstrate the practical worth of their social theories, human sciences, and behavioral technologies in making and shaping public policy" (Herman 1995, 5). Herman documents the process by which psychological experts became central to public policy formation in the postwar decades and "decisively shaped Americans' understanding of what significant social issues were and what should be done about them" (ibid., 6) in areas ranging from national security and Cold War politics to problems of poverty, race relations, and gender conflict. A key aspect of this institutionalization was psychology's shift from attending to "deviant" individuals and social groups and toward expanding "the market for therapeutic services among normal individuals" (ibid., 258). That shift was aided by the National Mental Health Act of 1946, the creation of the National Institute of Mental Health in 1949, and the 1955 National Mental Health Study Act, and by the Ford Foundation's generous support of behavioral research in psychology and related social sciences.

Increased government and foundation funding paved the way for a large-scale expansion of public mental health services and a surge in programs to train mental health professionals. Herman notes that between 1940 and 1970, the number of psychiatrists and psychologists in the United States "climbed astronomically" (ibid., 2). During that period, membership in the American Psychological Association grew by 1,100 percent, while the American Psychiatric Association's membership increased 760 percent (ibid., 2–3). Such growth continued into the 1990s. The United States boasted some 80,000 clinical social workers in 1990. By 1993 the American Psychological Association had approximately 75,000 members and the American Psychiatric Association claimed more than 38,000 (ibid., 3). The mental health industry expanded accordingly. Private treatment centers quadrupled between 1978 and 1984 (Peele 1989, 126) while profit-making psychiatric hospitals doubled in the years between 1984 and 1991 (Reeves and Campbell 1994, 40).

The number of Americans seeking psychological help followed this growth pattern. In 1960, 14 percent of the population had "sought therapeutic assistance for problems they defined in psychological terms" (Herman 1995, 2). By 1976 that number had increased to 26 percent, and by 1990, one-third of the population had received some kind of mental health service (ibid.; VandenBos, DeLeon, and Belar 1991, 442). The self-help industry also expanded dramatically in the 1980s. A 1988 Gallup survey found that one in three adults had purchased a self-help book (Wood 1988, 33). By 1990 some 15 million Americans were attending 500,000 "recovery" groups (Jones 1990, 16) and there were "close to 300 recovery book stores in the United States"—an increase of over 100 percent from the previous year (Rivkin 1990, 26, quoted in Simonds 1992, 240). Finally, a national survey published in 1994 in the *Archives of General Psychiatry* indicated that 48 percent of Americans had suffered from and sought help for a mental disorder at some point in their lives (Survey 1994).

Herman contends that the key period of the institutionalization of the "psychological worldview" occurred between 1945 and 1970 as "the federal government moved toward methodically governing the mental health of ordinary U.S. citizens, those ordinary citizens moved toward enthusiastically consuming psychotherapeutic services, and psychological experts moved to solidify their authority over every aspect of individual and social life implicated in the manufacture of normality and psychological well-being" (Herman 1995, 274).

Cushman argues that the phenomenal expansion of the psychotherapeutic enterprise in the United States suggests it "is so accurately attuned to the twentieth-century cultural frame of reference that it has developed an intellectual discourse and provides human services that are crucial, perhaps indispensable to our current way of life" (Cushman 1995, 6). From a functionalist perspective, this merely reflects the parallel path of individual and societal development. Such a perspective, however, fails to question the political implications of the historical rise of the therapeutic enterprise, which, in its focus on alleviating individual malaise, does not question its own place in the social conditions responsible for that suffering in the first place. It is from this latter stance that I consider the incorporation of the therapeutic project by *The Oprah Winfrey Show* and its special resonance for her predominantly female following.

The Therapeutic Quest for Women's Hearts and Minds

The therapeutic enterprise has from the beginning held particular significance for women. In his study of the late-nineteenth century–United States, Lears notes that the new "nervous ailments" appeared to disproportionately afflict educated business and professional men and their wives in the urban hearts of the industrial capitalist world. Although some, like Beard, believed that the striking increase in "nervousness" was a universal cultural infirmity of the age, others "dismissed neurasthenia as a spurious leisure-class complaint, confined primarily to society ladies who were either too coddled or too dissipated to shoulder their duties as wives or mothers" (Lears 1981, 51). Middle- and upper-class women became special objects of concern during this period, as they seemed to be stricken with an "epidemic" of "hopeless invalidism" (Ehrenreich and English 1978, 105). Whether or not women of this class stratum were more predisposed than their working-class counterparts to fall ill, they were certainly more likely to receive professional attention and more able to follow the typical "bed rest" prescription. Beard and fellow medical and psychiatric professionals threw themselves into diagnosing and treating the new ailments to which these women were prone: "hysteria," "sick headache," "nervous prostration." Given their proclivity for physiologically based explanations of emotional ills, they sought causes in women's biology—in particular, their reproductive organs.

Cushman suggests that the "epidemic" of nervous maladies among middle- and upper-class American women in the Victorian period can be read as a socially accept-able response to the narrow confines of their prescribed gender role. To the extent that women found those confines intolerable, but could not "articulate their anger and resistance"—or at least not as *political* complaints against the configuration of gender"—their "reactions would show up in forms that were accessible within the Victorian horizon of understandings: as somatic symptoms" (Cushman 1995, 103). Because most male doctors and psychiatric advisers accepted as natural the gender roles of their time, they failed "to make the connection between the sociopolitical restrictions from which their female patients suffered and their bizarre physical symptoms." The result, Cushman argues, "was the development of a new healing technology, an arsenal of healing techniques that did not address the moral framework and political structures that shaped women's maladies" (ibid., 104).

Freud was as myopic as Beard in his interpretation of women's neurotic symptoms and equally prone to take the particular contours of Victorian gender relations as reflecting universal features of male and female sexuality. Jessica Benjamin contends that Freud took for granted women's subordination to men because he conceived "the male as the model of the individual" (Benjamin 1988, 184) and made women's inferiority a fact of human nature. In Richard Lichtman's view, this led Freud to "reduce the social subordination of women to a category of nature and present a politi-cally structured relationship of domination and subservience as a natural anatomical fact" (Lichtman 1982, 169). Thus, Cushman notes, Freud assumed that "the power relations of gender in the Victorian family" was simply an expression of the eternal Oedipal drama (Cushman 1995, 114).[7]

Significantly, it was during this period that the New Thought movement exerted a powerful attraction for white middle-class women precisely because it took into account the "emotional and cultural tensions" confronting them in late-nineteenth-century America (Satter 1999, 240). Besides comprising the majority of students and followers of the various branches of the movement (e.g., Christian Science, Divine Science, Spiritual Science, Mental Healing, Mind Cure), women were also prominent as leaders, healers, teachers, and authors. As Satter notes, the appeal of New Thought for women issued from the tensions connected to late-Victorian ideals, which "were more problematic for white women than for white men." In fact, New Thought was at times referred to as the new "woman's religion" (ibid.).

While the failure to situate personal suffering within a "broader, more encompass-ing perspective on the historical and economic forces that frame and shape them" (Cushman 1995, 2) has been built into the theoretical assumptions and clinical practices of the therapeutic enterprise in general, it has had particularly deleterious consequences for women. In taking the individual psyche as their object of analysis, therapeutic techniques focus on remedying individual "dysfunction" through per-ceptual, behavioral, and physiological change. Insofar as individual problems are seen as either the effect of external, natural, and unchangeable forces or as the cause of societal problems, treatment is aimed at helping the patient adjust to those forces and/or to develop self-control over problematic tendencies so as to be a "productive" member of society. In a social order founded on inequitable gender roles and relations, the treatment of women's problems will be directed at helping them become more "healthy" by adjusting to their own domination. This would become the basis of the feminist critique of psychology and psychotherapy that emerged from the second wave of the women's movement in the 1960s and 1970s.

Assumptions about the natural basis of male power and independence and female dependence and weakness were firmly entrenched in the therapeutic professions by the mid-twentieth century. Herman argues that after 1945, the attention of psychological experts "shifted decisively toward the female gender" (Herman 1995, 277). In the late 1940s and 1950s, "blaming women for everything from children's misbehavior to the alarming state of Western civilization became a public ritual among experts" (ibid., 279). This obsession with women's psychological deficiencies was organized along two interrelated axes: women were charged with producing weak, dependent male offspring who grew into feminized men and, conversely, with valuing their own independence over their family obligations and becoming masculinized women. Brett Williams documents the demonization of women by the mental health industry in the 1950s, where mothers were held responsible for causing in their children both schizophrenia and the "disease" of homosexuality (B. Williams 1999, 71–72). In light of such judgments, it is not surprising that feminists in the late 1960s took on the psychological professions and "accused psychological theories and practices of contributing more than their fair share to the creation and maintenance of sexual inequality" (Herman 1995, 279; see also Showalter 1987).

The feminist critique of the therapeutic enterprise was extensive, from publications to public demonstrations to the creation of separate (and often separatist) caucuses and associations by women in the psychological professions. But if feminism denounced the psychology establishment for perpetuating sexism and naturalizing gender inequity, it did not reject the psychological worldview in general. As Herman points out, "the intellectual and clinical traditions rooted in the career of postwar psychological expertise inspired early feminist theory and mobilized feminist activism" (Herman 1995, 290). Although feminists declared war on psychological experts, they were susceptible to incorporating a "psychological sensibility" (ibid.) because their aspirations for women's liberation had certain parallels with the values espoused by the humanistic psychology movement that took root in the 1960s counterculture. Although humanist or existentialist psychology traces its birth to the late 1940s, its real gains occurred in the 1960s. Proposing itself an alternative to the determinist tendencies of behaviorism and traditional psychoanalysis, humanist psychology continued the American revision of Freud initiated by ego psychology. Rejecting the view that individuals were products of biological reflexes or instinctual drives, figures such as Gordon Allport, Carl Rogers, and Abraham Maslow insisted that human beings were motivated by a search for self-actualization. The "core imperatives" of the theory, Herman writes, revolved around individuals' quest "to grow, to become, and to realize full human potential" (ibid., 265). In contrast to Freud's notion of the ineradicable tension between an innately destructive human nature and an inherently repressive civilization, humanist psychology promoted "a benign conception of human nature" (ibid., 268) coupled with a vision of a society of abundance in which self-realization was eminently achievable.

Jacoby argues that if ego psychology was "neo-Freudian" in that it elevated the ego but retained the concepts of the id and superego, humanist psychology was "post-Freudian" in that it rejected entirely the existence of a dark psychic interior. Whereas Freud had "cast doubt on the autonomous subject," post-Freudians sought "to assuage any suspicion that the individual is not the master of the house" (Jacoby 1975, 46). Freud's focus on "the neurotic and the sick" was abandoned by humanistic psychology in favor of "the normal and the cheerful" (ibid., 50)—the "self-actualizers" who were "invested in their own psychological growth and development" (Herman 1995, 271). Humanist psychology thus purged the therapeutic project of all negativity and replaced it with an optimistic view of both the individual and society (see also Turkle 1980). In Jacoby's assessment, humanistic psychology "only affirms and confirms" (1975, 50) and "suggests liberation now without the sweat and grime of social change" (ibid., 47). In this respect, it has significant affinities with New Thought.

To the extent that humanist psychology positioned itself as a critical alternative to the psychotherapeutic establishment, presented its theory as a model of human liberation, and echoed countercultural values, it could be appended to feminist concerns. Both perspectives made subjective experience the cornerstone of theory and "emphasized introspection, emotional self-exposure, and the sharing of personal, experiential testimony" as the means by which individuals might achieve insight into their lives and problems (Herman 1995, 298). Feminists reasoned that "it was impossible to separate women's complaints about their lives and aspirations for change from an overall assessment of women's status as a gender category" (ibid., 300). Accordingly, consciousness-raising techniques encouraged women to use their personal experience to interrogate larger issues of gender domination. However, making women's subjective experience the foundation of theory and political practice also "confirmed the centrality of 'psychological oppression' to women's subordinated status and 'psychological liberation' to a vision of sexual equality" (ibid., 297), contributing to a "confusion between psychological and political change" (ibid., 300). Although many feminists were aware of the danger of turning the political quest for social equality into an individual search for mental health, the fact that the women's movement internalized premises of the psychological worldview made it vulnerable to the conflation of the political and the psychological. As the psychotherapeutic professions began to respond to and incorporate feminist concerns in the 1970s, the political edge of the latter was blunted. The result, Herman argues, was a hybridization of feminism and psychology that "reasoned that anything that was 'healing' and respectful must be both therapeutic and good for women" (ibid., 302).

Such reasoning falls back into the methodological individualism that defines the therapeutic enterprise, where healing is based on ameliorating individual suffering rather than changing structural relations of domination and subordination. Feminism hoped to expose the structural basis of gender inequity by encouraging women to explore their personal pain as a prerequisite to interrogating society. But because suffering is lived at the level of individual experience, therapy's intervention at that level can be powerfully seductive—perhaps more so than the institutional analysis mandated by feminism. Certainly therapy's individually based solutions seem more immediately achievable than feminism's call to transform the world. Thus, as Herman states, "The culture of psychology [has] not [been] adequately understood as a competitor for women's hearts and minds, peddling adjustment while feminism pledged genuine change" (313).

Elayne Rapping explores this competition for women's allegiance in her analysis of the "complicated interrelations between feminism and recovery" (Rapping 1996, 9). Although the "recovery movement"—which, I argue in subsequent chapters, served as the dominant frame of intelligibility in *The Oprah Winfrey Show* in its early years—is a product of the 1980s, its roots lie in the creation of Alcoholics Anonymous (AA) in the 1930s. Founded by two white middle-class professional men, AA was conceived as a lay fellowship based on Protestant religious principles through which chronic drinkers might support each other in overcoming their dependence on alcohol. Rather than seeing excessive drinking as an emotional or moral defect, AA defined alcoholism as a physiological response of certain individuals who were "allergic" to alcohol. The effect of this "allergy" was an inability to drink in moderation and an overwhelming desire to drink in excess. Hence, alcoholism was defined as a "disease" of addiction. Because this physiological propensity could not be altered, alcoholism was seen as a permanent, incurable illness. The only treatment was complete abstinence, which could be maintained only by ongoing support from fellow addicts committed to a strict set of guidelines for the never-ending battle against the temptation to drink. Those guidelines, of course, became the "12 Steps" of AA. Following those steps became known as "working the program"—a lifelong undertaking insofar as being alcoholic was not a description of one's behavior but of one's being. AA thus followed the path established by Beard, psychiatry and mental hygiene of conceiving psychological problems as a biological disorder.

Central to the 12 Steps of AA—and of all of its successors and offshoots—are two key premises: that overcoming addiction is predicated on admitting to being "powerless" over whatever one is addicted to and, in light of that impotence, turning one's "will and life" over to a "Higher Power" (i.e., God in some form). As Rapping (1996) notes, these foundational principles constitute a key contrast between the recovery movement and feminism. Although both begin from an acknowledgment of individual powerlessness, AA and its progeny consider this a permanent quality of the addicted person, while feminism sees it as the consequence of historically produced relations of gender inequality. The recovery model mandates embracing one's powerlessness as a prerequisite to receiving help from an external metaphysical force. Feminism, in contrast, proposes that women act collectively to change inequitable social arrangements and, through that essentially political process, reclaim their independence and power.

This difference would become increasingly blurred in the 1980s as the AA model of addiction and 12-Step technology of healing were extended to a wide array of individual behavior and social problems. For the first several decades of its existence, Alcoholics Anonymous membership was almost exclusively male. In the 1960s, the 12-Step model was expanded to drug abuse and food "addiction" with the creation of Overeaters Anonymous, which attracted significant numbers of women. The real growth of the recovery movement occurred in the 1980s, however, with AA's "success in promoting its ideas about 'disease' as the root of emotional dysfunctions which lead to compulsive behavior" (Rapping 1996, 76). As this disease model was extended to problems of family and gender relationships, women were drawn in large numbers to the proliferating 12-Step fellowships devoted to various kinds of "emotional addiction." One of the most influential of those new fellowships, the "Women Who Love Too Much" groups that grew out of Robin Norwood's book of the same name, was prominently featured in Winfrey's first season and definitively shaped the show's treatment of relationship conflicts. Recovery groups, publishing houses, books, periodicals, and bookstores also increased dramatically in response to this trend (Jones 1989, 1990; Rivkin 1990; Rapping 1996). By the 1990s, the AA-based model of addiction and recovery through abstinence and fellowship had been fully institutionalized within the medical and psychotherapeutic professions, government mental health policy, schools, churches, insurance providers, and business. As Rapping argues, it "has become a near-universal way of thinking about human troubles in the larger society and has, indeed, become widely sanctioned and invoked by the media and other social institutions, from the medical to the religious to the corporate" (Rapping 1996, 77).[8]

Along with the striking growth of the recovery movement, the 1980s and 1990s brought a renewed campaign by psychiatry to treat psychological distress as a biological malfunction. Although this physiological approach had defined psychiatry from its birth, the development of a series of new psychoactive drugs in the 1950s—the so-called drug revolution in the field—invigorated the psychiatric profession's quest to locate emotional disturbances in physical causes (Treacher and Baruch 1980, 146). By the mid-1960s, Peter Breggin contends, "psychiatry was well on the way toward its wholesale conversion to biochemical and genetic theories and to technological interventions, such as shock and electrotherapy" (Breggin 1991, 10). Over the next three decades, the "revolution in psychiatry" gained steam as more and more forms of unhappiness were attributed to "genetic aberrations" or "biochemical imbalances" and patients were increasingly "considered biologically and genetically defective," rather than beset by life difficulties (ibid.).[9] Thus, the nineteenth-century equation of the human mind with the physical organ of the brain was alive and well more than a century later. As Breggin writes, "This [equation] has become psychiatry's main promotional theme, aimed at selling biological and hospital psychiatry to the public and at garnering more money for research into the brain as the seat of personal, social, educational, and political problems" (ibid., 11).

These intertwined strands of the therapeutic enterprise have progressively claimed a powerful grip on the hearts, minds, and bodies of women. According to Breggin, "far more women than men develop 'careers' as mental patients, spending substantial portions of their lives on psychiatric drugs, in psychotherapy, or in mental hospitals" (ibid., 323). Women are diagnosed as depressed by a rate of two to one over men (ibid., 324), two-thirds of electroshock patients are women (ibid., 193), and women are lobotomized "at least twice as often as men" (ibid., 319). Scull similarly notes that "women are consistently found to be more prone [than men] to neurosis and manic-depressive symptoms and are much more likely to be taking psychoactive drugs" (Scull 1989, 271). In the early 1980s, women comprised nearly two-thirds of adult clients of community mental health facilities, psychiatric hospitals, and outpatient clinics, and an estimated 84 percent of private psychotherapy patients were female (Greenspan 1983, 5). By mid-decade, women were the target of more than two-thirds of annual prescriptions for psychoactive drugs. Between 1980 and 1985, women were estimated to have received 71 to 83 percent of prescriptions for antidepressants (Russo 1985, 20–21). Studies in the late 1980s found that women were also more likely than men to buy self-help books, especially on subjects of family, relationships, stress, and anxiety (Starker 1988; Simonds 1992, 23). And, according to publishing industry analysts, women were responsible for 75 to 85 percent of sales of "recovery" books by the end of the 1980s (Jones 1990, 20).

As the 12-Step–based recovery movement took off in the 1980s, so did its interpretation of women's unhappiness. Rapping argues that rather than merely replacing feminism's analysis of women's suffering, the recovery movement actually owes its success to feminism, which supplied "its main sources of power, the main reason why women are drawn to it" (Rapping 1996, 10). In her view, second-wave feminism succeeded in raising awareness of how sexism was built into societal institutions and woven into the fabric of social relationships and individual consciousness. The political changes the movement helped instigate constituted a "revolution that was begun and then thwarted, or at least stalled in its ability to deliver the goods we optimistically anticipated in the sixties" (ibid., 139). To the extent that the women's movement did partially succeed, however, feminist ideas have been "widely assimilated into the mainstream" of American culture (ibid., 153) and continue to inform the "demands of women and girls for changes in their social and personal conditions" (ibid., 139). By redefining women's problems as psychological rather than political in origin, Bette Tallen argues, the recovery paradigm "addresses many of the same concerns that we as feminists address, but without the high personal price of challenge and criticism" (Tallen 1990, 21). Judith Stacey (1990b) makes a parallel argument about the rise in the 1980s of "postfeminism," which she characterizes as "the simultaneous incorporation, revision, and depoliticization of many of the central goals of second-wave feminism" (339).

But if the appeal of both feminism and the recovery movement issues from the reality of women's struggles in their daily lives, they differ dramatically in their explanation of the causes of and solutions to those problems. Missing in the recovery agenda is an analysis of "the social context in which our suffering is born and grows" (Rapping 1996, 7). In its place is substituted a focus "only on the *effects* of our confusion and pain" (ibid.) and an emphasis "on how we can change *ourselves*" (ibid., 13). Although the modern-day mind-cure technology of healing begins from the assumption that the self is inherently perfect rather than "dysfunctional," it too envisions healing as willed self-transformation. Biopsychiatry is similarly dedicated to individual change, albeit at the level of physiology. Among all strands of the therapeutic enterprise, it has been least responsive to feminist concerns because it rejects at the outset any kind of social explanation for mental distress. Nevertheless, its clientele remains disproportionately female as ever-increasing numbers of women seek relief from their misery through drugs, psychosurgery, and electroshock.

The Therapy Talk Show and the Problem of "Empowerment"

Given that *The Oprah Winfrey Show* is organized around women's lives and problems, we should expect its diagnosis of those problems and its prescriptions for "empowerment" to be deeply entangled with these various strands of the therapeutic enterprise. Phil Donahue may have characterized his program as "the talk show for women who think" and sought "to entertain people as well as inform them" (Katz 1996b; Hall 1996a, 28), but Winfrey insisted that her show would do more than educate and entertain—it would also "empower" her viewers. That mission has been decisively informed by the therapeutic enterprise. In an early assessment of Winfrey, Maya Angelou described her as a "pathfinder" who was "paving the way for other young white, black, Hispanic, Asian, and Native American women to follow." Angelou cited as evidence a "loyal fan" of the show who had described Winfrey as "America's most accessible and honest psychiatrist" (Angelou 1989, 88). A quarter-century later, another fan echoed that view on Winfrey's web site: "The Oprah Show is one of the most important shows of our time. It has helped us in our lives, it has educated us, it has opened the door to our awarenesses [*sic*], and has literally embraced our souls. The Oprah Show has lifted us up to greet the challenges of the future" (lotus7 2002).

Such sentiments are common among posts to Winfrey's web site, letters to her show and magazine, and attendees' comments at her personal growth tours. As we have seen, a number of scholars also consider Winfrey's program uplifting and "empowering" and see it as an outgrowth of feminism. Shattuc (1997) argues that the therapeutic logic of talk programs issues from "American revisions of Freudian psychoanalysis—humanist therapy, the self-help movement, and feminist therapy" (113). This "self-determination" model of therapy, she suggests, undermines the authority of psychological expertise in favor of the "active/activist individual who has the capacity to think and disagree" and thereby "give[s] a voice to normally voiceless women" who "speak for themselves and are valued for their experience" (ibid., 136). The empowering potential of talk shows derives from their having borrowed the logic of the consciousness-raising group, which Shattuc claims has "always been a hybrid: part therapy and part political activism" (ibid., 128).

Conceiving consciousness-raising (CR) as a means for sharing personal stories so as to find common ground, Shattuc maintains that CR groups and "their talk show incarnation have been held together by empowering women through collectively constructing self-esteem" (ibid., 129). Masciarotte (1991) and Patricia Mellencamp (1990) similarly see talks shows as patterned on consciousness-raising techniques. The latter argues that this feminist legacy enables talk shows to direct viewers "away from the experts and toward self-help, away from individuality and toward a group or collective mentality" (Mellencamp 1990, 218). Rapping, in contrast, proposes that TV talk shows are a prime purveyor of the "master narratives" of addiction, powerlessness, and lifelong recuperation associated with the recovery movement, which she sees as part of a broader backlash against feminism in the 1980s. Insofar as talk shows "provide endless snippets and variation and versions of those narratives," they are a means "by which all of us, but especially women, are being taught how to analyze and take action upon our most troubling personal and social sorrows" (Rapping 1996, 33). From Rapping's perspective, therapy talk shows such as Winfrey's are politically disabling because they encourage female viewers to see themselves as ill, rather than as oppressed or exploited.

These opposing views of the aims and consequences of the therapy talk show invite a closer examination of the notion of empowerment—a term bandied about as if its meaning is self-evident. According to Shattuc, because feminism challenges inequitable gender relations of power, as well as assumptions about the innate passivity and dependence of women that legitimized such inequality, feminist therapy offered a view of women as "active, complex, and everchanging individuals who have capacity to choose, to assign meaning to their lives, and to be autonomous" (Shattuc 1997, 123). Feminist therapy therefore encouraged women to consider how they had been constrained by socially constructed gender roles so as to expand their possibilities for action and positively revalue themselves. That process, for Shattuc, constitutes "empowerment" (ibid.). The goal (and desired outcome) of this process, according to Jana Sawicki, is the bolstering of women's self-esteem, which is "a principal aim of feminism" (Sawicki 1991, 106).

This emphasis on building women's self-esteem is the basis of Winfrey's claim to empower her audience and of assertions by scholars that her program is feminist in some way. It is important to note, however, that it is entirely possible to feel more positively about oneself and capable of exploring a wider range of action without challenging the existing system of social relations. Indeed, it could plausibly be argued that such an empowered individual might feel more, rather than less, at home in the given social order. Nor is there any necessary connection between seeing oneself as "active," "autonomous," and free to choose, and adopting what Mellencamp (1990) terms a "collective mentality." In fact, such an autonomous, efficacious individual might actually be less inclined toward such a collective identification. Finally, although Mellencamp and Shattuc credit talk shows with encouraging female viewers to understand their shared condition through the lens of institutionalized gender inequality, it may equally be argued that the "master narratives" of the recovery movement so prominent in the shows promote a communal identification rooted in a disease explanation of women's troubles.

Thus, we should not simply take at face value Winfrey's claim to empower her audience, nor viewers' claims that they have been empowered by her. Rather, it is important to critically examine the meaning behind such assertions. How is power—and its absence—understood and deployed in *The Oprah Winfrey Show*? Who lacks power, who holds it, and why? By what means does one become empowered, and toward what ends? I suggest that there is a vital difference between conceiving empowerment at the level of individual well-being versus understanding it as a sociopolitical, hence collective, undertaking. This difference is especially significant given that the former conception is integral to the therapeutic enterprise. As Lichtman (1982) argues, "our society defines the function of therapy ... as the 'empowering' of individuals to minimize or overcome individual pain through the techniques of individual transformation" (269). Insofar as the therapy talk show is heir to the psychological worldview, we should anticipate that *The Oprah Winfrey Show* would define empowerment primarily in terms of individual transformation. Implicit in any promise of transformation and empowerment is a conception of a self in need of both. What, then, is the nature of the self that Winfrey's program proposes to transform, and with what healing technologies? To what extent is this configuration of self—and related curative techniques—compatible with a feminist political project?

If, as Rapping argues, second-wave feminism has made inroads into the larger culture such that its critique of gender relations informs women's experiences and expectations, the recovery movement, mind cure, and biopsychiatry have also become formidable competitors for women's loyalty. The differences between these configurations of self and related technologies of healing generate powerful tensions within any therapeutic project directed at women, including that of the "therapy talk show." Those tensions haunt *The Oprah Winfrey Show*, which from its first season wedded the ostensibly feminist goal of "empowering women" to conceptions of self and techniques of healing rooted in the recovery movement. This uneasy marriage traversed the program from its 1986 debut through the early 1990s, with its recurring display of addicted, diseased, and dysfunctional individuals.

Winfrey's professed weariness in 1994 with the seemingly infinite supply of human wreckage that washed ashore on her stage reveals the fragility of that union. Her decision in 1994 to "stop talking about how bad things are" and to instead emphasize "positive" messages suggests an awareness that the deficient self at the core of the recovery paradigm was an obstacle not only to her claims to "empower" and "heal" women, but to her aspirations for broader public legitimacy. Winfrey's response to that dilemma was to cast about for a conception of self more amenable to her quest for public acclaim as a healer. Marianne Williamson's modern-day mind-cure philosophy—with its vision of an "enchanted" self, waiting to be discovered and liberated—would provide the antidote to interminable dysfunctionality. It was through the rejection of the damaged dysfunctional self that Winfrey would attain the status of "inspirational phenomenon." That journey, I suggest, is reminiscent of the historical process of banalization by which Freud's dark, divided interior was replaced by a sanitized unconscious entirely at one with the world.

In the following chapters, I trace the parallel evolution of Winfrey's therapeutic enterprise and neoliberalism's political trajectory. In *Inventing Our Selves* (1998), Nikolas Rose argues that "the growth of the intellectual and practical technologies in Europe and North American over the period since the late nineteenth century is intrinsically linked with transformations in the exercise of power in contemporary liberal democracies." Thus is the history of psychology "intrinsically linked to the history of government" (11). As Rose reminds us, neoliberalism is not simply a political or economic philosophy. Rather, it "constitutes a mentality of government, a conception of how authorities should use their powers to improve national well-being, the ends they should seek, the evils they should avoid, the means they should use, and, crucially, the nature of the persons upon whom they must act" (ibid., 153). I propose that Winfrey's journey to a position of singular cultural authority has to do with the fit between the neoliberal strategy of governing and her configuration of self, illness, and technology of healing. The frames of intelligibility provided by Winfrey's various media undertakings, through which her followers are invited to make sense of themselves and the world, have proven eminently compatible with neoliberal visions of "national well-being" and the kinds of social subjects necessary to achieve it.

CHAPTER

~ *3* ~

*Backlash Politics, the Dysfunctional
Self, and the Recovery Cure*

Two weeks into her first season in national syndication, Oprah Winfrey introduced
an episode titled "Women: Life in the '80s" that aimed to "take the pulse of America's
women" (*Oprah Winfrey Show*, Sept. 26, 1986). A dozen women from twelve regions
of the country were invited to discuss "what they are thinking and feeling about their
lives, about their marriages, about their children." Selected, no doubt, to reflect the
composition of the audience, the women were overwhelmingly white, heterosexual,
currently or formerly wives (seven married, one divorced, one widowed, three single),
and mothers (ten of twelve). Seven worked outside the home, one was a farm wife,
and the remaining four were homemakers, including one mother on welfare. Three
of the working women held professional positions (reporter, broadcast consultant,
press relations director), while four had clerical or service jobs. The husbands of the
stay-at-home wives included the "billionaire" owner of the Houston Rockets bas-
ketball team, an unemployed electrical engineer, a state government employee, and
a farmer. One working woman was married to an unemployed miner; the spouses'
occupations of the other employed panelists were not identified.

Winfrey's introduction acknowledged changes wrought by the women's movement.
The show, she said, would pose the following questions to the panelists: "Are their
dreams coming true, or is life different from what they imagined it would be? Do
they feel they have more choices today, or are they just more confused? Is the quality
of our lives as women better than that of our mothers, and what kind of life do we
see ahead for our own daughters?" The fact that women's situation had undergone
historical change was evident in comparing the lives of the oldest and youngest
participants. Marie Newman, a retired widow and grandmother living on social
security, had grown up on a farm with an invalid mother. Her "prime ambition" as
a child was to become a nurse, but by the end of eighth grade she had quit school to
take odd jobs for $3 a day because her family needed the money. "Education wasn't

as important as it is now," she explained. Although Newman had worked most of her life, she never became a nurse. At age sixty, however, she did achieve her "main goal in life"—getting a high school diploma by taking the GED exam. Reflecting on Winfrey's question about attaining one's childhood dreams, Newman replied, "I'm thinking I was born at the wrong time" and admitted to feeling "cheated" by the limited possibilities that had been available to her. In contrast, twenty-two-year-old Linda Sypien, who had recently graduated from UCLA with a music degree, was looking forward to her future because she had "so many choices."

Sypien's statement is instructive in that "choice" was a central trope through which Winfrey, the panelists, and the audience understood both their lives and feminism. During the second segment Winfrey asked the women if they considered themselves feminist and whether they felt the women's movement had helped them. Doatsy Peifer, a Denver radio/TV consultant, applauded the movement because "it really reminds us that we do have choices, and you can decide not to take advantage of them or you can." Winfrey agreed: "My definition of what a feminist is, is that you just believe you have the right to make choices in your life that are equal to those of men." Such comments echo the central tenet of liberal feminism, which views gender inequality as a disparity of rights and opportunities. Solving that inequity means expanding women's choices to parity with men's without fundamentally altering the structure of society. Liberal feminism thus follows liberal political philosophy's conception of freedom as individuals' right to pursue their self-interest without constraints. But if Winfrey and Doatsy Peifer defined feminism in terms of expanding women's choices in general, others in the show identified it with a specific choice: working outside the home. Mary Allgood of Louisiana said that because she had never had to "make a choice" between her job and family, she saw herself as "a mix" of feminist and nonfeminist. Vermont homemaker Marilyn Johnson explained that being a mother and housewife was "the role in life I have chosen" and had "not sought to fight the feminist issue, because I'm very happy as a homemaker." A caller charged the women's movement with having "a negative effect" on her life because, having "chosen to delay my career and to be a full-time mother and housewife," she felt her choice was not respected.

In equating feminism with employment outside the home, these women implied that being a stay-at-home wife and mother automatically meant one was not a feminist. An audience member questioned that assumption:

A lot of things having to do with feminism have nothing to do with just being in the workplace. I mean, I think it's helped a lot in terms of things like networking.... The fact of the matter is it's not just feminism; in [these] economic conditions a lot of women have to get together to help each other. And I think the feminist movement has helped a lot of women to get together and find each other, who're working in the same fields, who want to advance each other and help each other along. But that doesn't necessarily mean that they don't want you to be a housewife or that they couldn't help you network as a housewife. I think a lot have gotten together as housewives, especially farm wives and other people who have been separated from each other have been brought together in consciousness raising and other kinds of groups.

This attempt to expand the purview of feminism and challenge was short-circuited by Winfrey, however, who stepped in to announce a commercial break. Further, she had previously undermined the idea of women coming together to "help each other along." A few minutes earlier, Winfrey had asked the panelists if they thought "women are more supportive of each other now"—a clear reference to one of the goals of the women's movement. Although three of the guests quickly answered affirmatively, Winfrey interjected, "Well, see, I'd say that women are very bitchy to a great extent" and proceeded to complain about female viewers who criticized her appearance.

That the question of "work versus family" arose early in the episode and dominated three of the show's eight segments suggests that this "choice" loomed large in the women's lives. Although the newly graduated Linda Sypien extolled her options, saying she could "do whatever I want because everything's so open," her optimism quickly gave way to anxiety. She confessed to fears she might not find a husband supportive of her desire for both career and family and worried that if she were to marry, she would become a divorce statistic. Sypien's concerns about navigating the dual demands of family and work were shared by many of the women onstage, in the studio audience, and among callers to the show. The third segment opened with a question from an audience member: "I'd like to know how can one do it all? How can one be a super career woman, a super wife, super mom, super daughter, super granddaughter, super friend, super everything?" One panelist replied, "You set your own priorities, don't let someone else say what you should be," to which the questioner retorted, "But aren't you cheating someone, aren't you cheating your husband?" Another panelist—one of the homemakers—broke in to assert that it was children who were cheated by mothers who went to work: "Mothers can't help it. They've got to be out there working, so they can't devote as much time to their children, but the children are suffering because of it." Winfrey then took a call from a new mother who said she was "beginning to think it's impossible to be both" (a mother and job holder). An audience member countered: "I think you can have it all, you can have it all at different times.... I have been all of these things at one time or another. I'm satisfied. I have wonderful children, a marvelous husband. I don't know if that makes me a feminist or not a feminist or whatever, but why do we have to have these labels?" Another audience member chimed in: "Yes, I think that's probably the biggest problem that we have as women, is we have been pushed into this, where we feel like we have to do it all. You don't have to do it all. Everybody has to reach down inside and decide what they want." At that point Winfrey interrupted: "How come I don't feel that? I don't feel I have to do it, I really don't feel that. I don't feel that pressure. Have I missed something?"

Winfrey's inability to identify with these women's almost palpable anxiety might have something to do with the fact that she had neither husband nor children, and certainly was not struggling with economic pressures given that her annual salary at the time was $30 million (Mair 1994/1998, 101). Her guests and audience were too polite or too intimidated to point this out, since no one responded, but neither did they drop the issue. When a caller complained about having to care for the "neglected" children of neighboring working mothers, Winfrey suggested that not all women who work are irresponsible parents, as did one of the job-holding panelists, who said "there are some irresponsible stay-at-home moms too." At that point, another panelist [unidentified in the transcript] jumped in:

> But I think we're neglecting what a part of the problem is, and the problem is that we have a government that does not support the role of motherhood. That allows a woman to have a career, but to have the time where she can have children if she wants to, or to provide the funds for adequate daycare, to give parents the chance to take the expense off their taxes, for instance, for adequate daycare. And I hope perhaps the new tax laws will allow us to do that. But the main problem is that we do not support motherhood, and we do not support children.

Panelist Michele Rucker, a single mother on welfare from North Carolina, picked up on this link between government policy and the lives of families. Noting that she had been a nurse's aide and secretary, Rucker explained that it was more difficult to support her two children by working at the low-paying jobs available to her than by receiving welfare because of the prohibitive cost of childcare, transportation, and health insurance.

This moment was ripe for exploring connections between the personal and political—which is the central aim of feminist consciousness-raising. Winfrey did not pursue this possibility but instead took a question from the studio audience that sent the talk in an unrelated direction. Nor had she responded to an earlier statement by Marie Newman, who said she found herself "really lean[ing] toward feminism" because of her experience with the social security system. When Newman's retired husband died, she was forced to take a cut in her benefits because her lifetime wages had been lower than his. She saw this as patently discriminatory because "it costs just as much for a widow to take care of her household, pay her utilities, rent, et cetera, as it does for a man to do the same things." Winfrey's silence in both cases is significant in that these were the only instances in the show that participants made explicit links between the circumstances of individual women and larger institutional structures in society. Her failure to explore such connections is not simply an oversight or limited to this particular episode, but, as I will argue throughout this book, is a defining feature of *The Oprah Winfrey Show*—claims about its feminist sympathies notwithstanding.

Further, the centrality of the notion of "individual choice" in framing the discussion of the women's lives helps keep at bay the connection between the political and the personal. Thus, working or staying at home are understood as purely individual inclinations, as are choosing to be on welfare versus being employed, or landing a satisfying career versus slaving at a dead-end job. In their study of *The Oprah Winfrey Show*, Debbie Epstein and Deborah Steinberg argue that "the notion of choice pervades virtually every programme," where "choice is equated with freedom, civil rights, America, feminism, personal responsibility, and growth" (1998, 83). At the same time, choices are understood strictly at the level of individual action and thus appear "to take place in a social vacuum" (ibid.). In the "Women: Life in the '80s" episode, Winfrey, the panelists, audience members, and callers referred to setting one's own priorities, not letting others decide what one should be, saying for yourself what you can or cannot do, being the kind of person you would like to be, "reaching into yourself" and being confident in whatever you do, and so on. Such statements would seem to support claims that Winfrey's program fosters women's self-esteem, encourages women to exercise their freedom, and validates the "active individual who has the capacity to think and disagree." In light of such claims, it is instructive to examine the concrete, as opposed to abstract, "choices" available to the twelve panelists.

Marie Newman's choice was to drop out of school at age thirteen to do day labor, which set into motion the trajectory of her life. Michele Rucker's choices were to stay on welfare to maintain her family at a subsistence level or seek work that paid too little to cover childcare, transportation, and medical care for her children. "I would like to have a career," she said, but this did not appear to be one of the actual options on her horizon. Mary Allgood chose to get married and drop out of college in her junior year to help put her husband through school. She worked for a grocers' association—an occupation, she said, that was "not what I had intended or envisioned"—to help support her family. She regretted not completing her education and would "really enjoy" having a job like Winfrey's. Donna Shoop chose to marry a farmer and have four children. After twenty-nine years, her family, like so many others, was losing its farm. She now had the choice of seeking employment in a world that did not seem to value the skills she had developed as a farm wife. Charlene Eldridge chose to marry a coal miner who, like so many others, had lost his job. She supported the family with her position at a local welfare office. Her life, she said, "could be better." Janice Twede, homemaker and mother of six from Utah, chose to be "a very traditional housewife." When her engineer husband was laid off, she had chosen to take in ironing to help feed the family. And Linda Sypien, the college graduate with "so many choices," was working as a retail sales clerk. While it is true that the lives of these women are the product of individual decisions and actions, it is equally true that those actions and decisions are the product of historically specific social conditions and relations that they did not "choose." It is to those conditions that I now turn, to examine "life in the '80s" through a different window so as to gain additional perspective on the "state of America's women."

Taking the Pulse of the 1980s: The Reagan Revolution and the Politics of Backlash

As these women gathered on Winfrey's stage, Ronald Reagan was midway through his second presidential term. Reagan's road to the White House had been paved in the 1970s by the rise of the "New Right" as a powerful organizational force within the Republican Party. Fueled by opposition to Supreme Court rulings on school prayer and abortion, the programs associated with Johnson's Great Society reforms, and changes wrought by the 1960s political movements, the New Right consolidated its power by forging an alliance of entrepreneurial capitalists from southern and western states, expanding and coordinating an array of emerging right-wing single-issue movements, and skillfully using direct mail technologies to generate supporters and funding. Its goal of mobilizing a "silent majority" of conservative voters was abetted by economic conditions in the 1970s. The post-Vietnam shift to a peacetime economy, the 1973 oil crisis, and the worldwide recession of 1974–1975—which brought to a close almost three decades of uninterrupted growth following World War II—launched a new period of stagnant growth, high inflation, deindustrialization, high taxes, rising unemployment, and a decline of organized labor. In combination, these conditions eroded support for Great Society programs and, according to Mike Davis, exacerbated divisions and polarization "not only between classes, but *within* classes, to create opposing camps of inflationary 'haves' and 'have-nots'" (1986, 178). "The stagflation of the 1970s," he argues, "transformed the objective terrain and subjective discourse of politics in America in a way which encouraged the growth of right-wing neo-populism" (ibid.).

The New Right's political strategy was to tap into those divisions and resentments and direct them against "big government," "big labor" (i.e., unions), and the "liberal establishment," which, along with women, gays, African Americans, and other racial/ethnic minorities were deemed "special interests," as opposed to "ordinary Americans" or "the little guy." By joining forces with the religious right and coordinating an array of conservative single-issue campaigns—anti-busing, anti–affirmative action, anti–gun control, anticommunism, anti–property taxes—New Right leaders "mobilized widespread support from classical New Deal, blue-collar constituencies, thus demonstrating that social conservatism, racism, and patriotism provided powerful entrees for New Right politics" (ibid., 170).

Meanwhile, the Democratic Party was itself veering rightward in the late 1970s. In 1977 the Carter administration and Democratic-controlled Congress imposed a freeze on social spending and raised interest rates, and over the next two years reduced the domestic budget, abandoned health care and labor law reforms, and curtailed urban jobs programs. Reagan's victory in 1980 should therefore be seen less as a radical reversal of Democratic policy than a continuation and deepening of trends already underway. As Nick Heffernan argues, "The adoption of tight monetary controls late in the Carter administration was the herald of the Reaganomics of the 1980s" (Heffernan 2000, 182; see also Meeropol 1998, 54–55, 85; Henwood 1997).[1] Despite diminishing the gap between the two parties and chasing after a "mainstream [that] flowed rightward with strong overtones of racial and sexual backlash" (Davis 1986, 179), the Democratic Party still came up empty-handed in 1980: "When the smoke had cleared, the Democrats had lost more than a quarter of self-described 'liberal' voters and almost half of trade-union households" (ibid., 177). Reagan's appeal among such constituencies stemmed from his campaign strategy of downplaying overt anti-union sentiments while playing up the pro-growth benefits of his "supply-side" economic program, thereby unifying white middle- and working-class voters around a conservative agenda that promised a brighter future for both.

The mutually reinforcing set of economic, political, and ideological practices that comprised the so-called Reagan Revolution marked the emergence of neoliberalism as a particular interpretation of, and response to, the structural crisis of capitalism in the 1970s. During the long post–World War II boom, the U.S. gross national product increased sixfold; labor productivity grew steadily each year; the annual rate of economic growth averaged over 5 percent; the yearly rate of increase in the profit rate held steady at 5 to 6 percent; real wages grew at a steady rate; and inflation averaged less than 3 percent a year and never exceeded 6 percent (Heffernan 2000, 27). Organized along Keynesian principles, U.S. economic policy during this boom included the development of the welfare state as a bulwark against economic crises such as the Great Depression; a commitment to full employment via government spending; state regulation of various sectors of the economy that "extended the field of activities freed from the necessity to maximize the profit rate (i.e., the 'market')" (Dumenil and Levy 2002, 50); and fine-tuning of the economy to manage the relationship of production and consumption (to avoid crises at either pole) while striking a relative balance of force between capital and labor.

This prolonged period of stability and growth from 1945 to the early 1970s has been characterized as the "Keynesian compromise" struck between "big government," "big business," and "big labor" (Harvey 1989; Lebowitz 2004). That compromise held as long as growth continued: the recession of 1974–1975, the deepest since the 1930s, marked the beginning of its unraveling. Capital was the first to defect as the annual rates of growth and profit began to slide and inflation climbed to 10 percent in the mid-1970s (Heffernan 2000, 27). The capitalist class, which had long seen Keynesian economics—especially its commitment to full employment through government expenditure—as an "encroachment on its power" (Dumenil and Levy

2002, 48), blamed Keynesianism for the downturn and cast about for an alternative economic agenda to restore its waning fortunes. Monetarism promised to do just that with its prescription for curing inflation by reducing state spending and cranking up unemployment.

"Reaganomics" was the implementation of this monetarist solution. As Joyce Kolko notes, monetarist or "supply-side" economics holds that to counter inflation, governments "must try to increase the supply of resources and the factors of production—that is, of capital—through greater incentives and tax concessions, and to decrease the cost of labor by lowering wages and enlarging the reserve army of the unemployed" (Kolko 1988, 32). Insofar as monetarism "depends on the notion that a national economy can and should be a self-regulating system that will naturally produce growth and prosperity if not interfered with by government" (P. Smith 1997, 163), Reagan presented his supply-side economic program as a return to the principles of the "free market" that had purportedly been strangled by the welfare state. In theory, monetarist policy was based on tightening the money supply so as to reduce inflation and encourage investment, thereby spurring economic growth—the benefits of which would "trickle down" to the general population. As Kolko states, the idea was "to put the economy 'through the wringer' in order to squeeze inflation out of the system" (1988, 33). Following this reasoning, Reagan, with the aid of a Democrat-controlled Congress, slashed government spending for social programs (military spending, in contrast, was dramatically increased by enlarging the federal debt);[2] engaged in an aggressive deregulation campaign, especially of the financial sector; instituted massive tax cuts, particularly for corporations and the wealthiest strata; and raised interest rates, which favored banks and speculators.

Through such measures, Reaganomics accelerated trends that had begun in the late 1970s: the export of jobs in search of cheap labor (both internally, in the migration of jobs from the unionized "Frostbelt" to the union-weak "Sunbelt," and externally, to peripheral nations that offered abundant low-cost, nonunionized labor and minimal regulation); a shift from relatively high-wage factory work in heavy industry to low-wage service occupations; and growing dependence on part-time and temporary employment. Between 1980 and 1985, 2.3 million U.S. manufacturing jobs disappeared; by 1986, 81 percent of new jobs were in service, the vast majority of which were near the bottom of the wage ladder (ibid., 309–310). Part-time, temporary, and home-based work—which rarely include benefits—grew at faster rates than full-time jobs in the 1980s. The number of part-time jobs increased 58 percent between 1980 and 1988 to comprise a quarter of all people employed in the United States (ibid., 311, 313). Of all the new jobs created in the 1980s, half paid a wage lower than the federal poverty figure for a family of four (Coontz 1992, 264). Unemployment rose dramatically. At the height of the 1982 recession there were 12 million Americans officially out of work, nearly 6 million laboring part-time involuntarily because full-time work was unavailable, and 2 million more "discouraged" workers who had lost hope of finding a job (Kolko 1988, 335). Meanwhile, federal cuts in unemployment insurance meant that 55 percent of those out of work in 1982 received no compensation at all (ibid., 339).

Poverty and homelessness climbed accordingly. According to Kolko, "five million additional Americans fell below the poverty level between 1980 and 1982 alone" (340–341). Two years later, 33 million Americans, or one in seven, lived below the poverty level—an increase of nine million since 1978 (Ferguson and Rogers 1986, 130). By the end of 1985 it was estimated that 3 million people were homeless (Kolko 1988, 340–341). The poverty rate in 1987 stood at 12.5 percent in urban areas, 16.9 percent in rural regions, and 18.6 percent in the inner cities, compared to the average poverty rate of 11.9 percent under both the Carter and Nixon/Ford administrations (Porter 1989, 3; Pollin 2000, 36). The combination of accelerating interest rates and cuts in federal programs under Reagan also contributed significantly to the farm crisis in the 1980s. Having been encouraged in the 1970s to borrow against their rising land values to expand their acreage and upgrade equipment, small to mid-size farmers were devastated by the triple blow of falling land and crop prices, skyrocketing interest rates, and withdrawal of federal aid. As Osha Gray Davidson notes, the pledge of the Reagan Revolution to "get government off the backs of the people" proved to be "most successful ... at knocking rural communities off their feet and onto their backs" (Davidson 1996, 66). As farm foreclosures became a common event across the country, the rural poverty rate grew from 13.8 percent in 1979 to 18.3 percent in 1983 (ibid., 75).

White-collar workers were not immune to the effects of this economic restructuring. Confronted with downsizing and the demands of the "reengineered workplace" amid a wave of corporate mergers and takeovers, they increasingly found themselves out of work, sometimes to be rehired as temporary contract employees without benefits (Uchitelle 2006). As both the quantity and quality of work retracted, many Americans found themselves holding more than one job and working more hours just to stay even. According to Kolko, the value of real wages "fell significantly in 1980, remaining at the point attained in the early 1960s and more than 12 percent below the 1972–73 peak, and were expected to fall in 1987 for the fifth year of the decade" (Kolko 1988, 318). The result was a massive increase in the ranks of the working poor. As Davis argues, by the mid-1980s, "at least a third of the 100 million U.S. labor force was ... trapped in a low-wage ghetto" (Davis 1986, 208). The number of people working full-time who still remained poor increased by nearly 57 percent between 1978 and 1987 (Coontz 1992, 273). By 1987 "more than a third of all American households were 'shelter poor'—unable to buy enough food, clothes and other necessities after paying for their housing" (ibid., 269). Falling wages made it increasingly necessary for families to have two wage earners. By the late 1980s both parents were working in over 50 percent of families with children, including half of all women with children under age six (Kolko 1988, 315). Coontz maintains that "without the work of wives, the entire bottom 60 percent of the U.S. population would have had real income losses between 1970 and 1986" (1992, 260). Another way Americans maintained family income was by going deeper into debt and using credit cards to pay for necessities such as groceries and medicine. As Kolko writes, by 1986, "consumer debt amounted to a record 19 percent of all take-home pay" (Kolko 1988, 318).

At the other end of the economic spectrum, Reaganomics yielded striking rewards. Thanks to Reagan's tax cuts, federal receipts from corporate taxes, which had averaged 27.6 percent in the 1950s, 21.3 percent in the 1960s, and 15 percent in the 1970s, had shrunk to 6.2 percent by 1983 (Ferguson and Rogers 1986, 122–123). The wealthiest 1 percent of the population nearly doubled its share of national income (from 8 percent to 14.7 percent) between 1980 and 1989. The net worth of the 400 richest Americans tripled, going from $92 billion in 1982 to $270 billion in 1989 (Brecher and Costello 1994, 29). By the beginning of the 1990s, the top 1 percent of families owned 42 percent of the net worth of U.S. households, including 60 percent of all corporate stock (Coontz 1992, 272). Compensation for top corporate executives grew astronomically in the Reagan years. In 1980 the average chief executive officer of a Fortune 500 company earned thirty-eight times the income of the average school teacher and forty-two times the wages of the average factory worker. Eight years later that already large disparity had ballooned to seventy-two times and ninety-three times, respectively (ibid., 273).

In practice, then, Reaganomics constituted a dramatic redistribution of wealth as the money supply was not just tightened but aggressively channeled upward through a combination of tax reductions that disproportionately favored the wealthy and cuts in government funding of social programs that disproportionately harmed those below. That redistribution is evident in comparing the bottom 20 percent of Americans, who between 1980 and 1984 saw their after-tax income shrink by 7.6 percent, to the top 20 percent, whose after-tax income grew 8.7 percent in the same period (Davis 1986, 234). A Congressional Budget Office report concluded that during the first four years of the Reagan presidency, low-income families lost $23 billion in income and federal benefits while their high-income counterparts gained more than $35 billion (ibid.). Through economic policies that amounted to a "massive subsidy of rich Americans," the distribution of income in the United States at the end of Reagan's first term "was more unequal than at any time since 1947, the year the Census Bureau first began collecting data on the subject" (Ferguson and Rogers 1986, 130).

The Reagan Revolution was not simply an economic program, however, but a political project to establish a new set of rules for governing the functioning of capitalism. That project involved replacing the "Keynesian compromise" that had given labor a greater share of national wealth with a new social compromise based on a reconfigured class coalition. Gerard Dumenil and Dominique Levy contend that the rise of neoliberalism under Reagan should be understood as "an attempt ... by a class of capitalist owners to restore, in alliance with top managers, its power and income after a setback of several decades" (Dumenil and Levy 2002, 53). During the structural crisis of the 1970s, they note, "low profits, low distribution of dividends and low interest rates, combined with large inflation rates, had considerably reduced the income of the ruling classes" (ibid., 54). Whereas during the postwar boom decades the richest 1 percent of U.S. households had held between 30 and 35 percent of the total national wealth, by 1976 their share had decreased to 22 percent. Neoliberalism sought to reverse that slide:

> Confronting the decline of their income and wealth, the ruling classes politically modi-fied the course of capitalism. From the mid-1980s onwards they were able to impose tight controls on the growth of wage costs and to enlarge, to an astonishing extent, their own "siphoning off" of profits. They restored their position dramatically, even *prior* to the appearance of the new upward trend in the profit rate. (ibid.)

Under Keynesian economic policy, working- and middle-class Americans benefited from government spending that made possible low unemployment, the expansion of the public infrastructure, greater access to education, and the social "safety net" of the welfare state (e.g., social security, unemployment insurance, Medicare, Aid to Families with Dependent Children, etc.). Keynesianism, in other words, gave workers a larger share of the national income by imposing certain limits on the power and proportion of wealth that accrued to capital. With the advent of the structural crisis of the 1970s, capitalists claimed that government spending had produced "an unduly low unemployment rate" (Kolko 1988, 53), which they saw as the sole cause of inflation. As Kolko writes, "Capitalism had only one medicine for the inflation virus. Lowering inflation invariably meant squeezing the working class—this was the simple logic behind 'wage restraints' and 'acceptable minimum' unemployment strategies—and led to the effort to re-create the reserve army of unemployed" (ibid., 33).

Expanding the ranks of the unemployed is a key means by which to drive down labor costs and increase profits. As jobs grow scarce, workers are more likely to consent to wage and benefit reductions, to work longer for less, and to accept speed-ups in the work process. Such inclinations were exacerbated in the 1980s by the declining power of labor unions—a result of the combination of deindustrialization, job flight to nonunionized regions, growth in service and temporary work, aggressive union-busting campaigns, and waning federal support for organized labor, as evidenced in cuts to government programs responsible for overseeing labor relations and conditions and, most vividly, in Reagan's summary firing in 1981 of striking air traffic control-lers. Through such "discipline," Reaganomics succeeded in driving down the cost of labor and increasing the profit margins of capital. The average hourly wage for nonsupervisory workers—which under Carter had been $13.51—dropped to $12.82 during the Reagan/Bush administrations. Similarly, the average wage for the bottom 10 percent of workers shrank from $6.32 to $5.68 (Pollin 2000, 37).

Neoliberalism can thus be understood as capital's cure for the economic crisis—one based on "contempt for the problem of unemployment and an overriding concern for price stability" in conjunction with "the unambiguous reassertion of the maximization of the profit rate in every dimension of activity" (Dumenil and Levy 2002, 48, 52). As Paul Smith argues, "for monetarists, unemployment is in a sense an irrelevancy, an issue deemed to be more of a hindrance at the level of public opinion than a genuine economic problem" (Smith 1997, 163). The neoliberal cure—with its bitter pill of high unemployment—could not simply be imposed unilaterally by the capitalist class, however. According to Dumenil and Levy, the success and sustainability of neoliberalism has depended on its ability to "establish a new social compromise in an environment of rising inequality" by "associating a broader social strata to the growing prosperity of the few, really or fictitiously" (Dumenil and Levy 2002, 45). It is therefore necessary to examine the ideological practices through which Reaganism sanctioned and legitimized this mounting inequality, destabilized the Keynesian compromise, and forged a new class coalition.

The ideological project of Reaganism involved fashioning an explanation for the economic downturn that would appeal to middle-class professionals and entrepreneurs while exploiting divisions within the working class so as to siphon off a bloc of Democratic support. That explanation identified three "causes" of national decline: the excesses of "big government" (e.g., high taxes, unrestrained spending, overregulation); the privileging of "special interests" at the expense of "average Americans"; and the deterioration of "traditional" American values of hard work, individual initiative, and self-sufficiency. Weaving together these elements, Reaganism constructed a narrative in which hard-working Americans were being penalized by a voracious government that took an unreasonable share of their money, handed it over to undeserving individuals and social groups, and thereby undermined the work ethic by punishing the diligent and rewarding the lazy. Accordingly, the solution lay in reversing this unfairness, restoring economic growth, and reviving appropriate values. That solution paralleled the neoliberal political-economic agenda, which was organized around:

(1) The "de-regulation" of free enterprise and the belief that only private capital, endowed with ample profit margins and tax breaks, can "reindustrialize" America; (2) the further remoulding of state expenditure and intervention to reinforce the subsidized position of the middle-strata and new entrepreneurs; and (3) the curtailing of Great Society–type income and employment programs targeted at minorities, women and the poor. (Davis 1986, 228)

That agenda is manifested ideologically in Reaganism's celebration of the free market, which, when freed from government interference, would purportedly offer everyone an equal chance to compete; and of the entrepreneurial spirit, which would blossom once people realized that their industriousness would be rewarded. Richard Reeves and Jimmie Campbell (1994) suggest that Reaganism can be seen as a revival of the nineteenth–century Horatio Alger myth, in which one's lot in life depends solely on individual gumption and effort (75). Robert Reich, who would serve as Bill Clinton's first-term labor secretary, argued in the late 1980s that the Alger myth explicitly "endorsed large disparities in wealth, since riches were the award for applying yourself, saving money and trading shrewdly" (Reich 1988, 106–107). It thus justified giving greater monetary rewards to those willing to take economic risks and denying benefits to those who lacked the will to better themselves. The logic of this "reverse Robin Hoodism," to borrow a phrase from Reeves and Campbell, was used to drive a wedge between the upper and lower strata of the working class, between the working class and the poor, between suburbanites and inner-city residents, and between whites and racial minorities (especially African Americans), and thereby to reconfigure class alliances through a "divide-and-conquer/unite-and-mobilize" strategy (Reeves and Campbell 1994, 75, 157).

Thomas and Mary Edsall contend that whereas Keynesian economic policy used "federal funding to unite the poor and the middle class," Reagan's monetarist neoliberalism "used opposition to federal tax burdens to unite the rich and the working class" (Edsall and Edsall 1991, 178).[3] Declining resources and the shrinking value of wages under high inflation also created "chasms of inequality between working-class strata" as wage differentials grew between skilled, unionized workers and unskilled, nonunionized and service employees (Davis 1986, 178). As Mike Davis argues, this "fragmentation of the class structure facilitated the recomposition of politics around the selfishly 'survivalist' axis favored by the New Right" (ibid.). As resources contracted in the late 1970s, "public spending and taxes increasingly became a terrain of division between suburbanized workers and middle strata, on the one hand, and inner-city workers and the non-waged poor on the other" (ibid., 198).

The tensions generated within this milieu of scarcity provided an ideal medium for the cultivation of New Right backlash politics. Playing the role of vanguard in the backlash were the myriad single-issue movements that emerged in the late 1970s. Dominated by white middle-class suburbanites from the technical, professional, and managerial strata, these movements (anti-busing, anti-ERA, anti–gay rights, anti-abortion, anti–property and income taxes) were "devoted to the sanctity of white suburban family life" (ibid., 170). Such campaigns also elicited working-class support, especially among white skilled workers living in the suburbs who joined the assault on busing, integrated housing, affirmative action, and property taxes. As Davis argues, "through the rise of these new movements, a broadly embracing 'Have' politics was forged which gave a political interpretation to stagflationary trends in the economy, stressing the immanent themes of privatization, redirected state spending and the new inegalitarianism" (ibid., 227). Through a strategy of "permanently shrinking the federal budget" to "deepen the schism between inner-city and suburban Democrats by increasing the competition for scarce revenue sharing," Reaganomics helped solidify this emerging cross-class alliance of haves against have-nots (ibid., 268–269).

Pitting the suburbs against the inner city was also central to Reaganism's efforts to "realign the electorate along racial, rather than class, lines" (Reeves and Campbell 1994, 157; also Macek 2006). As the attack on Keynesian economic policy was racialized, minorities—and African Americans in particular—were relegated to the category of "special interests," painted as beneficiaries of government largesse at the expense of whites, as privy to unfair advantages in a shrinking job market and preferential access to education and training, as a threat to "law and order" and the integrity of "community," as bereft of "family values." The ideology of Reaganism held that racism had been overcome—thus justifying the assault on affirmative action and other social programs aimed at disadvantaged racial groups—while espousing a "new racism" in which the problems of black Americans were deemed the result of cultural or individual pathology. At the same time, according to Reeves and Campbell, the 1980s saw the "right-wing appropriation of the celebrated mainstream media achievements of a handful of prominent African-American 'individuals,'" including Oprah Winfrey (Reeves and Campbell 1994, 100; see also Cloud 1996).

By denying the existence of institutionalized racism, attributing black failure to lack of initiative or impoverished values, and adulating black stars as proof that racial barriers to success had evaporated, Reaganism simultaneously tapped into historically deep undercurrents of racism in American culture and absolved whites of any implication in that history (see also Jhally and Lewis 1992). It thereby "facilitated the upward redistribution of wealth in the 1980s by releasing people in the suburbs from any responsibility for—or identification with—the economic distress in the inner city" (Reeves and Campbell 1994, 157). The consequences of this abdication were devastating. Taking stock in the late 1980s, Davis wrote, "Black America has been savaged by a new immiseration. Nearly half of all Black children are growing up in poverty, and in the upswing of the Reagan 'recovery,' the Black unemployment rate, which historically has been double the white rate, is now three times higher (at 16 percent)" (Davis 1986, 261). Further, 60 percent of employed African American men and half of working Hispanic men were concentrated in the lowest-paid occupations, particularly in the service and temporary employment sectors (ibid., 208).

Equally vital to the ideological arsenal of Reaganism was the backlash against the women's movement and feminism, which was appended to the defense of white suburban family life via the trope of "family values." Central to the backlash were campaigns against the Equal Rights Amendment, women's reproductive rights, affirmative action policies related to gender, and efforts to achieve pay equity for women. As the Reagan administration was dismantling federal offices and programs dedicated to women's issues and decimating the ranks of women in federal service in the 1980s, the media "issued a steady stream of indictments against the women's movement" that held "the campaign for women's equality responsible for nearly every woe besetting women, from mental depression to meager savings accounts" (Faludi 1991, x–xi). The various strands of antifeminism in the Reagan years, according to Susan Faludi, were woven into a unified message: that women had succeeded in achieving equality *and* were utterly miserable, hence, "women's equality [was] responsible for women's unhappiness" (ibid., 230).

But even as this message emanated from the news media, Hollywood, Madison Avenue, the medical profession, the academy, and the political arena, the actual conditions of women's lives belied its claims. By the late 1980s women constituted two-thirds of poor adults in the United States; the average female college graduate earned less than a male high school graduate; 80 percent of working women toiled in low-paying, traditionally "female" jobs; married women were still burdened with 70 percent of household duties (ibid., xiii–xiv); the pay ratio of women to men still hovered in the 50 to 60 percentile; the U.S. gender wage gap remained one of the largest in the advanced capitalist world (Coontz 1992, 260); and "relative poverty" was being "mass-produced" through "the incorporation of women into burgeoning low-wage sectors of the economy" (Davis 1986, 208–209).

Further, Faludi argues, surveys of women in the mid- to late 1980s contradicted claims that gender equality had been realized: "In poll after poll in the decade, overwhelming majorities of women said they needed equal pay and equal job opportunities, they needed an Equal Rights Amendment, they needed the right to an abortion without government interference, they needed a federal law guaranteeing maternity leave, they needed decent child care services. They have none of these" (Faludi 1991, xv). Nor were women blaming feminism for their problems: "In national surveys 75 to 95 percent of women credit the feminist campaign with *improving* their lives, and a similar proportion say that the women's movement should keep pushing for change" (ibid.). Further, public opinion surveys indicated that "women consistently rank their own *inequality*, at work and at home, among their most urgent concerns" (ibid.).

Despite such poll results, the antifeminist backlash succeeded in shifting the focus from women's rights to women's duties through the trope of "family values." As more and more social problems were laid at the feet of the "crisis of the family," women came under particular fire because the historical separation of the public and private spheres had made the family their special domain of responsibility. Wedding the attack on feminism to the notion of "family values," Reagan and the New Right portrayed the supposed decline of the latter as the consequence of the former. Within Reaganism's "orthodoxy of nostalgia" (Reeves and Campbell 1994, 2), "the family" implied a white middle-class nuclear unit headed by an employed father and his helpmate, the stay-at-home mother, who together instilled in their children appropriate values. Any variation on this ideal was destined to fall short, even though this family type was far from the norm in the 1980s. In fact, Coontz points out, by 1988 "the two-parent family in which only the father worked for wages represented just 25 percent of all families with children, down from 44 percent in 1975" (Coontz 1992, 18). Although the number of women in the workforce had grown each decade since the 1940s, the dramatic influx of mothers with young children into the workplace in the 1970s "is what link[ed] female employment to feminism and 'family collapse'" in the eyes of the New Right, which charged that mothers had been persuaded by the women's movement to "put their own selfish aspirations above duty to their children" (ibid., 167).

Feminism was thereby accused of encouraging women to betray their feminine nature, turning them into masculinized career-seekers, and, in the process, "dismantling the traditional familial support system" (Faludi 1991, 230)—a critique eerily reminiscent of the psychology establishment's attack on women in the 1950s. Such sentiments are exemplified by George Gilder—one of the Reagan administration's "house intellectuals" in Thomas Frank's terminology (Frank 2000, 34). Gilder's *Men and Marriage* (1986) called the women's movement a "menace" to "the sex roles on which the family is founded" and, by extension, to "the freedoms at the very heart of free enterprise" (108, 149). As Reaganism launched a frontal assault on women's efforts to achieve equality, the Democrats opted for a more indirect strategy, jumping on the anti–"special interests" and "pro-family" bandwagon after Mondale's defeat in 1984. In 1988, Democratic National Committee chair Paul Kirk declared that the Equal Rights Amendment and the right to legal abortion "had no place on the party platform"; the Democratic Leadership Council (birthplace of Bill Clinton's rise to national prominence and of "New Liberalism") dropped abortion rights from its agenda; and shortly before the November election the National Women's Political Caucus and Women's Vote Project sent out a mailing "that focused with virtual exclusivity on 'family' issues" (Faludi 1991, 274–276).

As both national political parties proclaimed their fealty to "the family" and "motherhood," women continued to pour into the labor force, driven not by selfishness but by economic necessity, thanks to the combination of high inflation, falling wage values, and mounting unemployment. As Coontz points out, without wives' employment, 80 percent of married-couple families would have suffered income declines between 1979 and 1986 (Coontz 1992, 260). Even in two-income-earner homes, according to Kolko, "household spending power fell in the 1980s" (Kolko 1988, 315). Further, the growth of female employment largely occurred in the expanding low-wage service sector and in temporary and part-time jobs. And, contrary to claims that sex segregation and pay inequity in the workplace had been overcome, the majority of working women in the 1980s toiled in traditionally "female" jobs, such as "salesclerking, cleaning services, food preparation, and secretarial, administrative and reception work" (Faludi 1991, 365). Moreover, these "female work ghettos" became even more female-dominated in the Reagan years. As Faludi argues, "a resegregating work force was one reason why women's wages fell in the '80s; by 1986, more women would be taking home poverty-level wages than in 1973" (ibid.).

Thus, at the same time that the economic practices of Reaganomics pushed more and more women into low-paying jobs and reduced or eliminated government support desperately needed by households at the lower end of the wage spectrum, the ideology of Reaganism attacked women for short-shrifting children and stealing jobs from men. Indeed, blaming women, people of color, and the poor for the national economic hardship and individual and familial crises resulting from Reaganomics was a key component of the political and ideological project of Reaganism. As Davis argues, "faced with a genuinely collapsing standard of living in many sectors of the traditional working class," skilled workers and the lower stratum of the white-collar middle class "increasingly visualized themselves ... as locked into a desperate zero-sum rivalry with equality-seeking minorities and women" (Davis 1986, 228). The Reagan Revolution fostered and capitalized on these anxieties and prejudices to forge a new class compromise uniting white skilled labor, the lower salariat, the professional-managerial strata of the middle class, nouveau riche entrepreneurs, and capitalist owners and upper management.

The Problems Facing Women, or Women with Problems?

Armed with this understanding of life in the 1980s, we can revisit the women on Winfrey's show and consider their "choices" in light of the objective conditions confronting them. Charlene Eldridge's unemployed miner husband was one of the millions of casualties of deindustrialization. Janice Twede's engineer husband may have been out of work because of corporate downsizing or cuts in government spending on public infrastructure. Donna Shoop's family was among thousands devastated by the farm crisis. Marie Newman belonged to the swelling ranks of the female elderly poor. Michele Rucker was trapped between the low-wage female work ghetto and a welfare system that had been decimated under Reagan. And recent college graduate Linda Sypien was working as a clothing sales clerk—a job dominated by women (83 percent) with the largest gender pay gap of any field, in which women were paid "less than men in any other occupation, including day laborers" (Faludi 1991, 378). Nor is it surprising that tensions arose in the show around the question of working mothers given the number of women in the workforce, the scarcity of adequate, affordable childcare and paid parental leave, and the fact that married women—employed or not—were shouldering the lion's share of the work at home.

Meanwhile, women were being informed from every direction that they had achieved full equality, that if they were unhappy it was their own doing, and that because of their selfishness, not only their families but the entire social fabric was falling apart. Women in the 1980s, in other words, were being told that they could "have it all" so long as they were willing to do it all. The extent to which women had internalized this message is evident in the episode as speakers agonized over the demands of the "superwoman" role or lashed out at working mothers for failing their parental duty. It is telling, for example, that nowhere in the program did anyone, including Winfrey, suggest that fathers had any responsibility for household duties, for children's care and emotional needs, or for the "crisis of the family." Further, that many of the participants in the "Life in the '80s" episode saw feminism as relevant only for employed women suggests that the antifeminist backlash had succeeded in framing the movement for women's equality as "antifamily" and shifting the focus from women's equality to women's maternal obligations.

If the lives and choices of these women were conditioned by the economic, political, and ideological practices of the Reagan Revolution, so too was *The Oprah Winfrey Show*, which must be understood as a cultural manifestation of its times. Contrary to claims that Winfrey's program constitutes "television at its most feminist," or that it espouses some version of liberatory politics, I propose that the show rarely challenged, and more often reinforced, the political and ideological agenda of Reaganism, including the latter's stance on women's problems; its conception of the family; its position on poverty, unemployment, and financial success; and its attitude toward state-funded social programs. In light of Winfrey's professed commitment to "empowering" women, the remainder of this chapter examines the program's treatment of some key issues confronting women in the 1980s.

The show's take on the "work vs. family" dilemma is exemplified in "Runaway Mothers," which aired a week after the "Life in the '80s" episode, and in "How Mom's Working Affects the Kids," which ran the next summer (*Oprah Winfrey Show*, Oct. 3, 1986, and July 17, 1987). Winfrey opened "Runaway Mothers" by introducing three panelists "who one day decided they just could not handle the pressures of their marriages and children." The first had left her husband and two children when the strain of holding a night-shift job and being responsible for all of the household duties and most of the childcare without the support of her "uncommunicative husband" had turned her into "an empty shell." The second panelist—at age twenty-one with two small children—had left her husband when she discovered he was a transvestite. Despite working seven days a week as a cocktail waitress to support her kids—with no help from their father—she could not make ends meet, lost her apartment, suffered a breakdown, and ended up in a mental hospital. In a drugged state, she was persuaded to sign over her children to her ex-husband. Upon her release, she learned she could recover her children only by returning to her husband, which she refused to do. The third "runaway," whose husband had seen to it that she "had everything," had disintegrated under the pressure of playing the "perfect wife" and "perfect mother." After getting hooked on cocaine and contemplating suicide, she handed over her two children to her own mother.

Although one caller—a young mother—accused the three panelists of being less than human because "you don't leave your kids" and a childless woman in the audience argued that "mom is always supposed to be there," two other callers and two audience members identified with the need to escape the "unbearable, overwhelming problems" and confessed that they too often fantasized about running away. Guest expert Phyllis Chesler, a feminist psychologist and author of *Women and Madness* (1972) and *Mothers on Trial* (1986), cited the double standard whereby fathers who leave but occasionally visit their children are considered "heroes," while mothers without custody who see their children regularly are "viewed as pariahs." Of those rare women who leave their children, she said, most "are forced out due to economic pressure, and terrible, overwhelming psychological pressure." Chesler also pointed out that "the majority of women stay and live on welfare, they work two jobs, they get no pension, no wages, no love life. . . . They stay with their kids under enormous pressure." Winfrey's response—"But aren't they supposed to stay with their kids?"—reiterated the double standard applied to men and women, which Chesler challenged:

> Well, who says so? The government that doesn't want to give us a family income? I mean, who says so, the husbands who don't want to help in a serious way to parent the children? Who says so? The husbands who will not pay child support even when they can afford to do so? So that the larger picture is that mothers are losing children against their will, for reasons that are very unjust, such as not having enough money.

As in the "Life in the '80s" episode, Winfrey was offered an opportunity to explore the relationship of the personal and the political that is central to a feminist perspective. And, as before, she switched the subject. And although Chesler and two of the panelists explicitly referred to the economic conditions under which women struggle with the "double shift" of work and family, Winfrey cast the issue exclusively in terms of psychological trauma. Although she expressed sympathy for the burdens faced by mothers, she treated those pressures as inherent to motherhood rather than a consequence of historically constituted social arrangements. Thus, even when handed an explicit feminist analysis of women's problems, Winfrey retreated into the apolitical domain of the therapeutic.

"How Mom's Working Affects the Kids" featured two working mothers, two mothers who had quit their jobs to stay at home with their children, four teenagers with employed mothers, and two guest experts. Winfrey introduced the episode as follows:

> Do children suffer when mothers work? Most, about 60 percent, of mothers do work these days, and for many it is a financial necessity. For others, work provides fun, excitement, independence and an escape from the restrictive routine of staying at home with small children. Later on we're going to talk with working mothers who say their children are just fine, thank you, and there is no need for them to quit work. And we'll meet mothers from a reportedly growing group of women who have sacrificed their careers because they feel that their children need them at home.

The first segment featured the four teenagers, all of whose mothers held professional jobs. While each said they occasionally wished their mothers were more available and sometimes resented their extra household chores, all stated that they had good relationships with their mothers, supported their moms' desire to work, and felt they were more responsible because they had to help out at home. At this point, the show seemed to be challenging the notion that children are harmed when mothers work.

That stance was reiterated by the two employed panelists: Ann Reese, a financial adviser for the European division of Mobil Oil, and Ilana Knapp, chief financial officer for a Wall Street securities firm. Both insisted their jobs did not harm their ability to be good mothers and enabled them to give their children advantages such as private schools and travel. This assessment was hotly contested by the stay-at-home mothers—Debbie Forst, who left her job in customer service at a grocery store to raise her children, and Cheryl Werner, a former buyer for a women's clothing store who had "put [her] priorities in order" by returning home to her four kids. Forst also insisted, correctly, that the two highly paid professional panelists did not represent "average families," who could ill afford housekeepers and nannies. Her observation about class differences among families went nowhere, however, as Winfrey cut to a commercial.

Winfrey's role in the episode largely involved provoking tensions between the two sets of women, especially egging on the stay-at-home mothers who repeatedly charged the working women with short-changing their children. Cheryl Werner, for example, said she quit her job "because I started to realize that the family net-work in itself is based on the mother. The mother ties everything together. The children need us, they need us at home." She then criticized Ann Reese for hiring a babysitter, who was no "substitute for the kind of nurturing love that a mother can provide." Winfrey broke in: "So, do you think you're a better mother? ... I want to get a real fat fight. Do you think you're a better mother than Ann because you stay at home?" Werner: "No, I just think that I have my priorities in place." Winfrey: "And she doesn't?" Reese interrupted: "I resent your talking about that." This exchange reflected the tone throughout the episode, with the at-home mothers accusing their working counterparts of failing "the most important job there is" and the employed mothers defending their parenting abilities. Late in the show, one of the working-mother panelists remarked on this dynamic. When asked by Winfrey if she would quit work if she did not need the money, Ilana Knapp responded,

Not anymore. I work because I enjoy working. I'm not angry. I always get the feeling that mothers who made the decision to stay home are so angry. I don't think you've made a right choice or a wrong choice—you made a choice that was good for you. I would work no matter what because it suits me to do so. And I'd like to raise another point. My ... our fathers all worked, and we didn't not love our fathers because they were out of the house all day.

Although Knapp attempted to introduce gender-based disparities in parental roles, she also defended herself by means of the notion of individual choice, which simultaneously located her decision within the discourse of individual rights and freedom and undercut a broader political-economic analysis of the issue.

Guest experts in this episode were Linda Burton, whose book *What's a Smart Woman Like You Doing at Home?* dealt with women who quit work to stay home with their children, and Barbara Berg, whose *The Crisis of the Working Mother* challenged the idea that society's ills were the fault of mothers who work. Burton's book, Winfrey said, focused on a "new breed of mothers" who differed from "the housewives of the '50s" or "the working mothers of the '70s" in that they "know how to put their children first without putting themselves last." Burton counted herself among "an emerging population of women" working part-time out of their homes so as to be "available to their children" and recommended this "middle ground" solution to put an end to "the bickering and controversy" surrounding working mothers. Berg countered that "mothers have worked throughout our national history" and asked why they were now "being blamed for a lot of what seems to be wrong with society." Further, she said, over 80 percent of employed mothers "are not doing it for the beach house or the carpet," but "because they really need that money, that money is putting bread and butter on their tables." Winfrey did not pursue this line of reasoning but instead sought to stimulate conflict: "But there seems to be the implication that they don't love their children as much because they choose to work." The two stay-at-home panelists seized this opportunity to continue berating working mothers for the remainder of the segment. One went so far as to suggest that women who chose to work outside the home should not have children in the first place.

Following a commercial break, Berg tried to put the issue into a broader social context:

> I think we've been very, very personal this morning ... and I think it's really important to make some points. First of all, almost every single study that has compared the way children of working moms and children of moms who are working in the home have turned out to show that these kids look absolutely identical in almost every way, and that sometimes the advantages seem to favor the kids whose moms have actually worked outside of the home. Children whose mothers work have been shown to be as tied and as bonded to their mothers as children whose moms have been home full time.

She also expressed concern about the "divisiveness" that had characterized the discussion:

> What women need is to respect one another's choices, and to fight for the kinds of things that we need in society. For example, why are we the only industrialized nation that doesn't have some form of paid parenting leave, so that mothers like you could

be home and then go back eventually if you want to? Why don't we have more quality childcare facilities on or near site? Why don't we have more flex-time and more cross-time arrangements? Why must we still juggle our lives so that we feel like we're pretzels to try and meet all our roles?

Finally, Berg questioned the assumption that only mothers are capable of properly caring for children: "Why can't we get dads into the picture more and have some kind of arrangements where dad could be home doing some of the nurturing and some of the things that we say only moms can do?" This attempt to expand the discussion to a consideration of broader gender arrangements was derailed by Winfrey, who switched gears to take a call from a viewer.

In the last few minutes of the episode, the experts were allowed a final comment. Berg reiterated that because most women were working out of necessity, "It's a luxury to sit around and say moms shouldn't be working or moms should be working. The fact is they need to work, they're going to need to work, and we as women better stop arguing with one another and get together and help us all out, or else we're going to be in trouble." Burton countered that "you really cannot legislate loving care" and returned to the theme of women's maternal instincts:

> For every study and statistic that they can show you saying it's wonderful to work, nobody's getting hurt, I can show you one that says that's not true. That isn't what we look toward when we decide whether or not we're going to be at home. It's toward the dictates of our consciences, the inclinations of our hearts, and the common sense observations of our own two eyes. And when mothers leave work to go home, that is the evidence they look at.

Emboldened by this statement, the two stay-at-home mothers had the last word in the show:

> FORST: That's right. Go home because your children are there. Love them because they really need us.

> WERNER: The mother's the pillar of the family. Everything really has to base on her.

On one hand, *The Oprah Winfrey Show*'s treatment of this subject obeys the journalistic dictate of presenting "both sides" of a controversial issue, and the individual stories of the guests are, by means of the expert testimony, associated with broader social trends—hence, the link between personal and political that would seem to qualify Winfrey's program as feminist in its approach. But closer examination undermines that assessment. As seen in these episodes, not only does Winfrey consistently fail to follow up on overt feminist analyses of the topical problem at hand, in some instances she takes a decidedly nonfeminist position. In the working mothers program, for example, an audience member suggested that corporations should do more to support employed mothers by offering flexible work schedules and on-site childcare. Winfrey responded: "Isn't one of the reasons why corporations aren't making it available is what happens when you've promoted a woman to an executive position and then she takes a maternity leave?"

Elements of the antifeminist backlash also surfaced in episodes where the women's movement was the central focus. "Male Chauvinism" (*Oprah Winfrey Show*, Jan. 14, 1987) featured Susan Brownmiller, author of *Against Our Will*, Emily Woo Yamasaki from National Radical Women, and four "male chauvinists": George Gilder, whose *Sexual Suicide* and *Men and Marriage* were key documents of New Right gender ideology; Langley Kirksite, professed "male supremist" and author of *Men First, Last and Always* who appeared in disguise to "protect his identity"; Patrick Finley Girondi, who argued that the women's movement was turning women into "scum like men"; and president of Men's Rights, Inc., Fred Hayward, who claimed that the more pressing problem was "female chauvinism." Two things immediately stand out in this episode. First, the male panelists were selected based on the extremity of their views and personalities to provide maximum conflict, shock value, and thus entertainment. Second, they utterly dominated the discussion. The men spoke more than twice as often as Brownmiller and Yamasaki, for substantially longer periods, and repeatedly interrupted and cut off the women. Brownmiller was interrupted fifteen of the forty-one times she attempted to speak, and her longest statement ran three sentences; Yamasaki was interrupted in half of her twenty-two utterances, the longest of which was four sentences. Winfrey herself contributed significantly to this imbalance: she elicited comments from, asked questions of, and responded to the male guests forty-six times during the show compared to nine times for the women; she specifically solicited comments from the men in the audience, but not from the female audience members; and she twice cut off Yamasaki in midsentence to give the stage to one of the men.

The episode was less a substantive examination of the problem of sexism than a platform for the male guests to express sexist views and attack the women panelists. Over the course of the show, the men became increasingly aggressive and insulting while the women grew increasingly silent. By the fourth of eight segments, Brownmiller had nearly disappeared from the discussion, making only two brief comments during the last third of the program. Yamasaki attempted to stay in the conversation—even going so far as to note that "a prime example of sexism or male chauvinism is how the women have been treated on this show, where every time I start to speak, I get interrupted"—but to little effect. The male panelists and Winfrey ignored Yamasaki's comment, and the men continued to cut her off, even in the middle of the above statement. She was also insulted and dismissed. When Yamasaki argued that gender discrimination "still exists" and tried to connect it to the exploitation of women's labor, Gilder interjected: "Bull. Bull." Moments later, when she raised the issue of the unpaid labor of housewives, Gilder and Kirksite cut in and ordered her to "stop whining."

Given the many outlandish statements by the "male chauvinists," the episode at times bordered on a circus. Kirksite, who considered women to be good only for "sex and service," argued that sex for procreation should be banned worldwide for ten years to counteract overpopulation—a problem he blamed entirely on women. Gilder opined that Kirksite would be less extreme if he would marry and become "stabilized" by the "civilizing" influence of a woman. Winfrey shot back: "Who would want him?" At one point, Brownmiller asked if Winfrey had recruited the male panelists "from central casting." But it would be a mistake to write off this episode as simply entertainment. Midway through the program, Winfrey told viewers that "what we're trying to do here … is to assess what the women's liberation movement has done, how far we've come." It became clear as the hour wore on that the assessment was not radically dissimilar to Reaganism's. Predictably, the "male chauvinists" found plenty wrong with the women's movement. Gilder argued that because the innately different roles of men and women were "indispensable to sustaining civilized society," any attempt to achieve gender equality threatened civilization. Girondi charged feminism with inducing women to abandon their children for work. "It's the feminists' fault," he said, "that the mothers in the home are unthanked." Kirksite insisted that "feminism has hurt the American woman more than anything that I know." Significantly, none of these assertions were challenged by Winfrey. Two men in the audience echoed such views. The first asserted that "every man agrees" that women should stay home and take care of children because "they're so good at it" and "it's too hard a job for a man to do." Although the second speaker did not object to women having careers and believed men should share the housework and childcare, he insisted that "the family has been degraded in value" because of the women's movement.

It was not only men who expressed such views. A female caller said she "agree[d] with most of the men" on the show. She had quit her "high-paying job" when she found a "strong man" who earned more than she. Further, she said,

> The women's movement was a bitter disappointment to me. It seems that they advo-
> cate strangers raising children, which fragments our society; they seem to advocate
> promiscuity … and that has only fragmented our society. I've gone back to feeling
> that the family unit is integral to the survival of our country right now, and I wouldn't
> have it any other way.

Winfrey had evoked this caller's association of feminism with family deterioration when she asked the men in the audience if they agreed with Girondi "that there's been a breakdown in the family as the result of women's lib." Winfrey's reply to the caller further cemented that causal connection:

I think you're absolutely right.... Without families, none of us are going to survive. And I think it's great you found somebody who makes more money than you, who can take care of you. It think it'd be great if every woman could find it, but the fact of the matter is, that's not going to happen.

After a commercial break, Winfrey returned to the caller's comments:

I think that a lot of women, a lot of women, agree with the caller who said that she tried it and she worked, and she was making money, and then found someone who she obviously felt good about, and who made more money than she, and she just decided that the family was an integral part of this whole process. And I think there are a lot of women who have tried, and they've tried and tried and tried with careers, and struggled and found out that they weren't getting paid as much and that they weren't as fulfilled, and they have decided that there needs to be a balance between, you know, women's lib on this side and the family on that side, but that the two should come together.

Winfrey thus reinforced the idea that the women's movement is relevant only for working women—more precisely, for those with careers—while also accepting the New Right argument that "women's lib" somehow stood in antagonistic relation-ship to the "family unit." Winfrey's comment also implied that feminism would be unnecessary if every woman could find a man to take care of her. Further, despite the many sexist—even misogynist—statements by the male panelists and audience members, Winfrey never questioned how *those* attitudes might affect the family. Nor was the "breakdown in the family" ever associated with men's behavior. Intentionally or not, then, Winfrey reinforced the New Right's stance on feminism—a point that one woman in the audience attempted to raise in the final minutes of the show:

The issue today got into whether there was discrimination, which I don't think is argu-able. Whether there is chauvinism, which I also don't think is arguable. But there's a way that things need to pull together—that is that all the different groups that are under attack from the right wing need to get together and fight back, or else we're all going to go down. And I think that's the most important thing, and feminism is very central to that.

Her statement provoked a brief free-for-all on stage as the male panelists vented their hostility toward feminism and Yamasaki made a last pitch for social equality. Winfrey closed the episode saying, "It's been quite interesting. I don't know what was accomplished, but at least we talked about it." Winfrey's professed confusion aside, I suggest that what was accomplished in this episode was the tacit endorsement of the notion that women are uniquely responsible for the vitality of the family, that the movement for women's equality is inimical to that institution, and that it is up to women alone to resolve that dilemma.

The women's movement was also the focal point of "Old-fashioned Women," which aired the following season (*Oprah Winfrey Show*, March 14, 1988). Winfrey opened by saying the program would address a subject that "I know every one of you out there has discussed at some point or another in the past five years: Should women go back to being more old-fashioned?" She warned viewers that the episode "may be full of bad news for all of the women out there who think that every man likes a successful, assertive, go-getting career woman." Panelists included Nick Nickolas, described as a "millionaire restauranteur," "one of the country's most eligible bachelors," and an "old-fashioned man" who believed the women's movement had made women "too tough"; Ty Wansley, a "modern man" who supported women's struggle for equality; Carol Isenberg, a TV producer who cited her equitable marriage as proof that men *could* change; Asa Baber, a *Playboy* columnist who claimed men wanted women to be "more feminine"; popular radio psychologist Toni Grant, whose best-selling book *Being a Woman* argued that women must be less aggressive and competitive if they wanted to attract and keep men; and founding editor of *Ms.* magazine, Letty Pogrebin, who maintained that being an "old-fashioned woman" was equivalent to being subservient to men.

Grant, Baber, and Nickolas were united in their complaint that the women's movement had caused a "war between the sexes" and that this conflict was entirely women's doing. Echoing the ideology of Reaganism, they argued that women had become aggressive and unfeminine, hostile to men, unable to form lasting love relationships, and, as a result, miserable. Their solution was for women to change—to be more "soft and sweet," "ladylike," and "feminine," and less "angry," "competitive," and "self-centered." These panelists also insisted that women were mired in confusion. When asked by Winfrey if he believed the women's movement had "hurt relationships between men and women," Nickolas replied: "I think mainly the women are confused now. You know, I think they're tired of climbing telephone poles and working construction and joining the army. That didn't work." Baber accused the women's movement of creating "total confusion in both sexes." Grant argued that "the average woman today" was "armored," "competitive," "antagonistic toward men," and "confused." Grant said she had written *Being a Woman* because she was "confused about being a woman" and "wanted to become more of a woman." In her view, being more of a woman meant realizing that competitiveness and assertiveness belonged in the workplace, not in relationships. Because women failed to recognize this, they were "always fighting with men" and had "trouble being a lady," even though what men really wanted was "some ladylike behaviors" and "to come home to some serenity." Women would be more successful in love, Grant insisted, and even "find relief," if they would remove their "Amazon armor" and "yield control to some man."

Wansley, Isenberg, and Pogrebin rejected both this diagnosis and the prescribed cure. Pogrebin argued that women's unhappiness stemmed from the fact that men were "short-changing women emotionally" and keeping them "economically dependent" so as to retain their male privilege. Wansley said women's "subservient" and "passive" role had "gone on too long." In his view, women deserved a "50–50 relationship" and men who resisted that arrangement were "cowards." Isenberg stated that gender-based "power and control issues" were "enormous" in a "culture that is much more geared toward men in a much more powerful role." Winfrey joined the fray when she described women who constantly wait on and cater to men as "slaves." Such apparently minor gestures, she said, were "symbolic of power and control in a relationship." This comparison provoked vehement objections from Grant, Baber, and Nickolas. Grant accused Winfrey of mistaking a "loving gesture" for subservience. Nickolas chastised her for "reducing those things to words like slave and servant. Nobody ever thinks that way." Baber argued that Winfrey's comment exemplified "the anger that men face." It was "so angry and unfair," he said, "to reduce us to … the slave/master relationship." Winfrey replied, "I didn't say you were slaveholders. I said there are women, there are some women, and I know this because I talk to them all the time, there are some women, a great majority of women, who are in relationships where they behave like subservient slaves."

This statement merits scrutiny. While Winfrey was obviously critical of women's subordination and thus appeared to be making a feminist critique of gender inequality, she laid the blame on women's behavior—not men's. The implication is that being a "subservient slave" is a voluntary undertaking or purely psychological disposition on the part of women rather than an effect of structured social relations. Winfrey also seemed to validate such subordination, implying in a question to Grant that struggling for gender equality and getting along with men were mutually exclusive: "Do we [women] want to be right or do we want to be loved?" Grant replied that women would surely opt for love and recommended they learn to use their "feminine power" to get it. She was adamant that being a feminist and being loved by men were incompatible, as was Baber, who argued that women "cannot be filled with feminist rhetoric and feminist self-absorption and knock us [men] and call us all sorts of names and expect us to be able to love them."

Pogrebin challenged that perspective, but to little avail, as Baber interrupted to complain that feminists "believe they are superior to men," and Grant claimed the feminists she knew were "desperately unhappy and lonely." Winfrey was silent during this exchange and never challenged the stereotype of feminists as miserable, man-hating malcontents. That some women had taken to heart this stereotype was evident in comments by two audience members. "I don't want to be a man's enemy," said the first, "I love men and want a man to love me." The second, who quickly noted she was no feminist, concurred: "I don't want to fight with men. I like men." The idea that women who sought equality would necessarily alienate men not only gained momentum as the hour wore on—it was presented exclusively as women's problem to solve. Winfrey reinforced this message in her summary statement near the end of the episode:

I think a lot of women who are out there working and being aggressive and trying to get positions in life are mistaken—mistaken in the notion that men want women who are successful. Because from what we're hearing from you and men like you, Nick, is that men don't care what position you have and they'd rather you didn't.

Winfrey thus made a man who preferred his women "soft and sweet" and who wished to "be in charge" in relationships into the representative of what "men want." Conversely, panelist Ty Wansley, who advocated gender equality, appeared to speak only for himself. Nickolas may have won the right to represent "men in general" because he was much more vocal, speaking forty-eight times to Wansley's nine utterances. But his prominence might have something to do with Winfrey, who engaged with him repeatedly, eliciting his comments, asking him questions and responding to him sixteen times versus four times for Wansley. Certainly Nickolas's numerous sexist statements provided more drama—and thus entertainment—that might account for Winfrey's greater interaction with him, but it is telling nonetheless that she gave so little attention to a male guest committed to the women's movement. Indeed, as in the "Male Chauvinism" episode, the antifeminist panelists received much more air time than their profeminist counterparts; the former spoke a combined 123 times to the 60 utterances of the latter. It is also noteworthy that Winfrey's own closing comments, as noted above, echoed the position espoused by the antifeminist trio, even though of the twenty-one panelists and audience members who spoke during the show, twelve expressed profeminist views.

What, then, are we to make of claims that *The Oprah Winfrey Show* represents a version of popular feminism that "empowers" women? If feminism seeks to dissolve the public/private divide by exposing and analyzing the relationship between personal experience and political power, the fact that talk shows publicize the private lives of women—who have historically been excluded from public discourse—might invite a homology between feminism and talk programs. But if both start from personal testimony, their destinations differ in crucial ways. For feminism, the purpose of examining one's experience is to achieve an analysis of women's lives in terms of structural gender relations of power and to derive a political program of collective action. For talk shows, self-revelation is an end in itself—the content, raison d'etre, and substance of the entertainment. If, in Jane Shattuc's estimation, these programs "articulate the frustrations of women's subordination in a 'man's world'" (Shattuc 1997, 136), they do so without examining the systemic nature and material foundations of those frustrations. As Shattuc has noted, therapy talk shows, including *The Oprah Winfrey Show*, "phobically avoid male bashing" (ibid., 129). Indeed, as we saw in the episodes analyzed here, women are much more likely to be the target of criticism as Winfrey and many female audience members strive not to alienate even the most overtly sexist male guests.

The feminism of talk shows, Shattuc writes, issues mainly from the fact that they make women's experience the primary content—hence, "the critique of masculine power is implied and rarely stated" (ibid., 129). But perhaps we should not equate addressing the experience of women with engaging in a feminist political critique. Talk shows typically avoid dealing with explicitly feminist topics in the first place, as Shattuc acknowledges, and in the relatively few episodes devoted to such topics, the host rarely takes an openly feminist stance. While Winfrey may have invited guests such as Chesler, Brownmiller, Berg, and Pogrebin to represent the feminist side of an issue, she did not align herself with them. Indeed, as seen in these episodes, feminist panelists received substantially less of her attention and interest than those who were hostile toward the women's movement. Further, in contrast to a feminist critique, *The Oprah Winfrey Show* does not move from the personal experiences of participants to an investigation of their political context and implications. Instead, Winfrey remains resolutely at the level of the personal, which allows her to direct the comments and interactions so as to evoke the maximum emotional response from her guests and audience. This is the hallmark of her particular style as talk show host—the very quality that enables her to differentiate her TV persona and product in a highly competitive genre. Her effort in the working-mothers episode to "get a real fat fight" by fanning the frustrations of the at-home moms and the extensive time accorded the "male chauvinists" and proponents of "old-fashioned women" help maintain the conflict and emotional intensity that keeps viewers tuned in for the fireworks.

The effect of corralling talk show topics within the confines of the personal is to circumvent an interrogation of the objective conditions and structural relations of power within which personal experience is constituted. This is the ideological work of talk shows generally and what, in the case of *The Oprah Winfrey Show*, makes it possible to "take the pulse of American women" without having to take the pulse of American politics and economics. This is also what allows Winfrey's program to turn the problems facing women into the recurring display of "women with problems." As I argue in the next chapter, the absence or devaluation of a feminist framework of interpretation opens the door to an alternative way of understanding women's lives and struggles: the therapeutic narrative of "recovery," whereby "women with problems" is transmuted into "the problem with women." This transmutation is the basis of the compatibility between "recovery" and Reaganism.

~ 4 ~

Recovery and Reaganism

The Psychologization of the Political and the Politics of Pathology

You know, I don't think there is a woman alive who has not been in a relationship at some point with a low-down dawg.... sometimes, you know, it takes time to spot a scoundrel. But today's show is all about women who are absolutely hooked on bad relationships
—"Women Who Love Too Much," *Oprah Winfrey Show*, Dec. 2, 1986

If Oprah Winfrey was reluctant to identify with guests forwarding a feminist critique of the political problems facing women, she showed no such timidity when it came to guests offering diagnoses of women's psychological problems. In December 1986, Winfrey welcomed Robin Norwood, whose *Women Who Love Too Much* (1985) had soared to the top of best-seller lists. Norwood claimed that the book grew out of her work counseling male drug and alcohol abusers and their female partners, from which she concluded that the women were also "addicted"—in this case to abusive men—and equally in need of "recovery." When Norwood appeared on *The Oprah Winfrey Show*, thousands of women across the United States were already attending Women Who Love Too Much (WWLTM) groups and identifying themselves as "man junkies" in need of help from a "higher power" to overcome their addictive inclinations.

In her introduction, Winfrey said she was "so glad to be doing this show, because women have called all around the country saying please do something on this subject." Indeed, so widespread was this problem that it apparently plagued her entire audience: "If you're a woman who is watching this show, undoubtedly at some point in your life you have experienced it too." Winfrey spent the first two segments exploring the troubled relationships of guests Denise Lane and Peggy Wilkins. Lane financially supported her boyfriend (and father of her two children), despite the fact that throughout their six-year relationship he routinely cheated on her and disappeared for days at a time. She remained convinced he would one day "wake up" and appreciate her love. Wilkins gave up a successful modeling career at her jealous lover's insistence and eventually became a "prisoner" in her own home. She had left him once but returned, even though "it was back to the same story but even worse." During the exchange, Winfrey revealed that she too had suffered from what she called "this 'down-on-your-knees' syndrome," but made it clear that, unlike her guests, she had long since "recovered" from her own "period of mental illness." Her goal was to get the two women to confront their pathology. "Do you think there's something wrong with you?" she asked Lane. "Do you realize you're one of these women [who love too much]?" she queried Wilkins.

It was not just the panelists who needed help. Before introducing Norwood, Winfrey recited the "typical characteristics of women who love too much" (to which I return shortly) and directed the audience "to see if you recognize yourself." She then asked for a show of hands from audience members who "heard yourselves in these comments." From the program transcript, it appears that many did, including Norwood, who said she had written the book "because I've been there." Indeed, her own professed recovery from "relationship-addiction" was key to the book's popularity (Faludi 1991, 253). Comments during the episode indicate that the studio audience was largely comprised of women who had read the book. While many remained mired in unsatisfying relationships and a few claimed they were on the road to "recovery," all who spoke identified with Norwood's diagnosis and saw themselves as "women who love too much."

The core message of Norwood's book is fairly simple: women from "dysfunctional families" choose "distant, damaged" men so as to replicate their childhood experience and gain another chance to win the love they were originally denied. They are obsessed with "fixing" their troubled partners and relationships, driven not by authentic love (which Norwood insisted is "so rare") but by a compulsion that is incomprehensible "if you don't look at it as addiction." During the show, Norwood compared women involved with hurtful men to alcoholics and drug addicts, all of whom "can't stop on their own" and "have to hit bottom." That this language issues from the world of 12-Step programs is to be expected, given that her book was dedicated to "the Anonymous programs in gratitude for the miracle of recovery they offer" (Norwood 1986, 27). The "cure" for "man junkies" was therefore the same as for alcohol or heroin abusers. When asked by Winfrey what women "hooked on bad relationships" should do, Norwood replied: "One of the things I know is that we don't get well from addiction on our own. We need something larger than ourselves.... Probably most women who love too much qualify for some of the anonymous programs—Al-Anon, which is for the partners, families and friends of alcoholics—that kind of approach to this helps more than anything I've ever seen."

But if "man junkies" could not conquer their "addiction" alone, they bore full responsibility for being in troubled relationships in the first place. In Norwood's view, "there aren't any accidents in relationships"—women "have to begin to say this is my pattern" and stop blaming men "if [they're] going to change." This is precisely what "women who love too much" failed to do: "What's so hard for us to accept is that this person is who he is," Norwood said. Women attracted to "dangerous men" ignore signs of trouble and throw themselves into trying to improve the relationship, which "is a very self-willed thing to do." Herein lies the pathology of "man junkies"—their effort to alter the terms of their relationships is a manifestation of their "addiction" to "emotional pain." What's more, such behavior is "oppressive" to men because "it's very smothering to be on the other end of a woman who is so desperately trying to make everything right." As Norwood told a caller to the show—whose boyfriend had someone beat her up because she went back to work against his wishes—whether men change or not "is none of our business. Our job is to change ourselves." Winfrey pressed this point with guest Diane Lane, asking why she stayed with her cheating boyfriend when "it's your choice, and we all, as Robin says, have to take full responsibility for the choices we make in life." Lane replied that by the time she realized he was "a manipulator instead of an appreciator," it was "too late." A few minutes later, as Winfrey similarly pressured an audience member, Lane broke in desperately: "It's so easy for you, Oprah, you recovered."

Norwood's answer to why women stay with hurtful men exposes the contradiction at the center of her analysis. On one hand, women are held responsible for entering, remaining in, and trying to improve bad relationships—a tendency, Norwood suggested, to which females are especially prone: "It has to do with this incredible will to change another person, to get him to be different. There's something so compelling about that in women." On the other hand, getting involved with "damaged" men is an addiction equivalent to substance abuse—something that women "can't stop on their own." Winfrey picked up on this contradiction when she asked, "Why can't we stop it though, because we all have free wills to make choices for ourselves?" Norwood's answer: "Well, if you understand what addiction is, you know that free will doesn't do it." Thus, "women who love too much" are chastised for having exercised their will by selecting a "damaged" partner *and* for exerting their will to try to change the relationship, which is a sign of their own disease. The only cure is to "let go of self-will" and "build your willingness to surrender" (quoted in Faludi 1991, 349). This amounts to saying that women's "will" is itself pathological—something that can be combated only by renouncing one's desires and conceding dependence on an external, metaphysical force.

That such a message runs counter to feminism's take on women's problems is obvious. Indeed, it is decidedly antifeminist in its recommendation that women accept men as they are, that their desire for men to change is a symptom of a specifically female mental disturbance, that they purge themselves of will and embrace powerlessness. The antifeminist thrust of Norwood's message is evident in examining the "Characteristics of Women Who Love Too Much," which Winfrey recited to her audience and that were (and are) routinely read aloud in WWLTM groups. Those characteristics, as presented by Winfrey, are as follows:

> You come from a home in which your emotional needs were not met. You are a caregiver, particularly to men who appear needy. Because your parents were not warm and loving, you are attracted to men who are like that and also whom you'd like to change by loving them. Terrified of abandonment, you'll do just about anything to keep a relationship going; nothing is too much trouble or expense if it will help your man. You are willing to wait, to hope and try harder to please. You're willing to take far more than 50 percent of the blame for any relationship. Your self-esteem is very low, and deep down, you don't believe you have the right to be happy. You have a desperate need to take control in a relationship and mask it by being helpful. In a relationship you're much more in touch with your dreams of how it could be than the reality of how it really is. You are addicted to men and to emotional pain. You may be predisposed to addiction to drugs, to alcohol, to certain foods, particularly sugary ones. By being drawn to people with problems you avoid focusing on yourself. You have a tendency towards depression. You are not attracted to men who are kind, who are safe, who are reliable and interested in you ... you find them boring.[1]

What is striking about this litany of "characteristics" is the extent to which what they label pathological symptoms might, from another perspective, be seen as responses to or results of structural relations of gender domination. Being afraid of abandonment by men and "doing just about anything to keep a relationship going," for example, may be reasonable actions in a world where millions of women are dependent on men for their (and their children's) financial security, and where gender inequities in education and employment are firmly institutionalized. Doing whatever it takes to hang onto a man makes sense in purely economic terms, given the findings of Lenore J. Weitzman's *The Divorce Revolution* (1985) that women and their children suffered a 73 percent decline in their standard of living following a divorce, while men reaped a 42 percent increase. Striving to please men seems equally understandable in light of the fact that male violence against women is unfortunately common. Being a "caregiver," trying to fulfill the needs of one's partner, taking most of the responsibility for relational difficulties, and focusing on other people's problems rather than one's own—which are here presented as personality defects—might just as easily be seen as consequences of women's socially prescribed gender role. All of these behaviors are examples of what Debbie Epstein and Deborah Steinberg (1998) call "kinship work" involving "the creation, mediation and even dissolution of relationships" (86). As they note, within the existing, historically constituted relations of gender, it is "primarily women who are expected to do this work" (ibid., 88). Thus, what Norwood decries as symptoms specific to "man junkies" are actually behaviors expected of women in general based on the gendered division of emotional labor. In this respect, all women could be potentially identified as pathological.

Similarly, the "desperate need to take control" portrayed by Norwood as an irruption of peculiarly feminine neurosis might more plausibly reflect women's awareness of and response to gender inequality. That women seek control indirectly (i.e., "by being helpful") could be interpreted as a result of their subordination, insofar as direct bids for power by subordinate individuals or social groups are often met with suppression and/or violence. "Low self-esteem" and a "tendency towards depression" are also logical consequences of an unequal gender order, where women are devalued and their range of acceptable actions restricted. As Paula Caplan notes, the self-denial cultivated in girls and expected from women "often goes hand-in-hand" with "low self-esteem" (Caplan 1985, 35). Such attributes also help defuse challenges to that order if women are demoralized and filled with self-doubt. Of particular interest is the claim that "women who love too much" are "much more in touch with [their] dreams of how it could be than the reality of how it really is." While Norwood is suggesting that "man addicts" deceive themselves about the true nature of their relationships, her diagnosis implies that learning to accept "how it really is" means letting go of one's "passion" (since she equates it with "suffering"), abandoning the will to affect one's circumstances, and ceasing to make demands on men. From an alternative perspective—a feminist one, say—it is certainly important to possess clarity about the actual nature of gender relations (hence the crucial role of "consciousness-raising" within feminism), but it is equally vital to imagine a different, more equitable gender order, because it is the latter that fuels political struggles for change.

The assertions that "women who love too much" are "addicted to men and to emotional pain" and "predisposed" to dependence on drugs, alcohol, or food bring together two powerful strands of the psychological worldview. The first draws on the long-standing belief that women are inherently masochistic. Susan Faludi argues that the psychiatric diagnosis of masochism, which first emerged in the late Victorian period, quickly "degenerated into a sort of all-purpose definition of the female psyche" (1991, 356; see also Ehrenreich and English 1978). While the assumption of an "innate feminine masochism" (Faludi 1991, 356) had diminished somewhat by the 1970s thanks in part to the feminist critique of psychology, it had not disappeared. The idea that women somehow seek out and relish suffering was, predictably, revived in the 1980s as feminism came under increasing political attack. In 1985 the male-dominated American Psychiatric Association (APA) added "masochistic personality disorder" to its professional bible—the *Diagnostic and Statistical Manual of Mental Disorders (DSM)*.[2] Given the historical association of masochism with women, it is not surprising that the nine characteristics used to define—and determine the presence of—this newly minted disorder "described only the self-sacrificing and self-denigrating sort of behavior that is supposed to typify ideal femininity" (Faludi 1991, 357). Both Norwood's book and the powerful psychiatric establishment thus reinforced the damaging notion that being a woman and being psychologically defective were synonymous.

By drawing a connection between being "addicted to emotional pain" and being addicted to alcohol, drugs, or food, Norwood's description of "man junkies" also incorporated (via AA) the well-established biological explanation of psychological functioning. *Women Who Love Too Much* attributed women's attraction to abusive men to "an interplay of cultural and biological factors," whereby women "try to protect themselves and avoid pain" through compulsive behaviors such as drinking, eating, and loving too much (Norwood 1986, 27). As Elayne Rapping notes, employing a "metaphor of biological addiction" as "an explanation for destructive sexual attractions" works to sever male/female relationships from their social and political context and "ensures that women's efforts to free themselves from unhealthy relationships with men will remain personal and spiritual, never political" (Rapping 1996, 151, 152). This resort to biology also legitimizes the "medicalization" of women's lives, whereby their emotions and behavior are "defined in terms of health and illness" and subjected to medical labeling and treatment (Riessman 1983, 5). As Catherine Riessman argues, "women are more likely than men to have problematic experiences defined and treated medically" because of their "structurally dependent" status (ibid.).

Furthermore, for all that Norwood purported to address relationship problems, her book is fundamentally nonrelational in its approach. One of feminist theory's major insights is that gender is not a neutral description of natural biological differences but a historically constituted system of meanings and practices rooted in social relations of power. When gender is conceived relationally, it is impossible to understand one gender in isolation from the other or from the hierarchy of power that binds them together. If definitions of masculine and feminine, the social roles assigned to males and females, and the actions of men and women are inextricably linked, any change at one pole of the gender order necessarily has effects on the other. Because that order *is* hierarchical, the dominant gender has greater freedom and resources at its disposal to direct change in its own favor, while the subordinate gender is expected to comply and adjust accordingly. Key to preserving this power imbalance is the capacity to represent a particular sociohistorical system of gender relations as natural, inevitable, and desirable (rooted in nature and biology, for example), to deny that a hierarchy exists in the first place (the separate-but-equal alibi), and/or to present it in camera obscura (e.g., women are morally superior, too pure for the public sphere, the "Cult of True Womanhood," etc.).

Norwood's analysis incorporates all three ideological strategies. Whereas men ("damaged" or not) simply "are who they are," women—despite their inherent compulsion to "get him to be different"—can either indulge in their penchant for pain and choose bad men or give up their will and passion and settle for "nice guys" who are "safe" and "boring." The one thing they cannot do—if they wish to embark on "recovery"—is expect or ask men to change. Such expectations are futile in any case, since there is no sense in Norwood's analysis that men are even capable of changing. They appear instead to be forces of nature to which women must simply adapt. Men's motives are not only none of women's business but also apparently beyond comprehension. When in the Winfrey episode guest Diane Lane asked if there are "men who love too much," Norwood replied: "There are men who love too much. I don't write about men because I don't understand men. I understand women." This is a remarkable statement from someone claiming to be an expert on heterosexual relationships and would seem to undermine her entire analysis. No one in the program, however, including Winfrey, found this revelation worth commenting upon.

Despite the fact that Norwood on occasion had compared WWLTM groups to consciousness-raising groups, her analysis ultimately reinforced rather than challenged the existing gender order because it conceived gender differences as innate and static, treated men and women as separate and merely different kinds of beings, and implied that women are ultimately superior because they—unlike men—can modify their behavior, albeit by surrendering to an external (and implicitly masculine) power.[3] Ironically, Norwood's prescription for counteracting women's putative masochistic tendencies—letting go of their will and passion—valorized yet another trait—passivity—that the psychological establishment had long considered inherent to femininity.[4]

Because Norwood failed to treat gender as a relational system of power, women's suffering was attributed to defects of their psychology that exist independently of men. Accordingly, as she explained on Winfrey's show, "women who love too much" must "get off of what he does and what he doesn't do" and focus solely on their own "recovery." What Norwood did *not* counsel is for women to simply leave abusive men. Late in the episode, a caller (and mother of three) described her eight-year marriage to a man who forbid her to have friends or connections with family members, to leave the house without him, or even to open the curtains when she was home alone. She said she had tried to leave but relented when he promised "things will change." Winfrey asked Norwood what the woman should do, to which Norwood replied: "Well, one of the things that women say to me often when they start seeing me is 'I need to leave, or I want to leave, or should I leave.' And my response is you need to stay until you learn the lesson that this relationship is trying to teach you." Such lessons apparently extended to physical abuse. When the caller revealed that her husband also hit her, Norwood stated that violence "is usually present in these relationships" because "women who love too much" are "very addicted to drama and excitement." In effect, Norwood accused this desperate, isolated, mistreated woman of seeking her own torment due to her particular psychological defects. Glaringly absent in the interaction was any criticism of the husband or attempt to explore the concrete life options available to the caller—her economic situation, her potential job skills, the ages of her children, whether she knew of local shelters or programs for abused women and their children, and so on. Instead, Norwood used this woman's horrendous circumstances as one more illustration of women's pathological "patterns of relating." Winfrey was equally insensitive during this exchange. After listening to the caller's pained description of a life of virtual imprisonment, Winfrey queried, "Is he just jealous, is that it?" and followed with, "How long will you stick around? It obviously—it's not bad enough to make you leave, is it?"

In the concluding minutes of the show, Winfrey asked Norwood whether "women who love too much" would even "be able to live with" a "perfectly nice guy." Norwood replied, "We have to get well before we can do that. . . . You know, we attract someone who treats us in a way that fits with how we treat ourselves." The program thus reiterated the double bind at the heart of what Paula Caplan calls the "myth of women's masochism," where qualities such as being selfless, nurturing, and endlessly patient, which are not only learned behaviors but constitute "the very essence of femininity in Western culture" (Caplan 1985, 35), are used as proof of female masochism. Caplan argues that while much of women's unhappiness stems from living in a "misogynist society," the myth of women's masochism is employed "to blame the women themselves for their misery" (ibid., 9). Through this myth, "women's problems can be attributed to our deep-seated psychological needs, not to the social institutions that really are the cause of the trouble" (ibid., 10).

Winfrey and Norwood did not address this double bind and its implications. They did not explore entrenched economic inequities that figure into women's dependence on men, question how and why women have been saddled with the majority of "kinship work," or ponder the effect on women's "self-esteem" of being told that performing the role for which they were trained is a sign of their mental illness and informed that the humiliation and abuse they endure at the hands of men stems from their own "addiction to pain." Equally significant is the fact that men escaped examination altogether, so that all relationship problems were laid at women's feet. This diagnosis faltered even in the cases discussed on the show, however. The men described by the panelists, audience members, and callers appeared to be no less "addicted" to their relationships than the women. Indeed, many of the women in the episode described husbands and lovers who became desperate—often to the point of violence—when their wives or girlfriends tried to leave. But since men's behavior was not at issue, the problem could be attributed exclusively to "women who love too much," rather than, as Bette Tallen puts it in her critique of Norwood, to "men who hit too much" (Tallen 1990, 21).

Winfrey's embrace of this disease explanation of women's struggles with men—she remarked at the end of the show, "if you think it's anything else [but addiction], then you're wrong"—reflects her ambivalence toward a feminist analysis of gender relations and her preference for the far less threatening recovery model. Harriet Lerner argues that "recovery" functions as "a sort of compromise solution" that "teaches women to move in the direction of 'more self' while it sanitizes and makes change safe, because the dominant group culture is not threatened by sick women meeting together to get well" (Lerner 1990, 15). The recovery paradigm thereby allowed Winfrey to tackle problems faced by her largely female audience without antagonizing male viewers or being accused of man-bashing. It is thus not surprising that "recovery" achieved the status of the dominant frame of intelligibility in *The Oprah Winfrey Show* from its first season. As a "structure of knowing," the recovery model (in conjunction with the deficient self on which it is based) attempts to manage social and political conflicts by translating them into personal, psychological troubles. This translation process, which constitutes the ideological work of the therapeutic enterprise in general, is evident in a subsequent episode devoted to "relationship addiction" that aired six months after Norwood's appearance.

Winfrey's introduction to "Obsessive Love" (*Oprah Winfrey Show*, June 12, 1987) was strikingly similar to her opening remarks in "Women Who Love Too Much":

> I am really, really excited about this show, because I think this is a show that affects just about every woman I know who's watching, to some extent. You've been down on your knees, begging him not to leave you, because you just cannot imagine life without him. He's been a low-down dirty dog, but you … still can't live without him. He's been unfaithful, but you still love him; you're tormented when you're with him, terrified of being without him. I'm Oprah Winfrey, and today we're going to hear from people obsessed with love and loving.

As in the Norwood episode, Winfrey suggested that the problem was universal to women: "I was talking to my producers this morning, and we were talking about how every woman, at some level, has felt these feelings of obsession." And, as before, the initial segments were devoted to recounting the horror stories of the three "ordinary" guests "obsessed with love." Two of the panelists, Barbara Weidman and Mary Mann, might have qualified for a slot on the "Women Who Love Too Much" show, having been "addicted" to unfaithful, abusive men, were it not for the fact that both had since left their partners. The third guest, Tony Toto, still pined for his wife even though she had tried to have him murdered and was serving time in prison for her crime. Toto presented a challenge to Winfrey's conviction that love addiction was a distinctly feminine malady, which she tried to resolve by treating him as an anomaly. The guest expert, in comparison, was much more difficult to reconcile with the "women who love too much" frame of intelligibility.

After introducing Dr. Stanton Peele as "a specialist in addictive relationships," Winfrey said she and the audience wanted to know "why it happens." Was it, she asked, simply a matter of "self-hatred, or insecurity"? Peele was likely targeted as a suitable expert for this topic because his book, *Love and Addiction* (1975), was listed in the appendix of *Women Who Love Too Much* as "required reading." It was immediately apparent that Winfrey expected him to reiterate Norwood's take on both addiction and love. Had she actually read Peele's book, however, she would have encountered an analysis wholly at odds with Norwood's. Although he uses the term *addiction* in association with relationships, Peele rejects outright the notion that addiction is rooted in biology, even in the case of drug and alcohol dependence. Indeed, he states in the book's introduction that his interest in the subject of addiction grew out of his concern that "people were misconstruing human problems as physical and biochemical problems" (Peele 1975, 16). In contrast to a biological approach, Peele characterizes addiction as a way of relating to the world arising from "a paucity of experience," an ingrained sense of inadequacy, and a lack of "confidence in [one's] capacity to come to grips with life independently" (ibid., 60).

In Peele's analysis, all of the above are socially conditioned phenomena rather than innate tendencies or purely individual flaws. As a way of relating to oneself and others, addiction is a logical result of "learned helplessness" that robs people of the means to resolve their problems and leaves them feeling powerless to affect the course of their own lives. Although feelings of impotence can afflict both men and women, Peele notes that structural gender inequality exacerbates women's sense of inadequacy and powerlessness: "The role mapped out for a woman symbolizes the addict's lot because it is predicated on inadequacy" (ibid., 173). He also links "the denial of financial independence and freedom of movement to women" to a "denial of [their] emotional independence, which is what addiction springs from in women and in men" (ibid.). Because women "have been channeled into a few basic involvements —marriage, family, home"—that constitute their "assigned sphere of activity," Peele maintains that "it is not surprising if, lacking other outlets, a woman defines herself by [these] relationships and depends on them to the point of addiction" (ibid.).

In contrast to Norwood's admonition to "man junkies" that their "self-will" is part of their disease, Peele views addiction as a deficit of will and passion in individuals who had been "systematically educated and trained into incompetence" by social institutions such as the family, education, and religion (ibid., 57). Their resulting sense of impotence leads them to seek external sources of strength in substances, activities, or people. Thus, from Peele's perspective, the "cure" for addiction is not *less* passion and will, but *more*. The "antithesis of addiction," he writes, "is a true relatedness to the world" that follows from "the development of . . . interests, joys, [and] competencies" (ibid., 17, 19). Further, although combating addiction begins with "gathering tools of self-analysis" (ibid., 18), it necessarily leads to an interrogation of the social sources of this mode of relating:

> The real cure for addiction lies in a social change which reorients our major institutions and the types of experience people have within them. If we are to do more than to liberate ourselves one by one . . . then we have to change our institutions, and ultimately our society. Just as we cannot begin to understand addiction without understanding people's relationship to their social setting, so we cannot begin to cure it in the absence of a more universal access to our society's resources, and to its political power. If addiction is based on a feeling of helplessness, it will be with us until we create a social structure that is sensitive to people's desires and their efforts at influence. (ibid., 206)

Given the clear contrast between the perspectives of Peele and Norwood—and Winfrey's strong identification with the latter—the "Obsessive Love" episode was marked by clashes between these competing frames of intelligibility. In response to Winfrey's question about the cause of love addiction, Peele suggested that the inability to discern good relationships from bad was a common human experience that "nearly every adolescent has gone through." We are susceptible to this confusion in our youth, he said, because "you get involved in relationships that aren't good for you and you don't have enough confidence in yourself to ask yourself 'Why do I feel bad?' and decide 'Well, this relationship isn't for me.'" Peele added that "most people get over that kind of puppy love" because "they grow up, they become more secure about themselves, they get involved in work, they develop friendships." By implication, people who continue a pattern of destructive relationships as adults can break that cycle only by "get[ting] involved in life, so that you get a real feeling that you're a better kind of person."

Peele's prescription differed dramatically from Norwood's: she encouraged women to turn inward and focus on their "disease" while he recommended turning outward to develop a richer set of experiences and connections to the world. And although Peele referred to "sick" or "addictive" relationships, at no point in his book or on Winfrey's show did he suggest that people in such relationships suffered from a disease. As the following exchange indicates, he also resisted Winfrey's attempts to make relationship addiction a specifically female phenomenon:

WINFREY: What is it about us, particularly women more so than men, Tony [Toto] is an exception to the rule in every aspect—but what is it about women in particular that causes us to believe the more we suffer, the more we can get him?

PEELE: Well, I think there's a male counterpart to every woman who's involved in . . .

WINFREY: You do?

PEELE: . . . in an addictive relationship. They just express it in a different kind of fashion.

Peele thus conceived troubled relationships *relationally* as an interplay of the actions of both parties. Winfrey's confusion here (i.e., "You do?") reflected her identification with Norwood's analysis, as did her continued use during this episode of the phrase "women who love too much," despite the fact that Peele himself never employed such language.

Peele also departed from Norwood in advising people in "disastrous," hurtful relationships to "get out of it." And, in contrast to Norwood's readiness to dispense a one-size-fits-all diagnosis (women are addicted to men and pain) and prescription (admit your powerlessness and get thee to a 12-Step program), Peele was obviously uncomfortable with such an approach, as this exchange with a young woman in the audience illustrates:

AUDIENCE MEMBER: But why do we find it necessary to give up all our friends, to not worry about our job? Why do we do this to ourselves?

WINFREY: You've done it?

AUDIENCE MEMBER: Yes, I have—my grades have gone down, my other friends, I've completely ignored them.

PEELE: Well, you're answering the question. Are those friends and are those other things important to you?

AUDIENCE MEMBER: They were. They very much were before I started in the relationship, until I gave up everything and had just him as my only friend, my only—

PEELE: What would you tell a friend who gave up her job and gave up her friends?

AUDIENCE MEMBER: A fool. But I—

WINFREY: Say, girl, you are stupid!

AUDIENCE MEMBER: But why do they do it? Why did I do it?

PEELE: How can I tell you why you gave up things that were supposedly important to you? Maybe they were causing you too much anxiety, and maybe you felt this was an easy way out. But what I would tell you is those are the things that are going to get you through life, and that if you were going to be in love, if somebody's going to really love you, they're going to appreciate you because you have friends and you're intelligent and you have a job.

Peele did pose possible reasons for this young woman's retreat into a suffocating relationship. But in keeping with his belief that addiction stems from a profound sense of inadequacy, he also validated her involvement in friendships, work, and school and affirmed her capacity for self-knowledge and action by implying that it was *she* who held the key to her self-understanding. It is worth speculating on how Norwood would have handled this guest. The young woman would likely be labeled a "woman who loves too much," told she was hooked on suffering, and encouraged to embark on a lifetime of trying to manage her "disease." Which of these responses should be described as "empowering"?

Despite the striking difference between Peele's view of addiction and Norwood's, Winfrey continued to conflate the two. Immediately following the preceding exchange, she told viewers they would "find out about the men who choose women who love too much in a moment." In the final minute of the show, Peele suggested, "when so many people have the same problem" in their intimate relations, "we're talking about a society and not just an individual." This attempt to understand the personal as constituted by the social was, as usual, fleeting. The real lesson of the show, Winfrey said as she signed off, was "to never give up your personal spiritual power to another person."

From the idea that relinquishing one's power to another person is a symptom of addiction, it is a short step to the notion of codependency. Emerging in the late 1970s from the AA technology of healing, *codependence* became an umbrella term for the ensemble of "enabling" behaviors associated with spouses (chiefly wives) and children of alcoholics. Given AA's disease model of addiction, according to Jo-Ann Krestan and Claudia Bepko, "it was not a difficult leap to decide that if the alcoholic had a disease, then so must the rest of the family. Gradually came the shift from describing a problem to ascribing pathology" (Krestan and Bepko 1991, 52). As the recovery movement exploded in the 1980s and the concept of addiction migrated far beyond the terrain of alcohol and drug abuse, codependency escaped its narrow identification with alcoholism. By the end of the 1980s, Lerner posits, the term had become "a label of such vast inclusiveness that we are all 'it'" (Lerner 1990, 15). *Basics of Codependency* (1983), for example, identified as codependent "anyone who lives in close association over a prolonged period of time with anyone who has a neurotic personality" (quoted in Krestan and Bepko 1991, 53). Sharon Wegscheider-Cruse, who appeared as a guest expert on Winfrey's earliest episode on alcoholism (*Oprah Winfrey Show*, Oct. 29, 1986), considered not only those from alcoholic families to be codependent but also anyone who "grew up in an emotionally repressive family" (quoted in Tallen 1990, 20). The concept was also appended to biopsychiatry. Joseph Cruse's *Painful Affairs: Looking for Love Through Addiction and Co-Dependency* (1989), for example, labeled codependence "a toxic brain syndrome" (quoted in Krestan and Bepko 1991, 53).

Rapping credits Cruse's *Co-dependency: An Emerging Issue* (1984) with "put[ting] the term 'co-dependent' into common therapeutic use as a description of the kinds of oppressive, 'dysfunctional' relationships which came to be called 'addictive'" (Rapping 1996, 197 n. 9). But it was Melody Beattie's best-selling *Co-dependent No More* (1987) that "made the term a household word" (Rapping 1996, 197 n. 9). Beattie's popularity, in Rapping's view, lay in not restricting the diagnosis to women. Codependents included anyone whose identity was based on trying to control, please, help, and rescue others. Although gender socialization made women more likely to be codependent, men were also susceptible to the "disease." As Rapping argues, Beattie's book "avoid[ed] even the twinge of feminist identification Norwood's book clearly had by being geared only to women, and appear[ed] to be an equal opportunity cure-all" (ibid., 154).

Given Winfrey's affinity for Norwood's diagnosis, and her own conviction that to give up one's personal power to others was the epitome of emotional illness, the concept of codependence found a warm reception on *The Oprah Winfrey Show*. Beattie's inaugural appearance on the program was as a guest expert in the first of twelve monthly episodes in 1989 devoted to alcoholism ("How to Leave a Dependent Spouse," *Oprah Winfrey Show*, Jan. 4, 1989). Characterizing alcohol dependence as "a disease [that] is ripping apart the foundation of our families and our businesses," Winfrey introduced guests Margaret and Jose (identified onscreen as "codependent spouse" and "alcoholic husband"), Lucy ("separated from alcoholic husband"), Dorothy Brown ("left alcoholic husband"), and Gwen ("married to alcoholic husband"). After spending four segments probing the experiences of these panelists, Winfrey introduced Beattie: "My next guest says that the person who lives with an alcoholic also has an illness. It's called codependency." Beattie promptly defined codependency as "a very painful condition" that afflicts those who hail from families "where there was dysfunction or alcoholism."

Contrary to Norwood, Beattie maintained that "men can get just as stuck as women," but like Norwood she did not recommend simply getting out: "Leaving isn't the only answer, because if we leave and don't begin recovery, we're going to find ourselves, chances are, right back in the same spot again. So—we need to stay right where we're at and start taking care of ourselves and start recovering." She offered few clues during the episode as to what that process might entail, however, other than "getting up in the morning, putting on our makeup, and going for a walk." Near the end of the show, a woman in the audience commended Winfrey for "bringing society into this" by "educating us through the TV and mass media." Winfrey seized on this opportunity to announce her plan to "devote a show every month to the disease" so as to examine its impact on "the alcoholics, their family, their friends, and the cures for it." But beyond eliciting the painful details of the panelists' and audience members' experiences in this premiere episode, neither Winfrey nor Beattie provided much substantive information about the subject.

This poverty of knowledge, I suggest, is endemic not only to the notion of codependency but to the larger recovery paradigm. When, as with Beattie, codependency is equated with letting oneself be affected by and trying to control the behavior of other people, autonomy and independence become the presumed model of human development, which makes women inherently inferior. Such a position denies the "value to human relationships" of women's "traditional 'other' focus" and "ignores the social, political, and economic factors that contribute to women's highly developed skills in these areas" (Sloven 1991, 196). Because Beattie simply accepted the binary of autonomy/dependence, which automatically privileges the first term as *the* measure of human maturity, her analysis pathologizes women for their focus on relationship (as well as men who exhibit such "dependent" tendencies) and legitimizes a gender order that devalues "the feminine." Further, given that Beattie considered all efforts to help others as symptomatic of disease, her own analysis precluded her from offering genuine aid to her fellow codependents. Because the disease of codependency entails being encumbered by the lives and needs of others, from which the patient must extricate herself if she is to embark on "recovery," the technology of healing associated with codependency makes the individual solely responsible for both her suffering and her cure.

At root, the notion of codependency—like that of "women who love too much"—is a new variation on an old theme: the autonomous individual's mastery of his own fate, upon which both liberal political theory and capitalism depend. Similarly to liberal feminism, the codependency paradigm extends this implicitly masculine model of the individual to women (see Benjamin 1988). It is by means of this extension, in fact, that the healing technologies of "women who love too much" and "codependency" can claim common cause with feminism, insofar as they appear to challenge the subordination of women's lives to the needs of others. Thus, focusing on one's own "recovery" and becoming "codependent no more" can be represented as paths to women's liberation. Tallen suggests that women have been drawn to the notion of codependency precisely because it "so accurately describes what many of us experience in our lives" (Tallen 1990, 21). That WWLTM groups were favorably compared to consciousness-raising groups and codependency books became best-sellers in feminist bookstores further testifies to the complicated relationship between feminism and the recovery movement.

Recovery, Reaganism, and the "Crisis of the Family"

The codependency diagnosis depoliticizes gender struggles by confining them to the realm of individual psychology and interpersonal relationships. Women's lack of independence and efficacy is thus seen as the consequence not of an inequitable political-economic order, but of familial pathology. It is here that the recovery paradigm and Reaganism meet. The explosion of the recovery movement during the Reagan era is no coincidence, in that the "dysfunctional family" and wounded self at the core of the recovery model turned out to be compatible with the "breakdown of family values" and the "irresponsible" or "immoral" self at the center of Reaganism's ideological agenda. For recovery, as for Reaganism, the malfunctioning of the family is seen as the seat of all forms of pathology. Hence, the cure lies in resuscitating that institution—restoring its values and making it "functional" once again.

This family-centered diagnosis of the cause of and cure for personal and social malaise operated as a central frame of intelligibility in *The Oprah Winfrey Show* throughout the reigns of Ronald Reagan and George H. W. Bush. Alcoholism, drug abuse, addiction, divorce, domestic violence, child abuse, crime, and even poverty were laid at the doorstep of the so-called dysfunctional family. Within this technology of healing, the offspring of such families were doomed to replicate their pathology—with dire social consequences—until they acknowledged their diseased condition and embarked on a lifelong pursuit of recovery. As a self-appointed healer, Winfrey's mission was to educate her audience about the true cause of their misery so as to combat the pathological symptoms that were "ripping apart the foundations of our families and our businesses" (*Oprah Winfrey Show*, Jan. 4, 1989).

Given that the historically constituted gendered division of labor has made women "emotionally central to the family" (Krestan and Bepko 1991, 55), the recovery movement's focus on the "dysfunctional family" and Reaganism's obsession with the "breakdown of the family" were guaranteed to capture women's attention and tap into their anxieties. But while both perspectives implied that women's behavior was a threat to their intimate and familial relationships, they offered diametrically opposed diagnoses and cures. For Reaganism, the crisis of the family issued from women's rejection of their natural role as nurturers and refusal to subordinate their desires and ambitions to the needs of the family. The recovery movement, in contrast, told women that abandoning their needs for the sake of others was the *cause* of their problems. In effect, what the recovery paradigm prescribed as the cure for codependence and "loving too much"—to stop thinking about others and focus on yourself—was the very thing that Reaganism held to be the source of familial crisis: women's selfishness. In light of these apparently contradictory messages, how are we to understand the relationship of Reaganism and recovery? The unity of these phenomena, I suggest, resides in their adherence to an ahistorical—indeed, mythological—notion of the family.

Within the ideological practice of Reaganism, what was in crisis and in danger of breakdown was not the postwar economic boom but the traditional family, conceived in terms of the male breadwinner, female homemaker, and dependent children constellation. By presenting this particular configuration of domestic relationships as natural, timeless, and universal, its purported breakdown was also located outside history—as the result of purely individual motives and actions (e.g., men's failure to exert their natural paternal authority, women's refusal to obey their natural inclination to nurture, children's misbehavior as a loss of these natural role models, and so on). In this way, family difficulties could be portrayed as the origin, rather than consequence, of social, political, and economic problems. Reaganism's relentless quest to defend and strengthen this hypostatized "traditional family" was intimately connected to the political-economic project of Reaganomics: both were organized around eliminating collective public responsibility for social life in favor of purely individual responsibility and private interest. Every conceivable social problem was traced back to the diminution of personal "values," and thus to the family, which was seen as singularly responsible for instilling values. State abdication of responsibility for social welfare and public infrastructure could then be justified in the name of restoring individual initiative and morality.

Key to rehabilitating the "traditional family" was returning women to their rightful place at the emotional center of domestic life—hence the political importance of the antifeminist (and anti-gay) backlash for Reaganism. Families who failed, or worse, refused, their duty to instill proper values became rhetorical scapegoats in New Right efforts to abolish welfare and slash social services, and in campaigns to restore "law and order" by means of the "war on drugs," harsh and racially discriminatory laws and sentencing procedures, the massive, privately funded buildup of the penal system, and an explosion of incarceration rates, especially among poor, non-white males. At the same time, by means of the New Right's "moral framing of economic distress" (Reeves and Campbell 1994, 103), increases in crime and domestic conflict and the growth of a drug-based economy in impoverished inner cities could be attributed to family decay rather than to political-economic policies. As Michaela di Leonardo points out, this "'blame-the-victim' rhetoric" directed at "the poor, particularly poor blacks and Latinos ... coalesced into a full-blown underclass ideology in the 1980s" (di Leonardo 1999, 58).

The recovery movement's emphasis on illness and healing may seem at odds with Reaganism's focus on transgression and punishment, but its conception of the family was just as myopic and ahistorical. Central to the recovery paradigm is the idea that the "dysfunctional family" is the sole cause of addiction and codependency and that the "wounded inner child" is the inevitable outcome of family dysfunction. Recovery therefore aims at healing the damaged "adult/child" through therapeutic techniques organized around reclaiming one's childhood trauma. Biology is frequently incorporated into this diagnosis when dysfunction and addiction are understood to be genetically transmitted.

Through *The Oprah Winfrey Show*'s adoption of the recovery paradigm, the dysfunctional family became common sense in the program's treatment of individual suffering. Winfrey, in league with guest experts from the therapeutic establishment, routinely began from the assumption that panelists' troubles originated in family disorder, even if the guests failed to recognize this fact. Announcing the debut appearance of John Bradshaw, one of the most prominent recovery gurus of the 1980s, Winfrey assured viewers that they would "find out how to help you, along with me, along with our [studio] audience, resolve a painful past even if you don't think you had one" ("Childhood Wounds Seminar," *Oprah Winfrey Show*, Sept. 5, 1990). That she assumed her entire audience *was* scourged with a painful past was clear: "If you're always in bad relationships, if you're depressed sometimes, often, if you're angry, you're plagued by addiction, or if you've survived sexual, physical or emotional abuse, or came from any kind of dysfunctional family, which I think all of us did, this show is for you." The Bradshaw episode featured exercises to help audience members "reclaim" and "champion" their "wounded inner child." The biological model of psychic distress also figured in Bradshaw's claim that childhood trauma "gets imprinted in your brain" and will dominate one's behavior "until we heal that brain."

Bradshaw's insistence that everyone carries a "wounded child" within, as well as Winfrey's assertion that "Beaver Cleaver's the only person that had a non-dysfunctional family," betray a crucial tension at the heart of the recovery paradigm. The larger therapeutic enterprise has historically justified itself as a recuperative practice directed at individuals who failed to integrate properly into society. The proportionately small number requiring therapeutic intervention confirmed both their aberrant status and the legitimacy of the larger social arrangements. Even Sigmund Freud, who considered any social order anathema to basic human instincts, sought to help patients find less neurotic responses to the demands of society. In contrast, isolated strands of psychology—for example, as proposed by Erich Fromm and some versions of feminist therapy—have argued that individuals' psychological distress is the result of a "sick" social order. From this latter perspective, the cure lies in changing society rather than helping people adjust to a world of repressive social relations. What is historically distinct about the recovery movement is that while it considers psychic pathology to be nearly universal, it sees this not as evidence of a malignant social order but as a consequence of the malfunctioning of only one institution: the family.

By the late 1980s it had become a truism of the recovery movement that some 95 percent of American families were dysfunctional, which in turn meant that nearly everyone was addictive and/or codependent. Despite the absence of any empirical evidence for this extravagant claim, this statistic was frequently cited by experts, panelists, and audience members on *The Oprah Winfrey Show*. In "Self-Help Addicts" (*Oprah Winfrey Show*, June 10, 1990), for example, an audience member justified her attendance at a plethora of 12-Step groups as follows: "I went out and got the only spiritual healing and nurturing I ever got in my life because I came from—95 percent of us came from—a dysfunctional family." Stanton Peele, in his second appearance on the program, retorted: "If there are 95 percent of us who have been brought up in dysfunctional families, do 95 percent of us need to join self-help groups?" The women's reply echoed the recovery party line: "I would say that 95 percent of us today deal with their emotions probably through some form of addiction." As in his first visit to the show, Peele attempted to move the discussion to a social level. Several panelists and audience members, as well as Winfrey, had characterized being dependent on self-help groups as a "positive addiction" because the groups gave people a place to talk about their problems. Winfrey attributed the appeal of TV talk shows to this same desire for communication. People "tell their innermost, deep, the most private and personal things" on talk shows, she explained, "because nobody else will listen." In fact, she noted, "we wouldn't have a show if it wasn't for self-help." Peele continued to press the issue, however:

But if we're having worse communication now, if we don't have the opportunity to talk to other people, we'll never be able to make that up, no matter how many groups we create. If we don't address the basic, fundamental problems of society and in groups and in communities that don't allow us to talk to one another, then the support groups are just an after-the-fact, almost addictive way of trying to resolve something that's just much more fundamental, just like drinking and other addictions can just be an addictive way to resolve a more basic underlying emotional need.

Winfrey had no reply to this statement, likely because the recovery model that commanded her allegiance tends to view social problems as fallout from individual psychological deficiencies originating in the dysfunctional family. Such families appear to have no origins, or simply to be the result of defective individuals who are themselves products of "dysfunctional" families. This tautological logic characterizes even those recovery books purporting to offer a broader social analysis, such as Anne Wilson Schaef's *When Society Becomes an Addict* (1987), in which society is conceived as an organic entity beset by addictive tendencies. Thus, despite its claim that 95 percent of families are dysfunctional, the recovery paradigm does not offer an analysis—much less a critique—of the social conditions that might have produced this extraordinary degree of pathology in a central societal institution. Rather, the notion of the dysfunctional family serves primarily to valorize its binary opposite—the "functional family"—against which the putative inadequacies of the vast majority of actual families are measured.

Interestingly, the "functional" family has superficial similarities to the "traditional" family exalted by Reaganism. As Krestan and Bepko point out, in the therapeutic establishment, "The functional family structure assumes the traditional, normative, white middle-class family balanced around a more overtly powerful working father, who has access to economic resources and many options for self-definition, complemented by a mother who is fully responsible for children and the family emotional environment" (Krestan and Bepko 1991, 58). But as many researchers have demonstrated, this family configuration has never constituted a majority of actual families in the United States—not even in its heyday in the two decades following World War II (Coontz 1992; May 1988; B. Williams 1999). What's more, the postwar, white, middle-class suburban family was heavily subsidized by urban working-class and poor families of all races through systematic revenue transfers and unequal distribution of public resources (Coontz 1992; B. Williams 1999). Indeed, as Brett Williams notes, white suburban families of the 1950s "were perhaps the luckiest welfare recipients in history" (B. Williams 1999, 70).

But if the traditional family model accounted for a minority of households in the 1950s—and by the late 1980s represented only 10 percent of American families (Stacey 1990a, 340) because the historical conditions that made it possible had passed—its power as myth lives on. Williams argues that the ascent of family values rhetoric in the

1980s depended on "inventing a golden age for families" to elicit nostalgia for "the ideal 1950's family" that helped "mask both historical and contemporary processes" (B. Williams 1999, 69; see also Peck 1996). This reification of the family not only was central to the political and ideological projects of Reaganism but also underpins the therapeutic establishment's conception of the "functional" family—an entity as emotionally seductive as it is practically elusive. As Krestan and Bepko argue, "fantasy is notoriously resistant to fact.... We still often subconsciously hold in our head a kind of mythic idealized version of the family that rarely exists today. It could be argued that it is in fact our *mythology* about what constitutes a normal family that gives rise to our notions that not living in one causes codependency" (Krestan and Bepko 1991, 55–56).

When addiction, codependency, and psychic distress of every variety are understood as the effects of having been raised in a "dysfunctional family," the cure requires restoring or re-creating the "functional family," in much the same way that Reaganism called for the return of the "traditional family" as the solution to myriad public problems. Whereas the New Right's quest to revive the traditional family openly touted the benefits of patriarchal authority and female domesticity, implicit in the recovery paradigm is the assumption "that there *is* such a thing as a functional family not influenced by gender inequality, and that if we could re-achieve this seemingly functional structure, codependency could become a diagnosis of the past" (ibid). In Tallen's view, the concept of the dysfunctional family obscures the social conditions and character of actual familial relations insofar as it "holds out the hope that it is possible to achieve a fundamentally healthy family in this society without challenging the basic institutions of capitalism, heterosexism, sexism, racism, and classism that produced the patriarchal family in the first place." It further "betrays the fundamental feminist insight that the patriarchal family itself is the primary institution in the oppression of women" (Tallen 1990, 21).

The recovery movement's focus on the "dysfunctional" or "toxic" family, like Reaganism's fetishization of the "traditional" family, ultimately shielded the historical institution of the family from critical examination even as it blamed "the family" for all individual and social problems. According to Mas'ud Zavarzadeh, "institutions of intimacy" (such as the family, marriage, and friendship) are primary sites through which "the ideologies that legitimate the social order are circulated and produced" (Zavarzadeh 1991, 139). When those institutions are threatened—as the family was claimed to be in the 1980s—"one of the most ideologically effective moves to preserve and prolong" them is "to deny that they have been historically formed in response to certain socioeconomic demands" (ibid., 139). Representing the family as natural and eternal, moreover, "privatizes the problems of intimacy represented in marriage, family, and parenthood as the failures of individuals" and "demonstrates that these institutions of middle-class life are in good shape and far from breaking down, saving them from sustained interrogation and enabling the continued mystification of their practices in contemporary thought" (ibid.).

The Oprah Winfrey Show participated in this mystification process through its appropriation of the recovery movement's conception of the dysfunctional family as the root of all ills. The extent to which the master narrative of dysfunction and recovery had been uncritically incorporated by the program is evident in an episode devoted to codependency. Titled "Codependency Conspiracy" (*Oprah Winfrey Show*, Apr. 17, 1991), the show featured a panel of three critics and three supporters. Identified onscreen as "Against Codependency Movement" were Dr. Stan Katz, coauthor of *The Codependency Conspiracy* (1991); journalist Wendy Kaminer, who had written *A Fearful Freedom: Women's Flight from Equality* (1990); and Skip Hollandsworth, who had explored several self-help groups after his relationship failed. Labeled as "Supports Codependency Movement" were psychologist Robert Subby, author of *Healing the Family Within* (1990); therapist Joy Miller, author of *My Holding Us Up Is Holding Me Back* (1990); and "recovering codependent" Lois Jordan. Ostensibly obeying the rule of journalistic balance, Winfrey introduced the episode as follows:

> Codependency. Once it used to mean the problems of people married to or directly related to alcoholics. But now, for many, it has become a universal movement. Hundreds of codependency experts are writing books and holding seminars on subjects ranging from sex to shopping. And a lot of them are saying that every one of us is probably codependent, and that we all come from dysfunctional families. But not everybody buys that argument. Has the codependency movement become a big rip-off? Well, some of my guests today say, yes, it has become a major scam.

Critics Katz and Kaminer were given the stage first. Eschewing the idea that codependency is a disease, Katz compared 12-Step programs such as Codependents Anonymous (CODA) to cults, in which people subordinate their wills to group dogma and substitute one addiction for another: addiction to "recovery." Kaminer concurred with the cult designation. Like cults, she said, the codependency movement "encourages people not to think for themselves" while it "immunizes itself against criticism by saying that anybody who criticizes it is simply in denial." Both panelists took issue with how the movement taught people they were powerless and required a lifetime of recovery.

Allowing Katz and Kaminer to speak first was not an arbitrary decision; it is standard practice in talk shows to open with the most compelling or controversial guest(s) to capture viewers' attention immediately. By pressing the cult comparison, Winfrey knew she would ignite fireworks onstage and in the studio audience. Immediately after the pairs' opening remarks, two audience members broke in (Winfrey commented that "they're starting early today"). One identified herself as "an adult/child" whose "life has turned around" thanks to 12-Step groups, while the other labeled herself "a recovering person." Both were offended by the critics' statements, and the second speaker accused Katz and Kaminer of "black-and-white thinking"—one of the standard slogans of 12-Step discourse. This challenging by means of personal testimonials from 12-Step devotees characterized the entire episode. The three "pro" panelists identified themselves as "codependent," a "recovering person," and an "adult/child" and defended the codependency movement in terms of their personal experiences. Subby had "been in self-help 17 years," Jordan had "been in recovery" for a decade, and Miller asserted that, like her, most people were codependent and in need of recovery.

The studio audience was particularly active and agitated during the show. As Laura Grindstaff (2002) notes in her study of talk shows, producers often "seek out specific groups of people [for the studio audience] with a vested interest in a topic." It is common for producers to "pepper" the studio audience with people who had been previously interviewed as potential panelists, because they "have a connection to, and a stake in, the subject matter" and enhance "the potential for dramatic interaction" (121–122). This particular audience was packed with people from recovery groups. Of the sixteen who spoke during the episode, fourteen described themselves as members of 12-Step programs, all objected vehemently to criticisms of the recovery movement, several insisted that their addiction was a disease from which they would have died were it not for "the program," and many identified their dysfunctional families as the source of their problems.

Although Winfrey maintained a moderator role for much of the episode, her inclination toward the recovery paradigm surfaced several times. At one point, Kaminer explained that her objection to the 12-Step movement was that while it "is supposed to be about building people's self-esteem, I don't know that you give people self-esteem by having them label themselves as being sick, addicted, weak and helpless." Winfrey replied: "Is that labeling, or taking responsibility?" When panelist Hollandsworth criticized recovery gurus Melody Beattie and John Bradshaw for telling people that all their problems stemmed from family dysfunction, Winfrey defended Bradshaw and said she found his visit to the show "very enlightening." And when Katz suggested that the 12-Step movement was "not really self-help" but "a doctrine" for people to obey, Winfrey retorted: "But what's wrong if people are empowered?" Katz's response to this question illustrates the tensions surrounding the notion of empowerment. "I want people to be empowered," he told Winfrey, but "the reality is that we're not powerless. We don't have to be in recovery, we don't have to buy the labeling of disease." He also questioned the gender ramifications of the codependency movement: "Women have made great strides in the last 20 years ... for achieving equality and parity. Now we have a movement saying women are codependents, they suffer from a disease, as opposed to saying that women have really been conditioned into lower-paying jobs, conditioned into ... the caretaker roles. I think it's a dangerous concept to embrace." Kaminer seconded Katz's critique:

Yeah, especially for women, this recovery movement turns political problems into personal problems. It says that virtually every woman who is married to an abusive man is by definition codependent, addicted, she's weak in some way.... I read about 40 codependency books, and it's in just about every one of them, that the woman is codependent, that's why she's in the relationship. Now, in fact, a lot of women stay in abusive marriages because they can't afford to leave, maybe because they haven't had the same employment opportunities as their husbands, maybe because they have three young children and no day care. Instead of trying to get in touch with her inner child, maybe she should get in touch with her congressman.

This is a provocative statement—one that we might expect to elicit further discussion on a talk show. Not so on *The Oprah Winfrey Show,* however, whose host promptly cut to a commercial. After the break, Winfrey took more testimonials from audience members who "couldn't have made it without the 12-Step program" and concluded with final comments from the panelists. Kaminer returned to the political consequences of the codependency movement:

We need to look at the effects that this movement has as a culture. And in order to do that, we have to step beyond how it's affected us individually.... Think about what the message of this movement is. The underlying message is that you are powerless, that you're diseased, any exercise in self-control is just another symptom of your disease. Imagine if this slogan of the recovery movement—"Admit that you're powerless and submit to a higher power"—imagine if that were a political slogan. That is not a slogan for a democracy. That's a slogan for a dictatorship.

The program transcript notes that Kaminer's comment provoked "crosstalk," indicating an outcry from other panelists or audience members. Winfrey turned over the floor to Miller, who described codependency as "a movement of self-responsibility and self-loving, and healing the child within. And I think this audience is an example of celebration." The audience reciprocated with applause. The final word went to Lois Jordan: "I want to say that a message prepared in the heart reaches a heart, and a message prepared in the mind reaches a mind. And people are out there with broken hearts. And this stuff needs to stay focused on heart-healing, not head-healing."

This heart/mind dichotomy is a fitting description for this episode, where every effort to analyze the social and political implications of recovery was quickly overwhelmed in a milieu that turns the social into the personal and the political into the psychological. In this regard, *The Oprah Winfrey Show* exemplified the dominant practice of the larger therapeutic enterprise, which Philip Cushman characterizes as the "location of the social in the private interior and the reduction of the social to the dramas of the interpsychic" (Cushman 1995, 283). While this strategy might be construed as appropriate in episodes dealing with seemingly psychic ills, it also characterized programs that addressed political and economic issues, including welfare, homelessness, unemployment, and poverty. Although—based on a topic list—Winfrey dedicated fewer than a dozen of some 1,000 episodes to these issues between 1986 and 1992, the way they were handled illustrates the ideological consequences of framing political-economic issues as individual problems. It simultaneously reveals parallels between the cultural politics of *The Oprah Winfrey Show* and the political culture of Reaganism.

The Deserving and the Undeserving

Winfrey opened "Pros and Cons of Welfare" (*Oprah Winfrey Show*, Nov. 17, 1986) by warning viewers to "hold onto your hats today, because this show is probably going to be pretty hot." Indeed it was, thanks in no small part to Winfrey's introduction:

> You know, welfare has become a way of life for millions of people in this country. We want to know how you feel about able-bodied welfare recipients sitting at home with their feet up, as you trudge off to work to support them with the tax dollars that are taken from your paycheck each week. Does it make you angry? A lot of people are.

Panelists included Lawrence Mead, a political science professor from New York University whose *Beyond Entitlement: The Social Obligations of Citizenship* (1986) argues that welfare recipients should be forced to work for their benefits; California State Senator Diane Watson, who compared "workfare" to slavery and was seeking to overturn the requirement that welfare recipients work in public service jobs without pay in her home state; and welfare recipient and single mother of three, Valencia Dodson.

Two things stand out in the episode: the extent of audience and caller involvement (twenty-seven audience members, four callers) and the depth of hostility directed at "welfare mothers" by callers, the studio audience, Mead, and Winfrey. Mead established the tone for the show with his opening proclamation that "welfare mothers are out of step with other mothers who are working today. It is normal for single mothers to work, and if welfare mothers do not work, then they're not part of the United States. They actually are outside of the mainstream." Watson tried to counter this accusation. Forcing welfare recipients to work in public service jobs without pay, she said, was not only "punitive" but "loses sight of the reason why welfare, AFDC—aid to families with dependent children—was designed, and that was to provide the necessary support for children." Watson would wage a lonely battle. Although panelist Valencia Dodson and several AFDC recipients in the audience defended their need for public assistance—which they described as inadequate to begin with—Winfrey's and Mead's introductory remarks set the stage for the ensuing assault. All four callers and sixteen of the twenty-seven audience participants accused welfare recipients of being "lazy," of procreating simply to boost their benefits, of getting paid to "sit on their butts," of lacking "incentive," of robbing taxpayers, of fostering a "socialist state."

Winfrey did little to conceal her own hostility to those who got money "for doing nothing." To an audience member who said of a friend on welfare with six children, "That's not an easy life," Winfrey responded: "Then why have all the babies?" When another woman in the audience said that most people on welfare would prefer to work, Winfrey retorted: "Then why do you think that more people don't try to work?" Watson tried to counter the audience's "misconceptions" that people on welfare were chronic parasites. The typical AFDC recipient, she said, was a young woman who got pregnant and dropped out of high school. Lacking education and skills, "Where is she going to find a job in a highly competitive society?" Further, Watson pointed out, the average California welfare recipient stayed in the program for eighteen to thirty-seven months: "They come on and leave." Winfrey interrupted: "That doesn't represent the rest of the country, though, does it? Because we read about and hear about and see people who—their mother was [on welfare] and they were and their children are," thereby cementing the misconception Watson had sought to dispel. Winfrey then contrasted welfare recipients with "people who come from other countries, and they work 24 hours a day with their brothers and they pair up and they cut grass and they wash dishes and they do whatever it takes to get ahead." Comparing these "inspiring" examples to those on public aid, she added: "I think what a lot of people don't understand is why wouldn't you be willing to start at the bottom."

Panelist Valencia Dodson was pummeled from all directions during the show. Dodson and her three children received $546 (which included $178 in food stamps) per month from AFDC. Trained as a cosmetologist but unable to find adequate work in her field, Dodson had labored at minimum-wage jobs but found she could not support her children and also afford child and health care. "Once you see that you can't make it," she told Winfrey, "where else is there for you to go?" She described welfare as comparable to minimum wage, but without the burden of having to pay for childcare. Winfrey replied: "But it's minimum wage for doing nothing. That's the way a lot of people perceive it." When Dodson said she would "love to go to work" if offered a job "that paid enough so I could support my family," Mead shot back, "Why does it have to pay enough?" He, Winfrey, and an audience member also chastised Dodson for living in Madison, Wisconsin, where rents were high and suggested she should move. An angry caller lashed out: "Look at her. I love the way you're dressed. Who paid for that [dress]? How do you feel?"

Dodson maintained her composure through most of these comments. Late in the show, however, when an audience member complained that taxpayers were footing the cost of her housing, Dodson replied, "Your tax dollars also pay for $3,000 [a year] for the defense department, and none of you are complaining about that." This was not the only attempt to connect welfare to broader political-economic policies. An audience member who opposed "workfare" argued that "this country perpetuates slavery" and suggested that Illinois governor James Thompson was overpaid. Another audience member asserted, "Look at where the taxes go to, okay? The taxes go right back to President Reagan." Such observations—while somewhat reductive and unsophisticated—might have become springboards to explore the disparate proportion of tax revenue devoted to social welfare versus defense spending. But not in this venue. Responding to the comment about Reagan, Winfrey said, "What does that have to do with you?" She added derisively, "on to presidents and governors in this audience." And when Dodson mentioned military spending, her accuser turned to Winfrey in confusion: "What is she talking about?"

This episode from Winfrey's first season typified the show's ongoing treatment of issues related to poverty. Success and failure were conceived as the consequence of individual attitudes and behavior. The poor were responsible for their fate and, with the exception of needy children, were not deserving of our assistance or our compassion. Those receiving or in need of public assistance were legitimate targets of rage from responsible taxpaying citizens. Political/structural explanations of poverty (and wealth) were routinely minimized or ignored, and the preferred solution to poverty was self-help and "personal responsibility" in most instances, or private charity in the case of the deserving few.

In "America's Poor" (*Oprah Winfrey Show*, Oct. 12, 1987), Winfrey announced that the program would examine the desperate circumstances of several families to bring viewers "face to face with poverty." One caller subsequently asked why the featured families had borne children they couldn't afford to care for. "I mean, there is such a thing as birth control. You can get an abortion," she said, adding, "I think these people are just too lazy." A second caller opined that the panelists were "not using basically common sense" and lacked "self-motivation" because there were "too many jobs out there" for those who wanted to work. "I think they want sympathy," she stated, "and that is crazy." An audience member suggested that the impoverished panelists should take "the same energy you're using to complain about not being able to work" to "go out there and get a job" and then "invest" their money rather than "blow[ing] it all." Another audience member, representing Reagan's President's Office of Employment Training, contended that people in need were simply "ignorant" of the many opportunities for training and employment and argued that it was their responsibility to "get the information" so as "to better your situation," because the federal government was "here to help those who help themselves." It should be noted here that the ignorant, self-pitying, incentive-lacking individuals to whom these remarks were directed included an uneducated woman living with her three children in a two-room apartment in the Chicago ghetto, whose sole income came from collecting aluminum cans; a woman who, since her husband walked out, was living in her car with her three kids; and a couple with five children who had both fallen ill, lost their jobs, and were facing imminent eviction.

"Homeless People" (*Oprah Winfrey Show*, Dec. 3, 1986) opened with four homeless panelists (a mother and her teenage daughter, a young woman who had spent most of her childhood in institutions, and an alcoholic man in his forties) recounting their struggles for existence. Winfrey then introduced Mitch Snyder, founder of Community for Creative Non-Violence, who had gone on a fifty-one–day hunger strike in 1984 to protest the Reagan administration's cuts to homeless shelters. Snyder was currently living in the streets of Washington, D.C., in his continuing effort to call attention to the plight of homeless Americans, whose numbers, he said, were greater "than we've ever seen at ay time since the Great Depression" due to "the cumulative effects of budget cuts, economic conditions, and the near disappearance of affordable housing."

Winfrey labeled Snyder "remarkable." She also treated him and the other homeless guests as if they were an exotic species of life and objects of curiosity. "So you're one of those guys we see on the street," she said to Chico, the homeless man. "Do you intend to always be on the street?" she asked. "What do you want to do with your life?" Chico's answer: "Survive. Do you know what that means?" She inquired of Snyder, "What's it like? Those of us who come from comfortable surroundings and pass homeless people on the street sometimes wonder, what do you do all day?" After listening to Snyder describe the monumental energy involved in just surviving a day without shelter, Winfrey asked: "Why do you do it then?" He replied:

> As long as there's large numbers of my sisters and brothers living out there like animals on the streets, most of them through no fault of their own, it seems to me it's my responsibility as a human being and as a citizen to, number one, reduce some of that distance between me and them; number two, feel in my own flesh at least some of the time what they're experiencing; and number three, do everything in my power to force those who have the ability to do something about it to do it. So we're out on the streets, we're trying to bring Congress' attention to bear.

Winfrey turned to a homeless man in the audience: "I heard that you said to one of our producers that you felt responsible for your situation." The man assented: "Yes, I feel responsible for myself, for me being in the predicament I'm in. And I feel that it's no one's fault and can't nobody else fault someone else for their mistakes."

Although one caller vented anger on the four homeless panelists who "look very healthy" and could get jobs if they "really want to," this episode displayed less hostility than "America's Poor," perhaps because of Snyder's presence. But structural interpretations of homelessness were sidestepped as usual, and Winfrey declined to pursue any of Snyder's political observations. In contrast to welfare recipients, however, the homeless were deemed worthy of some sympathy. The concluding segments focused on a young boy and his parents who had created a private shelter to "bring hope to the homeless" (the boy, Winfrey noted, had "been honored by President Reagan at the White House"), and Winfrey encouraged the studio and home audience to "go somewhere and volunteer." Not only did this episode fail to explore the human costs of Reaganomics, it validated Reaganism's solution to same: the privatization of responsibility for social welfare. Accordingly, Winfrey's fans were encouraged to enhance their self-esteem by voluntarily helping the deserving poor, without having to question their own place in the social reproduction of inequality.

"Three Generations of Underclass" (*Oprah Winfrey Show*, March 22, 1989) and "Angry Taxpayers/Angry Tenants: The Public Housing Controversy" (*Oprah Winfrey Show*, June 18, 1991) returned to the issue of the "undeserving" poor and those burdened by them. Winfrey opened the two episodes as follows:

> So, you know, we have all heard stories of how being on welfare takes a hold of some families, about two and three generations of mothers and daughters and sons that get stuck in a cycle of poverty that provides little inspiration to the next generation to do better. People who work and pay taxes have a lot of big gripes about those who spend decades and generations on welfare.... Today we asked families—mothers who have raised their children on welfare and their daughters who are also raising their children on welfare—why the cycle gets repeated. ("Three Generations")
>
> Well, in 1991, $27 billion—billions now—taxpayer dollars will be spent on public housing and yet the public housing that we pay for is literally falling down. The tenants are angry and so are the taxpayers. ("Public Housing")

Both episodes were refracted through the lens of "underclass ideology"—the notion that poverty and dependence are effects of defective cultural attitudes and weak familial values. Promulgated by books such as Lawrence Mead's *Beyond Entitlement* (1986), Ken Auletta's *The Underclass* (1982), Charles Murray's *Losing Ground: American Social Policy 1950–1980* (1984), and Michael Novak's *The New Consensus on Family and Welfare: A Community of Self-Reliance* (1987), this "new ideology of the 'minority urban underclass'" gained near universal acceptance in the 1980s, according to di Leonardo (1999, 59). By recasting poverty as the special province of "black Americans living in ghettoised neighbourhoods" (J. Smith 1997, 179), underclass ideology deflected attention from the general effects of deregulated markets and the redistribution of wealth and turned it into a pathology of a specific segment of the population.

In "Three Generations," Winfrey echoed this perspective by repeatedly referring to public aid recipients being stuck in a "cycle of poverty" caused by their "welfare mentality." In "Public Housing" she cited the "psychological programming" that afflicts residents of subsidized housing: "How do you even pull yourself up when your mother had lived there and her mother had lived there and ... you're in a deep hole? It's what we now refer to as, you know, the underclass system." In "Three Generations," guest expert Richard Williams, a former professor of health and author of *They Stole It, But You Must Return It* (1986), reinforced the idea that dependence on public assistance among African Americans was a cultural, rather than political-economic, problem. The legacy of slavery, he contended, was the emasculation of the "adequate male" in black communities: "The absence of the male ... is a key problem ... because the male plays a very important role in the development of the family." Adopting the view of sociologist William J. Wilson, who in 1987 had argued that the "underclass was caused by an absence of a 'marriageable pool' of traditional bread-winning males" (ibid., 179; see also Abramovitz and Withorn 1999)—Williams, himself African American, validated the assumption that the aberrant black family was responsible for the fate of the urban African American poor. Although Winfrey was amenable to tracing problems back to the family—and to holding women primarily responsible for children's behavior, given her statement that "we have a responsibility as mothers in the black community to teach our sons to really be men"—she took issue with Williams's reference to slavery. "I think a lot of people still use the slavery experience as an excuse," Winfrey said. "Some people are still walking around thinking that this system—now Mr. Bush owes them something because we were in slavery, and is that fair?" Williams concurred, explaining that it was entirely up to "black folk to rebuild those things that were taken and torn down themselves. As a matter of fact, I think they're the only ones who can do it." "Right," Winfrey replied.

This exchange—where historically constituted inequities rooted in race and class relations were reified as matters of cultural character, for which those who exhibited that character were unilaterally responsible—exemplifies underclass ideology. As di Leonardo argues, like "older culture-of-poverty formulations" such as that for-warded in the 1960s by Patrick Moynihan, underclass ideology functioned "to focus attention away from [the] political-economic production of poverty to the 'pathologi-cal' behavior of the poor" (di Leonardo 1999, 59; see also Abramovitz and Withorn 1999). Treating impoverishment as a personal pathology—a failure to develop healthy, productive attitudes and behaviors—dovetails readily with the assumptions of the recovery paradigm. Following the preceding exchange, an audience member asserted, "Welfare is like in a way alcoholism. It goes generation after generation because they think that it's all right. That's all they've been brought up as. If it doesn't change in one generation, it's never going to change because they think that's the way of life."

The notion that the poor could change their circumstances if they simply acknowl-edged and took responsibility for their psychological deficiencies was underscored when Winfrey introduced two African American panelists "who say they too grew up on welfare with mothers who collected checks and invisible fathers, but they say they have managed to break the cycle and become independent taxpaying citizens, and anybody who wants to can do it." Guest Bill Jarvis stated, "This is America. You can do anything you want. Just set your mind to it and you can do it." Panelist Sandra Frazier told Winfrey that the ability to overcome the welfare mentality "comes from within the person." So compelling was this "personal responsibility" stance—both in *The Oprah Winfrey Show* and the broader political culture of the 1980s—that alternative interpretations were nearly impossible to sustain. An exchange between Frazier, Winfrey, and a male audience member illustrates the difficulty of transcending the show's dominant framework of intelligibility:

AUDIENCE MEMBER: I think you're being really unfair—do you think that some people are just bad and they're on welfare and some people are good so they get off welfare? I think it's a whole system that perpetrates this, and I think there's a whole group of people who have been made impotent and have been made passive. And maybe they can get out and maybe they can't, but there's a lot [of] other things going on here besides bad people who are lazy who stay on welfare.

WINFREY: I did not say these people are bad.

Frazier: This country does not think very highly of blacks, and blacks do not think very highly of themselves. It's within you.... If you have a defeatist attitude about yourself, then the battle's lost before you even start it. You have to think positive.

AUDIENCE MEMBER: I agree with you ... but this whole issue we're talking about is much more complicated than just finding this thing within yourself.... There's a lot of other things going on, much larger things.

WINFREY: But where are you going to find it, though, if it doesn't start with you? Let me ask you that. Where's it going to come from if it doesn't come from you?

AUDIENCE MEMBER: I don't know where it's going to come from if it doesn't come from within you—right—but there's a lot of people who never ever find it, that thing you're talking about.

Condensed in this interaction is a central ideological strategy of *The Oprah Winfrey Show*, whereby those "much larger things" the audience member struggled to articulate remained outside the boundaries of the discussion, while the failures, inadequacies, and responsibilities of individuals were talked about endlessly.

This translation of social problems into personal flaws took a different form in episodes examining the effects of Reagan/Bush economic policies on middle-class "citizens." Whereas the travails of the poor were typically cast in moral terms, the economic dilemmas of middle- and upper-middle-class guests were conceived as solely psychological in nature. Richard Reeves and Jimmie Campbell note a similar distinction in their study of the Reagan-initiated "war on drugs." Analyzing eight years of network television news coverage of the "drug crisis," they found that white middle-class cocaine users were portrayed as "offenders" and "diseased soul[s] in need of therapeutic transformation" whereas poor non-white crack cocaine users were represented as "pathological others" and "delinquent[s] beyond rehabilitation" (Reeves and Campbell 1994, 40). The authors identify these contrasting media frames as a "discourse of recovery" versus a "discourse of discrimination" organized around the binary of "inclusion/exclusion." Inclusionary discourses, they argue, are "devoted generally to the edification and internal discipline of those who are within the fold." They are, in other words, "stories about Us" (ibid., 39). Discourses of exclusion, in contrast, are "preoccupied with sustaining the central tenets of the existing moral order against threats from the margins" (ibid., 41).

In contrast to the four episodes on welfare, poverty, and homelessness—in which the poor were portrayed as unfathomable, alien Others deserving pity at best and scorn at worst—episodes such as "Unemployment" (*Oprah Winfrey Show*, Sept. 7, 1987) and "How to Cope in Bad Economic Times" (*Oprah Winfrey Show*, Jan. 23, 1992) can be read as "stories about Us." In these shows, the effects of Reagan/Bush economic policies on those "within the fold" were treated as psychological traumas requiring therapeutic adjustment. In "Unemployment" and "How to Cope," losing one's job was characterized as a "personal tragedy" and "emotionally devastating." Panelists were encouraged to confess their feelings of humiliation, their battles with depression, and the effects on their sex lives, their children's emotional security, and their "self-esteem." Guest experts counseled the unemployed to develop "coping mechanisms," to attend support groups, to "network," to exercise to manage their anxiety, to be "persistent" and "positive," to be "flexible" about switching fields and lowering their salary expectations, and to enroll in retraining programs. In "Unemployment," this self-help approach to joblessness was countered by the late senator Paul Simon (D-Il.), who argued for expanding public-sector jobs and government-funded training programs and raising the minimum wage. "We can do much, much better in this country providing jobs for people," he told Winfrey, "and we're not doing it because we haven't made a priority out of putting our people to work and we ought to."

Simon was an atypical *Oprah Winfrey Show* guest, as the host acknowledged: "Normally we don't have politicians on the show," she said, but she had made an exception for Simon because "we like [him] a lot." His proposals were harder to love. Winfrey informed him that unemployment "seems like a problem we're never going to resolve." She was equally dubious about increasing the minimum wage and wondered if the senator was "presenting a false sense of hope" with his talk about full employment. Winfrey's inability to discuss unemployment as a political-economic matter—rather than a personal setback—was evident throughout the episode, as illustrated in this exchange:

SIMON: The jobs program would cost at the most $8 billion. That's a lot of money, but that is one-fourth of the increase asked this year for the defense budget.

WINFREY: Okay.

SIMON: The question is of priorities.

WINFREY: We'll be back with final comments in a moment.

The sole "final comment" after the break came from an audience member, who asserted that "the problem with most of these [jobless] people here, they got to take responsibility for their own actions and the things they need to do in life."

This personal responsibility mantra was thriving five years later when the show again tackled the problem of joblessness at the height of the 1991–1992 recession. Winfrey opened "How to Cope in Bad Economic Times" as follows:

> You see it every day in the headlines across America. There are layoffs and unemployment and economic hard times. If it hasn't affected you yet, you probably know someone it has affected. The economic slump we're in right now is the longest since the 1930's, and there's a recent Gallup poll that says almost half of all Americans are worried about losing their jobs.

This statement might lead us to anticipate an examination of unemployment as a historical, political-economic issue. In the next sentence, however, Winfrey dispelled that illusion. The show's focus, she said, would be "how to emotionally and financially battle these difficult economic times, because it really affects a lot of people psychologically first."

After nearly an hour probing the assorted psychic strains suffered by the unemployed middle-class panelists and audience members, Winfrey shared her own perspective on the problem in the penultimate segment:

> See, I have a personal, spiritual, religious philosophy in my own life. When trouble comes, instead of looking at the trouble as, "Oh my God, why is this happening to me," I try to ask for every single problem in my life, "What are you here to teach me?" and look at it as an opportunity to move on to the next level, whatever that level is. And the level may be something you never even thought you would end up doing.

Guest expert and financial columnist Jane Bryant Quinn chimed in with an example of an unemployed friend who had said she viewed losing her job "as the universe has just handed me a growth opportunity."

Both the episodes on poverty and those on unemployment mirrored the ideological project of Reaganism: the former by turning the social problem of deepening inequality into a moral problem of individual and familial pathology, the latter by counseling "those within the fold" to strengthen their internal discipline. *The Oprah Winfrey Show*'s prescription for economic distress thereby paralleled Reaganism's cure for the "drug crisis," which Reeves and Campbell characterize as "therapy and rehabilitation for some, and punishment and imprisonment for others" (1994, 45). As Joan Smith notes, a central feature of the New Right's political strategy has been to recast welfare recipients and the poor as "the creators of the problem of social order rather than its casualties, as dependents on society rather than claimants from society" (J. Smith 1997, 178).

Through discourses of inclusion and exclusion, the poor could be banished from the fold of "Us"—or, as guest expert Lawrence Mead put it, "not part of the United States"—and blamed for the social deterioration wrought by Reaganomics. *The Oprah Winfrey Show* participated in this ideological practice by promulgating the notion that the poor were parasites gobbling up an escalating share of the national wealth, during a period that federal support of public welfare was actually being gutted. Between 1980 and 1989, federal aid to cities—which had been a primary resource for poor urban neighborhoods—was reduced by 64 percent (Davis 2002, 247). The federal programs that suffered the worst retrenchment in the 1980s were those directed at the most disadvantaged citizens: subsidized housing was cut by 82 percent, economic development assistance by 78 percent, and job training by 63 percent (ibid., 249). Such facts were entirely absent from Winfrey's examination of both poverty and unemployment.

Like the vast majority of episodes of *The Oprah Winfrey Show* that dealt with individual and family dysfunction, these relatively rare installments on political-economic issues obeyed the show's general logic of reducing the social to the personal, the political to the psychological. That logic was entirely compatible with the ideological agenda of Reaganism, which blamed the objective decay of the social fabric on the subjective failure of irresponsible individuals and families bereft of values. The guiding precepts of the recovery paradigm—which supplied the dominant frame of intelligibility in Winfrey's program—facilitated this displacement of responsibility for individual suffering and social disintegration onto the "dysfunctional family" and its corrupted values.

Despite Winfrey's professed mission to "enlighten" and "empower" her followers, her program from 1986 through the early 1990s replicated the diagnosis and cure proffered by Reaganism. Women were encouraged to look inward for the cause of their suffering, to stop blaming and competing with men, to reconnect with their maternal nature, to rein in their desires and their will. The poor were advised to stop whining and being a burden on citizens, to develop incentive, to quit blaming politicians and society for their lot, to take responsibility for their character defects, to get a job, to "just do it." Such homilies served to reaffirm the "central tenets of the existing moral order" (Reeves and Campbell 1994, 41) by policing the boundary between the pathological margins and those within the fold. Rapping describes the recovery movement as a "subtle kind of social control" (Rapping 1996, 69) insofar as it encourages people to focus not on changing the world but on changing how they think about that world. This is an equally apt description of Winfrey's enterprise and of the ideological practices of the Reagan/Bush regimes. Hence the concomitant rise of recovery and Reaganism. As Rapping argues, "The recovery movement—with its insistence on imposing order upon wayward, morally weak, and diseased souls and its use of a confessional process which is at least somewhat coercive—has many features which fit very well with the most repressive and regressive political and moral attitudes in the American political system" (ibid., 77).

Reeves and Campbell suggest that the "discourse of recovery," which is primarily designed for and adopted by the middle and professional classes, is directed at "the psychic repair of the bourgeois soul" (Reeves and Campbell 1994, 40). In the early 1990s, Winfrey started to chafe at the sheer number of damaged souls clamoring for her therapeutic touch, because their psychic wounds were tethering her to the increasingly denigrated ranks of "trash talk" TV. Elevating her public persona would therefore require more than simply patching up the fractured bourgeois soul on a piecemeal basis; it would demand a makeover of that soul itself.

Mind Cure, the Enchanted Self, and
the New Liberal Covenant

It was not particularly surprising that Bill Clinton chose to kick off the release of his autobiography, *My Life* (2004), with an appearance on *The Oprah Winfrey Show*, where he was assured a congenial reception. His association with Winfrey dates to his first inauguration, when Winfrey joined a host of prominent African Americans at "A Call for Reunion"—the inaugural's opening ceremony at the Lincoln Memorial organized by her friend Quincy Jones—and read a passage from Thomas Jefferson's writings (Randolph 1993a). Winfrey stood by Clinton's side at his 1993 signing of the National Child Protection Act—legislation she had initiated two years earlier that came to be known as the "Oprah Bill" (Mair 1994/1998, 214; "President Steps Up" 1993). Six months later, she was a guest at the Clintons' first state dinner, in honor of the emperor and empress of Japan (Lague 1994, 38). First Lady Hillary Rodham Clinton twice visited *The Oprah Winfrey Show* during her husband's tenure—in 1995 to discuss children's rights and the following year to promote her book, *It Takes a Village* (1996). Winfrey also participated in Clinton's second inauguration activities, where she was one of several "great thinkers" invited to "hold seminars on weighty issues of the day" (Robinson 1996). In 2003 the former president was featured on Winfrey's special on AIDS and Africa; she and the Clintons attended Nelson Mandela's seventieth birthday party in South Africa where, Winfrey told her audience, she "danced the cha cha cha" with the former first lady and Bishop Desmond Tutu (Archerd 2003); and Hillary Clinton appeared on *The Oprah Winfrey Show* to tout her own autobiography, *Living History* (2003).

Winfrey evoked this history of association in Clinton's 2004 appearance—her first question to him was why she had not been mentioned in his book. Clinton spent much of the interview explaining his affair with Monica Lewinsky through the narrative of childhood trauma—its negative effects on his sense of self-worth and his marriage—and the liberation he had found through therapy (*Oprah Winfrey*

Show, June 22, 2004). Midway through the show, when Winfrey asked if his wife had forgiven him, Clinton replied, "She forgave me long before I forgave myself." Apparently fighting back tears, he fell silent—as did the studio audience—before Winfrey cut to commercial. Such moments, which "make visible the precise moment of letting go, of losing control, of surrendering to the body and its 'animal' emotions," constitute what Laura Grindstaff calls the "money shot" of TV talk shows (Grindstaff 2002, 20). At these points, the camera homes in to capture emotional nakedness for the viewing audience. As Grindstaff notes, talk show production strategies are strictly organized to generate the "money shot" because these "moments of dramatic revelation" have come to stand for authenticity on television (ibid., 250).

The fact that the object of this particular "money shot" was a former president of the United States is testimony to Winfrey's unique position in American culture. It is difficult to imagine Bill Clinton appearing on another daytime talk show, much less allowing the host to bring him to a state of inarticulate emotion. If Clinton capitalized on his history with Winfrey by choosing her show as a friendly environment to launch his book, she has also benefited from her association with the Clinton presidency. As I will argue in this chapter, the "values politics" of Clinton's "New Liberalism" constituted an ideal political environment for the makeover of Winfrey's place in American public life, the seeds of which were being sown during the same period that Clinton was plowing his path to the White House.

From Dysfunction to Enchantment

Because the recovery paradigm that had come to dominate *The Oprah Winfrey Show* was organized around the "dysfunctional family" and its necessary by-product, the "wounded child," it was inevitable that Winfrey's attention would gravitate toward the problems of children. She deemed 1990 "The Year of the Child" and devoted one episode a month to children's issues; the following year she produced and hosted a special on child abuse titled *Scared Silent.* In February 1991, Angelica Mena, a four-year-old Chicago girl, was raped and murdered by a paroled child molester. A month later, Winfrey aired an episode titled "Child Victims of Crime" (*Oprah Winfrey Show,* March 13, 1991). One of the guests was crime novelist Andrew Vachss, a crusader against child abuse who urged Winfrey to use her wealth and influence on behalf of children. She responded by hiring former Illinois governor James Thompson and the law firm of Winston and Shaw to draft legislation that would create a national database of convicted child abusers. Thompson persuaded Senator Joseph Biden (D-DE) to sponsor the bill, and Winfrey testified on behalf of the legislation before the Senate Judiciary Committee on November 12, 1991. She also appeared two days later on *The Today Show* to talk about the bill and her campaign against child abuse (Mair 1994/1998, 224–225). Although this bill failed to pass, it established Winfrey in the public eye beyond her popular identification as a TV talk show host. It also established her relationship with Biden, who would push through the "Oprah bill" in 1993 and appear on Winfrey's show in one of her special post–September 11 episodes.

While passing a law to track known child abusers might help protect some children, it did not dislodge one of the articles of faith of the recovery paradigm: that abusers were also victims of the "dysfunctional family" and could never be completely cured because they were plagued by a lifelong affliction. Given that 95 percent of families were considered dysfunctional within that paradigm, the prognosis for children was grim indeed. In the recovery framework of intelligibility, then, the best hope for 95 percent of us is that we might spend our lives admitting to and "recovering" from our dysfunctionality. This might be good news for TV talk shows—it meant a potentially infinite supply of guests—but it was also a source of critics' increasingly vocal denunciation of the programs. Being designated "queen" of the genre was thus a dubious honor for Winfrey. Having won significant positive attention for her involvement in child abuse issues, Winfrey was primed for an alternative framework for making sense of the problems addressed on her show. Marianne Williamson would be the catalyst for that new configuration of self, illness, and technology of healing.

Oprah Winfrey's relationship with Williamson began the same year that Bill Clinton captured the presidency after a dozen years of Republican rule in the White House. Williamson made her debut appearance on *The Oprah Winfrey Show* in February 1992, when Winfrey invited the former cabaret singer to promote her book, *A Return to Love: Reflections on a Course in Miracles* ("My Life Is Driving Me Crazy," *Oprah Winfrey Show*, Feb. 4, 1992). Thanks to Winfrey's ardent endorsement—"I have never been as moved by a book," she told viewers—*Return to Love* shot to the top of best-seller lists, and the episode generated record-breaking viewer mail.[1] Three months later, Williamson was asked back to "answer specific questions" about how to achieve the "total inner peace" she espoused ("Understanding 'A Return to Love,'" *Oprah Winfrey Show*, June 24, 1992). In the opening minutes of this second episode, Winfrey read the following letter from audience member Joyce Austin:

> A couple of months ago, you had Marianne Williamson on your show talking about her new book, *A Return to Love*. That show truly impacted my life and my situation, and once I read the book, all I think about now is "How can I change my life and situation by following the purpose—inner peace?" I'm 33 years old and married. My husband and I have four children. My husband is unemployed due to a back injury he received while working, and since that time, he's not been able to find employment. I'm the only one working, trying to make ends meet. I go to church. I truly believe in God. It seems that the more I try to rely on God and things to work out, it seems as though they get worse. It's starting to look like separation and welfare are our only choice.... Thank you for the opportunity to write, and believing that it was something positive for me, I'm just going to believe that something good will come out of this. Maybe there is a possibility you could have Marianne back on your show for questions and answers.

Austin's story was not unlike those of hundreds of others who had populated *The Oprah Winfrey Show* over the years. Had it been located within a recovery framework of intelligibility, Austin's problems would have easily fit into a diagnosis of family dysfunction and she would have been encouraged to acknowledge her addictive, codependent tendencies so as to begin the lifelong process of recovery. Conversely, from the ideological stance of Reaganism, Austin and her husband could have been charged with failing to uphold the "traditional family" ideal. In particular, her husband's joblessness and her intimation that she might move out and go on welfare could have provoked accusations of laziness and irresponsibility. Neither of these things occurred in the episode. Instead, Williamson empathized with Austin and beseeched Winfrey, the studio audience, and viewers to "join their minds" and "pray for a miracle" to "reverse and transform" the family's problems.

Although Winfrey's public proclamation that her show would cease focusing on people's dysfunction in favor of "what's of value in the world" was some eighteen months away, these 1992 appearances by Williamson signaled the beginning of the shift in the show's technology of healing. In contrast to recovery and Reaganism, both of which located problems in the psychological or moral deficiencies of the individual and left society out of the equation altogether, Williamson's cosmology conceived individuals as innately perfect and relegated all imperfection to the external world. Overcoming one's problems did not begin with changing that world, however, but with changing one's beliefs and perceptions about it, because what appears to us as "reality" is simply an effect of our perceptions.

In her introduction of Williamson, Winfrey observed that the goal of attaining total inner peace was "easier said than done." Her choice of words was a bit off the mark, however. In Williamson's psychospiritual philosophy, words and thoughts take precedence over deeds and action, as the introduction to *Return to Love* makes clear:

> When we were born, we were programmed perfectly. We had a natural tendency to focus on love. Our imaginations were creative and flourishing, and we knew how to use them. We were connected to a world much richer than the one we connect to now, a world full of enchantment and sense of the miraculous. So what happened? Why is it that we reached a certain age, looked around, and the enchantment was gone? Because we were taught to focus elsewhere. We were taught to focus unnaturally. We were taught a very bad philosophy, a way of looking at the world that contradicts who we are. We were taught to think thoughts like competition, struggle, sickness, finite resources, limitation, guilt, bad, death, scarcity, and loss. We began to think these things, and so we began to know them. ... The thinking of the world, which is not based on love, began pounding in our ears the moment we hit shore. (Williamson 1992, xix–xx)

Williamson's psychospiritual cosmology is organized around a fundamental opposition of love versus fear: "Love is what we were born with. Fear is what we have learned here. The spiritual journey is the relinquishment—or unlearning—of fear and the acceptance of love back into our hearts" (ibid., xx). From such a perspective, "total inner peace" follows naturally from rejecting fear, which has been artificially imposed by the "thinking of the world," and returning to love, which is our authentic, original state of being. As Williamson told Winfrey's audience, "Love is real and nothing else truly exists.... Love is always available regardless of what is appearing to happen on the earth plane" (*Oprah Winfrey Show*, June 24, 1992). The key to transforming the transitory "earth plane" is to purge oneself of externally imposed—and thus false—perceptions, and reconnect with "the intuitive knowledge of our hearts" (Williamson 1992, xxi). Choosing "inner peace"—which for Williamson *is* a matter of choice—means replacing the "thought system of this world" with the "thought system we were born with" that is "still buried within our minds" (ibid., xxii).

Midway through the episode, Williamson attempted to demonstrate the power of mind by applying it to Austin's case. Stating that she was "very touched" by Austin's letter, she turned to the audience and inquired, "What does this lady need?" Winfrey interjected, "She needs a miracle." Williamson concurred and urged Winfrey and the audience to help her make it happen:

> The real issue here is a matter of faith and belief for everybody in this room and everybody watching this show. Do we or do we not believe that there is a power greater than the power of this world? This is really what the issue is. We have faith in this back injury of your husband's. We have faith in a recession which makes it difficult for a lot of people to get work even when they don't have physical injury. We have faith in the fact that there's only limited resources. You only have so much money and four kids to feed, plus you and your husband. We have faith in the limitation and the negativity of this world. What we need is to withdraw our faith from the negativity and finite belief system of this world and to instead open ourselves to the faith that God has the power to break through this limitation, to break through this negativity to open up so that there are infinite possibilities as opposed to the finite possibilities that we see now. (*Oprah Winfrey Show*, June 24, 1992)

Williamson told studio and home viewers they could shatter that negativity by joining minds and praying for a miracle. Winfrey reminded those who felt uncomfortable that they need not participate and then took Austin's hand while Williamson prayed for God to "enter here to completely reverse and transform this situation from one of darkness to light. In our minds at this moment, we hold to this possibility." At the conclusion of the prayer, Winfrey confessed it had been "the first time I prayed on TV." It would not be the last.

Although Williamson's technology of healing gradually displaced the recovery paradigm that had previously served as the dominant framework of intelligibility on *The Oprah Winfrey Show*, it would be inaccurate to describe her blend of psychology and religion as a new development. The roots of Williamson's diagnosis of what ails us—as well as her cure—are over a century old, a legacy of the nineteenth-century New Thought or "mind-cure" movement. Like Winfrey's enterprise, mind cure was not born in a social vacuum. It developed in conjunction with the rise of industrial capitalism in the late nineteenth century and the culture of consumption that was necessary to its success. Mind-cure therapies took root and flourished during the period that Martin Sklar (1988) characterizes as "the passage of capitalism from its proprietary-competitive stage to its corporate-industrial stage"—a historical development that "established the fundamental conditions of what many historians regard as the mass culture society and also as the organization of bureaucratic society with its concomitant rise of a professional, managerial, and technical middle class" (3, 441). In William Leach's assessment, the initial success and subsequent historical endurance of the core tenets of mind-cure issue from its pragmatic orientation and its agility at adapting religious themes and practices to the priorities of capitalism: "These faiths wanted to make religion work in the modern era, to integrate it with secular and scientific aspirations, and to accommodate it to ever-expanding material desires" (Leach 1993, 227). In particular, mind curists and positive thinkers embraced a philosophy of abundance where, by tapping into its inner riches, the self would also reap "the full abundance of the universe" (ibid.).

In his historical account of mesmerism, Robert Fuller notes its promise of mind's triumph over matter: "It taught that there was no material need or lack which could not be met by cultivating the proper frame of mind" (Fuller 1982, 156). Conceiving God as "an unlimited supply of bounty," New Thought proponents envisioned a world where to achieve material abundance was "to live in accordance with the divine" (Cushman 1995, 127). This is not to say these religious systems simply advocated crass material acquisition. Given their insistence that the material world was illusory and only spirit was real, striving after material wealth as an end itself would be to fall into spiritual error. Rather, living "in accordance with the divine" would necessarily result in happiness and freedom from want. Because mind-cure theologies took root and flourished within a social class stratum that was already comfortably removed from the realities of material deprivation, it was possible to imagine that one's material comfort was the natural result of correct thinking. Conversely, to dwell on worldly problems, such as hunger and poverty, was to fall into spiritual error by granting reality and power to such illusions. Any effort to help the poor was therefore not only detrimental to mind curists' spiritual well-being but also contributed to the poor's mistaken belief in the power of the material world.[2]

Beginning in the 1890s, according to Leach, "corporate business, in league with key social and political institutions, began the transformation of American society into a society preoccupied with consumption, with comfort and bodily well-being, with luxury, spending and acquisition" (Leach 1993, xiii). He examines the elaborate complex of institutions and practices developed to counter crises of overproduction that accompanied the expansion of the capitalist industrial production system. Myriad public and private efforts were devoted to solving the "distribution problem," or the need to coordinate increases in the production of commodities with a concomitant expansion in consumption. This entailed more than changing people's buying habits; it involved cultivating a new kind of social subject for whom commodities might represent fulfillment, happiness, self-worth, and identity (see also Marchand 1985). It also involved eliminating or reinterpreting values that were at odds with such an equation.

Leach contends that both mainstream religion and the new spiritual/therapeutic philosophies ultimately accommodated the emerging culture of consumption—traditional religion indirectly by "fail[ing] to fully confront the moral challenges posed by that culture" (Leach 1993, 221) and mind cure directly by actively promoting "a new outlook more in tune with the dominant business culture" (226). Even as mind-cure therapies promised individual liberation, according to Jackson Lears (1981), they "concealed new patterns of self-manipulation and new modes of accommodation to the emerging corporate order" (54). The new configuration of self proffered by mind cure was amenable enough to the requirements of consumer culture that its emphasis on "psychic abundance" was readily adopted by economists and "corporate ideologues" of the era who "shared the interest of mind curists in liberating repressed impulses" (ibid.).

In Sklar's analysis, the reconstruction of U.S. capitalism around the turn of the century was facilitated by a new political leadership "composed of capitalists recently engaged in organizing or directing corporate enterprise, and people from social strata with an interest in the emergent property relations or in their broader social effects or implications, among them lawyers, intellectuals, journalists, educators, clergy, engineers, and professional politicians" (Sklar 1988, 24). It is among these constituencies that mind cure—with its emphasis on self-fulfillment, abundance, and progress—would find a strong following (Lears 1981; Leach 1993; Caplan 1998; Satter 1999). As I argue in later chapters, Winfrey's modern-day mind cure and Clinton's New Liberalism also appeal to a contemporary professional middle-class stratum.

Philip Cushman (1995) maintains that the proliferation of mind cure in the late nineteenth century issued from its ability to provide "a compensatory political solution . . . for the moral and economic problems of the times. Its discourse and practices were a response to the emotional and social consequences of a political system—industrial capitalism—that was gaining preeminence and creating a great deal of human wreckage in its wake" (131). Its appeal resided in the ability to explain people's psychological distress, to offer prescriptions for easing it, to "further construct and guide the self most in synch with that system," and to do so "without overthrowing, or even upsetting, the social and political structures that caused the suffering" (ibid.).

A century later, Winfrey has to contend with the human wreckage of the so-called postindustrial capitalist society and has responded with her own latter-day technology of healing. Referring to Winfrey's personal growth seminar, Mimi Avins states:

She has ingested this human-potential seed so completely that she can easily spit it out, in full bloom. She doesn't claim her message is new, only that it may heal the heart-sickness so many of her fans write her about.... She's synthesized from the best, from Eastern and Western philosophy and the gurus of New Age enlightenment. (Avins 2000)

In truth, Winfrey's cure for heart-sickness is neither Eastern nor new. It is steeped in the peculiarly American synthesis of capitalism, religion, and the therapeutic enterprise that spawned nineteenth-century mind cure and its twentieth-century offspring, from Norman Vincent Peale's positive thinking to Robert Fuller's power of prayer, to *A Course in Miracles* and Marianne Williamson's "spiritual psychotherapy." Early mind-cure philosophies had similarly preached "a new upbeat psychology" (Leach 1993, 228) and "renounced all negative thinking" (ibid., 229) that might impede one's infinite possibilities. Fear was deemed a particularly damaging state of mind—a "self-imposed or self-permitted suggestion of inferiority" that stood in the way of plenitude and success (ibid.). Williamson's contemporary condemnation of fear propagates this basic tenet of mind cure.

Winfrey's appropriation of this cosmology is evident in the conception of self that drives her growth and empowerment mission, which has certain parallels with mind cure's nineteenth-century configuration of the self. Both technologies of healing are based on an enchanted expansive self that need only be rediscovered and set free. Compare statements by mesmerist Phineas Quimby—"All good things are found within" (Cushman 1995, 125); New Thought's Horatio Dresser—"All development is from an inner center or seed ... the only cure comes from self-help and the only freedom through self-knowledge" (ibid., 128); the Unity movement's Emilie Cady—"the source of all knowledge" is "latent within ourselves" (Cady 1894, 8); and Positive Thinker Ralph Waldo Trine—"Within yourself lies the cause of whatever enters your life" (Trine 1897, 16) to typical Winfrey comments. She remarked at one of her personal growth seminars: "I'm defined by my spirit, which comes from a greater spirit.... I'm hoping that you leave this place feeling a sense of empowerment that comes from inside. It doesn't come from me, because I don't have any power over your life. But you do" (Avins 2000). In *Omni* magazine, Winfrey described her view of utopia: "The boundaries and limitations that prevent us from living our Utopia are those we have created in our own mind and have made a part of our own reality" (Long 1988, 106). The philosophy of abundance is also compatible with Winfrey's cosmology, as is evident in comments such as, "What we think is what manifests in reality for all of us" (Cameron 1989, 215); "In Utopia, my life would be exactly the same as it is right now.... I'm telling you there would be no difference because I truly believe you can have it all—and all in one lifetime" (Long 1988, 106); "I think we become what we believe, and I often say that the reason why I've been able to accomplish what I have in the world is because I did not believe what I was told about being poor and black and female in Mississippi in 1954" (*Oprah Winfrey Show*, Oct. 30, 2000).

This is not to say that nineteenth-century mind-cure therapies and Winfrey's contemporary personal empowerment philosophy are identical, which would run counter to my argument that her project must be situated in its particular historical context. If Winfrey's modern-day cure bears explicit traces of the expansive self of mind cure, the explanation for this continuity must be sought in the character of our own times. Hence the need to examine Winfrey's enterprise in light of the social values, political commitments, and economic priorities of Clinton's New Liberalism, which coincided with and provided the political-economic context for her dramatic ascent in the 1990s to "prophet" status. The New Liberal conception of human subjects, I will argue, has significant affinities with Winfrey's revamped configuration of the self. Both are organized around a doctrine of "personal responsibility," a belief in the power of individual will to overcome material obstacles, a vision of "community" that eschews social division and conflict, an unbridled commitment to "growth" and "progress," an embrace of consumer culture, and a refusal of historical limits. If early mind-cure therapies and Winfrey's contemporary psychospiritual project are technologies of healing the private individual self, New Liberalism can be understood as a healing technology directed at the public collective "self" (i.e., the polity or the "community"). That there are definite parallels between the two is not coincidental: they are part of the same "cultural package" and thus "interrelated, intertwined and interpenetrating" (Cushman 1995, 7).

The Therapeutic President

During the 1992 Democratic convention, *New York Times* columnists Maureen Dowd and Frank Rich compared Bill Clinton to "a psychiatric social worker" who "sprinkles his interviews with the trendy language of co-dependency." Were he to win the election, they wrote, Clinton would become "the first post-therapy president ever to inhabit the White House" (Dowd and Rich 1992).[3] On the eve of the inauguration, Howard Fineman wrote in *Newsweek,* "America gets a New Age president this week," one who "can speak in the rhythms and rhetoric of pop psychology and self-actualization" (1993). Looking back on the campaign, Richard Levine wrote in *Mother Jones* of Clinton's appearance on *Donahue,* where the candidate "struck a number of therapeutic chords ... in exactly the right confessional tone" and "reached out to the rest of us in what I've come to think of ... as Oprahland, a place populated by victims of one darn thing or another" (Levine 1993). In Clinton's initial months in office, a *Washington Post* writer characterized him as "the first chief executive whose values were shaped by the therapeutic movement that has come to dominate the way Americans think about themselves, not to mention the daytime talk shows" (McNichol 1993). The headline of this latter story—"The New Co-Dependent Covenant"—was a play on Clinton's campaign platform, "A New Covenant with the American People," which was peppered with therapeutic/spiritual sentiments.

During the 1992 campaign Clinton marketed himself as a new brand of Democrat offering "a new kind of leadership" that was "not mired in the past, nor limited by old ideologies" (Clinton and Gore 1992, 191). Indeed, so "new" were he and his running mate Al Gore that they were "neither liberal nor conservative, neither Democrat nor Republican" (ibid., viii). Clinton thus characterized his political vision as a "Third Way"—affiliated neither with "those who said government was the enemy" nor with "those who said government was the solution." In the former camp Clinton placed Reagan/Bush conservatism; in the latter, traditional Democratic liberalism affili- ated with Roosevelt's New Deal and Johnson's Great Society. His "Third Way," in contrast, would champion the middle class, "provide more opportunity, insist on more responsibility, and create a greater sense of community" (Clinton and Gore 1992, 191). The "New Covenant" would not only restore the "American Dream," it would "heal America" (ibid., 229). If elected, Clinton said in announcing his candidacy, he would create a "government that offers more empowerment and less entitlement" (ibid., 226), make it "more efficient and effective," reinstill it with "values," and "give citizens more choices in the services they get, and empower them to make those choices" (ibid., 196).

Values, healing, opportunity, responsibility, community, empowerment. These are central tropes of Clinton's political discourse, which has also been characterized as "values politics" and as a "politics of meaning." It is a political discourse deeply inflected by the therapeutic ethos in which individual transformation is causally tied to societal transformation. The label "politics of meaning" emerged in Clinton's first 100 days in office. Interestingly, a *Time* magazine article compared the final week of this presidential "honeymoon" period to "a special edition of the Oprah Winfrey show titled 'Presidents Who Try to Do Too Much and the People Who Love Them'" (Duffy 1993, 32). Doing her part to advance her husband's New Covenant agenda, Hillary Rodham Clinton delivered a speech on April 6, 1993, at the University of Texas, where she spoke of a "crisis of meaning" in the United States. She appealed to Americans to develop a greater sense of community by "redefining what it means to be a human being in the 20th century, moving into the new millennium." Such a new kind of human being demanded a new kind of politics: "We need a politics of meaning," she asserted (Schorr 1993).

This phrase was not Hillary Clinton's creation—she had taken it from a book of the same title by Michael Lerner, a psychotherapist, activist, and founder/editor of the liberal Jewish journal *Tikkun*. Lerner characterized the politics of meaning as "a religious perspective on politics" that "promotes ethical sensitivity" and responds to "the hunger that most Americans have for a society that supports rather than under- mines loving relationships, ethical life and communities" (Lerner 1993). Combining psychology, theology, and ostensibly progressive politics, Lerner held that the qualities rewarded in the "world of work"—competitiveness and calculated manipulation—had produced "a crisis in values, the decline of family life, the instability in relationships and friendships," and a "deep sense of alienation and loneliness that leads people to hunger for communities of meaning that will transcend me-firstism" (ibid.). In his view, because Democrats had "never understood this level of pain," the Republican right had succeeded in fashioning its own "version of a politics of meaning," which "offered a vision of community along with attacks on blacks, women, gays, etc." He called on Democrats to create an alternative "liberal, pro-family" politics of meaning if they were to seriously challenge Republican political hegemony (ibid.).

Hillary Clinton took up that call. A few weeks after her Texas speech she invited Lerner to the White House to tell him that she and her husband had been reading his work since 1988, when Bill Clinton sent Lerner a letter from the Arkansas governor's mansion stating, "you have helped me clarify my own thinking" (Allen 1993). "It's amazing how we seem to be on the same wavelength," the first lady said to Lerner. "Am I your mouthpiece or what?" (Schorr 1993). The alignment of their thinking may be less amazing than Mrs. Clinton assumed. The seeds of "values politics" that Clinton would so skillfully employ in his campaign had been sown in the alliance of the political and religious right that brought Reagan to power and sustained Republican control of the presidency for the next dozen years. Those seeds had also taken root within the Democratic Party, eventually blossoming into the Democratic Leadership Council (DLC)—the vehicle that would launch Clinton onto the national political scene and propel him to the White House. Among the principles listed in the DLC's founding document was an endorsement of "the moral and cultural values that most Americans share" (Wilgoren 2004). As a member of the DLC and its chair in 1990–1991, Clinton was well-versed in "values politics"—indeed, council executive director Al From said of Clinton, "This guy understood the importance of values politics better than anybody else" (Klinkner 1999, 15).

Clinton's mastery of values language and its resonance with the "politics of meaning" were not lost on Lerner. In a *Washington Post* op-ed piece in June 1993, Lerner argued that in contrast to many Democrats who had interpreted deprivation solely in economic terms, "Clinton himself embodied and articulated a sensitivity to this hunger for meaning and justice." Because the new president "linked the mechanisms for economic recovery to our taking greater social responsibility," he was uniquely positioned to "help us imagine a moral community" (Lerner 1993). Thus, Lerner argued, the adoption of a "politics of meaning" was potentially "the most important development of the entire Clinton administration." Lerner was especially enamored of Clinton's "visionary" programs and ability to instill "joy and hopefulness" in the public. He interpreted the Clintons' affinity for the politics of meaning as their "attempt to change the dominant discourse of this society from the language of selfishness to the language of caring, social responsibility and ecological sensitivity" (ibid.).

While Lerner may have been engaging in a bit of defensive hyperbole here—Mrs. Clinton's embrace of his ideas had been skewered by the establishment press, and she ultimately distanced herself from him (Allen 1993)—Bill Clinton had indeed painted himself as the embodiment of hope and possibility in his run for the presidency. Doug Henwood (1997) points out that this was precisely the image Reagan had projected so effectively in 1980 and 1984. In contrast, after Reagan's first victory "the Democrats became the party of fiscal orthodoxy." Democratic contenders Walter Mondale and Michael Dukakis "were full of rhetoric about a country living beyond its means, and held out the promise of little more than tighter belts" (162). Henwood describes "a bizarre kind of political cross-dressing" during the 1980s, where "the Republicans had become the party of optimism, growth, and exuberance" and the Democrats "the party of gloom and restraint" (ibid.). Clinton reversed this pattern. As Henwood writes:

> Unlike his predecessors, [Clinton] did not run as the candidate of austerity. Quite the contrary—his economic message was expansive. He would raise the levels of public physical and social investment, rebuilding a tattered national infrastructure, jack up spending on education and health care, and propose policies (details largely unspecified) to boost employment and wages. The numbers were tiny, but at least greater than zero. Politically, he had in large part appropriated the optimistic mood, if not the substance, of Reagan's economic message. (ibid., 163)

Clinton's New Covenant campaign rhetoric—with its emphasis on empowerment, growth, and renewal—has certain affinities with mind cure's promise of progress, abundance, and fulfillment. Gloom and austerity were also anathema in mind cure's cosmology, which Leach characterizes as "wish-oriented, optimistic, sunny, the epitome of cheer and self-confidence, and completely lacking in anything resembling a tragic sense of life" (Leach 1993, 225). Whereas mind cure succeeded by tapping into the desire for individual transformation, Clinton's success was the product and expression of a political transformation—a "makeover" of the Democratic Party initiated in the 1980s in response to the Reagan Revolution.

Values Politics and the Making of New Liberalism

According to Jon Hale, the 1980 election was "the worst disaster for the Democrats since the New Deal," with an incumbent Democratic president ejected and the Republicans in "control of the Senate for the first time since the 1952 election" (Hale 1995, 2). Echoing Henwood, Hale argues that with its "new conservative agenda," the GOP was "perceived as the party of ideas, the party with a sense of mission" (ibid.). Reeling from the 1980 defeat, a group of House Democrats initiated an effort to examine the party's national identity and develop strate-gies for the future. Representative Gillis Long (D-LA), newly elected chair of the House Democratic Caucus, created the Committee on Party Effectiveness (CPE) in 1981, which "became the first organizational embodiment of the New Democrats" (ibid., 3). The CPE—with a membership of thirty-six policy-oriented, self-described "centrists" mainly from southern and western Sunbelt states—met for the next two years to "discuss new directions for the Party" (ibid.). The committee created task forces, held forums, and produced policy papers. Among its reports was a paper on long-term economic policy written by Representatives Tim Wirth (D-CO) and Richard Gephardt (D-MO), which argued for "a reorientation of Democratic economic policy away from an emphasis on redistribution and toward an emphasis on the twin goals of restoring growth and opportunity." Wirth and Gephardt specifically called for policies to "encourage investment in new high-tech industries"—an augur of what, in the late 1990s, would be christened the "New Economy" (ibid.) and hailed as the accomplishment of Clintonomics (Henwood 2003; Frank 2000).

Henwood suggests that one of Reagan's most "lasting achievements" may be "the transformation of the Democratic Party" (Henwood 1997, 161)—an achievement that would have been impossible without the avid participation of many Democrats. If the CPE signaled the birth of that transformation, the Democratic Leadership Council would nurture it to maturity. The DLC was founded in February 1985, shortly after Reagan's victory over Mondale. The formation of the council was announced at a Capitol Hill press conference; in attendance were Al From, a former aid to Gillis Long and now the newly appointed executive director of the DLC; Gephardt, the organization's first chair; and founding spokespersons Senators Sam Nunn (D-GA) and Lawton Chiles (D-FL), Representative James Jones (D-OK), and Governors Chuck Robb (VA) and Bruce Babbitt (AZ). Other prominent Democrats affiliated early on with the DLC were Senator Al Gore (D-TN), Senator Joseph Biden (D-DE), and Georgia Governor Zell Miller. Henwood notes that the DLC's "cause was quickly endorsed by pundits, who universally held that the Democrats lost" in 1984 because Mondale "had been too liberal" (ibid., 161). The group's "cause," Nunn explained at the council's inaugural press conference, was "to try to move the party—both in substance and perception—back into the mainstream of American political life" (Hale 1995, 6). According to Hale, the DLC specifically sought "to reconstruct the identity of the national party to make it more appealing to mainstream voters who had been deserting the party in recent elections" (ibid., 5). After Dukakis's defeat in 1988, the DLC became more activist in its quest to shape "a specific mainstream alternative identity for the party" (ibid., 8).

Although Bill Clinton had been associated with the DLC from its early years, he became much more active in the organization after 1988—the year he and his wife read Michael Lerner's book. In 1990, when Clinton was looking to boost his national visibility, he assumed the chair of the DLC. In Hale's estimation, "It was a perfect fit, given Clinton's interest in policy and his national aspirations" (Hale 1995, 11). As council chair, Clinton oversaw the founding of two dozen new state chapters and a burgeoning membership. In 1989 the DLC had 219 members. By spring 1991, when Clinton completed his chair duties, that number had grown to 400. A year later, when his presidential campaign was in full swing, DLC membership numbered 700 (ibid., 9). The returns on Clinton's investment in the DLC were significant: "He received key early money, campaign workers, and endorsements," and the council's "policy development efforts provided Clinton with the ready-made messages and agenda of the New Democrats to use in his campaign" (ibid., 11; see also Kramer 1992a). The key tropes of Clinton's platform and campaign—opportunity, responsibility, community—were taken directly from DLC position papers. According to Hale, "every major issue position" in Clinton's October 1991 announcement speech "was in agreement with the New Democrat agenda" (ibid.).

What, then, is the substance of that agenda? What underlies the quest to "reinvent" the Democratic Party? From the perspective of the DLC, the party had fallen from public grace through its identification with traditional liberalism. *The Politics of Evasion*, a 1989 report by the council's think tank, the Progressive Policy Institute,[4] charged that because of the party's own failings

> since the late 1960s, the public has come to associate liberalism with tax and spend policies that contradict the interests of average families; with welfare policies that foster dependence rather than self-reliance; with softness toward perpetrators of crime and indifference toward its victims; with ambivalence toward the assertion of American values and interests abroad; and with an adversarial stance toward mainstream moral and cultural values. (Galston and Kamarck 1989, 3–4).

The DLC's efforts to move the party "to the center of the political spectrum" (Hale 1995, 1) followed from its view that "the traditional liberalism espoused by the Democratic Party from the 1930s to the 1960s was no longer relevant or politically practical" (Klinkner 1999, 12). After 1988 the organization accelerated its efforts to transform the party. Through annual meetings, a magazine aptly named *The New Democrat*, regular media contacts, and generous funding from members, executives, lawyers, lobbyists, and corporations representing the energy, healthcare, insurance, pharmaceutical, retail, and tobacco industries, the DLC "became the political vehicle for publicizing the new centrist alternative" (Hale 1995, 8). So successful were these coordinated activities that by the end of the 1980s, "new Liberalism had come to dominate Democratic Party politics and discourse" (Klinkner 1999, 12). The core message of that discourse, according to Philip Klinkner, was that "the only way for the Democrats to win at the presidential level and to govern effectively was to shed their traditional support for and identification with the poor, the working class, and minorities and to reach out to the right on issues such as crime, affirmative action, welfare, and economic justice" (ibid.).

In effect, New Liberalism validated Reaganism's charge that the Democratic Party had lost touch with "ordinary" or "mainstream" Americans in favor of "special interests," which in both cases meant labor unions, the poor, minorities (especially African Americans), women, and gays and lesbians. Henwood contends that the "ideological and electoral aim" of the DLC was "to distance itself from the poor and the black in order to woo the rich and white" (Henwood 1997, 161). Certainly New Liberalism was designed to appeal to white middle- and working-class voters—especially suburban swing voters who had responded to the racialized rhetoric of the Reagan/Bush campaigns. But the Democratic Party's move to the "center" was underway well before the DLC achieved dominance. Throughout the 1980s, certain factions in the party tried to shed the "special interest" label employed so effectively by the political right. As we saw in Chapter 3, the party apparatus had backed away from feminist stances on women's issues and adopted a safer "pro-family" platform. In 1988, Democratic National Committee chair Paul Kirk moved "to weaken the institutional strength of liberal activists" by withdrawing official DNC support of party caucuses representing women, blacks, Hispanics, Asians, gays, liberals, and business/professionals (Hale 1995, 7). The DLC, then, was less a maverick force than evidence of a growing struggle *within* the party between "traditional" liberals and "New Democrats"—the latter's strategy for recapturing the White House being to beat the Republicans at their own game.

Reagan and Bush had won by forging an alliance among the rich, the white professional middle class, and significant blocs of the white working class, especially those living in Sunbelt state suburbs, and had done so by explicitly capitalizing on racial and gender divisions and anxieties. New Liberalism sought to win back—or convert—white voters from the professional, middle, and working strata, as well as to recoup its losses in the South. That is, the DLC was dedicated to recapturing "Reagan Democrats." The political and ideological practices of New Liberalism and its premier candidate Bill Clinton were crafted to appeal to these constituencies. Hence, the embrace of "values politics"—the ground on which the Republicans were perceived "to hold a decisive advantage" (A. Greenberg and S. B. Greenberg 2000, 1). Shortly before the 2000 presidential election, Anna Greenberg and Stanley Greenberg—the latter having been Clinton's first-term pollster—argued that while Americans might respect Democrats' "openness to new ideas," their "commitment to community," and their "defense of tolerance and individual rights," they are "more impressed with the Republicans' insistence on personal responsibility, discipline, and teaching children about right and wrong." To capture voters' hearts, the Greenbergs contended, Democrats must offer "a family-centered progressive discourse on values" (ibid.). Stanley Greenberg had made a similar argument for values politics in 1996. In his assessment, "Conservatives have been winning the battle to gain the support of working people because they, at least, seem to be able to identify with the personal responsibility and initiative and the progress people are making" (Greenberg 1996a). Democrats must therefore construct a narrative that puts at its center "the virtues of working- and middle-class Americans" and focus especially on their "self-reliance" and "responsibility." What New Democrats lacked, Greenberg asserted, was a "discourse about virtue" (ibid.).

The values politics of New Liberalism was therefore organized around the virtue of "mainstream" Americans, as opposed to "special interests." Adolph Reed Jr. argues that because New Liberalism's definition of "special interests" included "the labor movement, feminists, gays, secularists, civil libertarians, poor people and nonwhite minorities," it followed that "mainstream means relatively well-off, white, and male, in some combination or another" (Reed 1999d, 1). We might add to this list "suburban." White working- and middle-class suburbanites—a crucial bloc of Reaganism's support—became an even more potent political force during the 1990s. As Mike Davis points out, although denizens of suburbia had constituted "a majority of the white electorate since at least 1980," by 1992 they had become "the political majority in the United States" (Davis 2002, 256). Thanks to the "surburbanization of economic growth" in the 1990s, residents of burgeoning suburbs and "edge cities" acquired both unprecedented political power and "political autonomy from the crisis of the core cities." This geographical divide is also a political one, according to Davis, in that Republican Party affiliation has become "a direct function of distance away from urban centers" (ibid.). Fred Siegel suggests we might view the politics of suburbia as "not so much Republican as anti-urban" (Siegel 1991, 177). But, because "urban" has acquired what Davis terms "semantic identity" with "non-white," political appeals to the suburban "mainstream"—whether expressed by Republicans or Democrats—are invariably racially coded (Davis 2002, 255; see also Macek 2006).

The tropes of New Liberalism's values discourse—opportunity, responsibility, community—were therefore designed to bring the (white) "mainstream" back into the Democratic fold, and it was simply assumed that the "special interests" would vote Democratic by default. Reed contends that the "devotion to this mainstream" that formed the basis of New Liberalism "is a symbolic meeting ground for several tendencies that rest uneasily" within the Democratic Party (Reed 1999d, 1). Those tendencies include a "neoliberal element" dedicated to economic policy and the free market; a "communitarian tendency" that believes "public policy should enforce, or at least reinforce, putatively majoritarian values"; and Southern Democrats, who had grown increasingly restive with left-liberal and black constituencies in the party (ibid., 2). These three strands of New Liberalism have certain differences: neoliberals are chiefly concerned with economic policy and inclined to be "libertarian" on social issues; communitarians may support economic regulation to make business operate in the community interest—an anathema to free marketeers; and Southern Democrats' segregationist legacy and "antiegalitarian" inclinations may offend the "progressive sensibilities" of neoliberals and communitarians (ibid., 3–4). Philip Klinkner argues that as the first presidential contender to emerge from the DLC and cast himself as a "New Democrat," Bill Clinton is "a textbook example of the New Liberalism in practice," representing a synthesis of neoliberal, communitarian, and Southern Democrat sensibilities (Klinkner 1999, 12). Indeed, Reed contends Clinton's "political genius is that he has variously and simultaneously embodied each of the main strains—neoliberal, communitarian, and southern conservative—that constitute the New Liberalism's base" (Reed 1999d, 7).

The rise of neoliberalism within the Democratic Party was predicated on a rejection of "New Deal liberalism" and its affiliated Keynesian economic policies. Beginning in 1980 a number of Democrats began claiming that the United States had entered a new "post-industrial" stage that demanded a new economic paradigm.[5] Contrary to Keynesianism's emphasis on federal management of the economy and redistributive policies to prevent economic crises and maintain stability through the capital-labor compromise, neoliberal Democrats called for "a return to economic growth as the first principle of liberalism" (Rothenberg 1984, 45). In neoliberals' view, social justice—a traditional concern of the Democratic Party—would follow from economic growth; it was a matter of growing a bigger "economic pie," rather than redistributing the existing pie (Wicker 1981, 31). Neoliberals held Keynesianism responsible for the economic stagnation of the 1970s, arguing that it privileged stability and security over innovation and risk-taking. In the view of investment banker Felix Rohatyn, a leading Democratic adviser and influence on neoliberal thought, Johnson's Great Society program in particular had produced a "risk adverse" society because "by attempting to reduce the element of risk, it succeeded in eliminating many of the incentives to create wealth" (Rothenberg 1984, 148). The key to reviving economic growth, then, was government policies and practices that favored "disequilibrium" over stability to encourage and reward risk-taking.

Such assumptions are shared by Reaganomics' monetarist, "trickle-down" version of neoliberalism and by the Democratic New Liberal variant. In both cases, the major impediment to growth is "big government," which is blamed for removing incentives to innovation and investment through excessive regulation and redistributive programs that foster dependency.[6] Both strands of neoliberalism consider individual competition the primary engine of growth and progress. Democratic neoliberals argued that the United States had entered a "new post-industrial paradigm" involving "a transition from the high-volume mass production economy of the industrial era to an economy based on information and high technology" (Rothenberg 1984, 52). They were therefore inclined to valorize the high-tech entrepreneur, given their belief that an information-based economy was the "solution to the dilemma of maintaining growth without befouling the environment or abusing diminishing natural resources" (ibid., 80).

Neoliberals also welcomed the global reach of the information-based economy, which they saw as having "transformed the world from independent national economic units to an interdependent global economy" (ibid., 52). For neoliberal Democrats, national economic growth depended on U.S. dominance in a global, information-based economic order, and this required a transformation of the American workforce. Hence, the centrality in neoliberal thinking of the concept of "human capital," a term derived from Chicago economist Gary Becker to refer to the sum of an individual's knowledge, skills, and training. Becker proposed that all social behavior could be conceptualized along economic lines—as "calculative actions undertaken through the human faculty of choice in order to maximize human capital" (Rose 1999, 483). Randall Rothenberg notes that one of the "most pervasive axioms" among Democrat neoliberals is "that the post-industrial economy is 'human-capital intensive,' meaning that the rapid pace of industrial change demands not workers skilled at single, repetitive tasks, but workers with the knowledge, education, and ability to adapt to a variety of tasks as the needs of industry shift" (Rothenberg 1984, 87). If the United States was to lead the global economy, it was imperative that government invest in cultivating its stock of "human capital" through education and training. The concept of human capital also marks a decisive break with traditional liberal theory, which had "stressed not the market advantages, but the non-market advantages of education and training" (ibid., 87). Indeed, one of the defining features of neoliberalism is its tendency to view the world entirely through the lens of economics. As neoliberals gained ascendancy in the Democratic Party, according to Rothenberg, the party's "great issues of the past—school busing, national health insurance, welfare, equal employment, labor law reform, consumer protection, environmentalism, and the First Amendment—had receded. The new issue, the only issue, it seemed, was economics" (ibid., 18).

Because it begins from a conception of society as the sum of rational, competitive "entrepreneurs" seeking to maximize their advantage, neoliberal theory eschews the "antagonism" of "interest group politics" (or class-based politics) in favor of "cooperation" and "community," whether between nations, between management and labor, or between the private and public sectors—hence neoliberalism's distance from organized labor and other "special interests" and its enthusiastic support from business and industry. This emphasis on community and cooperation forms a bridge to the communitarian wing of New Liberalism. Drawing on the ideas of Robert Bellah, Amitai Etzioni, and Robert Putnam, communitarians interpret social disorder as a result of a "decay of the networks of civic trust" (Rose 1999, 479) that purportedly provide a sense of individual responsibility and mutual obligation. From a communitarian perspective, traditional left-liberal Democratic politics "erred in not honoring majoritarian notions of virtue and desert and has alienated its natural base by coddling and rewarding those who fail to honor dominant norms" (Reed 1999d, 2). Like Reaganism, communitarianism rests on a "narrative of moral degeneration," which warrants an "agenda of moral rearmament" (Rose 1999, 470). In contrast to the technocratic solutions favored by neoliberals, communitarians support the creation of "a new moral contract ... based on the strengthening of the natural bonds of community" (ibid., 479). Given their faith that "government action can produce specifically virtuous outcomes," (Reed 1999d, 2), communitarians are not averse to recommending punitive measures for those who fail to uphold those bonds.

Whereas neoliberals view people's actions through the lens of "human capital," communitarians employ the concept of "social capital"—seen not as a quantifiable personal possession but as the intangible by-product of interpersonal relations. University of Chicago sociologist James Coleman developed the term to denote feelings of cooperation between members of social groups. In his formulation, "Groups whose members manifest trustworthiness and place extensive trust in one another will be able to accomplish more than comparable groups that lack trustworthiness and trust" (Coleman 1990, 304). It was Harvard political scientist Robert Putnam, however, who popularized the concept of social capital by using it to describe the rewards of participating in civic and community associations. In a paper presented at a Nobel Symposium in 1994, which was subsequently published in the journal *Democracy* and later expanded into a book, *Bowling Alone: The Collapse and Revival of American Community* (2000), Putnam contended that a decline in group membership—and hence of American social capital—was the central cause of a vast range of problems, from the health of individuals ("Your chance of dying over the next year is cut in half if you join just one group. Isolation is as big a [risk] factor as smoking") to the health of democratic society ("Society doesn't work as well when there is an absence of social capital") (Ellison 2000). The cure for this malaise born of disconnectedness is more "community." It was therefore the responsibility of the state to foster community-building efforts for the purpose of "renewing civic culture" (Rose 1999, 486).[7]

The communitarian valorization of connectedness rests on the assumption that inclusion mandates responsibilities and obligations. Conversely, disconnection implies a lack of responsibility toward the community. Nikolas Rose argues that from a communitarian perspective, "the excluded" require "ethical reconstruction" so as to be "reattached to a virtuous community" (ibid., 489). Conversely, for those who refuse this process of moral improvement, "harsh measures are entirely appropriate. Three strikes and you're out" (ibid., 488). The communitarian embrace of "majoritarian notions of virtue" (Reed 1999d, 2) and resulting tendency to frame social problems in terms of individual "dependency, license, idleness, irresponsibility" (Rose 1999, 479) form a bridge to the third pillar of New Liberalism's base. Southern Democrats had been ambivalent toward the increasing prominence of African Americans in the Democratic Party dating from the passage of the Civil Rights and Voting Acts and resulting defection of Wallace Democrats in the 1960s. They were also uneasy with the "rise of environmentalists, civil libertarian, gay rights, abortion rights, and other feminist constituencies" within the party (Reed 1999d, 3). Southern Democrats thus welcomed New Liberalism's emphasis on "majority" values, with its implicit appeal to white male voters.

As one of the "architects" of the Democratic Party's "rightward move" (Henwood 1997, 161) under the banner of New Liberalism, Bill Clinton "exemplifies the mind-set and program of the New Liberalism in power" (Reed 1999d, 7). Neoliberal, communitarian, and Southern Democrat sensibilities are woven into Clinton's political discourse and practice. The neoliberal perspective was prominent in his campaign platform outlined in *Putting People First* (Clinton and Gore 1992), where he declared his commitment to economic growth and faith in "free enterprise and the power of market forces" (1). His administration, Clinton asserted, would "encourage small business people and entrepreneurs to take risks" and "reward" those who "create new jobs" (ibid., 146). From the outset, Clinton embraced the benefits of a global economic system, which the United States would command by developing a "national economic strategy to invest in people and meet the competition" (ibid., 6). A primary goal of his presidency would be to pare down government by reducing spending, fostering public/private partnerships to promote efficiency, and encouraging private investment.[8]

Aside from the reference to government support for the American workforce (investing in "human capital"), Clinton's economic vision was not far removed from that of Reaganomics. In the 1980s, in fact, Arthur Schlesinger Jr. charged neoliberal Democrats with having "more or less accepted" Reagan's economic framework. As Schlesinger wrote, "they have joined in the clamor against 'big government,' found great merit in the unregulated marketplace, opposed structural change in the economy and gone along with swollen military budgets and the nuclear arms race" (quoted in Rothenberg 1984, 19). By 1992, with the Cold War officially dead, Clinton could include defense cuts in his plans to streamline government. At the same time, his neoliberal orientation was apparent in his tendency to view social problems through an economic lens. In his New Covenant speech at the 1992 Democratic convention, Clinton stated, "The most important family policy, urban policy, labor policy, minority policy, and foreign policy America can have is an expanding, entrepreneurial economy of high-wage, high-skill jobs" (Clinton and Gore 1992, 217).

Communitarian principles also infused Clinton's political sensibilities, as evidenced in his affinity for Lerner's "politics of meaning." William Galston, coauthor of the DLC's *Politics of Evasion* report and one of Clinton's domestic policy advisers, was a dedicated communitarian and close associate of Amitai Etzioni. In 1991 Galston and Etzioni organized a conference on communitarianism, published a manifesto for the movement, and founded the journal *The Responsive Community: Rights and Responsibilities*. Shortly after Clinton's election, the journal published a series of "recommendations to help ensure that the new president's communitarian spirit will not be suppressed" (Wieseltier 1993). In summer 1993, Etzioni wrote a piece for the *National Civic Review* titled "Is Bill Clinton a Communitarian?" which argued that "the links between the communitarian movement and the Clinton administration are well established, and we might expect continued communitarian messages from the White House" (Etzioni 1993, 224). As president, Clinton also formed a relationship with Robert Putnam in 1994 and, in the process, elevated Putnam's "bowling alone" thesis to the status of statecraft.[9]

The communitarian vision is central to Clinton's deployment of values politics. In announcing his candidacy, Clinton asserted, "We need a new spirit of community" (Clinton and Gore 1992, 196). The Reagan/Bush administrations, he charged, had "betrayed the values that make America great: providing opportunity, taking responsibility, [and] rewarding work" (ibid., 3). Here Clinton employed a "discourse about virtue" designed to appeal to "mainstream" values. Those who belong to the "virtuous community" (i.e., the hard-working, self-reliant, and responsible) were distinguished from those who lie outside it (i.e., the irresponsible, lazy, and dependent). This "discourse about virtue" provided Clinton with one of his most potent campaign promises: that his administration would "strengthen families and empower all Americans to work" and "break the cycle of dependency and end welfare as we know it" (ibid., 14). His support for capital punishment and increased funding to hire more police and put more criminals behind bars were also directed at a "virtuous mainstream" that saw itself as victimized by lawless outsiders. The adoption of communitarian principles thereby enabled Clinton and New Liberalism to recolonize phrases such as "law and order," "traditional values," and "personal responsibility" that Republicans had used so effectively to appeal to white middle- and working-class voters.

Clinton's mantra of personal responsibility, his attack on welfare, his support for "law and order," and his pro-business stance also issue from his Southern Democrat roots. As a Sunbelt governor, Clinton promoted Arkansas's right-to-work law as a lure to capital investment, had a "history of indifference or hostility toward organized labor," and lavished "tax and regulatory indulgence" on the state's nonunionized chicken industry, whose environmental and labor practices had been widely criticized (Henwood 1997, 163, 164).[10] On his road to the White House, Clinton capitalized on opportunities to boost his appeal to the white "mainstream." Under his leadership, the DLC at its 1991 convention approved a platform opposing racial "quotas" and made a point not to invite Jesse Jackson, who represented for New Democrats "the most visible embodiment of the liberal policies and strategies they rejected" (Baer 2000, 183). In January 1992, Clinton left the campaign trail to attend the Arkansas execution of a brain-damaged black man convicted of murdering a white policeman. During the Los Angeles riots a few months later, Clinton echoed President Bush's line that the uprising stemmed partly from "'the culture of poverty' and dependency in inner cities" (Klinkner 1999, 16). On the day of Southern primaries, Clinton posed for a photo with Senator Sam Nunn in Stone Mountain, Georgia—a place known as the "second home" of the Ku Klux Klan. With "the graven images of the generals of the Confederacy looming in the background, and in the middle distance, a chain gang of black prisoners," the photo of Clinton and Nunn appeared in newspapers across the South (Wypijewski 2004, 88; Gray 2004, 99). In June 1992, in an address to Jesse Jackson's Rainbow Coalition, Clinton criticized Jackson and the organization for having provided a forum for singer Sista Souljah, whose comments about the LA riots had sparked a furor in the white media. In Klinkner's assessment, Clinton's public attack on Jackson was "part of a planned and deliberate strategy ... to reassure white voters of his toughness with Democratic Party special interests" (Klinkner 1999, 16, 17).

Out of this synthesis of neoliberal, communitarian, and Southern Democrat priorities, Bill Clinton and running mate Al Gore fashioned a New Liberal "economic and values-based agenda" (Greenberg 1997a). As one of their 1992 TV campaign advertisements stated, Clinton and Gore were "a new generation of Democrats.... They don't think the way the old Democratic Party did. They've called for an end to welfare as we know it.... They've sent a strong signal to criminals by supporting the death penalty" (Klinkner 1999, 19). The Clinton/Gore victory in 1992 seemed to justify and validate the "makeover" of the Democratic Party, marking the ascendancy not only of New Liberalism but of a new form of politics and government.

Nikolas Rose describes this shift as the emergence of "etho-politics," in which "features of human collective existence—sentiments, values, beliefs—have come to provide the 'medium' within which the self-government of the autonomous individual can be connected up with the imperatives of good government" (Rose 1999, 477). Etho-politics conceives human beings first and foremost as "ethical creatures," whose behavior can be governed "through ethics and in the name of ethics" (ibid., 474). Rose suggests that the politics of the "Third Way" is organized around "acting upon the ethical formation and the ethical self-management of individuals so as to promote their engagement in their collective destiny in the interests of economic advancement, civic stability, even justice and happiness" (ibid., 475). Michael Lerner's "politics of meaning"—and its appropriation by the Clintons—exemplifies etho-politics. Early in Clinton's first term, Lerner had sent the president a memo urging him to hold a "summit conference on ethics, community, and the politics of meaning" (Allen 1993).

Adolph Reed argues that the "language of responsibility" allowed New Liberalism to manage the "centrifugal tendencies" within the three poles of its support (1999d, 4). Neoliberals, for example, emphasize the responsibility of individuals to acquire the knowledge and abilities necessary to make good choices as producers and consumers. Communitarians believe the rewards of inclusion in the community should accrue only to those who fulfill their responsibilities to that collective. And for Southern Democrats, "personal responsibility" functions as a racially coded appeal to white voters hostile to the idea that white racism continues to be embedded in social institutions.

New Liberalism embraced the notion of "personal responsibility" to distinguish itself from traditional Democratic politics, which it accused of eroding individual initiative. Although New Democrats also sought to differentiate themselves from Reagan/Bush–style neoliberalism through an emphasis on interindividual obligation (i.e., "community"), the "language of responsibility" marked the continuity between Reaganism and New Liberalism. The parallels were significant enough that as early as 1981, a *New Republic* writer questioned whether neoliberal Democrats were merely advocating "Reaganism with a human face" (Kaus 1981). Arthur Schlesinger Jr. echoed that charge in 1986, referring to the Democratic Leadership Council as a "quasi-Reaganite formation" (Schlesinger 1986b). And in 1990, Senator Howard Metzenbaum and three dozen senatorial and congressional colleagues formed the Coalition for Democratic Values to counter the DLC, which they characterized as "the fine-tuning of Reaganism" (Baer 2000, 184).

In the rhetoric of the Third Way, Rose argues, "one can see the signs of the emergence of a new *moral* vocabulary for politics: the recurrence of terms freighted with values: partnership, civic society, community, civility, responsibility, mutuality, obligations, voluntary endeavour, autonomy, initiative" (Rose 1999, 474). This vocabulary through which the political "discourse about virtue" is elaborated is the basis of the conjuncture between Bill Clinton's New Liberalism and Oprah Winfrey's mind-cure technology of healing. Here we find the compatibility of etho-politics and the therapeutic enterprise, both of which are concerned with self-management for the sake of social integration, stability, and well-being.

The Makeover of Oprah Winfrey: Constructing a "Message of Goodness"

In January 1995, Winfrey appeared on *Larry King Live*. Early in the interview, King raised the specter of the sorry state of TV talk shows.

KING: Daytime television has become kind of like—it's a joke.

WINFREY: It's diseased.

KING: You say daytime television, and you think: "My aunt slept with my sister's boyfriend while I was out with my own mother." What happened?

Although Winfrey defended the genre for bringing "taboo" subjects "out of the closet" and getting "the country talking," she also conceded, "I think it's unfortunate that it's gone to this extreme" (King 1995, 367).

At the time of this interview, more than twenty talk shows crowded the airwaves. Many of them, especially those aimed at a younger audience, were competing for ratings with titillating topics and outrageous behavior by some of the guests. Popular press criticism of "trash talk TV" heated up in response. Two months after Winfrey's interview with Larry King, a gay guest at a taping of a *Jenny Jones* episode titled "Secret Admirers" confessed an attraction to his heterosexual neighbor, who was seated beside him on the stage. The unwilling object of desire murdered his "admirer" three days later and blamed the show for his actions. The incident and ensuing trial received abundant coverage, with commentators speculating that talk shows—rather than the killer—were actually on trial (Crain 1995; Goodman 1995; Braxton 1996). As

Laura Grindstaff notes, "The murder thrust talk shows into the national spotlight and intensified the pressure on them to clean up their act" (Grindstaff 2002, 28).

By December 1995, William Bennett, former secretary of education under Reagan, and prominent New Democrat Senators Joseph Lieberman and Sam Nunn joined forces in their "Empower America" campaign to rid the airwaves of the "cultural rot" of talk shows, which they charged had "mainstreamed trashy behavior" (Bennett 1996a, 1996b; Daley 1996). Asked by a reporter if he worried about "being lumped in with the Republicans on 'family values' issues," Senator Lieberman responded, "I'm very happy as a Democrat to have this opportunity to work with Bill Bennett.... Democrats care as much about values, and the impact culture has on values, as anyone else" (Hamilton 1996). Besides holding press conferences, supplying opinion pieces to the mainstream press, and producing radio and TV spots, the trio put pressure on advertisers, some of whom withdrew ads from talk programs to avoid adverse publicity (Beatty 1995; Gellene 1995; Johnson and Bash 1995).

Significantly, *The Oprah Winfrey Show* escaped this reinvigorated assault on talk television. Winfrey's program was conspicuously absent from Empower America's hit list of egregious shows. Nor was she targeted in the press coverage of Bennett's crusade or the *Jenny Jones* murder and trial. Indeed, Winfrey was frequently held up as the exception to the general debasement identified with talk shows. As one TV critic put it, "She's trying to inject some class into the raunchy, raucous world of daytime talkies" (Jubera 1995; see also Goodman 1995; Johnson and Bash 1995; Marks 1995; Page 1995; Priest 1995a, 1995b; Strauss 1995; Graham 1996; Mifflin 1996; Bennett 1996a, 1996b). That the undisputed "queen of talk" emerged unscathed from this full-scale attack on the genre was no accident. Winfrey had spent the previous year assiduously distancing herself from what she called the "trash pack" (Lorando 1994). Beginning with Marianne Williamson's appearance in January 1994—when Winfrey declared her intention to focus on "what's of value in the world"—*The Oprah Winfrey Show* began injecting more "uplifting" topics into its lineup, with titles such as "Random Acts of Kindness" (Feb. 15, 1994), "The Power of Prayer" (April 6, 1994), "Love Letters to Your Parents" (April 22, 1994), "There Are Angels Around Us" (July 6, 1994), "How to Live Your Dreams" (Aug. 17, 1994), "Only Good News" (Aug. 22, 1994), and "Thank You Day" (Sept. 19, 1994).

Winfrey explicitly identified 1994 as a turning point for her and for her show: it was, she said, a year of "profound change for me, emotionally, spiritually, and physically" (Adler 1997, 223). A key event was the departure of her longtime executive producer, Debra DiMaio. In the face of growing competition, ratings for *The Oprah Winfrey Show* in the May 1994 sweeps "dropped to the lowest point they had been in three years" (Mair 1994/1998, 340). Whereas Winfrey was determined to do "uplifting programs about spirituality, the meaning of life, world peace and building self-esteem," DiMaio favored "a return to talk show basics, namely, tough hard-edged topics for which the genre is infamous" (ibid.). Winfrey won that argument. DiMaio abruptly resigned on June 22, 1994, with a hefty severance settlement, and her boss was free to pursue uplift without opposition (Kubasik 1994). In a series of interviews that year, the language of responsibility loomed large in Winfrey's effort to reposition her show and recast her image. Not only did she vow to "be more responsible," to "do shows that are going to be a benefit" (Lorando 1994), and "to do responsible television" (Adler 1997, 78), she also expected "more responsibility" from her guests (Kennedy 1994, 28). "We're not gonna book a show where someone is talking about their victimization," she told *Entertainment Weekly* (ibid.). "I cannot listen to other people blaming their mothers for another year," she confided to *Redbook* magazine (Kest 1995, 77). "It's time to move on from 'we are dysfunctional' to 'what are we going to do about it,'" Winfrey said in another interview (Lorando 1994).

Perhaps Winfrey's most savvy decision as she sought to separate herself from the talk show critique was to tackle the issue head on. She kicked off the 1994–1995 season with back-to-back episodes titled "Are Talk Shows Bad?" (*Oprah Winfrey Show*, Sept. 12 and 13, 1994). The featured guest was Penn State sociologist Vicki Abt, who had published a study critical of talk shows a few months earlier. Titled "The Shameless World of Phil, Sally, and Oprah," the study appeared in the *Journal of Popular Culture* and was subsequently covered in the *New York Times*. Also appearing in these episodes were *Washington Post* TV writer Tom Shales—a long-standing critic of talk shows—and *People* magazine's David Hiltbrand, who was more sympathetic to the genre. Representing the views of "ordinary" people were Winfrey's studio audience and small groups of viewers participating via satellite from Boston, Atlanta, and San Francisco. Winfrey introduced the first episode by saying she was putting herself in the "hot seat" in order to address Abt's claim that "talk shows are harmful to society." She noted that Abt's study, along with her "own observation" of "some talk shows," had given her "a renewed mission of striving to improve all of our lives and spirits through this show."

In contrast to most popular press criticism that exempted Winfrey's program, Abt's research focused specifically on *The Oprah Winfrey Show, Donahue,* and *Sally Jesse Raphael*. The study claimed that the three programs featured "guests with deviant, bizarre and unusual behavior"; "desensitized [viewers] to bizarre, horrible and sick behavior and [left] them feeling no responsibility to intervene or to care"; "turn[ed] criminals and bad people" into "celebrities" and "encourag[ed] viewers to do the same thing to get on TV"; created "an insincere atmosphere of caring and helpfulness"; and were guilty of "tearing away at the family structure as more people turn to TV for personal communication" ("Are Talk Shows Bad? Part I," *Oprah Winfrey Show*, Sept. 12, 1994). Winfrey's response to these charges was multilayered: she granted legitimacy to the study's concerns ("I thought it made some very valid points"), acknowledged the possibility of her own culpability and a desire to make amends ("if I'm doing anything to cause harm through this show, I certainly want to know what that is and what to change it"), disparaged the excesses of other talk programs ("I'm embarrassed by some of the topics I see on certain shows"), and defended her own motives ("My goal is to uplift, encourage and enlighten you in some way").

Along the way, Winfrey elicited support for each of these strategies from the studio audience, Hiltbrand, Shales, and even from Abt herself. A woman in the Atlanta studio contrasted Ricki Lake—whose topics are "trashy" and "the few good topics that she has she doesn't handle well"—to Winfrey: "If Oprah were handling them, they would be done well." When Winfrey asked the panelists and studio audience, "What can we do with TV, with this show, to help the world?" a woman in the San Francisco studio volunteered: "Oprah, you do not need any advice from Vicki. I think you're doing just great on your own." *People's* Hiltbrand commented, "If anything, we owe talk shows like yours and some others a debt of gratitude" for airing issues that previously were not discussed publicly. Although Shales several times supported Abt during the discussion, he too treated Winfrey as an exception. In the second episode, after concurring with Abt's claim that talk shows "exploit people," Shales added, "I'm sorry we've turned into a referendum on Oprah because this is an awfully outstanding show. It's like we're going to talk about TV news and then all we talk about would be the 'CBS Evening News.' Well, what about 'Inside Edition' and 'Current Affair' and all that crap, if I may use that word?" This is a critic who in the late 1980s had specifically cited Oprah Winfrey as a purveyor of "talk rot." Even Abt, perhaps in response to the considerable hostility she encountered from the studio audience, drew a distinction between Winfrey and other talk show hosts: "You [Winfrey] started something that I think you realized that you could do better things for us. And I don't think your imitators care about people the way you care about them." Implicit in Abt's comment, as in Shales's, is that Winfrey had indeed undergone some kind of metamorphosis—that she may have once belonged in the category of "trash TV" but now occupied another realm altogether. I suggest that the purpose of these two episodes was precisely to validate that perception and further solidify the exceptional status of Winfrey and her program.

In closing the second installment, Winfrey affirmed the value of studies that "point out the immense power that we have, those of us who do television, to influence so many people." She distinguished herself from other talk show hosts: "I've been one to try and take risks.... I truly want this show and my life to serve the world and not belittle it." She incorporated the other participants in that noble mission: "I would like to thank you for doing the study and thank you all who had comments, and I will try to use this to upgrade, uplift, enlighten and encourage people." And her closing statement simultaneously dissociated her from the talk show critique and foreshadowed her ascendance to cultural icon: "I want you to know *The Oprah Winfrey Show* is going to continue. I am going to continue to try to strive to be a light to the world and to offer self-enlightenment to those who choose to watch. So thanks to all of you who watch because you feel we do achieve that goal, at least most days" ("Are Talk Shows Bad? Part II," *Oprah Winfrey Show*, Sept. 13, 1994).

Shortly before these episodes aired, *Entertainment Weekly* published an interview with Winfrey titled "Oprah Act Two: After a Year of Personal and Professional Turmoil, TV's Richest Woman Is Changing Her Life and Her Show" (Kennedy 1994, 21). Other writers have noted this shift in Winfrey's program in 1994 and 1995. Grindstaff argues that in response to the talk show critique, Winfrey "dropped conflict-based topics entirely and began a regime of moral and spiritual uplift" (Grindstaff 2002, 24). In Mair's view, "in contrast to the direction of all the other daytime TV talk programs," Winfrey "successfully re-created the Oprah show, shifting from trailer trash topics ... to self-fulfilling and enlightening topics" (Mair 1994/1998, 354, 352). Grindstaff suggests that Winfrey's move can be understood as part of a "struggle for distinction between the elite and popular media that goes back to the very origins of journalism" (Grindstaff 2002, 26). The divide between "legitimate" and "tabloid" journalism had fueled the critique of topical daytime talk shows since the genre's beginnings with *Donahue*. In Grindstaff's view, the proliferation of talk programs in the 1990s and resulting "general shift toward tabloid fare" triggered a "reproduction of the classy/trashy binarism internal to the genre itself" (ibid., 26). Through Winfrey's self-conscious efforts of reformulation, *The Oprah Winfrey Show* would come to epitomize the "classy" pole of the genre—hence, her conspicuous absence from the onslaught of criticism that besieged talk TV in 1995.

To say that Winfrey differentiated herself and her show by reducing conflict-based topics or eschewing "sleaze" does not on its own explain why the "queen of talk" would become a cultural heroine by the end of the decade. To understand that metamorphosis, it is necessary to examine the mind-cure technology of healing that has come to define her enterprise and its intersection with the political, economic, and ideological practices of Bill Clinton's New Liberalism. It is fitting that Winfrey would begin and end a year of remaking herself and her show with appearances by Marianne Williamson. Introducing Williamson as "one of the wisest people I know," Winfrey opened the December 14, 1994, episode promising to reveal "how a secret weapon can help with every single problem before you." That weapon was prayer. "By the time this show's over we're going to be so spiritually uplifted," Winfrey exclaimed (*Oprah Winfrey Show*, Dec. 14, 1994).

This episode is significant for two reasons. First, like the "Are Talk Shows Bad?" installments, it was intended to counter the talk show critique. All of the "ordinary" guests had previously appeared on the program and were invited back because they remained mired in dysfunction: a family of sisters who had staged "one of the biggest fights on the air" ("5 Sisters with 500 Problems," Sept. 29, 1993), a woman who had confronted her husband's murderer but was still unable to forgive and move on ("Set Free to Kill Again," Nov. 20, 1992), and a depressed mother on welfare ("I Kicked Welfare, You Can Too," Jan. 19, 1994). The purpose of the guests' return was to demonstrate that in contrast to "trashy" talk shows, Winfrey's program could truly "enlighten" and "empower" people to move beyond dysfunction. Second, the episode explicitly contrasted the mind-cure technology of healing with the limitations of the recovery paradigm. In introducing the program, Winfrey referred to past shows where "the therapists did all they could" to no effect. She said she had invited back some of these seemingly hopeless cases "to help them in a way that we feel is more effective than any expert in the world." Thus, she explained, "we're invoking the power of prayer today" under the guidance of Williamson, "one of America's foremost spiritual teachers."

Throughout the program, Williamson articulated mind-cure principles: "internal power is greater than the power of the external"; "prayer enables us to take the power of God and bring it down to the plane of our actual earth experience"; "a little bit of violence in the mind ... is contributing to the violence of our times"; through prayer, "the mind is lifted up to a new kind of thinking." She told the unhappy welfare mother that her problem lay in thinking that depression and being on welfare were "more powerful than God." Rather than thinking "I'm the victim," Williamson told the panelist, she should think, "I have within me the power to break through these constrictions." As in Williamson's earlier appearances on *The Oprah Winfrey Show*, the episode included group prayers for the beleaguered panelists and ended with a "Prayer for America." This time, Winfrey read the closing petition from Williamson's latest book, *Illuminata* (1995), a "collection of thoughts and prayers and rites of passage" that she had promoted throughout the episode.

Three weeks later, when Winfrey appeared on Larry King's show, she cited this episode with Williamson as exemplary of her mission to "lift people up." In the early days of her program, Winfrey told King, she was "not as evolved." Now, in contrast, she said she was "concerned about using my life and my show to really have a message of goodness" (King 1995, 369, 368). A few days later, Winfrey admitted during a taping of her show that she had tried cocaine in her twenties. In subsequent press coverage, her confession was framed through the language of responsibility, which enhanced Winfrey's reputation as a "responsible" talk show host (Edwards 1995). By early 1995, then, the public makeover of Oprah Winfrey was well underway. Meanwhile, Bill Clinton was undertaking his own project of self-transformation in response to the beating his party had taken in the November 1994 midterm election, the decline of his popularity in polls, the failure of two of his key initiatives, and the displeasure of the Democratic Leadership Council, which was accusing him of abandoning the New Liberal agenda that had put him in the White House in the first place.

The Makeover of Bill Clinton: Reinventing Democratic Politics

Winfrey and her viewers were not alone in seeking Marianne Williamson's help to invoke the secret weapon of prayer and conquer their problems. The same month that Williamson visited *The Oprah Winfrey Show*, she put in an appearance at Camp

David at the invitation of the president and first lady, who hosted her and fellow "self-help gurus" Stephen Covey, author of *Seven Habits of Highly Effective People,* and "peak performance coach" Anthony Robbins. Although the trio declined to divulge the substance of their session with the head of state and his wife, political pundits speculated that the Clintons were "reinventing" themselves in response to the electoral debacle that saw the Democrats lose control of both houses of Congress for the first time in four decades (Coleman 2000, 145; Kakutani 1995; DeWitt 1995; Smalley 2002). A *New York Times* article suggested the Clintons were indulging in a time-honored American preoccupation: "From the 1800's treatise 'Self-Help' by Samuel Smiles to 'The Power of Positive Thinking' by the Rev. Norman Vincent Peale, politicians, business executives, and millions of other Americans have gravitated to the message and messenger who tells them that the proper state of mind can produce physical, material and spiritual treasure" (DeWitt 1995). In truth, Bill Clinton's strategy after the 1994 election was less a full-scale "reinvention" than a reaffirmation of his New Liberal roots. According to DLC historian Kenneth Baer, with a 43 percent electoral plurality, a House evenly split between Republicans and Democrats, and his own party ideologically divided between traditional and "new" liberals, Clinton "was compelled to vacillate between Old and New Democratic policies" during his first two years in office (Baer 2000, 228). By November 1994, the DLC was frustrated enough with its protégé to interpret the Republican landslide as proof of the public's displeasure with Clinton for "straying from the New Democratic line" (ibid., 230). The White House bought this interpretation and the president promptly made tracks for "the New Democratic fold" to "rejuvenate [his] popularity and his prospects for reelection" (ibid.). Much as Winfrey used the 1994 "talk show wars" to emerge with her reputation not just intact but significantly enhanced, Clinton would take advantage of the crisis of the 1994 election to "resurrect both [himself] and the New Democrats" (ibid., 228).

Central to Clinton's political rebirth was his recruitment of another "guru"—Dick Morris—shortly after the 1994 election. Morris crafted what he termed a "triangulation" strategy by which Clinton might not only weather the GOP landslide but also secure a second term: "steal the Republicans' thunder, draw down the deficit, reform welfare, cut back government regulation and 'use Gore's reinventing government program to cut the public sector's size'" (Cockburn and St. Clair 2004, 46). This strategic shift was evident in Clinton's 1995 State of the Union address, where "New Democratic public philosophy dominated the speech" (ibid., 238).[11] In the address, Clinton revived the 1992 New Covenant terminology, reiterating his commitment to "reducing the deficit, reforming welfare, and shrinking the size and scope of the federal government" (ibid.). Prominently featured in the speech were sentiments drawn from Robert Putnam's "bowling alone" diagnosis of America's ills. Like Williamson, Covey, and Robbins, Putnam had been summoned to Camp David for an audience with Clinton in late 1994. According to a *Washington Post* writer, the communitarian political scientist had "clearly made an impact on the president"—so much so that "'Bowling Alone' was unmistakably the inspiration for key passages of the State of the Union speech" (Powers 1995).

Invoking the New Liberal trinity of "responsibility, opportunity and community," Clinton suggested that "citizenship" was the logical outcome of these three virtues (Clinton 1995a). In his diagnosis, the nation's troubles were the result of an eroded "civil life," a fraying of "the common bonds of community," a decline of "cooperation" and "association." The cure for this malaise was more responsibility: "we have to do more to accept responsibility for ourselves, and for our families, for our communities, and yes, for our fellow citizens," Clinton said. A lack of responsibility, he argued, was most apparent in people who treated welfare as "a way of life," in an "epidemic of teen pregnancies and births where there is no marriage," in individuals who failed to display "responsible parenting," in the media's promotion of "incessant, repetitive, mindless violence and irresponsible conduct." Conversely, the reward for embracing responsibility was "community," which, following Putnam, Clinton considered the source of "bonds of trust and cooperation."

Significantly absent in the president's address was any mention of corporate or governmental responsibility. Rather, government was defined primarily as an impediment: "Our job is to get rid of yesterday's government so that our own people can meet today's and tomorrow's needs," Clinton said. In place of the federal government taking responsibility for public resources and programs, he argued, "states and communities and private citizens in the private sector can do a better job." Thus, the federal government "should get out of the way and let them do what they can do better." Under the auspices of the New Covenant, "resources and decision making" would be shifted from government to citizens, thereby "injecting choice and competition and individual responsibility into national policy." Clinton characterized this shift as an expansion of opportunity, as a means of empowerment, as "taking power away from federal bureaucracies and giving it back to communities and individuals" (Clinton 1995a).

The 1995 State of the Union address signaled Clinton's return to the bosom of New Liberalism. Rather than continuing to seek alliances and compromises with the traditional liberal arm of the Democratic Party, he turned his gaze rightward, making "both symbolic and policy appeals to religious conservatives and moderates" (Guth 2000, 209) in anticipation of the 1996 election. From this point, Clinton adopted increasingly conservative social positions (Baer 2000, 240). He began referring regularly to his religious faith, announced an initiative favoring religious activities in public schools, renewed a call for "school choice," advocated the V-chip "so that parents could censor television programs for their children," and declared his support for a bill to outlaw gay marriage that had been pushed through Congress by religious conservatives (ibid.). By January 1996, Clinton had purged himself of all vestiges of traditional liberalism, delivering a State of the Union address that a decade earlier would have been unrecognizable as a Democratic president's. "The era of big government is over," he declared at the beginning of the speech. In its place was a "new, smaller government" operating "in an old-fashioned American way, together with all of our citizens through state and local governments, in the workplace, in religions, charitable and civic organizations" (Clinton 1996a).

Predictably, the 1996 address was saturated with "values politics," or the "discourse about virtue" recommended by Clinton pollster Stanley Greenberg. A year earlier the president had characterized the "old way of governing" as one driven by divisions of "interest, constituency and class" (Clinton 1995a). In 1996 those putatively antiquated divisions had now been surpassed, replaced by the real "foundation of American life": the family. Accordingly, much of the 1996 address was organized around strengthening the virtues of the family. Clinton spoke of the need for more parental "responsibility"; the benefits of the V-chip; the problem of teenage pregnancy; the merits of "school choice," charter schools, and national standards of educational measurement; and the need for more police and harsher punishments to protect families from "crime and gangs and drugs" (Clinton 1996a).

In addition to endorsing a balanced budget and smaller government—"our federal government is the smallest it has been in 30 years and it's getting smaller every day," Clinton boasted—he promoted an activist, internationalist foreign policy, a strong military, and stepped up policing and prosecution of illegal immigrants. That this "Republican-sounding 'values agenda'" (Harvey 2000, 129) was invoked by a Democratic president indicates the extent to which Clinton and New Liberalism had appropriated the ideological and political strategies of the GOP (Feldman 1996). Doug Henwood argues that Republicans' deep enmity toward Clinton issues in part from his successful co-optation of their own political agenda. Clinton, in contrast, viewed Republicans not as "the opposition" but "simply as friends he [hadn't] quite made yet" (Henwood 1997, 166).

A centerpiece of the "discourse about virtue" in the 1996 State of the Union address was Clinton's renewed pledge to "end welfare as we know it." To "those of you who are on welfare," he warned, "Congress and I are near agreement on sweeping welfare reform" (Clinton 1996a). Blaming welfare for having "undermined the values of family and work," the president issued a "challenge" to welfare recipients "to make the most of this opportunity for independence." Eight months later, Clinton would make good on that promise by signing the Personal Responsibility and Work Opportunity Reconciliation Act (PRWORA)—legislation engineered by Contract With America Republicans that abolished the sixty-year-old Aid to Families with Dependent Children (AFDC) program. Just as Reaganism consolidated a cross-class alliance by tapping into race- and gender-based divisions, Clinton also exploited racial tensions by using the issue of welfare reform to placate "mainstream" voters as he headed into the November election. Elaine Brown notes that Clinton's 1992 victory was "attributed to his campaign proposal to give welfare mothers a choice of working or being removed from the rolls, which brought Reagan Democrats back into the fold" (Brown 2002, 94). The *New Republic*'s Mickey Kaus had gone so far as to blame the Republican sweep in 1994 on the president's failure to push for "welfare reform rather than health care reform" (Kaus 1994, 1). Although Clinton's call for welfare reform was couched in the language of responsibility, independence, and opportunity, its political potency issued from the same underclass ideology that had fueled Reaganism. Taking a page from Reaganism's divide-and-conquer/unite-and-mobilize strategy, Clintonism sought to secure white middle-class allegiance by "bashing the poor"—a sector of the population with negligible political power (Abramovitz and Withorn 1999, 151; also Piven and Ehrenreich 2005).

Clinton's reelection in 1996 seemed to validate not only New Liberalism's control of the Democratic Party but also its reading of the American polity—at least that portion of the polity deemed worthy of attention. As Mimi Abramovitz and Ann Withorn note, by 1996 "a demonstrated hostility to the poor and a willingness to cut 'failed' social programs became a 'bottom-line' ticket of entry into 'responsible' politics in both parties" (Abramovitz and Withorn 1999, 168). Clinton's 1996 victory—the first time an elected Democratic president since Harry Truman had won a second term—marked the culmination of his New Democrat makeover. He and fellow New Democrats took his reelection as proof that channeling the diminishing resources of an ever-shrinking federal government to the "deserving" middle class, so as to enhance its human and social capital, while continuing to slash the already meager allotment to the "undeserving" poor, was the sole viable electoral strategy for Democrats. As I argue in the next chapter, the theory of the underclass, which by the 1990s captivated both conservative and liberal commentators and social scientists, provided an ideological rationale for this political strategy.

At the point that making good on his promise to end welfare was speeding Clinton toward reelection, Oprah Winfrey was launching Oprah's Book Club, the vehicle that would transport her decisively from the "trashy" to the "classy" side of the cultural divide. Expressing a recurring sentiment within the extensive press coverage of the book club, D. T. Max wrote in the *New York Times Magazine*, "When Winfrey says, 'Reading changed my life,' millions who see where she has gotten listen. Women from the inner city to the suburbs rush out to buy Oprah's pick" (Max 2000, 37). Although not empirically substantiated, such assertions about the universal membership of Oprah's Book Club have become part of the conventional wisdom that Winfrey's appeal transcends divisions of class and race. The singular role of the book club in elevating Winfrey to the status of cultural icon will be treated more fully in Chapter 7. In the next chapter, I take a closer look at Winfrey's relationship with the "inner city" and examine parallels between her treatment of welfare, race, and poverty and Clinton's handling of these issues so as to unpack the racial politics that unites both enterprises.

CHAPTER

～ 6 ～

"Transcending Race"

The Racial Politics of Oprah Winfrey and New Liberalism

On April 19, 1995, Oprah Winfrey introduced her show by referring to Bill Clinton's televised press conference from the previous evening: "Many of you might have seen the president's speech last night asking the GOP to help him with welfare reform—asking us all, actually. Well, that's what we're talking about today" ("Should Welfare Pay for Her Kids?" *Oprah Winfrey Show*, Apr. 19, 1995). Winfrey then introduced four panelists—current welfare recipients Linda and Dellamarie, and former AFDC beneficiaries Connie and Star—whom she characterized as follows:

> Both Linda and Della say that all of us owe them a welfare paycheck because they are performing a woman's most important job: raising children. Now I would definitely agree the most important job is raising children. We'll discuss the other [claim]....
> [Connie and Star] are incensed by what they call the "give me, give me, give me" attitude of some welfare recipients.... [Connie] says anybody who lives like this is just a leech. Star blames welfare for supporting her irresponsible habits, including carefree sex and drugs.

Unlike the vast majority of pre-taped *Oprah Winfrey Show* episodes, this session was broadcast live, suggesting Winfrey felt motivated enough by the issue to break with her normal production routines.[1] As she informed the audience, "these days America is rethinking its welfare experiment. We thought it was time, too, to question whether this experiment has failed."

Clinton's television appearance the night before was also a departure from routine, being only the fourth prime-time TV news conference in his two-plus years in the White House. The *Wall Street Journal* speculated that Clinton used this special venue to take advantage of "an issue with widespread populist appeal" and thereby "gain back some of the political momentum that the Republicans took from him in

November" (Wartzman and Stout 1995). Clinton had opened the press conference by citing his common ground with the Republican-controlled Congress: their mutual desire to reduce the deficit, shrink government, get "tough on crime," and cut taxes (Clinton 1995b). This emphasis on commonalities set the stage for the main point of the address: to revive his promise to "end welfare as we know it," an issue on which Democrats and Republicans "should be able to agree." Reminding viewers that in 1994 he had "introduced the most sweeping welfare reform ever presented to Congress," Clinton noted similarities between his and two GOP-sponsored bills—"All of these bills are based on the same idea: the fundamental goal of welfare reform is to move people into the work force and to make them independent." He then issued a challenge to Congress to "pass a bipartisan welfare reform bill and put in on my desk by July 4, so that we celebrate Independence Day by giving Americans on welfare the chance, the opportunity, the responsibility to move to independence" (ibid.).

This special broadcast was another leg of Clinton's journey back to his New Democratic roots as he charted a strategy for reelection. As the *Wall Street Journal* noted, the president "set out last night to reclaim welfare reform as an issue on which he can not only blast the Republicans but also offer a positive alternative and demonstrate leadership." By throwing down the gauntlet before the GOP-dominated Congress, Clinton "positioned himself to take credit on a subject that is hugely popular" (Wartzman and Stout 1995). Welfare itself had never enjoyed huge popularity. Unlike other programs created by the 1935 Social Security Act, it was "never proclaimed as a social advancement" (Withorn 1996, 497). But the creation of this public assistance program, Ann Withorn argues, had represented a political acknowledgement that "modern society creates a subset of the citizenry to whom government assistance must be given if the spillover effects of poverty are to be prevented from creating broader harm in the society at large" (ibid., 498). The far right wing of the Republican Party[2] had been a bitter foe of welfare from the beginning, but criticisms of AFDC—for example, its meager benefit levels, which were never high enough to elevate recipients above the poverty line, its emphasis on "relief" rather than "prevention and rehabilitation" (Patterson 1994, 131–132), and its complicated relationship to both structural sources of poverty and racial politics—had issued from across the political spectrum over the years (see Patterson 1994; Hamilton and Hamilton 1997; Brown 1999b; Gilens 1999). In the 1980s, as the Reagan administration "intensified its assault on poor people and welfare programs for political and ideological gain," welfare moved to the top of the national political agenda (Abramovitz and Withorn 1999, 154).

In 1982 Congress passed the Omnibus Budget Reconciliation Act, which tightened AFDC rules. Prohibiting recipients from working while continuing to receive food stamps and Medicaid, the legislation forced thousands of "working poor" off the rolls (ibid.). The 1988 Family Support Act (FSA) went further, transforming AFDC from an entitlement-based income maintenance program into "a mandatory work program offered in exchange for income support" (ibid., 155), but provided no funds for education, training, or childcare to help recipients successfully navigate this shift. Emboldened by the passage of FSA, states began implementing laws to "control the marital, childbearing and parental behavior of women on welfare" (ibid., 156), such as denying benefits to children born after their mothers went on AFDC, providing cash bonuses to welfare recipients who married, refusing aid to teenage mothers unless they lived with their children's grandparents, and tying benefits to children's school attendance (ibid., 156–157).

That the Family Support Act and related state initiatives received enthusiastic bipartisan support indicates the degree to which Democrats had backed away from their commitment to a liberal welfare state and accepted the premises of underclass ideology. As Withorn argues, "the theory of the underclass emerged in the early 1980s with a surprisingly wide spectrum of liberal support—the first sign of changing times" (Withorn 1996, 501).[3] Underclass theory, jointly forwarded by conservative and liberal journalists and social scientists, focused on a specific sector of the poor: people living in core urban areas marked by high rates of poverty, crime, drugs, joblessness, and school dropouts, as well as high rates of female-headed households, teenage pregnancy, out-of-wedlock births, and use of welfare. This distinctive "underclass" was distinguished from the "ordinary" poor in that it was "depicted as a rootless population that functioned outside mainstream values and institutions, whose dependence and antisocial behavior was transmitted generationally (in homes headed by women) and which was stubbornly resistant to change" (ibid.). The portrayal of the underclass was further linked to a second element of the emerging discourse on poverty in the 1980s: that the very existence of welfare violated "core American values" and therefore could not win support from "mainstream" Americans (ibid.). This assumption, as we have seen, was a central tenet of the New Liberal agenda to "reinvent" Democratic politics.

Both conservative and liberal strains of underclass theory rest on implicit racial and gender premises, in that the underclass is identified with core urban neighborhoods and female-headed households. Thus, the purportedly self-reproducing nature of the underclass is attributed to women's failure to instill responsibility and morality in their offspring. Christopher Jencks, for example, posited the existence of a "reproductive underclass" of female welfare recipients whose failure to "make responsible reproductive decisions" perpetuated both poverty and dependence (Withorn 1996, 502). This "cycle of poverty" (Mills 1994, 867) thesis—adopted from Daniel Patrick Moynihan's *The Negro Family* (1965) with its claim that black families were mired in "a tangle of pathology"—identifies "women's living and reproductive practices as the transmission belt that drives the cycle" (Withorn 1996, 191; also Zinn 1990, 365). Thanks to this "feminization" of the underclass, Withorn argues, "welfare mothers were discussed in the same breath as drug users, criminals and other antisocial groups" (Withorn 1996, 502). In the 1980s, the image of the "crack mother" pervaded media portrayals of drug problems in poor urban neighborhoods,

THE AGE OF OPRAH

becoming a potent symbol in Reaganism's "war on drugs" and contributing to the demonization of poor women—and especially poor minority women (Reeves and Campbell 1994, 207–216).[4]

As many critics have observed, the notion of the underclass is "racially coded," despite its veneer of social scientific neutrality, in that it provides a "way of talking about blacks (and, increasingly, Latinos) without talking about blacks" (Mills 1994, 859; see also Reed 1999d; Brown 1999; Abramovitz and Withorn 1999; Reeves and Campbell 1994; Roediger 2002; Macek 2006). At times these racial premises are made explicit, as in Mickey Kaus's assessment in *New Republic* that Clinton's failure to accomplish welfare reform was responsible for the 1994 Republican landslide. In Kaus's analysis, welfare was universally "despised" by voters because it was

> implicated in America's most difficult social problem—the existence of whole neighborhoods, mostly African American, where there are precious few intact, working families. Welfare may or may not have caused this underclass, but welfare is clearly what sustains it. And the underclass, in turn, drives the crime problem, the race problem, the "urban crisis" and the general sense of social decay. (Kaus 1994, 18)

According to Adolph Reed Jr. (1999d), by the mid-1990s such conceptions of the underclass had "taken hold of the public imagination" and achieved the status of "deeply entrenched common sense"—a legacy of the long rightward shift in "public debate about social welfare" that began under Reagan (179). In that political sea-change, both conservatives and liberals came to share the view that "the underclass was not merely poor, disorganized and marginal, but also deficient and deviant" (Withorn 1996, 502). Liberals were more inclined to employ the therapeutically inflected term "pathological," while conservatives opted for "immoral," but both camps defined use of AFDC benefits "as welfare dependence, and socially harmful exactly because it provided financial support for the underclass" (ibid.). This shifting national "common sense" regarding welfare is evident in public opinion poll results from 1985 and 1995. When asked whether the U.S. public assistance system "works well," 56 percent of respondents in 1985 said no, whereas ten years later, 72 percent replied negatively. On the question of whether public assistance "discourages people from working," 55 percent agreed in 1985, compared to 73 percent in 1995 (Weaver, Shapiro, and Jacobs 1995, 611). A number of studies have explored the media's contribution to this change in public opinion through habitual linkage of "homelessness, destitute urban neighborhoods, poverty, public housing, and welfare reform" with "deviance, dangers, and moral deficits of inner-city communities" (Macek 2006, 170; also Gray 1989; Reeves and Campbell 1994; Rivers 1996; Gilens 1999; Entman and Rojecki 2000). Further, as Steve Macek observes, television news coverage of poverty, welfare, and the underclass escalated "during the national debate over so-called welfare reform that preoccupied Congress and the White House during much of the Clinton era"

(Macek 2006, 175). Winfrey's handling of welfare, as well as poverty, public housing, and crime, reflects both tendencies.

Become All You Can Be: Winfrey Takes on the "Welfare Mentality"

Defining one segment of the population as inherently pathological or immoral and pitting it against those who "play by the rules" gave a humanitarian gloss to attacks on welfare and welfare recipients. Thus, Clinton could present the end of welfare as beneficial to poor Americans on the grounds that public assistance "undermines the work ethic, causes family breakup, promotes illegitimacy, induces dependence, and encourages irresponsible behavior" (Withorn 1996, 501). Winfrey's treatment of welfare, poverty, and race in the 1990s must be situated within this broader political milieu. As we saw in the "Three Generations of Underclass" episode discussed in Chapter 4, her attitude toward welfare had marked affinities with that of guest expert Lawrence Mead, an avowed conservative whose writings identified social welfare programs as "the source of antisocial behavior among recipients of benefits," held that "welfare programs must be abolished or rendered punitive or work-oriented for the benefit of the poor," and suggested that blacks, in particular, were "the group whose behavior most needed improvement" (ibid., 506).

Like the earlier "Three Generations of Underclass" episode, "Should Welfare Pay for Her Kids?" in 1995 was framed through underclass theory, blaming welfare for fostering dependency, violating American values, and exacerbating, rather than ameliorating, poverty. Introducing panelist John Goodman, who was identified on-screen with the tagline "Thinks Welfare Encourages Immoral Behavior," Winfrey said he viewed welfare as "a mistake" because it "rewards people for perverse behavior and encourages them to have illegitimate kids and forgo work." Indeed, Goodman blamed welfare not only for promoting immorality but for *creating* poverty, and at taxpayers' expense no less. "We are spending $350 billion every year combating poverty," he said. "That's $3,500 for every household in America. That's what we're spending. And each year we get more and more poor people." Goodman provided no evidence for these inaccurate and misleading figures and Winfrey asked for none, which left viewers free to imagine that $3,500 of their previous year's income had been pocketed by lazy deviants.

Such suspicions were reinforced by African American panelist Star Parker (tag-line: "Former Welfare Mother Now Opposed to Welfare"), who offered herself as proof that welfare "creates a cycle of dependency" because it allowed her "to live very irresponsibly," to obtain government-funded abortions and dump her daughter at "government paid-for daycare" while she spent her time "taking drugs" and "hanging out" at the beach. Parker described the welfare system as "sick," as "infectious," as "a cancer" that "steals the incentive from people to look within yourself." Not only did government assistance erode personal incentive and responsibility, in her view, it discouraged people from turning to superior sources of support: families and churches. As Parker asserted, "What happened to our faith in God? What happened to our faith in each other? What happened to our faith in our churches? But what's happening—the government is competing with the very helping institutions established." If this solution sounds eerily similar to President George H. W. Bush's "thousand points of light" philosophy of social welfare—in fact, one of the episode's pro-welfare panelists pointed out that Parker had been traveling the country as a "mouthpiece" for the Republican Party's antiwelfare crusade[5]—it also jibes with the communitarian-based critique of welfare embraced by Clinton and the New Democrats.

Panelist Linda Ray, an AFDC mother and member of "Welfare Warriors," a national coalition fighting for "economic justice," attempted to widen the discussion by raising the issue of "corporate welfare" and the national distribution of wealth: "We have one percent at the top who have 39 percent of all the resources. We have 80 percent at the very bottom, which I would guess that most of us are in that 80 percent, and we're fighting over 14 percent of the resources.... There's a disparity between the very rich and the very poor in this country, and that's what causes the problem." Fellow panelist Dellamarie (tagline: "On and Off Welfare for 18 Years") concurred: "It's a sad state of affairs when we have corporations getting big subsidies. The workers are paying more in taxes—working people are paying more in taxes than corporations are. They are not being paid a livable wage."[6] At that point, Connie—the panelist who had called AFDC recipients "leeches"—interjected, "But Della, you're not a working person." Linda Ray again tried to steer the conversation to women's economic situation: "A woman making minimum wage in 1979 made enough to support herself and her two children," she said. "A woman working today at minimum wage lives at three-quarters of the poverty level." Star Parker interrupted, "But America's not designed to keep you at minimum wage. This land is full of opportunity. You're supposed to move up."

This kind of short-circuiting, where ideas are undeveloped and statements of fact are countered by expressions of opinion, is standard in the talk show format. It is what makes the genre at once frustrating and seductive. Because this episode was aired live, the exchanges were even more disjointed and chaotic than usual; panelists cut each other off, studio audience members interrupted frequently, and Winfrey struggled to maintain order and make room for commercial breaks. Although the episode included a nominal balance of pro- and antiwelfare guests and Winfrey at one point asked whether ending welfare would put women and children "out in the streets," her support for "welfare reform" was clear. Citing poll results that placed her in the majority on the issue, Winfrey told the audience, "89 percent of you Americans support a law to cut back on welfare after two years." She also resisted efforts to connect welfare to broader economic issues.

Midway through the program, Winfrey introduced panelist Marian Kramer of the National Welfare Rights Union as follows:

> For the last 30 years Marian Kramer has been fighting for the rights of people who receive welfare. She says everybody in this country is on some kind of welfare. Middle-class citizens get income tax deductions for their home mortgages, while the rich take advantage of complicated tax shelters. Please tell me where they [tax shelters] are, would you, please?

Analyses of the ways social class figures into the distribution of public resources and the creation of public policy are abundant and well documented (e.g., May 1988; Coontz 1992; Lipsitz 1998; Entman and Rojecki 2000; Brown et al. 2003). An exploration of this link might go a long way toward providing the enlightenment that Winfrey claims is the mission of her show. By following her introduction of Kramer with a humorous aside about tax shelters, however, Winfrey avoided that exploration. Instead, her remark accomplished two things: it made light of Kramer's position and denied that "the rich"—a category to which Winfrey indisputably belongs—receive any benefits to which they are not entitled.

Like Linda Ray and Dellamarie, Kramer tried to expand the welfare debate by connecting it to corporate tax cuts, financial speculation, industrial plant closings, and the transfer of jobs outside the United States. In every case, Winfrey showed no interest in pursuing this line of analysis. In none of these instances did she utter a single comment or question. Immediately following Kramer's discussion of the social effects of massive plant closures in the Michigan auto industry, Winfrey excitedly announced that the upcoming segment would feature a "fascinating" guest from a previous episode who had gone home "a changed woman" after appearing on the show. The transformed panelist was none other than one of the "three generations of underclass" featured in 1989.

Winfrey prefaced her introduction of Jamie, who with her mother and daughter had represented the intergenerational transmission of dependence, with an excerpt from the earlier episode. In the taped excerpt Jamie described welfare as "a cycle" that "you can't hardly break." Whereas her tagline in 1989 had read "On Welfare," when Jamie walked onstage in 1995 she was identified thus: "Quit Welfare After THE OPRAH SHOW"—a graphic testimonial to the empowering effects of Winfrey's program. But if Jamie was intended to illustrate the transformative power of *The Oprah Winfrey Show*, her story fell somewhat short of inspirational. She had indeed quit welfare after appearing on the show and gotten a job at a temporary agency. That she had found a place in the contingent workforce was perhaps predictable. By the early 1990s, temporary employment was one of the fastest growing sectors of the labor market, Manpower Inc. was the largest employer in the nation, and women and people of color—such as Jamie—were overrepresented in that employment sector, in that African Americans comprised "ten percent of the total workforce, but 16 percent of the temp agency workforce" (Collins and Yeskel 2000, 109, 110). Jamie had since left temporary employment and was currently working two jobs—one full time and one part time. Winfrey did not ask why she held two jobs, although it is not unreasonable to speculate that, like millions of other Americans, Jamie had found she needed more than one job to make ends meet. Nor could she unambiguously fulfill Winfrey's claim that it was possible to "break the cycle." When Jamie revealed that her granddaughter had recently applied for welfare, thus making it "four generations," Winfrey broke for commercial.

At the close of "Should Welfare Pay for Her Kids?" Winfrey promised to "do another show about welfare," because "we never got to: How do you resolve it? What is the real answer to reform? ... We need solutions." In fact, Winfrey was not at a loss for solutions to the problem of welfare, as she had made clear the previous year. On January 19, 1994, five days after she had accepted Marianne Williamson's invitation to eschew "negativity" in favor of "positive" programming, Winfrey hosted an episode titled "I Kicked Welfare, You Can Too." This program featured women who had managed to leave public assistance offering advice to those who "don't think they can get off the welfare system." Reinforcing the equation of welfare and "dependence," the terminology of addiction figured prominently in the episode. Former AFDC recipients were identified as having "kicked" welfare, while their counterparts on public assistance were labeled as wanting to "quit"—as if public aid were a drug. Further, both being on welfare and leaving welfare were defined through the lens of individual psychology. Women who remained in the system suffered from depression, lacked "self-esteem," were trapped "in a rut," did not believe in their "possibilities," and erroneously perceived themselves as "victims." In contrast, women who managed to "kick" welfare "dependence" possessed "self-esteem" and "self-respect," were able to "move forward" because they recognized they had "alternatives."

The first two panelists personified the latter category: Sherry Peterson (tagline: "Kicked Welfare and Became a Lawyer") and Allison Barnett ("Kicked Welfare and Became a Doctor"). Winfrey introduced the pair as "women of strong character" who had "pulled themselves up by their bootstraps" and contrasted them to "their welfare twins," Marcy Dillon and Linda (last name not given). Although the stories of the two professional women who had extricated themselves from poverty and found their way off welfare rolls were impressive, it should be noted that both Peterson and Barnett had made that transition many years earlier. Barnett, for example, had been on welfare in the 1970s, when she passed the GED exam and received financial help getting into college. Peterson had combined welfare benefits and university-provided financial aid to make her way through school. Both had left welfare prior to the deep cuts in social services carried out under Reagan, when AFDC was turned into a "mandatory work program offered in exchange for income support." Such facts are irrelevant, however, when getting off welfare is treated as a matter of individual choice, attitude, and integrity.

Early in the program Winfrey vented her frustration with "young people who are impoverished" but "don't understand there's a process to success." She was equally annoyed with people who "blame society or they blame whoever is president at the time" and take the stance, "'I am the victim and the system ought to be doing better for me.'" Such attitudes violated what Winfrey described as "one of the things I believe in the very fiber of my being ... that you can become whatever you wish to do in life." This belief—the foundation of mind cure—served as the episode's dominant framework of intelligibility. As Winfrey elaborated:

> Not only that what you wish but what you expect of yourself is what usually comes true. And so today, we're talking to women who pulled themselves up by their bootstraps, who used to believe there was no way out, who had no education.... And they are talking to women who are on welfare right now who believe as you once believed. And we all know, anyone who attains any level of success and happiness in life is—knows that you become what you believe you can be, right?

This statement prefaced Winfrey's introduction of Marcy Dillon, who had applied for welfare two years earlier after leaving her husband. She and her four-year-old daughter—who were living with Dillon's mother and ailing grandmother—received $497 a month in AFDC and food stamp benefits, amounting to an annual income of $5,964, or approximately 60 percent of the federally designated poverty level in 1994 for a family consisting of a single parent and one child (United States Census Bureau 2003). Although Dillon had previously worked as a data entry clerk and wished to return to work or go to school for more training, she faced the problem of what to do with her daughter. She pointed out that childcare cost $130 to $140 a week—an amount exceeding her total monthly welfare benefits. Were she to return to full-time work, the cost of childcare would devour most of her paycheck and leave her without medical care for her daughter. Winfrey, panelist Sherry Peterson, and several audience members suggested Dillon turn to the "helping institutions" of family, church, and private charities. Dillon explained that her mother worked full time, that her grandmother was too ill to care for a four-year-old, and that churches she had contacted might help with an occasional bill or groceries but would not "take care of your kids on a day-to-day basis."

Although Winfrey conceded childcare was "a major issue for women in this country," the conversation quickly returned to Dillon's personal deficiencies: "You need a plan for your life," Winfrey told her. Sherry Peterson concurred: "You have to do a certain amount of problem solving yourself." Winfrey seized this opportunity to reiterate her position: "I know it's all—it sounds very simple, but there are some basic physical laws that work in the universe, what you put out comes back all the time." Dillon, she said, must recognize that "Every time you get knocked down, come back again. But what so many people seem to do that's so frustrating to me—I want to pull my hair out—is that people move through life as though life has control of them. It does not. It is about you deciding what you want for your life and believing that you can get it." Panelist Allison Barnett chimed in: "That's absolutely correct. It boils down to a sense of empowering [*sic*]."

Winfrey's message of empowerment through correct thinking did meet with occasional resistance. Guest Connie Tolbert had "kicked" welfare by being appointed to the Maryland governor's Commission on Welfare Reform. Because Tolbert was intended to represent a woman of "strong character," Winfrey sought her participation in framing welfare as chosen dependence. Their exchange is illustrative.

WINFREY: What about the woman who just said there are a lot of people who are lazy and want to be on [welfare]?

TOLBERT: Well, I don't think anybody wants to be on AFDC.

WINFREY: But if not want, would you not say that a lot of people are trapped in the—in the cycle of it?

TOLBERT: Exactly.

WINFREY: Yeah.

TOLBERT: They're trapped, literally. Right now Oprah—I don't think you—a lot of people know this—in the state of Maryland, a minimum wage job pays—AFDC pays more than a minimum wage job in Maryland.

WINFREY: And—and so would you—would you admit, though, that there are a lot of people who take the "I am the victim" theory for their lives and therefore, because they believe that they're victimized, can no longer move forward or don't move forward?

TOLBERT: Well, that may very well be true in some instances, but I don't think that's the majority, Oprah.

WINFREY: You do not?

TOLBERT: No, I do not believe that.

Tolbert's disagreement did not deter Winfrey from reasserting her conviction that rising out of poverty comes down to "a decision you have to make inside yourself somewhere." She was, however, amenable to viewing poverty and welfare as effects of psychological malaise. Guest expert Sharon Bilotti, who had worked with public aid recipients for thirty years, argued that the "stresses" of people living in poverty are so "monumental" that "many of them sink into what we are now being able to recognize as real medical depression." Winfrey was open to this diagnosis, she explained, because she had witnessed conditions in the Chicago public housing projects the previous summer while filming the television movie *There Are No Children Here* (Loynd 1993). "Just the physical being there is depressing to your spirit. It really is," she said. The antidote to this depression of spirit was "self-esteem." Given that Winfrey had once identified "lack of self-esteem" as "the root of all the problems in the world" and in 1990 had produced and hosted a special titled *In the Name of Self-Esteem* that aired on ABC, it was logical that she would envision the cure for welfare "addiction" as a regimen of self-esteem building ("Everybody's Talking!" 1992, 34).[7] This diagnosis/cure, moreover, would become the framework for one of her most ambitious projects, Families for a Better Life.

On September 13, 1994, Winfrey staged a press conference to announce the creation of a program that would take 100 families off welfare within two years. The idea for Families for a Better Life (FBL) originated in Winfrey's 1993 encounter with the Chicago housing projects during the filming of *There Are No Children Here*. There she met two families whom she subsequently helped move into their own homes. Families for a Better Life, which would target residents of Chicago Housing Authority developments and provide them with family and financial counseling, job training, health care, and educational opportunities, was intended to reproduce this success story on a large scale. Winfrey committed up to $6 million to the project—based on the estimate of $30,000 per year per family—which was to be administered by the Jane Adams Hull House Association. FBL would seek out families "who are motivated to change," she told reporters and camera crews. Accordingly, applicants would be carefully screened and subjected to drug testing, background checks, and home visits. Hull House organizers would develop a pilot program by the end of 1994, when the first ten families would begin their eight-week preparation course. In creating the program, Winfrey explained, "It is my intention to take people out, to change their lives. But more importantly than changing their lives, I want to change the way they think about their lives. I want to destroy the welfare mentality" (McRoberts 1994b).

The response to Winfrey's press conference was immediate. The following day, some 20,000 people from across the country called Hull House pleading to be included in the program. The organization's public relations director interpreted the deluge of calls as proof that people "want to get off welfare and better their lives" (Golab 1994). Press coverage hailed Winfrey's generosity and her commitment to helping welfare recipients "get on the road to independence" (McRoberts 1994b). A *Chicago Sun-Times* editorial applauded Winfrey's stated intention to "destroy the welfare mentality, the belief in victimization." As a "holistic program," the editorial said, Families for a Better Life was "bound to be the envy of state social service agencies whose fragmented approach to 'fixing' families rarely achieves long-term success" ("A shining star named Oprah" 1994, 29). The Harlem newspaper *New York*

Amsterdam News echoed this antigovernment stance. Because Winfrey was "determined to provide something government fails to provide—a way out," the editors opined, "many sectors of this society ... might want this project to fail, because if it succeeds it would show that a serious commitment to the elimination of poverty and the welfare class was largely successful, and cost less time and money than is now being spent" ("Oprah Winfrey helps" 1994, 28).

Beyond embodying Winfrey's mind-cure philosophy, Families for a Better Life must also be understood as part of her broader makeover campaign. Winfrey made a point to promote the program in interviews with Larry King and *Good Housekeeping* in 1995. FBL, she told King, was something she was "the most proud of myself for" because it was designed to "break the cycle of poverty." While Winfrey made sure to cite her considerable financial outlay, the more important point of FBL was to show "how you change the way people think. Breaking the cycle of victimization is what I'm trying to do." She elaborated, "What I think I'm giving is a sense of belief in themselves" (King 1995, 373). Winfrey reiterated this sentiment in a *Good Housekeeping* interview later that year. After commenting that FBL was "going to cost me millions of dollars," she asserted, "but it's not the money that's most significant. I really believe I can change the way people who have been on welfare all of their lives think about themselves" (L. Smith 1995, 192). Families for a Better Life, then, was yet another venue for validating her empowerment mission and winning acclaim beyond her identification as mere talk show host.

Because being on welfare, living in public housing, and by extension, being poor, were defined from the outset as psychologically based problems, Families for a Better Life was organized around principles of positive thinking and self-help. The pilot program finally got underway in June 1995, when Hull House administrators had identified seven suitable families to begin the eight-week "personal development" course. Participants attended a weekly three-hour class that began with an introductory video created by and featuring Winfrey, who also sat in on several sessions. Topics from making decisions to dealing with change were presented through a mix of self-help terminology and strategies from corporate human resources training. Each session also included practical lessons and homework. Between classes, Hull House employees visited the families at home to talk about "what they had learned." At the end of eight weeks, participants were expected to work toward the goals they had set in the preparation course (Kiernan 1996). Through this process, Winfrey insisted, welfare families would reject victimization in favor of empowerment, and thus serve as models for future waves of FBL participants.

By September 1995, the seven families had completed the preparatory course. Random House and Capital Cities/ABC had recently donated $500,000 apiece to the program, and Hull House President Gordon Johnson proclaimed that FBL was "going very well." If the inaugural families succeeded in achieving their goals, he said, Hull House would "begin phasing in 10 families per month" in January

(Ihejirika 1995). However, one year later, the point at which Winfrey had predicted 100 families would have broken "the cycle of poverty," Families for a Better Life was put "on hold" and Hull House officials said Winfrey's participation—and the future of the program itself—were in doubt. After an expenditure of $1.3 million—of which $843,000 had come from Winfrey—five of the original seven families had completed the program. All were headed by single mothers—four African American and one Latina—with an average of two children each. When they started the program in June 1995, all of the families were living in public housing and receiving AFDC benefits, with three parents working part-time or attending classes. By September 1996, two parents worked full-time, two part-time; one of the latter was attending nursing school, and the fifth mother was enrolled in a computer training program. Three of the families had left public housing, a fourth was in the process of moving out, and the fifth remained in a CHA project. The most "notable success" among the families was a mother who had gotten a $22,000-a-year job, but Hull House officials said they had seen changes in the attitudes of all of the parents, who had demonstrated "gains in the sense of control over their lives" (Kiernan 1996).[8]

Explanations for the discontinuation of Families for a Better Life included the unanticipated length and high cost of the screening process.[9] Hull House organizers also cited the challenges faced by participants who "lived so close to the edge" that "each crisis—whether transportation, illness, violence or a family dispute—threatened to plunge them into a financial and emotional abyss" (ibid.). Additionally, because the parents initially lacked high school educations or significant job experience, they had trouble finding and keeping work in the short time they were expected to develop "self-sufficiency" (ibid.). These explanations, however, were trumped by what became the official diagnosis of the program's failure: that it was seemingly impossible to "destroy the welfare mentality." Isabel Blanco, Hull House vice president for planning and research, expressed what would become a common theme in press coverage of the program's demise: "Even though we screened them, there was this mind frame of entitlement. We had to keep emphasizing that this is not about what you get. This is about what you do" (ibid.).

In news reports and editorials about FBL's failure, "welfare mentality" and/or "mind frame of entitlement" were recurring phrases, coupled with praise for Winfrey's admirable intentions. A *Chicago Tribune* reporter wrote that Winfrey "single-handedly took on poverty" (Kiernan 1996); the Peoria *Star Journal* described FBL as Winfrey's "poverty relief program" ("Winfrey-aided poverty effort" 1996); the Tacoma *News Tribune* cited her "hopes of providing a national model for lifting inner-city families out of poverty" ("Oprah's welfare idea" 1996); the *Tampa Tribune* remarked that the talk show star had donated her name and money to "tackle one of the nation's most vexing problems: poverty" ("Oprah's difficult welfare lesson" 1996). By contrasting Winfrey's noble motives to the problematic attitudes of the program's participants, press accounts arrived at similar conclusions. As a *Chicago Tribune* reporter put it,

THE AGE OF OPRAH

"At its most basic, the lesson of Families for a Better Life may be that the lives of the poor are so chaotic and infused with a 'mind frame of entitlement' that they defy even programs specifically designed to overcome these obstacles" (Kiernan 1996). The *Tampa Tribune* editorial seconded this assessment: "Many in the [FBL] project seemed determined to turn their lives around but were so accustomed to government safety nets that they failed to accept personal responsibility" ("Oprah's difficult welfare lesson" 1996). In other words, poor people (that is, the "underclass") are so disorganized and deficient that not even Oprah Winfrey could move them "off welfare and into productive lives" (ibid.). Given this verdict, welfare reform was not only justified but also an altruistic necessity. As an editorial in the Tacoma *News Tribune* stated, the fate of Winfrey's FBL project "tends to buttress the argument for welfare reform with tough provisions for limiting the amount of time people can spend on welfare.... Too much can be made of this one experiment, of course. But it does suggest that ending the culture of dependency fostered by welfare requires tough love" ("Oprah's welfare idea" 1996).

In contrast to the fanfare with which she announced the creation of Families for a Better Life in 1994, Winfrey held no press conferences to mark its termination in 1996. When Hull House officials announced in mid-September that the program had been put on hold, Winfrey refused to even be interviewed. Eleven days before that announcement, however, she had told a *Chicago Sun-Times* columnist she was "discouraged" by the results relative to the expenditure. "A million dollars didn't last long," Winfrey said. "That's why I prefer to make my donations direct, with no intermediaries. I believe Michael Jordan terminated his foundation for the same reason" (Kupcinet 1996). To my knowledge, this is Winfrey's only public statement about the demise of Families for a Better Life. Welfare would subsequently disappear as a topic on her show, as it would from public political discourse when Bill Clinton finally made good on his promise to "end welfare as we know it."

Triangulating the Road to Reelection

Contrary to popular perceptions, welfare rolls were actually shrinking in 1995, down to 12.8 million from a peak of 18 million in the 1991 recession, and the total budget for Aid to Families with Dependent Children was a fraction of the federal budget, amounting to "only 14 percent of the amount devoted to Medicare, a middle-class entitlement" (Cockburn and St. Clair 2004, 49; also Piven and Ehrenreich 2005, 78). As the Republican-controlled Congress was crafting legislation to further pare AFDC, Labor Secretary Robert Reich and Health and Human Services Secretary Donna Shalala were advising the president that the lack of training for unemployed and underemployed Americans was a more pressing national problem than the cost of welfare. The NAACP had drawn similar conclusions. While agreeing AFDC needed significant overhaul, the organization opposed a 1995 Republican welfare reform bill, arguing that its "measures focus largely on saving money, and not on saving children or making families more self-sufficient through adequate jobs and child care." It thus urged Clinton to "veto this woefully inadequate attempt to reform an imperfect welfare system" ("NAACP opposes welfare reform" 1995).

The president did veto that bill, as well as a subsequent version passed by the Republicans in early 1996. As the national political conventions drew near in summer 1996, the GOP-led Congress forwarded a third welfare reform bill. At that point, some 14 million Americans were receiving AFDC funding—94 percent were single mothers and children whose benefits averaged 60 percent of the amount needed to lift their incomes above poverty level (Withorn 1996, 497). More than half of these women (55 percent) did not possess a high school diploma; most had been employed prior to seeking AFDC; and 68 percent used welfare to weather an immediate crisis and typically stayed in the program less than two years, although about half would find it necessary to return because their jobs ended or were impossible to keep because of life and family pressures (ibid.). On July 30, 1996, Clinton gathered his top advisers and cabinet members to solicit their views as to whether he should sign the third GOP bill. Part of the discussion centered on a White House–commissioned study conducted by the Urban Institute, which reported that the bill "would push 2.6 million people further into poverty—1.1 million of them children." The Urban Institute predicted that under a best-case scenario, "11 million families would lose income" if the legislation were to become law (Cockburn and St. Clair 2004, 50). Clinton's cabinet urged him to veto the bill. Even Treasury Secretary Robert Rubin, chief architect and cheerleader of the administration's neoliberal economic policies, believed the bill "would harm too many people" and said the president would "show an act of courage to veto it" (ibid.).

Many congressional Democrats—even those who agreed the welfare system needed reform—opposed the bill as placing "undue hardship on poor women and children" (Wright 2000, 228). Ironically, one of the most vocal opponents was Senator Daniel Patrick Moynihan, who in 1965 had painted the black family as "pathological" and in 1988 had helped usher the Family Support Act through Congress. Moynihan was disturbed that Clinton was prepared to repeal the federal guarantee of aid to fatherless children—something no president had considered in the sixty years since the passage of the Social Security Act. "I cannot understand how this could be happening," Moynihan said, accusing fellow Democrats of participating "in the dismantling of the New Deal." In Moynihan's view, Clinton had to veto the bill "if he's to have any credentials as a progressive" (Lawrence 1995). Given Clinton's twenty-seven-point lead in the polls over Bob Dole in July 1996, and the fact that Democrats had reason to believe they might regain control of the House in November and have a chance to craft a less punitive version of welfare reform, many House Democrats expected a presidential veto (Cockburn and St. Clair 2004, 50).

As historian Kenneth Baer notes, however, Clinton considered his endorsement of the legislation a "highly symbolic act" because it fulfilled his 1992 campaign promise and validated his New Democratic allegiance to the "mainstream" (Baer 2000, 240). On this count, he had the support of Al Gore, who privately urged the president to sign the bill (Cockburn and St. Clair 2004, 50). More important, welfare reform was a centerpiece of Dick Morris's post-1994 makeover plan for winning reelection in 1996—his "triangulation" strategy of outflanking the Republicans by implementing their policies. As Morris himself put it, Clinton's plan for 1996 should be to "fast-forward the [Newt] Gingrich agenda" (quoted in Schell 1999). In particular, he told the president that vetoing the Republican welfare bill would cost him the election (ibid.). On August 22, 1996, Clinton chose the White House Rose Garden as the setting in which to sign into law the Personal Responsibility and Work Opportunity Reconciliation Act (PRWORA). Outside, "the angry voices of massed protesters" conveyed popular opposition to the legislation. Conspicuously absent from the ceremony were "at least half of the presidential White House staff," chair of the Democratic National Committee Senator Christopher Dodd, and "most of the Democratic leadership in Congress" (Hohenberg 1997, 177). Also missing was Marian Wright Edelman, head of the Children's Defense Fund and a friend of the Clintons, who called the president's signing of the bill a "moment of shame" and "the biggest betrayal of children and the poor" (Lipman 1996).

The 1996 welfare reform act replaced AFDC with Transitional Aid to Needy Families (TANF), capped federal welfare spending at $14.6 billion a year, shifted all responsibility for public assistance to the states in the form of block grants—which Austin, Texas, columnist Tom Teepen predicted would ignite "a bidding war among states to lower support for their neediest" (Teepen 1995)—imposed strict time limits and work requirements, and stripped the program of entitlement status (Lipman 1996; Pringle 1996; Ross 1996; Stevens 1996). Thus did a Democratic president accomplish what his Republican predecessors could only have dreamed of, while at the same time stripping his opponents of a powerful political weapon. As Clinton stated on the evening before signing the bill, "Welfare will no longer be a political issue. The two parties cannot attack each other over it" (Schell 1999). Casting welfare as a cause of "dependency" that destroys self-esteem and undermines personal responsibility allowed Clinton to conceive welfare reform as a means to "empower" people. Beneath this rhetoric of empowerment lurks the racial politics that unites Clinton's New Liberal agenda and Winfrey's mind-cure mission.

The "Transcendence of Race" or the Return of the Repressed?

Both Bill Clinton and Oprah Winfrey have been hailed as unusually gifted at bridging the black/white racial divide in American society. The fact that the majority (81 percent) of Winfrey's audience is white is regularly cited as proof of her unusual cross-racial appeal (Mediamark 2003). A 1988 *Savvy* magazine profile said Winfrey had "proven that a black woman (and her concerns) can appeal to an enormous, national audience" (Mosle 1988, 20). In 1991, *Ebony* dubbed Winfrey, Bill Cosby, and Arsenio Hall entertainers who "transcend race" ("Television" 1991, 51). Toni Morrison—who saw three of her novels become Oprah's Book Club selections—has characterized Winfrey's book club as "revolutionary" because her ability to get people to read "cuts across class and race" (Max 2000). Announcing the birth of *O: The Oprah Magazine*, Hearst publisher Alyce Alston said the magazine's success was virtually guaranteed because corporate market research showed Winfrey's "consumer reach ... cuts across race and class" (Feeney 2000).

Bill Clinton also enjoyed significant cross-racial support. In 1992 he won 39 percent of the white vote and 82 percent of the black vote (Kim 2002, 64). At his first inauguration, a "record number of Black Americans ... flocked to the nation's capital," where Spelman College president Johnnetta Cole described Clinton as "a president who has given us all kinds of signals that this will be an administration far more inclusive than in the past" (Randolph 1993a, 116). Clinton improved on those numbers in 1996 when he captured 46 percent of white voters and 84 percent of black voters (Kim 2002, 70). During the Monica Lewinsky scandal and ensuing impeachment proceedings in 1997–1998, African Americans threw their support behind the president. A fall 1998 *Washington Post* poll, for example, found that 94 percent of blacks, compared to 62 percent of whites, approved of Clinton's performance (Connolly and Pierre 1998). According to Randall Kennedy, the fact that black politicians, intellectuals, and businesspeople were among the president's most vocal defenders during this period suggests Clinton had "been embraced by some blacks as 'one of their own'" (Kennedy 1999). Indeed, author Ishmael Reed in 1998 pronounced the president "a white soul brother" (Connolly and Pierre 1998). The same year, Toni Morrison wrote in the *New Yorker* that African American men identified with Clinton because he "displays almost every trope of blackness: single-parent household, born poor, working class, saxophone-playing, McDonalds-and-junk-food-loving boy from Arkansas." In Morrison's view, "white skin notwithstanding, this is our first black President. Blacker than any actual black person who could ever be elected in our children's lifetime" (Morrison 1998, 32).[10]

In a society where racial segregation of housing and schools continues to be a severe social problem—70 percent of black and Latino students attended predominantly minority schools in 2000 (Cashin 2004, 218) and African Americans "continue to be the most residentially segregated group in the U.S." (Brown et al. 2003, 15; Massey 2004); where the racial wealth and income gap remains dramatic—in 1998, "black incomes were 54% of white incomes" and "black net worth (including residential) was 12%" (Henwood 2003, 125; also Dreazen 2000; Conley 2001); and where successful presidential candidates have capitalized on white racism to consolidate electoral support, what does it mean to say that an entertainer or a politician has transcended race?

Kennedy suggests that blacks' support for Bill Clinton was "based on the perception that he has been supportive of them" (Kennedy 1999). Clinton did appoint more African Americans to judicial, cabinet, and subcabinet administrative positions than any previous president (Kim 2002, 63). Against the wishes of the Democratic Leadership Council, he supported affirmative action, although not especially vigorously (Kim 2002; Kennedy 1999). And in 1997 he commissioned a national "initiative on race" to promote dialogue and "racial healing" (Bennet 1997a and 1997b). Such gestures, coupled with Clinton's attendance at black churches and his affinity for black music, were interpreted as signs that the president seemed to "genuinely like black people"—no menial perception in a nation where interracial friendships are still far from the norm (Kennedy 1999).

Similarly, Oprah Winfrey appears to genuinely like white people. How else to explain the degree to which she is described as a personal friend by her predominantly white followers, most of whom can probably claim no other black friendships? As Winfrey explains this phenomenon,

> I transcend race, really. I believe I have a higher calling. What I do goes beyond the realm of everyday parameters. I am profoundly effective. I know people really, really, really *love* me, *love* me, *love* me. A bonding of the human spirit takes place. Being able to lift a whole consciousness—that's what I do. (Adler 1997, 261)

Winfrey's ability to elicit this "intimacy at a distance" (Horton and Wohl 1976) from her majority white audience reflects her skill at embracing her black heritage while staying at arm's length from aspects of the black historical experience that might alienate her white fans. As a *Newsday* article stated early in her career, "Though she makes race an undercurrent of her message, and it is part of her bearing, it does not define her following. She has what the business calls broad appeal" (Firstman 1989). That broad appeal, I suggest, rests on a strategic balancing act whereby Winfrey's "empowerment" mission emphasizes individual aspirations rather than collective political goals. As Quentin Fottrell observes, "While embracing the philosophies of Eleanor Roosevelt and Martin Luther King," Winfrey "subtly distances herself from feminist politics and the radicalism of the Civil Rights movement" (Fottrell 2000).

Although this could be seen simply as the business savvy of an entertainer seeking a large heterogeneous audience, I propose it reveals a fundamental ambivalence toward race at the heart of Winfrey's enterprise and her popularity with whites. A similar ambivalence characterizes the DLC's "reinvention" of the Democratic Party and what David Roediger calls its "confused and confusing analysis" of race and race relations that "allowed the Clinton administration to move away from both race and class politics" (Roediger 2002, 57–58). For Winfrey as for Clinton, I suggest, the "transcendence" of race entails handling race-related issues in a way that placates whites by valorizing "mainstream virtues" and downplaying racial injustice—strategies at which both figures are skilled. Writing in 2003, sociologist Douglas Massey observed, "One of the pleasant fictions that helps justify the Bush administration's opposition to affirmative action is the pretense that America has left behind the evils of segregation and achieved something approaching a race-blind society" (Massey 2003; also Brown et al. 2003; Entman and Rojecki 2000). The notion that the problem of race in the United States is receding—lingering mainly as isolated individual attitudes rather than institutionalized practices—is not unique to George W. Bush. It figures prominently in Oprah Winfrey's enterprise and in the New Democratic political agenda.

New Liberalism and the "Problem of Race"

Lyndon Johnson famously predicted in the mid-1960s that the passage of the Civil Rights and Voting Acts would ultimately "cost Democrats the south" (Toner 2004b). In 1968 Richard Nixon's political strategist Kevin Phillips seized the opportunity to cut into the Democratic Party's historical southern advantage by painting it as the "Negro party" (Greenberg 1996a, 107)—a strategy greatly aided by George Wallace's segregationist independent candidacy. Johnson's prophecy proved correct; that year, four of five white southerners voted for Nixon or Wallace (ibid., 108). In Paul Krugman's assessment, "essentially the South switched sides after the passage of the Civil Rights Act" (Krugman 2005). A victorious GOP refined this racialized campaign strategy and, with the exception of Jimmy Carter's election in 1976, handily won the presidency through the 1980s. A key impetus for the formation of the Democratic Leadership Council, then, was its largely southern conservative membership's desire to counter the growing influence of African Americans in Democratic politics and the party's identification with black interests and issues.[11]

In 1985, the year the DLC was born, Samuel Huntington called for the remaking of the Democratic Party. Writing in *Public Interest* that Reagan in 1984 had won 75 percent of the southern white vote, 67 percent of young professional voters, and 52 percent of moderate income voters, he urged Democrats to aggressively pursue these constituencies if they were ever again to be a "majority party" (Huntington 1985, 76–77). While granting that creating policies and platforms to entice these groups "might produce less enthusiasm for the Democrats among blacks, women, Hispanics and the poor," Huntington contended that the potential loss of support was "likely to be more than outweighed by the ticket's broader appeal to erstwhile defectors and independents" (ibid., 78). Besides, he noted, "with the possible exception of Hispanics," it was doubtful that blacks, women, and poor people would ever turn en masse to the Republican Party (ibid.).

In retrospect, Huntington's call for "a redrawing of the lines of coalition and cleav-age within the Democratic Party" (ibid., 76) looks like a blueprint for what Al From termed the DLC's "bloodless revolution," including its strategy for handling the issue of race (Greenberg 1996a, 204). According to Claire Kim, that strategy began from the assumption that black Americans had effectively been "captured" by the Demo-cratic Party, thanks to Republicans' "indifference or outright hostility" (Kim 2002, 57). With black loyalty to the party guaranteed, there was little risk in emulating the GOP's track record in using race as a "wedge issue to draw whites" (ibid., 60).

Six months before the 1992 election, the Los Angeles riots gave Clinton a chance to test this strategy. Predictably, President George H. W. Bush responded with moralism; surveying the aftermath of the revolt, he called for "a national discussion about family, about values, about public policy and about race" (Bremner 1992). A spokesman for the president suggested the seeds of the riots had been sown by Johnson's Great Society programs, whereas congressional Democrats pointed the finger at the urban policies of the Reagan and Bush administrations. The Bush camp geared up for the approaching election with a law-and-order theme. Several aides confided they "would not be surprised" to see campaign ads featuring a "white truck driver" to evoke the beating of Reginald Denny during the riots. Bush also seized the opportunity to paint Clinton as a "return to the failed, big spending solutions" associated with President Johnson (Kramer 1992a). As a White House aide outlined Bush's campaign strategy and its embedded racial logic,

> Clinton can say, "That's not me," but before he can get to what he's really for, he's going to have to distance himself from the Democrats in Congress. And when he does that, he'll jeopardize his base by upsetting the blacks he needs to turn out in droves. When he turns back to capture them, we'll hit him for supporting the conventional Democratic response of throwing money at the problems. The people who vote, the middle-class swing voters, hear "city" as a code word for blacks and decay, for everything they've run to the suburbs to avoid. (ibid.)

Clinton, however, failed to play his assigned part in this script. Besides echoing Bush's proposal to remedy urban social problems with market-based solutions (e.g., urban "enterprise zones," privatization of public housing, etc.), Clinton "preach[ed] a credo of discipline and self-help over state assistance" and called for increased po-licing to make cities safe for business (Bremner 1992). He thus presented an elusive target for what had become standard Republican electoral tactics. Mike Davis notes that "in the aftermath of the Los Angeles rebellion, neither *Business Week* nor the *National Journal* could locate a significant dividing line between the Clinton and Bush approaches to urban policy" (Davis 2002, 258). As one Bush campaign official complained of Clinton, "I can't figure out a way to run against him from the right" (Pitney 2000, 168).

Mindful that Mondale and Dukakis had been undone by the GOP's race ploy, then, Clinton "mimicked the Republican electoral strategy" of courting the white vote through "a symbolic distancing from and rejection of black interests and leaders" (Kim 2002, 60)—hence his conservative stands on crime, capital punishment, welfare, and the LA riots, and his carefully choreographed attacks on Jesse Jackson. The extent to which Clinton was redrawing the lines of coalition and cleavage in his party was evident in his campaign manifesto "Putting People First," which "did not mention race at all except in the context of denouncing 'racial quotas'" (ibid., 62), and in the Democratic Party platform, the "first in almost thirty years to make no mention of redressing racial injustice" (ibid., 63; also Hacker 1993, 14).

Because Clinton and the DLC considered "Reagan Democrats" to be "the single most important factor in the elections of the 1980s" (Edsall 1992, 43), the 1992 campaign was crafted to appeal to this constituency by "forcefully disidentifying with black interests and concerns and aggressively courting white voters" (Kim 2002, 61). An important architect of this strategy was Stanley Greenberg—the Yale political scientist who would become Clinton's pollster and campaign adviser in 1992. Greenberg could claim special insight into the *Weltanschauung* of this coveted electoral bloc because he had been asked to take its pulse following Reagan's reelection. In early 1985 the Michigan State Democratic Party recruited Greenberg to conduct focus group discussions with voters in Macomb County, a white suburban enclave on the outskirts of Detroit. Once lauded as the most Democratic suburb in the United States, Macomb had become a stronghold of Reagan support, and Greenberg was hired to find out why (Greenberg 1996a, 25). What he found among these "traditional Democratic voters" was deep frustration and cynicism. He reported that they felt "squeezed and neglected," had little faith in government to improve their lives, and believed they shouldered the lion's share of the tax burden. As Greenberg characterized his informants, they were "the middle class that is quite literally 'cramped' and 'supporting both ends,' the hardest working and the most virtuous, yet the least honored" (ibid., 36).

A key target of Macomb residents' wrath was African Americans, as Greenberg observed:

> These white defectors from the Democratic Party expressed a profound distaste for black Americans, a sentiment that pervaded almost everything they thought about government and politics. Blacks constituted the explanation for their vulnerability and for almost everything that had gone wrong in their lives; not being black was what constituted being middle class; not living with blacks was what made a neighborhood a decent place to live. (ibid., 39)

The semantic identity of "urban" and "black" that successive Republican campaigns had forged and exploited was a prominent theme in the focus groups:

For these white suburban residents, the terms *blacks* and *Detroit* were interchange-
able.... Detroit was just a big pit into which state and federal governments poured tax
money, never to be heard from again.... These suburban voters felt nothing in common
with Detroit and its people and rejected out of hand the social justice claims of black
Americans. They denied that blacks suffer special disadvantages that would require
special treatment by employers or the government. They had no historical memory of
racism and no tolerance for present efforts to offset it. They felt no sense of personal
or collective responsibility that would support government anti-discrimination and
civil rights policies. (ibid.)

Further, white Macomb County voters evinced a hostility toward government and
sense of racial victimization cultivated by Reaganism:

Almost all these individuals perceived the special status of blacks as a serious obstacle
to their personal advancement. Indeed, discrimination against whites had become a
well assimilated and ready explanation for their status, vulnerability, and failures. ...
The federal government that had once helped create their world was now wholly biased
against them. For the men, particularly those over thirty, the feeling took on a special
intensity. When asked who got a "raw deal" in this country, they responded succes-
sively and every more directly: "It's the white people," "white, American, middle-class
male[s]." (ibid., 40, 42)

Clinton's New Covenant, with its repeated invocation of the virtuous and neglected middle class, its emphasis on responsibility, and its interpretation of equality
as "equality of opportunity, not of results" (Baer 2000, 265), was designed to appeal to such voters—including their sense of racial victimization.[12] In other words,
it was a way of talking about race without having actually to talk about race. Ditto
for Clinton's reticence to address the economic crisis facing U.S. cities after twelve
years of disinvestment and neglect under Republican rule. Davis argues that the
Reagan and Bush administrations' "de facto war against the cities"—which aimed
to erode traditional strongholds of Democratic support and shift federal monies to
the suburbs—had been "one of the strategic pillars of modern conservative politics"
(Davis 2002, 245). In Clinton's zeal to appease "Reagan Democrats," he cut a wide
path around the issues of urban problems and race to "reassure white suburbanites
at every opportunity that he was not soft on crime, friendly with the underclass, or
tolerant of big city welfare expenditures" (ibid., 257).

In January 1993, Thomas Edsall, whose book (written with Mary Edsall)
Chain Reaction: The Impact of Race, Rights, and Taxes on American Politics (1991)
was "suggestive in laying the basis" for New Democrats' "effortless transition from
white working-class to middle-class concerns" (Roediger 2002, 64), applauded the
president-elect's efforts to expand the party's support in white suburbs and working-
class neighborhoods. To that end, Edsall observed, Clinton "is determined to distance

himself from policies seen as redistributing income and tax dollars from the working class to the poor" (Edsall 1993). To shed the Democratic Party's identification with "special interests" and its identity as "the political home of black Americans" (Baer 2000, 82), Edsall noted that Clinton was engaging in a "subtle strategy" of "challenging such liberal interests as feminist and black organizations while maintaining a commitment to racial and sex diversity. The inherent danger of the strategy is the risk of appearing duplicitous, of seeking to have it both ways" (Edsall 1993).

Claire Kim suggests that by figuring out how to "develop and pursue systematic strategies for managing the racial breach and maximizing white and black support," Clinton did succeed in having it both ways (Kim 2002, 57). In her analysis, Clinton banked on black "capture" by the Democratic Party, that is, that blacks were "unable to make a threat of defection and thus unable to exercise influence over the party's policies" (ibid., 60), which freed him to engage in "breach management" strategies consisting in "first, an initial electoral strategy of courting white support, in part through symbolic rejection of blacks; and second, an adjusted governing/reelection strategy of pleasing whites with substantive action on racial policy issues and placating blacks with largely symbolic gestures of support" (ibid., 57). The success of those strategies, according to Kim, exemplifies a fundamental reformulation of thinking about the problem of race in American society at the end of the twentieth century. This philosophical shift reflects an emerging consensus between New Liberals and conservatives on the "race problem" that paralleled their convergence around the notion of the "underclass." In the new consensus, Kim argues, "the American race problem no longer consists of White racism, which is steadily declining, but rather of racialism, defined as the misguided tendency of minorities (especially Blacks) to cry racism and/or emphasize their racial identity as a strategy for getting ahead" (ibid., 8; also Brown et al. 2003, vii–viii).

It is a short step from here to the idea that whites—subjected to policies that penalize them for long past transgressions—are now victims of racism at the hands of minorities who have embraced a "cult of victimization" (Kim 2002, 62). This stance is not only common currency among conservatives such as Dinesh D'Souza, Charles Murray, and Shelby Steele, but is also found in the writings of New Liberals, as seen in Mickey Kaus's pronouncement that the black "underclass" is responsible for the "race problem" in the United States, or Joel Kotkin's claim in the DLC's *New Democrat* that "the greatest threat comes not from white bigots bent on segregation but from 'racialists' pursuing positive discrimination in favor of selected minority groups" (quoted in Kim 2000, 8). This reinterpretation of race and race relations served as New Liberalism's philosophical framework and shaped Clinton's campaign and presidency. In Roediger's estimation, "the 'new Democrats' of the Clinton administration developed their electoral strategies largely around claims to be uniquely well attuned to voters 'fed up' with race- and gender-specific policies" (Roediger 2002, 56). Thus, Clinton's "values language" that emphasized "personal responsibility"—like his attacks on welfare and Jesse Jackson—were calculated appeals to voters like those in Macomb County who believed their "raw deal" was a direct result of black gains won illegitimately through the "cult of victimization" (Kim 2002, 62). Like Bill Clinton, Oprah Winfrey must navigate the black/white racial breach to maintain and maximize her market reach—a task that becomes particularly delicate when dealing with race and racialized issues such as welfare and affirmative action. To that end, Winfrey has employed breach management strategies that resemble Clinton's.

Be All You Can Be: Winfrey on the "Slave Mentality"

As we have seen, Oprah Winfrey takes offense at people who exhibit what she terms the "I am a victim" mentality. In 1989 she was among twenty-four public figures asked by *Omni* magazine to share their "personal blueprints for Utopia." In Winfrey's vision, "The crucial element lacking in today's society, the thing that works so powerfully in holding Utopias back from coming into being is a failure—or a refusal—by some members of society to take responsibility for their own actions. If people want to solve their problems they must sooner or later reach inward to bring about a positive difference in their lives" (Long 1989, 106). This mantra of "personal responsibility" takes on particular salience in Winfrey's views of race and racism.

In February 1987, Winfrey traveled to Forsyth County, Georgia—where blacks had been officially banned since 1912—to shoot a live episode at a restaurant in the county seat. Forsyth County had made the headlines in January on Martin Luther King Jr. day when a "brotherhood march" of blacks and whites had been met with "Ku Klux Klan–inspired rock and bottle throwing." A week later, 25,000 predominantly black demonstrators marched through the county accompanied by Georgia state police and National Guardsmen ("Brotherhood march" 1987; "Oprah's show on Ga. march" 1987). In a controversial move, Winfrey decided to ban African Americans from the episode, claiming it was to be a forum exclusively for residents of Forsyth Country so they would feel comfortable speaking openly (Brown 2002, 242). Further, according to George Mair, Winfrey worried that "allowing militant blacks" on the show "would have been disruptive" (Mair 1994/1998, 126).

A number of African Americans, including Reverend Hosea Williams, the Atlanta civil rights leader who had organized the previous two marches, picketed outside the restaurant. Williams claimed his group "had been misled [by Winfrey] into believing they would have an opportunity to express their views" ("Brotherhood march" 1987, 9). He and seven other African American protestors were arrested during the live broadcast for disturbing the peace. Inside the building, according to Mair, Winfrey "quickly cut off several more liberal members of the audience because she feared they might bring retribution down on themselves with their pro-black comments" (Mair 1994/1998, 126). Afterward, Winfrey said she was "disappointed" Williams was arrested, but made no apologies for excluding blacks from the show ("Blacks picket" 1987). That Winfrey chose Forsyth County as the site for her first broadcast outside Chicago could be attributed to its prominence in the national news. It also made a fitting topic for Black History Month. But the fact that February also happened to be a ratings sweeps month did not pass unnoticed. An *Atlanta Journal-Constitution* headline proclaimed it "a stroke of programming genius" (Plott 1987, B1), and *Chicago Tribune* columnist Clarence Page remarked, "The stunt paid off: With one bold stroke, Winfrey's show suddenly became major news. Phil Donahue must have turned green with envy" (Page 1987, 3).

African American critics subsequently interpreted her exclusion of blacks from the broadcast, her silence about the arrests, and her conciliatory attitude toward Forsyth's white residents as proof Winfrey "was not the liberal civil rights crusader she would like some people to believe" (Mair 1994/1998, 127). Anyone who has closely examined Winfrey's career, however, would not mistake her for a civil rights crusader. From the beginning she has pointedly disassociated herself from "black people who are angry and bitter" (ibid., 174)—a stance that has been amply documented in interviews, unauthorized biographies, popular compilations of Winfrey's thought, and in her talk show, web site, magazine, and public appearances. Together these materials comprise an intertextual narrative of Winfrey's public persona—one in which her fans are likely well versed.

In a 1987 interview with *People Weekly*, Winfrey revealed that she "hated" her time at all-black Tennessee State University, where she "did not relate well to the racially militant mood" of fellow students. They "hated and resented me," she said, "because I refused to conform to the militant thinking of the time" (Richman 1987, 56). Winfrey contrasted herself to other TSU students who were "into black power and anger," whereas she was "just struggling to be a human being." She also described being ostracized as a child by other black youngsters because she did not speak in dialect and wanted to "excel," and as a high school student, where she was labeled an "oreo" for refusing to work with African American students organizing votes for a student council. "I thought their candidate wasn't the best qualified," she explained in the interview. Throughout her teenage and college years, Winfrey recalled, "whenever there was a conversation on race, I was on the other side, maybe because I never felt the kind of repression other black people were exposed to." Consequently, she explained, "Race is not an issue. It has never been an issue with me. ... Truth is, I've never felt prevented from doing anything because I was either black or a woman" (ibid.).

These sentiments, which have been replicated in a variety of venues over the years, help solidify Winfrey's relationship with her white following. While on one hand Winfrey denies the significance of race—being black, she insists, has had no effect on her accomplishments—she also acknowledges its role in the success of her enterprise:

I hear this a lot. I hear that I don't hug the black people the way I hug the white people, that I go to the white people in the audience first. First of all, there are *more* white people. There just are more! I could not survive with this show if I only catered to black people. I just could not. I couldn't be where I am if I did. (Mair 1994/1998, 174)

Winfrey's choice of language is instructive, in that she has cultivated her appeal to whites in part by reassuring them that she does not "cater" to blacks. Her routine condemnations of people who "blame society" or "blame whoever is president at the time," who see themselves as victims or fail to "reach inward to bring about a positive difference in their lives" (Long 1989, 106) figure prominently in this process.

In 1990 Winfrey appeared on the syndicated national TV program *Ebony/Jet Showcase* and took aim at "Blacks who bash other Blacks in public." Such behavior, she suggested, was evidence of a "slave mentality" ("Oprah Winfrey tells why" 1990, 60). Evoking "the ancestors," who "don't deserve" descendents who "sit and try and tear each other apart," Winfrey said the antidote to the "slave mentality" was the "freedom to believe that you can really do anything that your mind can conceive" (ibid., 61). Rather than criticizing each other, she said, blacks needed to take responsibility for their own shortcomings. "I see us as a people doing things to ourselves and our children. I see the drug problems. I see abusiveness toward ourselves," Winfrey stated (ibid., 62). A major impediment to blacks' advancement, in her view, was their "self-hatred" and failure to recognize that "the only thing that can free you is the belief that you can be free" (ibid., 62, 61).

As Mair observes, Winfrey "believes many blacks in America are hurt by a low self-image and view themselves as victims who cannot help themselves" (Mair 1994/1998, 354). Her diagnosis of black "self-hatred" deflects criticism from fellow African Americans, underscores her image as a champion of empowerment, and serves as an explanation for blacks' unwillingness to overcome the victim stance and take personal responsibility. As Winfrey has stated,

A small but vocal group of black people fear me. Slavery taught us to hate ourselves. I mean, Jane Pauley doesn't have to deal with this. It all comes out of self-hatred. A black person has to ask herself, "If Oprah Winfrey can make it, what does it say about me?" They no longer have any excuse. (Mair 1994/1998, 183)

This statement, I propose, goes to the heart of Winfrey's racial breach management strategy, which involves associating herself with selected black "ancestors" (e.g., Frederick Douglass, Sojourner Truth, Martin Luther King Jr.), distancing herself from openly critical black political stances, holding up her own success as proof that white racism is largely a thing of the past, and castigating blacks who embrace the "cult of victimization." Through this strategy, Winfrey embodies and validates the conservative/New Liberal consensus on the "race problem." I suggest her "transcendence of race"—which is a euphemistic way of saying white people like her—derives in no small part from her adherence to this new consensus. Winfrey's ascent to cultural heroine has entailed not only that she not cater to black people but that she explicitly cater to whites, without whom, as she says, "I couldn't be where I am" (Mair 1994/1998, 174). As we have seen, this strategy is also true of Bill Clinton, despite the fact that without black support he could not be where he is, either.

Black Self-Help Ideology and the Conservative/New Liberal Convergence

Claire Kim argues that although New Democrats characterized their "Third Way" as an alternative to traditional liberals—whose handouts to the disadvantaged had purportedly fostered dependency—and to conservatism's indifference to the needy, in fact they "simply adopted Republican positions on many race-related issues such as crime, welfare, and affirmative action in a considered effort to distance themselves from blacks and court white votes" (Kim 2002, 61). This could also be said of Winfrey, whose positions on these issues mirror New Liberalism's and whose "philosophy of being responsible for yourself and that you are what you make of yourself flies in the face of the concept of the welfare state" (Mair 1994/1998, 180). In both cases, the populist rhetoric of "empowerment" masks an ultimately conservative stance that denies the political-economic sources of racial inequity by fixating on individual values and behavior. In the process, moreover, Winfrey and Clinton play to and reinforce white racism, even as they claim to be emissaries of racial "healing."

David Roediger (2002) points out that Clinton's strategists began from the assumption that white working-class voters were "so obsessed with race as to be unable to enter into coalition politics unless issues of racial justice were removed from the agenda" (57). But if racial justice was off the agenda, racial politics was not. As Martin Gilens argues, crime and welfare reform are "widely viewed as 'coded' issues that play upon race (or, more specifically, upon white Americans' negative views of blacks) without explicitly raising the 'race card'" (Gilens 1996, 593). In his study of welfare and racial politics, Gilens found that whites significantly overestimate the percentage of African Americans who are poor and who are on welfare, and that negative perceptions of blacks—in particular the view that blacks are "lazy"—was the strongest predictor of opposition to welfare among whites.[13] In Gilens's words, "The white public's thinking about welfare is inordinately shaped by highly salient negative perceptions of blacks" (ibid.)—perceptions that are powerfully shaped by media representations. In Gilens's estimation, "race coded" issues such as welfare afford politicians an opportunity to "exploit the power of racial suspicion and animosity while insulating themselves from charges of race-baiting" (ibid., 602).

Welfare and crime functioned in precisely this way in Clinton's breach management strategy. Seeking to demonstrate that New Democrats were not "soft on crime,"

Clinton made passing a crime bill a top priority of his first term (Kim 2002, 65). The Clinton Crime Bill, signed into law on August 11, 1994, expanded the list of federal crimes to draw the death penalty, created harsher sentencing guidelines and mandatory sentencing for repeat offenders (the "three strikes and you're out" stipulation), provided for adult prosecution for children as young as thirteen for certain offenses, and included funds to hire 100,000 more police officers and vastly expand the prison system. The NAACP and the Congressional Black Congress opposed the bill, calling some of its provisions "excessively harsh" and citing racial inequities in sentencing in light of the historically disproportionate number of blacks who receive the death penalty. Although Clinton promised to "issue an executive order calling for 'racial fairness' in the application of the federal death penalty," in the end this language was deleted in committee, and he acceded to even harsher provisions to secure Republican votes (ibid., 66).

Two months later, Winfrey broadcast live back-to-back episodes from a Detroit theater titled "Violent Children: Detroit" (*Oprah Winfrey Show*, Oct. 3 and 4, 1994). By setting the show in Detroit—the "big pit" decried by Macomb County Reagan Democrats and one of the most racially segregated cities in the United States—and calling it "paralyzed by the crimes of violent children," Winfrey reinforced the semantic unity of urban, black, and criminality. During the broadcast she described child crime as a "national crisis," suggested the juvenile justice system was "antiquated" because it had not been created for "child murderers," cited a Gallup poll that found that "60 percent of the people surveyed think a teenager convicted of murder should get the death penalty," and quizzed the featured child offenders and their families about their values. She thus implicitly endorsed the necessity of a Clintonesque crackdown because, as she stated near the end of the second installment, "these children have not been raised up in the way they should go."

The effects of Clinton's crime bill were dramatic. America's prison population exploded to more than 2 million by the end of the 1990s, "a highly disproportionate number of whom were black males, particularly young black males" (Brown 2002, 179). In fact, more people were imprisoned under Clinton than under any previous U.S. president (ibid., 374). Assessing the outcome of this "get tough" agenda at the end of Clinton's presidency, the Milton S. Eisenhower Foundation issued a policy paper deeming it "immoral" that "the rate of incarceration of African American men in America today" was "four times higher than the rate of incarceration of black men in pre-Mandela, apartheid South Africa" (ibid., 180). Although from its passage in 1994 to the present, Clinton's crime bill has come under criticism as inequitable and ineffective, its symbolic power yielded the desired political dividends, which had also been true of the 1996 welfare reform bill. As Kim notes, the "Democrats' approval ratings on crime—which necessarily included support from some black Democrats, who were also concerned about mounting crime rates—rose from 50 percent in 1994 to 70 percent in 1997" (Kim 2002, 66). As Gilens points out, because "the symbolic power" of welfare or crime derives "in large measure from its racial undertones," using racially coded issues "as devices with which to mobilize and stimulate antiblack sentiments among the white electorate" amounts to "an insidious politics of racial division" (Gilens 1996, 602).

Welfare also provided Oprah Winfrey with an opportunity to curry favor with her predominantly white audience, given that AFDC is one of the "least popular components of the U.S. welfare state" and that "racial considerations are the single most important factor shaping whites' views of welfare" (ibid., 601). At the same time, it allowed her to distance herself from blacks who refuse to "bring about a positive difference in their lives." In this respect, she bears more resemblance to a Reagan Democrat than to a civil rights crusader. Mair argues that Winfrey "holds different views of race than many believe she has" and "agrees more with … Armstrong Williams than with Hosea Williams" (ibid.). That Winfrey would be linked to a figure who has been described as "an indefatigable propagandist" for the "hard right" of the Republican Party is not accidental. Armstrong Williams, a "staunch advocate for conservative and Christian values," is a longtime friend and business associate of Winfrey's fiancé, Stedman Graham. Were she to finally wed Graham, in fact, Williams would be their best man (Ford and Gamble 2002; Mitchell 2005).[14]

Along with figures such as Clarence Thomas, Glenn Loury, Thomas Sowell, and Shelby Steele, Armstrong Williams[15] is among a phalanx of black conservatives cultivated by the Reagan/Bush administrations in the 1980s and funded by right-wing foundations and think tanks (e.g., Scaife Foundation, American Enterprise Institute, Heritage Foundation, National Center for Public Policy Research, etc.).These black conservatives have been "in the forefront of establishing a self-help ideology" that "combines a suspicion of government-based approaches to black subordination with a concern for the plight of poor urban blacks" (P. H. Smith 1999, 258). Replete with phrases such as "self-reliance" and "individual responsibility," this ideology asserts that "the source of black problems came, and certainly their alleviation should come, from *within* the black community" (ibid., 257). Virulently critical of civil rights organizations and of government aid—both are blamed for promoting dependency and undermining individual autonomy—black conservatives embrace underclass theory and hold the welfare state responsible for the "moral breakdown" and "crisis of dependency" among the black urban poor (ibid., 267, 268).

Armstrong Williams exemplifies this perspective, labeling welfare a form of "slavery" and citing as core concerns the "reform of welfare and affirmative action programs" and the "restoration of morality in society" (Williams 2005). In 1995, as Clinton renewed his pledge to "end welfare as we know it" and Oprah Winfrey asked her audience whether welfare was a failed experiment, Williams published *Beyond Blame: How We Can Succeed in Breaking the Dependency Barrier*—a book that "explored the plight of young African-American males and the ideas of the American political right and advocated adopting Christian values, working hard, and assuming personal responsibility for their actions as the best ways for young blacks to succeed" (ibid.). In Williams's view, blacks are as guilty as whites of racial stereotyping and are quick to "blame whites for the ills of the black community" (Mair 1994/1998, 175) when they should focus on "helping [them]selves and self-motivation" (ibid., 121). He dismisses his numerous black critics with the charge they dislike him because he "refused to blame whites for what's wrong with blacks" (Williams 2005).

Although Williams is part of the Republican right and shares its hostility toward Bill Clinton, his stance on the "problem of race" is strikingly similar to that of Clinton and Winfrey—a testament to the GOP/New Democrat convergence. Preston Smith describes black conservatism as characterized by a "disdain for government aid" and preference for market-based solutions to black poverty (P. Smith 1999, 258), a diagnosis of the welfare state as the cause of "moral breakdown" in urban black families (ibid., 267), a tendency to minimize the relevance of racial discrimination in the problems of poor blacks (ibid., 262), a belief that "individual responsibility" is the key to black "upward mobility" (ibid., 258), and a commitment to privatism, voluntarism, and entrepreneurialism. According to Smith, while this rhetoric purports to advocate for poor African Americans, it contains an unspoken premise:

> Once the poor's ability to act for themselves is established in principle, then their behavior becomes fair game and can be identified as an important cause of their own plights. And the concern with what poor blacks do *for* themselves as subjects is easily shifted to what they do *to* themselves. Black conservative populist ideology restricts the poor's legitimate actions to either private, bootstrap activities or self-destructive behavior. (ibid., 259)

Given these options, "empowerment" involves choosing the former path. It then falls to figures such as Winfrey, Williams, and Clinton to encourage that choice by removing obstacles to "independence"—whether institutional (government support) or psychological (the "slave mentality")—and by serving as role models.

Smith contends that the notion of role modeling—a central component of black conservative self-help ideology—"confers moral superiority on those who have economic resources" and entitles them to "mentor" those of "lower status" (ibid., 264). Armstrong Williams, Oprah Winfrey, and Stedman Graham are enthusiastic practitioners of this "elite-led moral uplift" (ibid., 260). Williams regularly identifies himself—a teetotaler who condemns premarital sex—as an example of "right living" and attributes his success to "personal responsibility, economic independence, thrift, a strong work ethic, [and] an essential optimism" (Williams 2005).[16] He clung to his self-image as a role model even after it was revealed in 2005 that he received $240,000 from the U.S. Department of Education to promote the Bush administration's No Child Left Behind initiative (Hamburger 2005; Kirkpatrick 2005).

Graham similarly offers himself as a model of success—especially for young black men—in speaking engagements, seminars, and self-help books (e.g., *You Can Make It Happen: The 9-Step Plan to Success* [1997]; *Teens Can Make It Happen* [2000]). Indeed, he was "the catalyst" for Winfrey's Families for a Better Life project, which was "inspired by his guidance" (Adler 1997, 258). Graham's advice to black Americans: they can achieve anything they want if they "set a vision," "tap into this American free enterprise system," and forget about race, which is merely "a state of mind." People who "are so focused on the color of their skin," he says, "can't get past their own lack of achievement" ("Africans in America" 1998).

Winfrey epitomizes the "role model"—a female Horatio Alger who began at the bottom and achieved phenomenal success.[17] In her endlessly circulated biographical narrative, Winfrey is portrayed as having overcome the obstacles of race, gender, and class entirely through self-determination and individual "bootstrap" activities. Since the early days of her career, she has been fond of quoting Jesse Jackson's statement that "excellence is the best deterrent to racism" (R. C. Smith 1986) and opined in a 1988 interview, "The greatest contribution you can make to women's rights, to civil rights, is to be the absolute best at what you do" (Mosle 1988, 20). The rhetoric of empowerment defines Winfrey's enterprise. Not only is her program meant to "empower people" and be a "catalyst for people beginning to think more insightfully about themselves and their lives" (Adler 1997, 62), she is herself empowerment personified. Thus, her wealth and fame are the fruits of throwing off the "slave mentality," rejecting victimhood, and taking responsibility for her life. She is living proof of her claim that "you can be poor and black and female and make it to the top" (ibid., 278). By implication, all those other poor black females (and males) could, if they were willing to take "personal responsibility," make it to the top too. And if they do not, as Winfrey says, she is a constant reminder that "they no longer have any excuse" (Mair 1994/1998, 183).

Bill Cosby, another "role model" credited with "transcending race," delivered a similar message at the commemoration of the fiftieth anniversary of the *Brown vs. Board of Education* decision, where he lambasted "lower economic [black] people" for their defective parenting of offspring who are "going nowhere." A member of the black conservative organization Project 21 subsequently thanked Cosby for "speak[ing] out against the self-inflicted malaise that's destroying our community" and for refusing to "defer our problems to external factors rather than the natural consequences of our behavior" (Fritsch 2004; also Street 2005). Such comments by prominent black celebrity "role models" reinforce the new consensus claim that integration and racial equality are accomplished realities and the socioeconomic gap between blacks and whites is the result of moral or behavioral failure. Thus, in addition to being beacons of moral uplift for poor African Americans, Winfrey, Cosby, and other exemplars of "stratospheric black success" (Cashin 2004, xii) serve an important ideological function, according to Paul Street: "The majority of whites love to see black middle- and upper-class authority figures blame non-affluent blacks for their own problems" (Street 2005).

New Age Racism

This returns us to the question of what it means to say Winfrey has transcended race. While Winfrey cites her fans' devotion as evidence she transcends race, and observers take the fact that 80 percent of her following is white as proof she is correct, perhaps some skepticism is warranted. Like *The Cosby Show*, which was crafted to supply "positive images" of African Americans through the lovable Huxtable family and was scoured of anything that conveyed what Cosby termed "downtrodden, negative, I-can't-do-I-won't-do" (Miller 1988, 73), Winfrey's enterprise is designed to deliver an upbeat "message of goodness." Further, the fact that these black entertainers have attracted a majority white audience is interpreted as a major advance in American race relations. Just as Cosby sought to instill good feelings in his audience, Winfrey's viewers, readers, and seminar attendees are meant to feel enlightened, uplifted, and empowered. They are encouraged to esteem themselves, to "live their best life," to treat their suffering as an opportunity for personal growth, because, as Winfrey never tires of reminding us, we are "responsible for our own lives." What Winfrey's followers are not asked to do is to consider how they might be implicated in (and even benefit from) the suffering of others, or to take responsibility for this possibility. They are not, in other words, ever made to feel *uncomfortable*. And this, I propose, is the real basis of Winfrey's "transcendence of race": that her white fans feel relentlessly *comfortable* with her. This is what allows them to imagine that racism has been vanquished, or is about to be, because, after all, they invite a black woman into their homes on a daily basis and really, really, really *love* her, *love* her, *love* her.

Perhaps whites' embrace of black celebrities reveals more about the power of television than about the actual state of American race relations, however. Because the United States remains a highly racially segregated society, many whites' primary encounter with African Americans comes through television—a medium, Street argues, that "presents a dangerously schizophrenic image of black America split between super-successful and largely admirable (not-all-that) black superstars (Oprah being the best of all) and dangerous (all-too) black perpetrators" (Street 2005). According to Leonard Steinhorn and Barbara Diggs-Brown (1999), the repetitive character of TV programming and its domestic context of reception give "white Americans the sensation of having meaningful, repeated contact with blacks without actually having it"—a phenomenon they term "virtual integration" (146). In their view, "Virtual integration enables whites to live in a world with blacks without having to do so in fact. It provides a form of safe intimacy without any of the risks. It offers a clean and easy way for whites to establish and nourish what they see as their bona fide commitment to fairness, tolerance, and color blindness" (ibid., 157). If through virtual integration "whites have made room in their lives for black celebrities" and take their affection for figures such as Winfrey and Cosby "as evidence of their own open-mindedness and as proof that the nation isn't so hard on blacks after all," Steinhorn and Diggs-Brown point out that this same color-blindness is "almost unattainable for blacks in the real world" (ibid.).

Preston Smith (1999) contends that black conservatives suffer from a "critical blind spot about the real workings of the American political economy" (269). Missing is any reference to the effects on black urban communities over the past quarter-century of deindustrialization, draconian budget cuts, disinvestment, the polarization of labor markets, deunionization, and the resurgence of sweatshops and growth of the informal economy.[18] Indeed, he argues, black conservative self-help ideology in the 1980s was specifically designed to "shape new normative orientations that help to underwrite and adjust to the massive Reaganite disinvestment, public and private, in black communities." Thus, black conservatives "have used self-help's populist and democratic allure to shroud its socially regressive agenda for poor African American citizens" (ibid., 259).

Oprah Winfrey has an equally glaring political economic blind spot and similar propensity to "valorize individual voluntarism approaches to systemic social problems" (ibid., 288)—particularly on issues related to black poverty. In episodes dealing with welfare, poverty, public housing, crime, and affirmative action—heavily racially coded topics all—she is inclined to feature conservative black and white guest experts who promulgate underclass theory; blame government aid for fostering "dependency"; wax on about "values," the "work ethic," and "personal responsibility"; and prescribe self-help and empowerment as cures for poverty.[19] In infrequent episodes that do include black experts offering a critical, structural analysis of such issues, Winfrey tends to distance herself from them and seek the audience's affirmation, as in the 1995 episode, "Is Affirmative Action Outdated?" (*Oprah Winfrey Show*, Apr. 11, 1995), which featured four white panelists who claimed they had been discriminated against. After hearing each of their stories, Winfrey turned to the predominantly white studio audience members and asked, "Is that fair?" to which they shouted, "No." Like Bill Clinton—whose electoral and governing strategies aimed at "pleasing whites with policy decisions on key racial issues" (Kim 2002, 65)—Winfrey courts her core white audience by disidentifying with anything that smacks of black political "militancy." At the same time, she retains her image as a "healer" by proclaiming her desire to help people throw off the "slave mentality" and empower those who have not recognized that their own behavior is the biggest obstacle to their success.

Although drawing parallels between Winfrey and black conservatives may seem at odds with her image as a liberal (Schorow 1994), the distance between conservatism and New Liberalism has become increasingly imperceptible. This is especially true on matters of race and poverty. As Smith notes, "the self-help/empowerment discourse and punitive policy agenda" of the Reagan/Bush administrations were "easily extended into the Clinton era. Under the guise of 'empowering' the poor and promoting 'new social contract' policies such as welfare reform, the Clinton administration expect[ed] impoverished blacks to ask less of the state and do more for themselves with still less" (Smith 1999, 288). In a May 1996 profile of the "New Age President" in the *New York Times Magazine*, Dick Morris suggested the nation's "most enduring" problems were essentially "behavioral problems" that defied solution by government programs. In Morris's assessment, "The problems we face, not the symptoms, but the causes, are fundamental causes best dealt with by altering the way people think and act and do" (Henwood 1997, 171). This pronouncement—equally at home in self-help ideology, empowerment rhetoric, and mind-cure theology—could as easily have been uttered by Bill Clinton, Oprah Winfrey, Marianne Williamson, Armstrong Williams, Bill Cosby, or, for that matter, George W. Bush. In each case, moreover, the people most likely to be condemned for the way they "think and act and do" are those at the bottom of the political-economic hierarchy, who can be blamed for a laundry list of social ills precisely because of their political powerlessness.

According to the 2000 U.S. Census blacks were twice as likely as whites to be unemployed, the poverty rate for blacks was more than double that for whites, median black household income ($27,000) was less than two-thirds of white household median income ($42,000), and a 2004 report found black families' median household net worth ($11,800) was less than 10 percent that of whites' ($118,300). Because a disproportionate number of African Americans find themselves in this unenviable position, and because the new consensus on race has declared institutionalized white racism dead, poor blacks, more than any other social group, have been judged in need of a moral and behavioral makeover (Street 2005; "Facts and Figures: African Americans" 2006). This judgment is facilitated by the coupling of underclass theory and self-help ideology, which provides an explanation for black poverty, an alibi for the continued contraction of the state, and a scapegoat for working- and middle-class whites also caught in the juggernaut of neoliberal restructuring. Clinton's particular genius lay in skillfully deploying this ideological couplet in his racial breach management strategies, which allowed him to maintain extensive black support even as he was "pandering to the DLC's stereotype of the Reagan Democrat" (Davis 2002, 257).

Elaine Brown (2002) labels the fusion of underclass theory and self-help ideology under Clinton's New Liberalism "New Age Racism," which "promulgated the idea that the fault for the continuum of black misery lay not in the scheme of things in America, but in some flaw in blacks themselves" that could be overcome with "intro-spection and self-healing" (176). While Clinton introduced and enshrined in policy this "kinder, more palatable" (ibid.) strain of racism, its legitimacy and efficacy have also depended on "the complicity of blacks" (ibid., 219). For Brown, this complicity is a legacy of the "mentality of slavery"—a concept quite different from Winfrey's similar-sounding "slave mentality." Brown draws her terminology from Malcolm

X's contrast of the "field slave" and the "house slave," whose roles within slavery and relation to slaveholders differed significantly. Field slaves—the vast majority of blacks—performed hard labor and were housed apart from their owners, whereas house slaves led a less brutal existence in close proximity to the master and were more prone to accommodation to keep their few privileges. Malcolm X argued that this model of black social relations had survived into the twentieth century: the modern field slaves were "the black masses ... cordoned off in their southern shanty towns or new northern ghettos," while the contemporary house slaves were small business owners and professionals who served a largely black clientele. In his analysis, according to Brown, the latter "often harbored the mentality of the old House Slave, particularly in fear and hatred of the Field Slave, and in obsequiousness toward the Master" (ibid., 211). Although this formulation is problematic as a description of the real historical practices of slavery and the actual distinctions between field and house slaves, it does point to the complex intersections of race and class that have shaped both black/white relations and relations between African Americans.[20] For Malcolm X, the most damaging legacy of slavery was the internalization of class antagonisms that "divided and contained blacks" and interfered with their ability to "unite in a single struggle toward freedom" (Brown 2002, 211). Extending this argument metaphorically, Brown characterizes black proponents of underclass theory and self-help ideology as "New Age House Negroes" whose "significance" and "very livelihood" depend on their willingness to "round up the lazy black Field Slaves, the unwed welfare mothers and their children, the criminal predators, and the rest of the postindustrial black residue" (ibid., 212).

Adolph Reed argues that "black public figures' embrace of self-help rhetoric emboldened" the Democratic right by providing Clinton and the DLC with "a stamp of liberal, race-conscious black authenticity, a form of insurance against charges of racism" (Reed 1999b, 126). William Julius Wilson, for example, provided this seal of authenticity to Clinton's quest to end welfare. Early in his first term, Clinton sought advice from the University of Chicago sociologist, whose 1986 book, *The Truly Disadvantaged*, argued that the crisis of the black family stemmed from the absence of the disciplinary, moralizing influence of work. Described in the *Minneapolis Star-Tribune* as "the national poverty guru that President Clinton is quoting these days," Wilson praised the president for "developing a vision based on my work" (Hopfensperger 1993). While Wilson's analysis had parallels with Daniel Patrick Moynihan's earlier assessment of the pathological nature of the black urban poor—a writer in the *New Yorker* called Wilson "a black reincarnation of Moynihan" (Remnick 1996, 96)—he was immune to charges of racism by the fact of being African American, and this immunity extended to Clinton. In Reed's assessment, Wilson thereby played a "role in legitimizing underclass ideology for Clinton-era liberals ... by giving a black, putatively liberal seal of approval to a fundamentally racialized explanation for inequality" (Reed 1999d, 24).

Armstrong Williams and fellow black conservatives have been groomed and rewarded by the Republican right for performing this same legitimizing function. *Chicago Sun* columnist Mary Mitchell contends that "the majority of people who appreciate [Williams's] rhetoric are white, not black" (Mitchell 2005). Winfrey has proven equally eager to win public acceptance by distancing herself from the "field slaves," from those who "haven't learned to break the chain of poverty for themselves" (Adler 1997, 62), from "black people who are very angry and bitter" (Mair 1994/1998, 174), and from "the militant civil rights strata of black American life" (ibid., 180). Hence her repeated claim to be the sole author of her fate. As Brown points out, however, the irony of the latter-day "house slave" is that he or she has been "elevated to the house on the back of black struggle" (Brown 2002, 212). Winfrey is no exception. Despite her distaste for "militant blacks," her life has been indelibly shaped by the political gains achieved through black activism. Born the year of the *Brown vs. Board of Education* decision—to an unwed mother who worked as a domestic and periodically relied on welfare—Winfrey would reap opportunities unavailable to earlier generations of African Americans, thanks to civil rights crusaders. At age fourteen she won a scholarship for black youth to attend a private high school in Milwaukee as "part of a late sixties experiment ... to desegregate schools by ferrying children from mostly black neighborhoods to mostly white suburban schools" (Mair 1994/1998, 16). She completed school at East Nashville high, a white middle-class school and one of the first in Nashville to integrate. While in school she worked part-time at a white radio station where she was a "twofer" (female and black) at a time when the radio industry was being pressured by the civil rights and women's movements (ibid., 33). As a student at Tennessee State University she was recruited by Nashville's CBS affiliate looking for its first minority hire, which, with her subsequent TV news job in Baltimore, reflected broadcasters' need to respond to the "FCC's pressure to desegregate" (ibid., 42). Aware that she was a beneficiary of the civil rights movement's push to open up jobs in broadcasting, Winfrey later remarked, "Sure, I was a token, but honey, I was one happy token" (ibid., 36). Thus, while the young Winfrey may have possessed ambition and talent, it is the protracted, collective struggle of African Americans in their quest for racial justice and equality that made it possible for her to put them to use.

The Political Uses and Abuses of Empathy

As the first president to fully imbibe the therapeutic ethos, Bill Clinton "regularly empathized with the 'pain' and 'feelings' of American citizens" and "habitually employed emotivist language when justifying particular policy proposals or positions" (Nolan 1998, 235). As Elizabeth Drew writes, "Clinton's empathy, actual or feigned, became one of his trademarks" (Drew 2004, 95). This skill at appearing to share the feelings of his interlocutors helped earn Clinton the startling monikers of "the first woman president" and "the first black president" (Burnell 2000, 239; Kiefer 1999). Empathy is also one of Oprah Winfrey's trademarks—the foundation upon which she has built a media juggernaut. Having tapped deeply into the American self-help strain of the therapeutic enterprise, both figures have fashioned themselves as healers; diagnosing what ails us as the ways we "think and act and do," they prescribe a dose of "personal responsibility" so that we might be cured and "empowered." This universal prescription—dubious in any case—is particularly problematic when applied to socially structured inequalities of race (and class and gender). And therein lies its ideological value: it legitimizes those inequities by denying the existence of historically constituted structural constraints.

Clinton's "Initiative on Race," launched in 1997, exemplifies this ideological practice. Framed in lofty language about the need for "racial reconciliation" in the service of "a more perfect union" (Peterson 1997), the initiative upheld the new consensus that "intrinsic racial/cultural differences," rather than institutionalized racism, was the source of racial divisions, sidestepped connections between racial inequality and injustice, and treated the "problem of race" in largely individual terms. Casting race as a cause of civic disunity and the goal as a unified America, Clinton stated, "Money cannot buy it, power cannot compel it, technology cannot create it. This is something that can only come from the human spirit" (Kim 2000, 11). Having defined the race problem as one of "intergroup communications," the logical solution was the talking cure. Hence, the initiative's call for "a great and unprecedented conversation about race" among citizens (Kim 2002, 77)—an approach, ABC reporter John Donvan told the president, that critics were calling "little more than Presidential Oprah" (MacArthur 1997). Steinhorn and Diggs-Brown (1999) also suggest that Clinton forsook leadership on the problem of racism and opted instead for the role of "the Oprah Winfrey of our national racial conversation" (212). In conjunction with the therapeutic reduction of the social to the personal, "the notion of dialogue as an activity of private citizens," Kim argues, "fitted nicely with the New Democrats' vision of a 'reinvented' or streamlined government and with whites' clear opposition to new government programs designed to redress racial inequality" (Kim 2002, 77). By framing racial tensions in the United States entirely through a cultural—as opposed to political-economic—lens, Clinton's Initiative on Race succeeded in "closing off any meaningful challenge to existing political and economic arrangements" (ibid., 12).

It is to those arrangements that we now turn to assess the legacy of the nation's first therapeutic presidency. Surveying the entirety of Clinton's economic program, Robert Pollin concludes that "Clintonomics" amounted to "down-the-line neoliberalism: global economic integration and fiscal austerity, with minimum interventions to promote equity in labor markets or stability in financial markets" (Pollin 2003, 75). The real beneficiaries of Clintonomics were those at the top, for whom "wealth exploded" in the second half of the decade (ibid.). The primary engine of economic growth during Clinton's second term was a "debt-financed consumption boom" fueled by a dangerously overheated stock market (ibid., 65). Nearly all of this consumer activity, moreover, occurred among the richest 20 percent of households, while the majority of Americans struggled to stay even or cope with economic decline as wages "remained below their level of the previous generation" (ibid., 67, 75). The economy's "exceptional" performance in the latter half of the 1990s, as Federal Reserve Chairman Alan Greenspan told Congress, was due in large part to "a heightened sense of job insecurity and, as a consequence, subdued wages" (ibid., 53). In Pollin's estimation, this heightened sense of job insecurity "lies at the very foundation of the Clinton administration's economic legacy" (ibid., 54).

For those at the bottom, Clinton's record is rather grim. As Pollin notes, the average wages for nonsupervisory workers and the earnings of those in the bottom 10 percent decile "not only remained well below those of the Nixon/Ford and Carter administrations, but were actually lower even than those of the Reagan/Bush years" (ibid., 42–43). In fact, wage inequality under Clinton "increased sharply … even relative to the Republican heyday of the eighties" (ibid., 43). Near the end of Clinton's first term, Brown writes, the U.S. Census Bureau reported "the gap between the richest 20 percent and the rest of the population had become wider than at any time since WWII." Indeed, "the income gap in America had grown faster during the first two years of the Clinton administration than in all eight years of Ronald Reagan's presidency" (Brown 2002, 184). The end of welfare in 1996 pushed millions of poor and unskilled women into the labor market, "exerting a downward pressure on wages" when the minimum wage was already "too low to allow even a full-time worker to keep just herself and only one child above the official poverty line" (Pollin 2003, 30). Although the poverty rate for African American households did drop by seven percentage points from 1995 to 2000, black median income never reached two-thirds that of whites in this period ("Facts and figures: African Americans" 2006). In Brown's assessment, "the Clinton era was in many ways more detrimental to black Americans than the Reagan and Bush years had been" (Brown 2002, 184). Between Clinton's inauguration in 1992 and the day he left office, "700,000 more persons were incarcerated, mostly minorities" (Wypijewski 2004, 89). At the end of his presidency, nearly one-quarter of America's black citizens were living below the poverty line—a rate double that of whites—while the median white family income was twice that of black families (Brown 2002, 79, 184).

Shortly before Bill Clinton took office, outgoing Bush budget director Richard Darman reminded the president-elect that the U.S. political system had "accepted the reforms that affect the poor" but not those that "affect the rich" or the "broad middle" (quoted in Davis 2002, 262). Clinton needed no such reminder. As Colin Campbell and Bert Rockman (2000) note, Clinton and the New Democrats "knew the votes were with the broad middle-class base of society and that ... is where they went hunting," even if this meant turning a blind eye to "the needs of those on the bottom rungs ... who had become unfashionable and dispensable" (xvii). Davis contends that the restructuring of the U.S. economy since the end of the 1970s has involved a bipartisan strategy of "mobilizing the mass middle strata" by "expanding its claims to the national income" (Davis 1986, ix). In his view, "Democratic neo-liberalism as well as Reaganism asserts that the first function of the state is to provide welfare to the well-to-do and preserve a dynamic frontier of entrepreneurial, professional and rentier opportunity." A casualty of this political realignment, both between and within the two parties, was "the relinquishment of any serious appeal to full employment politics or social equality" (ibid.).

The rhetoric of empowerment promulgated by Clinton's New Liberalism, then, represents a kinder, more palatable version of Reaganism's overt blame-the-victim ideological agenda. As Preston Smith observes, the "conservative, market-based policies" embraced by both Republicans and New Democrats "have not empowered, nor are they likely to empower, poor black citizens.... Under a black conservative self-help agenda or a Clintonesque neoliberal, social responsibility agenda, the black urban poor will remain poor" (Smith 1999, 289). Perhaps the most telling consequence of this bipartisan political-economic convergence—and joint embrace of the new consensus on race—is the declining interest in the very subject of poverty, black or otherwise. Once the 1996 welfare reform bill had passed, Henwood observes, political interest "shifted to getting the poor off of the welfare rolls; even though most of those who lose their public assistance remain quite poor, no one in a position of intellectual or political authority really cares" (Henwood 2003, 107).

The "reinvention" of the Democratic Party under Clinton with its redrawing of the lines of coalition and cleavage thus involved making the party increasingly indistinguishable from its Republican counterpart. In the mid-1990s, columnist Tom Teepen charged that Clinton's "cave-in to Republican anti-welfare legislation" was "evidence that there is no Democratic Party left in Washington worth bothering about" (Teepen 1995, A15). In Gore Vidal's assessment, the United States at the end of the twentieth century appeared to be governed by "one political party, the Property Party, with two right wings, Republican and Democrat" (Vidal 2004). Even George Stephanopoulos, Clinton's 1992 aide and first-term communications director, later remarked that the administration had worked "to complete Reagan's agenda" (Wypijewski 2004, 90; see also "Republicans and the President" 1994; Feldman 1996; Harwood 1998; Meeropol 1998; Schell 1999; Miroff 2000, Harvey 2000; and Perlstein 2005). Reflecting on Clinton's record, Randall Kennedy in 1999 pondered African Americans' loyalty to the president and his party, given the absence of "any episode in which he risked considerable political capital on behalf of a fight for racial justice that would benefit black people" (Kennedy 1999, 2). In light of that record, Kennedy concluded, "for black Americans (like for many Americans) the appropriate response to Bill Clinton is neither gratitude nor admiration but disappointment" (ibid., 4).

The Transcendence of Race Revisited

At the point of Clinton's reelection, Oprah Winfrey had completed her exodus from the ranks of trash talk TV hosts and was well on her way to becoming "a cultural icon of mainstream America" (Brown 2002, 242). For Eva Illouz, that journey represents a signal advance in U.S. race relations and confirmation of Winfrey's transcendence of race. As Illouz (2003) writes:

> To the extent that Oprah symbolizes the very values that are promoted in the white middle class to account for success (hard work, self-help, endurance, altruism, more self-improvement), she not only offers a powerful alternative to the stereotypical images of black women but also has become a symbol of power and moral strength for all women. That a black woman would become a model and a guide for mainstream white women is ... unprecedented in American history. (228)

Elaine Brown agrees that in the 1990s Winfrey was welcomed into the heart of the American mainstream, but she is less sanguine about its significance. In Brown's view, Winfrey's entrée to mainstream adoration was achieved by "providing comfort to what became her core audience of white women, in the form of 'lifestyle' and glamour 'makeovers,' diets, and New Age self-healing readings and practices and endless self-deprecating discourse over her own weight and 'nappy' hair." At the same time, Winfrey "carefully avoided using her unparalleled power and voice on behalf of black women, even as the political agenda pounded poor black women and their children ever deeper into poverty and degradation" (Brown 2002, 243).

Certainly Winfrey's interest in black poverty appeared to dissipate from the moment Clinton signed the welfare reform bill and she deemed Families for a Better Life a lost cause. At that point, she was busy hatching a new project that could not be sabotaged by the chaotic lives of the poor and thus offered a safer, more direct route to the public acclaim she craved. Unveiled on September 16, 1996, Oprah's Book Club would definitively catapult Winfrey to the "classy" pole of the cultural divide and launch the full-scale creation and proliferation of the "Oprah brand." As I argue in the following chapter, the extraordinary success of the book club—a potent cocktail of mind cure, marketing, and the mythology of the reading subject—played a pivotal role in consolidating Winfrey's cultural power and expanding the size and reach of her media empire.

The Oprah Brand and the Enterprising Self

When a beloved television personality persuades, convinces, cajoles hundreds of thousands of people to read books, it's not just a revolution, it's an upheaval.
—Toni Morrison (*Oprah Winfrey Show*, Sept. 22, 1997)

Reporter: Are you ever concerned with oversaturation? Winfrey: Actually, no. I'm not concerned about that. (Ward 2000)

Oprah is such a profitable enterprise that it rivals the cash flow of a small country. (Albiniak 2004)

In April 2005, Word of Mouth, a group of 158 authors, penned an open letter to Oprah Winfrey begging her to reinstate her original book club's focus on contemporary fiction. Three years earlier, Winfrey had abruptly halted the phenomenally successful Oprah's Book Club, saying she had found it "harder and harder to find books on a monthly basis that I feel absolutely compelled to share" ("Open letter" 2005; Word of Mouth 2005).[1] Although she had reconstituted the club in June 2003, the new incarnation focused on "classics" by authors such as Faulkner and Tolstoy. The Word of Mouth writers lamented that sales of contemporary fiction had plummeted since the dissolution of the original book club. Without Winfrey's direction, the writers' group insisted, "the American literary landscape is in distress.... Readers have trouble finding contemporary books they'll like. They, the readers, need you. And we, the writers, need you.... Oprah Winfrey, we wish you'd come back" (ibid.). Five months later their wish was granted. Embarking on her show's twentieth season, Winfrey said she would once again include contemporary authors and announced her selection of *A Million Little Pieces*, James Frey's memoir of his treatment for drug and alcohol addiction. Publishers were elated, anticipating a surge of book sales. ABC News told writers to "rejoice" ("Oprah's book club returns" 2005). The Word of Mouth authors celebrated the "wonderful news" that Winfrey had renewed her mission to "encourage literacy, thought and intellectual curiosity" and reclaim her title as "a champion of contemporary fiction" (Word of Mouth 2005; also Thompson 2005).

The return of Oprah's Book Club was monumental, Word of Mouth member Paula Sharp argued, because "Getting people to read is about the most important contribution that anyone can make to American society" ("Open letter asks" 2005). While this could be dismissed as a writer's vested interest in boosting book sales, grandiose pronouncements have accompanied Oprah's Book Club since its inception in 1996. Among Winfrey's various efforts to renovate her public image in the 1990s, the book club played a seminal role in elevating her to iconic status, due in large part to its tapping into the mythology of reading and literacy in the Western historical imagination. I argue in this chapter that Winfrey's genius lies in wedding that mythic narrative to her mind-cure technology of the self and, in the process, laying the foundation for the "Oprah brand" that could be replicated across other platforms (e.g., her web site, made-for-TV movies, magazine, the Oxygen network, personal growth summits, etc.). As Winfrey won the adulation of the print media establishment for her contribution to literacy, she also solidified her appeal among the upscale, educated, professional market that by the late 1990s became her core following—the same sector of the populace that Bill Clinton hoped to woo to his New Democratic agenda.

The Mythic Significance of the Reading Subject

The West treasures few moments in its history the way it treasures the story of the democratization of print. [Eighteenth-century] men of letters commonly linked the spread of letters to the growth of knowledge and to the democratization of power.... In their eyes, the citizen's reading took on a mythic significance it has never lost, even to the present. (Warner 1990, 7)

In her show's 1996 season premiere, Oprah Winfrey unveiled her plan to "get the whole country reading again." Thus was born Oprah's Book Club, which by any measure was a stunning success. Every title rapidly achieved best-seller status, and her web site boasted in 1998 that "booksellers have credited Oprah with rejuvenating the publishing industry." Meanwhile, publishers and literary agents gushed over her salutary effect on book sales and the expansion of the market for "good fiction" (Graham 1996; Streitfield 1997). In the club's inaugural year, Winfrey was deemed "the most powerful figure in American publishing" and *Time* included her among "America's 25 Most Influential People of 1996." The following year *Newsweek* named her "the most important person in books and media" (Katz 1996b), and in 1999 she received the National Book Foundation's fiftieth anniversary gold medal for her "contribution to reading and books" ("Oprah Winfrey's biography" 2006).

Ironically, Winfrey had been skeptical when one of her producers first suggested the idea of a book club. Assuming a book discussion would be "too boring for TV," she anticipated her show would "die in the ratings" (Clemetson 2001, 45; Kinsella 1997, 276). She consented to test the idea, however, because a book segment could be incorporated into the redesign of the program in the direction of a magazine format with shorter segments and more lifestyle and celebrity features. In retrospect, that Winfrey's viewers embraced her entreaty to discover the joys of reading comes as no shock. More surprising was the ardent response to the creation of Oprah's Book Club among reporters, columnists, literary critics, and editorialists, who are known for their suspicion of television in general and their particular enmity toward TV talk shows.

The assumption of an unbridgeable divide between television and books, typically conceived as "passive" viewing versus "active" reading, was a recurring theme in the print media's initial treatment of the club. A book columnist for the *New York Times* described Winfrey's "attempt to merge genres that usually seem at war—television and books"—as "radical" because it implied "television's power can be used to entice people to read" (James 1996). In an effort to make sense of the book club, the *Times* columnist resorted to oppositions—book/television, readers/nonreaders, "high-art content"/ "down-home manner"—and suggested that Winfrey's accomplishment lay in surmounting these binaries through her popular appeal. Indeed, the extensive print media coverage of Oprah's Book Club in its first seasons betrayed awe and envy that a TV personality—a talk show host no less—had managed to turn a "mass" of "watchers" into a "nation of readers" (ibid.).

The opposition of books versus television was also invoked in the book club episodes. On several occasions, studio audience members and viewers selected to dine with Winfrey and the author commented that reading the book club selection meant less time for watching television. Winfrey reiterated this binary in a *Newsweek* interview, where she revealed her stepmother had limited her television viewing and required young Oprah to write reviews of the books she read: "I was only allowed to watch for an hour. 'Beaver' and 'Andy Griffith.' The rest was reading" (Gates 1996). A *Life* magazine profile the following year noted the "queen of television" "rarely watches television" because she believed it "'promotes false values,'" preferring instead to "spend her evenings reading" (Johnson 1997). The presumed incompatibility of television and books was simultaneously challenged and endorsed in the first book club season finale, where Winfrey told her audience,

> We started this book club in September, and since then I've mentioned six different books and it's gotten very big. You are all reading. You have proven a lot of people wrong who said people who watch TV also don't read. They didn't think you all knew how to read, but you've proven them wrong. (*Oprah Winfrey Show*, May 9, 1997)

In another episode, Winfrey seconded an audience member's suggestion that people should forsake television in favor of books, although she pointedly exempted her own program from that prescription (*Oprah Winfrey Show,* Jan. 22, 1997).

According to Eva Illouz, "If Oprah's show had until then a sensationalist flavor, the Book Club gave it a definite aura of respectability and even gentility" (Illouz 2003, 103). Thus did a figure whose name was synonymous with the widely denigrated "low culture" form of TV talk shows come to be hailed as a "savior" of the esteemed "high culture" realm of literature (Katz 1996a). An editorial in the *Christian Science Monitor* is typical of the popular press's early response to Winfrey's literacy campaign: "We find it ironic—but very heartening—that the leading lady of daytime television is doing what book publishers, educators and parents have been trying to do practically since the beginning of time: getting people to read more books" ("Reading with Oprah" 1996). For those who make their living from the written word, the value of "getting people to read more books" is so obvious as to need no elaboration, resting as it does on cherished assumptions about the relationship of the reading subject and the written object. Among these assumptions: reading is an inherently beneficial, liberating activity; it liberates by unleashing the free play of subjective imagination; when combined with "literature" it takes on the liberatory qualities of both; and by enriching the individual and nourishing her autonomy, reading has inevitable benefits for society.

This narrative of the combined empowering effects of the spread of letters, expansion of the reading public, and diffusion of literature is deeply embedded in contemporary understandings of reading and the written word. Popular and scholarly conceptions of literacy have long attributed awesome benefits to the diffusion of reading and writing—including individual progress, socioeconomic development, and political liberty. Terry Eagleton (1996) suggests that under the influence of Romanticism, literature was privileged as an anti-instrumental enclave of creativity, imagination, and spontaneity—an autonomous realm for the exercise of individual freedom and, by extension, a means of social enlightenment. Cathy Davidson (1986) similarly grants literature a special place in the democratization of knowledge. The novel, she claims, "subjects to review the forms of the society in which it is written and read" (44), giving readers "an increased sense of autonomy" that "signified a new relationship of the audience to authority and different possibilities for political action and social change" (72).

The notion that reading literature requires and facilitates the development of modes of reasoning necessary to an enlightened public also finds support in Jurgen Habermas's (1989) account of the rise of the bourgeois public sphere, which he argues was predicated on an expansion of literacy and the amount and kind of printed information in circulation. With the growth of the publishing industry in the early eighteenth century, "philosophical and literary works and works of art in general were produced for the market and distributed through it" and "became in principle accessible" (36). As these cultural goods proliferated, escaping the control of church and court and losing their "sacramental character," he contends, "the private people for whom the cultural product became a commodity had to determine its meaning on their own (by way of rational communication with one another), verbalize it, and thus state explicitly what precisely in its implicitness for so long could assert its authority" (ibid., 36, 37).

By the mid-eighteenth century, amid the growth of public libraries, book clubs, reading circles, and publications devoted to professional literary criticism, novel reading had "become customary for the bourgeois strata" (ibid., 51). These artifacts and institutions "formed the public sphere of a rational-critical debate in the world of letters within which the subjectivity originating in the interiority of the conjugal family, by communicating with itself, attained clarity about itself" (ibid.). Thus, literacy and participation in the "world of letters" are taken as the ground on which private individuals acquired and honed the skills of interpretation, analysis, abstraction, and argumentation required for the "rational-critical debate" central to an efficacious public sphere. As Habermas writes,

> Even before the control over the public sphere by public authority was contested and finally wrested away by the critical reasoning of private persons on political issues, there evolved under its cover a public sphere in apolitical form—the literary precursor of the public sphere operative in the public domain. It provided the training ground for a critical public reflection still preoccupied with itself—a process of self-clarification of private people focusing on the genuine experiences of their novel privateness. (ibid., 29)

Those "genuine experiences" were nowhere reflected more consistently than in the realm of literature. Habermas suggests that the emerging bourgeois reading public in the eighteenth century—"a public passionately concerned with itself"—found "genuine satisfaction in the literary forms of the domestic drama and psychological novel" (ibid., 43). In such works, the experiences and forms of subjectivity constituted within the bourgeois family became both the content of "literature" and the basis of public discussion between private persons. Thus did a specifically bourgeois subjectivity come to stand for a universal human subject.

Reflecting on accounts of the history of reading and literature, Michael Warner (1993) suggests that to imagine "the spread of print discourse as ensuring the triumph of the individual and empowerment of the people" is to construe the history of literacy through a "telos [of] emancipation" (9, 10). For Dana Salvino (1989) that telos represents an "ideology of literacy" based on a series of interlocking premises, beginning with the equation of knowledge and freedom. Within this equation, literacy is the means of acquiring knowledge, which leads to individual freedom and advancement. Further, reading literature and discussing with others is assumed to produce the forms of subjectivity and modes of thought conducive to informed citizenship, a democratic polity, and societal progress. The ideology of literacy has played a central role in popular press and scholarly treatments of Oprah's Book Club, given that, in Illouz's estimation, the "reverence for literacy" that underpins the club "resonates deeply with a society that makes the written word paramount not only in the ways knowledge is transmitted but also in defining moral competence" (Illouz 2003, 199).

In the early seasons of Oprah's Book Club, the mythic significance of the citizen's reading loomed large as its founder was praised for "reassuring viewers that books are user-friendly and relevant to their lives" (James 1996) and "drawing all kinds of people into the book stores ... creating a sense of excitement about books and authors that no well-meaning literacy program or reading campaign has ever before generated" (Berman 1996). As a Baltimore *Sun* article proclaimed, "Oprah democratizes and demystifies reading" (Lippman 1997). Prominently featured in early press coverage and book club episodes were testimonials from "virgin readers" and those who had rediscovered the joys of reading through the club. Winfrey often quoted on-air from letters and e-mails sent by new and reborn readers as evidence of the power of books.

Academic treatments of Oprah's Book Club have also emphasized its liberatory potential by conceiving the book club—and Winfrey's enterprise more generally—through the high culture/mass culture dichotomy. Noting that anxieties about mass culture have historically targeted cultural forms produced for and enjoyed by subordinate social groups (i.e., women, the working class, people of color), scholarly analysts are inclined to represent Winfrey's "literacy initiative" as a democratic corrective to high cultural elitism. Thus, Cecilia Konchar Farr (2005) deems Oprah's Book Club a "leap into cultural democracy." Winfrey, she says, is not only "shaping and advocating cultural democracy in her push to get America reading again" but "advanc[ing] on Old World privilege and elitism with her guerilla force of women readers behind her" (107–108). Ted Striphas (2003) makes a parallel argument about the inherently democratic impulse of Winfrey's book club. In his analysis, "Oprah's Book Club advanced a particular protocol for engaging with popular literature ... whereby women were encouraged to use books and book reading as vehicles both to step outside of and to interrogate critically values and routines" (297–298). The book club, he argues, offers "a set of symbolic and material resources with which feminist cultural producers might begin piecing together a feminist aesthetics" (297). Conversely, Striphas dismisses critiques of Winfrey's club as "reproachful responses" that "provide a kind of cover under which are smuggled demeaning attitudes toward women and the cultural forms they engage" (ibid.). Even Kathleen Rooney's more critical study of Oprah's Book Club describes it as an "implicitly feminist" undertaking engaged in "promoting the cultural visibility of underclass readers and readers of color" (Rooney 2005, 22).

Despite the mythology surrounding the "citizen's reading," however, modern conceptions of the relation of reading, subjectivity, and social order are haunted by an internal tension. Alongside the notion of literacy as "powerfully enabling" (Salvino

1989, 144) runs an equally deep historical current that has viewed it as fraught with danger in the hands of an unregulated, untrained public. Histories of literacy and reading have documented efforts of social elites to control access to the tools of reading and writing, the conditions and manner in which they are employed, and the objects to which they are applied (Graff 1979, 1995; Disch 1973; Soltow and Stevens 1981; Ohmann 1985; Davidson 1986; Denning 1987; Salvino 1989). These studies suggest that the institutional provision of literacy for the masses has long been used as a means of social control. As Harvey Graff writes of the nineteenth-century U.S. movement to create mass public education,

> Literacy was hardly a goal, for isolated from its moral basis, literacy was feared as potentially very dangerous.... Moral precepts formed the basis of tutelage in literacy, and instruction was properly to teach and inculcate the correct rules of social and economic behavior in a changing and modernizing society. Literacy became a crucial vehicle for that process, as reformers seized upon the socializing powers of print. (Graff 1979, 35, 40)

"Literature" has similarly been recruited for such socializing purposes. Terry Eagleton (1996) proposes that the "rise of English" as an academic enterprise in the nineteenth century was intended to cultivate the middle class—whose political-economic power had yet to be tempered by corresponding cultural refinement—and to discipline the working class by instilling in it a reverence for "the moral riches of bourgeois civilization" and "middle class accomplishments" while curbing "any disruptive tendency to collective political action" (22; also Williams 1961; Radway 1997).

This tension has surfaced in the print media's coverage of Oprah's Book Club. Commentary on the club highlighted the fact that Winfrey has gotten her viewers not simply to read, but to read books that are *good* for them. A *Houston Chronicle* reporter applauded Winfrey for having made "reading serious fiction popular" (Schaeffer 1997), while a story in the *Detroit News* praised the fact that "Oprah's book club picks are selling across the country in mass market stores like Sam's Club and Kmart, drawing audiences that typically gravitate more to Stephen King and Danielle Steele than Nobel-prize winners like Toni Morrison" (Berman 1996). A *Newsweek* article commended Winfrey's choice of Morrison's *Song of Solomon* as evidence that she did not intend to "dumb things down" (Gates 1996). A *New York Times* reporter hailed the inclusion of the Nobel laureate's books as "a giant leap from middlebrow to high art" and praised Winfrey for encouraging her viewers to "appreciate ... the literary qualities" of novels (James 1996). A former *Times* book review editor credited Winfrey with displaying "perfectly respectable literary judgment" (quoted in Lippman 1997), while the London *Guardian* labeled her selections "far from the standard airport fare" (Katz 1996a). A book critic for the San Francisco *Chronicle* described Morrison's first appearance on the show as a "decidedly literary discussion" in which "audiences learned something about developing a critical eye for literature and examining the true gifts of a writer" (Holt 1997a, 2).

If reading is good in and of itself, and reading "literature" is even better, discussing books with other readers amplifies the benefits of both. Thus, Oprah's Book Club was congratulated not just for getting people to read, but for fostering discussion among readers. A *Christian Science Monitor* story on the growth of book clubs and reading groups in the United States noted that publishers considered Oprah's Book Club "a key influence in the increase of book groups" (Holmstrom 1998). Winfrey capitalized on this boom by adding reading groups to her studio audience during book club episodes (*Oprah Winfrey Show*, Sept. 22, 1997). The notion of reading as a site (and condition) of interaction and debate was also built into the book club. In addition to a televised dinner discussion, onstage interview with the author, and follow-up questions from the studio audience in the book club episodes, Winfrey's web site has featured online chats with the authors and invites viewers to post comments about the books. As Jacquelyn Mitchard, author of Winfrey's first selection, *The Deep End of the Ocean*, stated: "Oprah is making reading a topic of gossip and conversation in a way that it hasn't been for probably a hundred years" (quoted in Berman 1996). Through such discussion, it is assumed that book club members will not only acquire an appreciation for what Rooney terms "the kind of seriousness and stimulation the best contemporary literary fiction has to offer" (Rooney 2005, 175) but also hone their capacity for participating in public deliberation beyond the strictly literary sphere.

This link between private reading and public citizenship—and the role of Oprah's Book Club in strengthening both—was made explicit in a *Washington Post* editorial titled "Will Oprah save the book?" (Schwartz 1996). Editorialist Amy Schwartz cited Winfrey's book club as part of a "rising wave of a broader return to reading" and connected it to the state of American politics. Posing the question, "What's sending people in such numbers—what's sending TV, of all media—back to the pages of books that are non-disposable?" Schwartz replied that it was not the "staleness of politics" but the increasing emphasis on "personal responsibility" in public discourse that accounted for the resurrection of reading. She further argued,

> As the president [Clinton] keeps saying—"give people the tools" to take advantage of their opportunities. Is one of these tools reading—maybe a central one? In David Denby's *Great Books*, in which the fiftyish author goes back to Columbia to study Western Civ, Prof. Edward Taylor urges the class on the first day, "You're not here for political reasons. You're here for very selfish reasons. You're here to build a self." Whatever you think of the ... endless Clinton calls for "personal responsibility," you can't expect an upsurge of private action to take place if it isn't powered by that private and unfashionable engine of initiative and responsibility, an inner life. It's probably too much to hope, but maybe Americans, urged from every side to do things that require a

well-developed inner life, are making for the bookshelves because they need the fuel. (Schwartz 1996)

That is, a key consequence of reading is its power to nurture the type of "inner life" suited to a political-economic order organized around individual "initiative and responsibility."

Both the "literacy as enabling" and the "literacy as dangerous" positions attribute great power to reading and the written word. In the first instance, literacy, reading, and literature are assumed to naturally produce enlightenment and individual autonomy. In the second, these are potential outcomes that can be contained and directed through the very tools of literacy, reading, and literature. While the print media establishment applauded Winfrey for "democratizing reading" (Lippman 1997), assuring viewers that books are "user-friendly" (James 1996), and "drawing all kinds of people into bookstores" (Berman 1996), such praise turned on the fact that her fans were reading "serious literature" and being instructed in how to read it properly (Gates 1996; Holt 1997a; Katz 1996a; Schaeffer 1997; M. E. Williams 1999b). Winfrey may celebrate books and reading as inherently valuable, but she has also exercised great control over her club. She personally selects all of the books, tells viewers what to look for when she announces a new selection, explains the lesson to be learned from each book, posts on her web site official book reviews and lists of questions to guide book group discussions, and chooses the four viewers who appear on the book club episodes based on the compatibility of their interpretations with her own. As the Word of Mouth writers pointed out, readers depend on Winfrey to provide this very guidance.

Thus, even as Oprah's Book Club provides an opportunity for the subjective play of imaginative freedom, it also constitutes an occasion for exercising the socializing power of the written word. As Graff reminds us, literacy—past and present—is a "crucial vehicle" for cultivating "the correct rules of social and economic behavior," which is to say that "tutelage in literacy" is also always involved in the production of social subjects (Graff 1979, 40). Hence, D. T. Max's characterization of Winfrey's book club as "a vast experiment in linked literary imagination and social engineering" (Max 1999, 37; see also McNett 1999). It is therefore important to explore what exactly is being "engineered" by Winfrey's "literacy campaign."

The Book Club as Ideological Practice: The Importance of Being Oprah

Oprah Winfrey uses culture as a form of therapy . . . as a set of resources to make sense of our suffering and to build a coherent self reflexively. She puts culture quite literally into action, showing that it is the ensemble of resources we should pull together to build selves. (Illouz 2003, 239–240)

In her study of Oprah's Book Club, Kathleen Rooney (2005) confesses disappointment that Winfrey "underestimates her audience's ability to appreciate intelligent discussion" of the books and "resorts instead to the imposition of various extraneous narratives—including those of her show, herself, and her readers—upon the novels" (22). I propose, however, that those narratives are not extraneous to the purpose of Oprah's Book Club but are rather its raison d'etre. That is, Winfrey's literacy initiative—in conjunction with her larger enterprise—is primarily concerned with "building a self," that beneficent outcome of reading endorsed by the *Washington Post* editorial. The question is, what kind of self is being built here?

An early *Los Angeles Times* story about Winfrey's book club referred to her as "the nation's girlfriend"—a play on her frequent use of the term to address viewers and guests and a reference to the way Winfrey's fans see her. The article quoted a fan whose perception of Winfrey exemplifies this relationship:

> She's like the friend you always connect with, the one who catches you up on her life; you know, the one you can confide in. She's down to earth, a real natural. When she talks, you don't just listen. You want to listen.... She's like the one friend you trust, the one you know has good taste. You stick with a girlfriend like that, you know. (Braun 1997)

A literary agent explained Winfrey's power to move books in similar terms: "People trust Oprah, they feel comfortable and familiar with her. It's like a friend saying, 'Hey, check out this great book.' That's always been the key to her success" (quoted in Graham 1996). The director of merchandise for Barnes and Noble concurred: "Even before the Book Club, people would come in and say Oprah had this author or that author on the show. It's as if they mean 'my friend Oprah'" (quoted in Kinsella 1997).

These sentiments are not anomalous. Winfrey receives hundreds of thousands of letters and e-mails a year from devoted viewers seeking advice and/or money; pouring out their life stories; offering tips about clothes, hair, and weight; or commenting on the program. In the first year of the book club, she received 50,000 letters about the club alone (*Oprah Winfrey Show*, Sept. 22, 1997). The sheer volume of communication suggests that viewers feel on intimate terms with Winfrey—an effect, in part, of the formal and representational codes of talk TV (Peck 1995). But this is not an intimacy of equals. This is, after all, a woman who heads her own multimedia empire, hosts the most successful talk show in American television history, and is one of the richest individuals in the world. Winfrey's appeal resides in managing to be both down-home "girlfriend" and world celebrity without apparent contradiction. As a *Los Angeles Times* reporter notes: "To her fans, Winfrey is the understanding girlfriend who knows their hidden emotional scars, their dietary yo-yoing, their love for unabashed romance, seemingly one of them even though she is what they are not—a talk show host-film star-studio executive who oversees an entertainment powerhouse worth $415 million" (Braun 1997).

This sense on the part of Winfrey's fans that she is "one of them" was central to the success of her program in the 1980s and early 1990s. As we have seen, however, she yearned to be more than a successful talk host. If being loved by millions of "girlfriends" had once sufficed, Winfrey's aspirations had expanded exponentially by the mid-1990s. As she described her mission to *Boston Globe* reporter Peter Canellos at the end of the book club's inaugural season, "It's about being able to inspire other people to have the highest vision for their own lives." According to Canellos, over the prior three years Winfrey had "succeeded at changing the meaning of her career." In his view, "Where once 'Oprah' connoted the spilling of toxic revelations about corrupt relationships, now her first name—as noun, verb or adjective—might stand for self-improvement." In this makeover of Winfrey's public image, "affirmation replaced dysfunction, and to the surprise of many, millions of Americans began toning their lives to her new themes: Responsibility, gratitude, and respect" (Canellos 1997).

For Canellos, Oprah's Book Club was a vital ingredient in transforming Winfrey into "one of the defining voices of her era." Rooney concurs with that assessment: "Whatever else it may have been, OBC [Oprah's Book Club] was certainly part of Winfrey's larger mission to transform the character of her show" (Rooney 2005, 28). Having achieved "widespread admiration" by eschewing dysfunction in favor of "affirmation" and "self-improvement" (Canellos 1997), it was only to be expected that Winfrey would organize her literacy initiative around these same principles—which is to say that Oprah's Book Club was logically subsumed under the mind-cure technology of healing, and the enchanted self on which it depends, that came to define her larger enterprise in the 1990s.

In the very first book club episode, Winfrey exclaimed: "That's why I love books. You read about somebody else's life, but it makes you think about your own" (*Oprah Winfrey Show*, Oct. 18, 1996). This sentiment—which she would reiterate numerous times over the course of the book club—constitutes the framework of intelligibility through which her audience was to apprehend reading and literature. Rooney observes that Winfrey consistently directed her readers to apprehend the selections through the lenses of "human interest and empathy" (Rooney 2005, 28). Typical book club discussions, according to Max, focused on what readers "thought of the book—especially and extensively—its relevance to their own lives. Could they be friends with the main character? What did the book teach them about themselves?"(Max 1999, 36). In Rooney's estimation,

> The problem with this technique was its failure to direct its audience to look beyond what these rather rudimentary methods can reveal. By encouraging her readers to sympathetically impose their own stories over the ones they encountered in books,

Winfrey caused OBC to have less to do with the books and more to do with the self-help narrative of her show itself. (Rooney 2005, 28)

While Rooney accurately identifies the book club's preferred method of reading, she fails to recognize it could not have been otherwise, given that this is the dominant mode of comprehension within Winfrey's enterprise more generally. As Illouz points out, literature—indeed, the entire cultural milieu—is for Winfrey a therapeutic toolbox, "a set of resources to make sense of our suffering and to build a coherent self reflexively" (Illouz 2003, 240). Thus, the travails of characters in books become a means to cultivate self-knowledge and self-esteem. This approach to reading also guides Winfrey's selection of novels. As Laura Lippman wrote in the *Baltimore Sun*, "Oprah's picks focus on stories that would make good Oprah Shows." The selections reflect "a taste for the tragic ... with an obligatory note of uplift" (Lippman 1997). Reflecting on her first three selections (*Deep End of the Ocean, Song of Solomon,* and *The Book of Ruth*), Winfrey said she chose the novels "because they are readable, poignant, thought-provoking. Our audience is predominantly female; all three books I've picked are strong stories with strong women" (Rooney 2005, 119). This statement could serve as a synopsis of a typical episode of *The Oprah Winfrey Show,* a promotion for the book club selections, a fan's description of Winfrey, or Winfrey's description of herself. It is not hard to imagine the assorted protagonists of "Oprah's Books" appearing as guests on the show, in that the majority of the novels feature women from "dysfunctional" families who, through prolonged suffering, finally achieve self-knowledge and emerge as better persons in the end. As individuals who undergo a change of mind and heart (who move from "fear" to "love"), the characters become models for building an improved self.

That the purpose of reading literature is to augment and enrich one's self is repeatedly stressed by Winfrey. In announcing each new book club selection, she typically tells viewers what to look for in the novel and how they will benefit from reading it. The chief benefit, of course, is that reading about the lives of others makes us reflect on our own. In the episode on Sheri Reynolds's *Rapture of Canaan,* Winfrey asked viewers: "How is Nina's [the protagonist's] life like your own? That's always the interesting thing when you're looking at characters, because I believe that for you to be drawn into a character, there has to be some character association with your own life" (*Oprah Winfrey Show,* May 9, 1997). In announcing Ernest Gaines's *A Lesson Before Dying,* she advised the audience: "Although many of you, your life may be far, far removed from the characters' lives, I think it makes you think about your own life. And that's what I love about books" (*Oprah Winfrey Show,* Sept. 22, 1997). This, in effect, is the lesson to be learned from every novel, given that books exist to enrich the reader's self. As Winfrey asserted during one episode, "The object of writing is to create characters with character, who help other people [readers] to develop their character" (*Oprah Winfrey Show,* Oct. 17, 1997).

Winfrey's insistence that novels are to be used as "springboards for self-reflection" (Max 1999, 36) is what Rooney decries as the "imposition of extraneous competing narratives" (Rooney 2005, 27). As Rooney observes, "In episode after episode, Winfrey instructed her audience to experience the book in terms of how they personally related to the main characters, focusing less on the novels themselves and more on how their own life stories could be understood and improved in the process" (ibid., 24). For instance, Ursula Hegi's *Stones from the River*—which documents the rise of Nazism in Germany through the eyes of Trudi, a young dwarf—became in Oprah's Book Club a "lesson" about being "opened up" to "embrace the differences" between individuals and "change your perceptions of the little people." Winfrey compared Trudi's desire to be tall with her own childhood dissatisfaction with the shape of her nose and her subsequent triumph over this lack of self-acceptance (*Oprah Winfrey Show*, Apr. 8, 1997). For Winfrey, such self-discovery through identification with fictional characters is the most significant consequence of reading: "That's what books do for you. It takes you to a world you never would have expected to have gone to" (*Oprah Winfrey Show*, Oct. 27, 1997). What the reader should look for in that new world, however, is always the same thing: herself.

The self that is the object of this quest has triumphed over fear and negative thoughts, the root causes of individual and collective "dysfunction," and the chief barriers to self-love. Although Winfrey had built her show and fame on precisely such character weaknesses, by the mid-1990s she had grown impatient with those who continued to be mired in negativity. In the episode on *The Book of Ruth*, Winfrey described the novel as "Ruth's discovery of herself over a long period of time, living in a mostly dysfunctional home with her mother, then marrying a dysfunctional guy, who ends up committing a terrible act of violence" (*Oprah Winfrey Show*, Jan. 22, 1997). In the taped dinner discussion, Winfrey confessed to author Jane Hamilton that while she had identified with Ruth when she first read the book, "after seven years of doing *The Oprah Winfrey Show*, I was not so empathetic with Ruth this time." She explained her frustration: "I've seen Ruth so many times in the street, and on my show, and so I've heard the stories. And now I just feel … get out, see it, move on, get out." Significantly, Winfrey's prescription for what ailed Ruth, and actual women like her, was "to see a few Oprah shows. They need to stop watching *Bewitched* and turn on the Oprah show." Whereas in discussing *Stones from the River*, Winfrey advised viewers to "embrace the differences," she was far less forgiving of Ruth's "difference" from what constitutes an acceptable self. Rather, Ruth was held up as everything one should *not* be, or, to be exact, as the opposite of Winfrey, who stated flatly: "I have grown and Ruth did not" (ibid.).

Here is the ideological project of Oprah's Book Club at its baldest—the valorization of a particular form of subjectivity through the act of "reading literature." This ideal subject is not simply endorsed—it is given embodiment. That is, the "self" consistently universalized and held up for emulation in *The Oprah Winfrey Show* and Oprah's Book Club is none other than Winfrey herself. Thus, even as Winfrey instructs her viewers to treat novels as occasions to think about themselves, Rooney observes that "the most dominant biographical narrative associated with the novels is her own sentimentalized, made-for-TV one"—so much so that it "fairly overshadowed" the narratives of the novels (Rooney 2005, 156, 157). In the episode on Wally Lamb's *She's Come Undone*—the story of an obese woman from a "dysfunctional" family who learns to love herself—Winfrey quoted her favorite line: "Accept what people offer. Drink their milkshakes. Take their love." She then confided to the audience,

> It's a great lesson for me. I used to, like—every time people would come up to me and say, 'I watch you, I love you,' I'd always, like, not hear it, dismiss it, try not to—put myself in another place: 'What does that *really* mean?' And now I try, with every person that has a kind thing to say to me, to honestly receive that and to fill myself with whatever it is they're trying to give me. (*Oprah Winfrey Show*, Feb. 28, 1997)

Winfrey thereby enacts the ideal self who, by consistently moving in the direction of self-love, deserves the love of millions. Through this self-referential approach to reading, Rooney argues, Winfrey not only encouraged "her audience to harbor infantile fantasies about becoming fictional characters" but also "indulged in the means to make herself over in said characters' images, thereby making each and every book she saw fit ... effectively about her" (Rooney 2005, 160–161). Rooney's frustration stems from her belief that literature provides an opportunity to get *outside* of one's self, to "engage intimately with a strange and complex other-consciousness" (ibid., 29) and encounter "human suffering in all its unresolvable complexity" (ibid., 142). Winfrey, in contrast, treats novels as "corollaries to her program's doctrine of mindless American optimism" and "stepping stones to a better lifestyle" (ibid.).

Rooney's critique is valid if Oprah's Book Club is intended to help readers develop a critical eye for literature, nurture their capacity for rational-critical debate, provide them an "increased sense of autonomy," a new relationship to authority (Davidson 1986, 72), or hold up a critical mirror to society. Under such expectations, the club could be considered a failure—little more than the "promotional lovefest" marked by "studiously immature" discussion that Rooney condemns (Rooney 2005, 153, 159). But if we consider Oprah's Book Club an ideological practice that embodies and valorizes Winfrey's mind-cure technology of the self while facilitating the makeover of her public persona, it looks more like an unqualified success. By definitively establishing her removal from the ranks of tasteless talk show hosts, Oprah's Book Club endowed Winfrey with the cultural legitimacy to pursue a more "respectable" audience. Most important, her newfound image as a "champion of literacy" would become the foundation of the "Oprah brand."

Building Brand Oprah

In July 1999, Hearst Magazines announced it had signed a deal with Winfrey to publish a new magazine for women "offering an Oprah-patented stew of features on family, relationships, spirituality, work, health, beauty and books" (Hamilton 1999). *Newsweek* business reporter Kendall Hamilton judged it a "very smart venture by Hearst," which had not only bought access to Winfrey's "built-in audience" but "in essence, licensed an established, powerful brand." For her part, Winfrey could add another jewel to the crown of her "burgeoning multimedia empire." In addition to owning Harpo Entertainment Group and partnering with ABC/Cap Cities to produce a series of TV movies and Internet content, Winfrey had recently ponied up $20 million for a 20 percent stake in Oxygen Media, an Internet/cable venture aimed at women. Her web site, Oprah.com, launched in fall 1998 and receiving 6 million page hits per month, would join Oxygen's network. A magazine would significantly enhance the "synergy" among these platforms. As Hamilton observed, "Once everything's up and running, Oprah's show will push the magazine, which will push the Web site, which will push the cable channel, creating an integrated media universe in which all roads lead to Oprah" (ibid.).

Upon the debut of *O, the Oprah Magazine* in April 2000, the *Boston Globe* reported that the publication would "carry Winfrey's trademark message of hope and empowerment" but wondered "whether it will also carry her box-office clout" (Jurkowitz 2000b). For Christine Miller, executive vice president of marketing for the Magazine Publishers of America, *O*'s success was beyond doubt "if you think, as we do, that the key to being a sure-fire winner is being a brand." With the creation of *The Oprah Magazine,* she said, Winfrey was wisely "extending her brand" (ibid.). Mississippi State University professor Samir Husni described the new venture as the "extension of the brand" and the "missing link" in Winfrey's media empire that "sort of closes the circle on everything" (Feeney 2000).

Publicly, Winfrey eschewed such market-driven motives. Responding to tensions among Hearst employees regarding her zealous control during the creation of the magazine's first issues, she asserted, "I know that to you guys the Oprah name is a brand. But for me, it's my life, it's the way I live my life, and everything I stand for" (Lippman 1997). This distinction is beside the point, however, in that Winfrey's life and everything she stands for are precisely what constitutes the Oprah brand. John Grace, executive director of Interbrand, said of the fusion of market value and personal values that defines Winfrey's enterprise, "As long as the basis for the relationship with her audience is trust and honesty, the audience will come back" (ibid.). This equation of brand with values, trust, and intimacy reflects a shift in thinking in the marketing profession that blossomed in the 1980s and flourished in the "new economy" of the 1990s. According to Naomi Klein (2000), in the shift toward "a psychological/anthropological examination of what brands mean to the culture and to people's lives" (7), corporations came to see themselves as producers of brands, rather than makers of products. Klein argues that as the brand came to represent the "meaning," "identity," "consciousness," or "soul" of the corporation, business success involved finding ways for brands to "establish emotional ties with their customers" (ibid., 20; see also Frank 2000). Or, as expressed by the vice president of marketing for Starbucks, "a great brand raises the bar—it adds a greater sense of purpose to the [consumer's] experience" (ibid., 21). Having been a Calvin Klein brand consultant, John Grace was well-versed in this new marketing philosophy—hence his recognition of the "emotional ties" and "sense of purpose" that define the Oprah brand. Naomi Klein suggests that in this new model, "the brand, and the selling of the brand, acquired an extra component that can only be described as spiritual" (Klein 2000, 21). Indeed, some marketing professionals began using the term "soul branding" to describe a strategy by which a corporate brand might acquire a "halo," or "an aura of positive feeling and receptivity" that would not only "buoy" its products but also create a "potent, direct emotional link" to consumers and investors (Maio 1998, quoted in Travis 2005, 6).

Perhaps no other corporate entity was better positioned than Winfrey to capitalize on this spiritualization of the brand, given that she was already "almost a religion" (Lebowitz 1996). Thus, Winfrey's image makeover in the 1990s was not simply a personal endeavor but a financial one; her ascent to the position of "prophet" paralleled a meteoric rise in her profits during the same period. Trysh Travis (2005) proposes that Oprah's Book Club can be understood as a dialectic of "re-enchantment" and "rationalization," where readers were encouraged to seek transcendence by reinventing themselves through reading, even as the club itself was a vital instrument in a broader business strategy of "audience building" (4). As Travis points out, irrespective of what the book club means to individual participants, it "was also part of a long-term and carefully planned strategy ... to differentiate Brand Oprah within the marketplace and to enhance the relationship consumers had with the brand" (ibid., 5).

In fact, Winfrey's halo was in need of polishing at the end of the 1995–1996 season, despite her efforts to upgrade her image over the previous two years. Her audience share, which in fall 1991 had been 34 percent, had shrunk to 23 percent by summer 1996. Competition from youth-oriented programs like *Ricki Lake* and the new *Rosie O'Donnell Show* had eaten into Winfrey's ratings, there were reports of internal staff tensions at Harpo, and industry insiders were speculating that *The Oprah Winfrey Show* had become stale and predictable (Braun 1997). The inauguration of Oprah's Book Club in September 1996 was part of a major overhaul of the program to counter this audience slippage. The old format, with the entire hour devoted to a single topic, was replaced with "faster-paced" shows of two or three segments. This shift to "tighter, shorter" units allowed producers to test the book club idea, which was initially packaged as a ten-minute segment at the end of the episode. The revamped format appeared to do the trick, staving off further audience erosion. By March 1997,

Winfrey's share had increased to 24 percent and she held "a commanding lead among total households and women viewers," especially among women ages twenty-five to fifty-four (ibid.).

More important, the commercial success of Oprah's Book Club provided a powerful boost to Winfrey's stature in the culture industries. As Stephen Braun wrote in 1997 in the *Los Angeles Times*, "These days the queen of talk is doing more than talking. She is advising her audience on what to read, what to listen to, how to live. And by the hundreds of thousands, Winfrey's devotees are taking her advice" (ibid.). The reinvention of *The Oprah Winfrey Show* not only stabilized her audience but "magnified her influence. She is no longer merely the nation's most popular talk show host. She is fast becoming a cultural tastemaker." Thanks to this turnaround, Braun writes, "veteran programmers have begun to refer to Winfrey as the personification of 'branding'" (ibid.). Vicki Abt—the Penn State sociologist who three years earlier had accused Winfrey and fellow talk show hosts of fostering social deviance—was now effusive: "Oprah right now is a God," Abt said. "She probably has the highest Q rating . . . of anyone on television. There may be better interviewers and smarter people elsewhere on television, but no one markets charisma like Oprah does" (ibid.).

Oprah's Book Club, then, was the cornerstone of the Oprah brand, with its consolidation of the mythic narrative of citizens' reading, Winfrey's representation of her enterprise as a "ministry" (quoted in Lowe 1998, 126), the economic rebound of her program, and her awe-inspiring power to shape consumer behavior. Thanks to this fusion, Travis notes, Winfrey's "'brand halo' seemed unassailable" in the latter half of the 1990s (Travis 2005, 10). Emboldened by praise for her contribution to literacy, Winfrey spent the remainder of the decade honing and extending her brand—that constellation of her "message of goodness" and the "tentacular structure" of her media enterprise united through the persona of "Oprah" (Illouz 2003, 5). *Time* reporter Christopher Farley has noted that Winfrey had "avoided the voyeuristic label" that plagued other talk show hosts "partly because her primary subject has always been her own life" (Farley 1998, 83). Illouz similarly observes that "more than any other public persona, Oprah has used her own life to shape the meaning of her performance." Winfrey's biography, she argues, is permeated with "the meanings that are central to her show" (Illouz 2003, 18). For *New Republic*'s Lee Siegel, "Oprah has revolutionized the presentation of self on television through the total deployment of every dimension of her life" (Siegel 2006). *Fortune* writer Patricia Sellers concurs: "Oprah's life is the essence of her brand," which can be distilled into a "simple message": "You are responsible for your own life." In Sellers's view, Winfrey's unwavering dedication to "making herself and her struggles central to this message" accounts for both her popularity ("she taps deep into the American psyche and its desire for self-reliance") and the success of her "business powerhouse" (Sellers 2002, 54).

Although Winfrey reportedly dislikes talking about business—as she told Sellers, "I don't think of myself as a business woman" (ibid., 50)—the elaboration of the

Oprah brand was clearly driven by a shrewd business strategy. In the words of Jeff Jacobs, Harpo president, Winfrey's personal agent, and architect of that business model: "We are an intellectual property company, and our partners (ABC, Hearst, Oxygen) are distributors. Core content is developed here and has *never* left our base" (ibid., 54). The "core content," of course, is Winfrey herself. It is why everything she is involved in bears her name and/or image, why she has refused to sell any part of her business or her name. This fusion of persona and enterprise is explicit in her comment to Sellers: "If I lost control of the business, I'd lose myself.... Owning myself is a way to be myself" (ibid.). As a *Broadcasting and Cable* writer noted, Winfrey "has shown no interest in developing her brand in ways that don't trade on her persona" (Grossman 2006).

Following on the success of Oprah's Book Club and the revamped *Oprah Winfrey Show*, the continued fortunes of the Oprah brand depended on seeking out new platforms and partnerships through which to distribute its core content. As Travis states, "Embracing rapidly evolving technologies and the possibilities of synergy, Harpo developed complementary media outlets; underwritten by cross-media corporate sponsorship, they disseminated common and mutually reinforcing content" (Travis 2005, 8–9). The trajectory of Winfrey's enterprise through the remainder of the decade reflects this business model, with its endless reiteration of the core message of the Oprah brand.

The 1997 season premiere of *The Oprah Winfrey Show* marked the birth of what would become Oprah's Angel Network, where viewers were asked to donate spare change for college scholarships and Habitat for Humanity. A month later, Winfrey released "Oprah: Make the Connection"—a video version of the best-selling 1996 book, *Make the Connection: Ten Steps to a Better Body—and a Better Life*, which she had coauthored with her fitness coach, Bob Greene. The first ABC/Harpo coproduction, *Oprah Winfrey Presents: The Wedding*, also aired in 1997. All three ventures embodied the values of responsibility, self-improvement, and literacy associated with the Oprah brand and won Winfrey the expected industry and popular endorsements. *Newsweek* named her the "Most Important Person" in books and media, and she garnered the People's Choice Award for "Favorite Television Performer."

Change Your Life TV: Marrying Marketing and Mind Cure

Buoyed by acclaim for these ventures, Winfrey embarked on her thirteenth season with yet another "makeover" in what she promoted as "the best year yet." The season premiere of *The Oprah Winfrey Show* on September 8, 1998, unveiled not only a "new look"—a remodeled studio, redesigned graphics, and a new theme song/music video performed by Winfrey herself—but a new mission: "We are launching Change Your Life TV," she announced. In the introduction, Winfrey said she had spent the previous year pondering whether to continue the program. Significantly, she couched her quandary in a critique of television: "I normally don't watch TV. TV is bad. It's a lot of bad shows on the TV. I'm not naming no names, but y'all know what I'm talking about." In opposition to the rest of television, which she said was "going straight down the tube," Winfrey vowed, "We're gonna try to raise ourselves to the highest vision possible for our lives and for those of you who are watching. We want to be an inspiration to you." This announcement was followed with scenes from earlier episodes, in which panelists credited *The Oprah Winfrey Show* with saving their marriages, their health, their literacy, even their lives. When the camera returned to Winfrey, she reiterated her intention "to try and do television that inspires us to make positive changes in our lives. This year we're gonna continue an even more significant and profound way and with even greater commitment to say something meaningful every day."

In addition to a plethora of "uplifting" topics (e.g., "People Who Did the Right Thing," "Design Your Dream," "The Best Thing I Ever Did For Myself"), plentiful celebrities (Robin Williams, Cuba Gooding Jr., Julia Roberts, Brad Pitt, John Travolta, etc.), another appearance by Marianne Williamson, episodes promoting the premiere of *Beloved,* and installments of Oprah's Angel Network and Oprah's Book Club, the new season featured multiple appearances by a bevy of self-help gurus. John Gray, author of *Men Are from Mars, Women Are from Venus,* tutored viewers on how to "find [their] soul's desire and personal success." Suze Orman promised the key to "opening the door to financial freedom" and developing "the courage to be rich." Iyanla Vanzant explained how "all healing begins with your ability to love yourself first" (Sept. 11, 1998). Phil McGraw—whose relationship with Winfrey began earlier that year when he served as the jury selection expert in her "mad cow trial" in Texas—injected a no-nonsense demand for "personal responsibility." Sarah Ban Breathnach, whose earlier book, *Simple Abundance,* had been the impetus for Winfrey and viewers to keep "gratitude journals," returned in October 1998 with *Something More*—a guide to "excavating your authentic self," this time with the aid of "discovery journals" (Oct. 13, 1998). Gary Zukav, whose *The Seat of the Soul* Winfrey anointed "one of the most powerful books I've ever read, except for the Bible, of course," instructed guests and viewers on how to obtain "real power" by discerning "the direction your soul wants to sail" (Apr. 23, 1999).[2] "Change Your Life TV" also introduced a new feature, "Remembering Your Spirit," a five-minute, end-of-episode segment designed to teach viewers how to "center" themselves, "find real joy and real peace," and "connect to spirit" through meditation. Introducing the first installment in the season premiere, Winfrey intoned, "everything starts with knowing who you are." If she had been "defined by the world as a talk show host," in reality, she confided, "I am much more. I am spirit connected to the greater spirit." The new feature, she insisted, would help her followers achieve this same epiphany (Sept. 8, 1998).

For Kathleen Lowney, the "Change Your Life" season represents Winfrey's decision to turn her show into a full-blown "testimonial to the benefits of the self-help movement" and her arrival as "the quintessential talk show evangelist" (Lowney 1999, 140, 139). Certainly, religious themes and language became a prominent feature of the program, as Winfrey referred regularly to God, prayer, the Bible, and so on. The regular guest experts were equally forthcoming about the religious dimensions of their self-improvement programs. John Gray attributed his success to having "prayed to God." "Spirit," he said, was "the part of us that can connect to God" (*Oprah Winfrey Show*, Sept. 9, 1998), whereas suffering resulted from "having forgotten that basic relationship to God." Gray also revealed that he practiced "laying-on-hands healing" (*Oprah Winfrey Show*, Oct. 7, 1998). Iyanla Vanzant described herself as "a unique and divine expression of God" and promised viewers they could become likewise (*Oprah Winfrey Show*, Sept. 11, 1998).[3] Sarah Ban Breathnach described people's longing for "something more" as "divine discontent" (*Oprah Winfrey Show*, Oct. 13, 1998). Gary Zukav counseled that our souls speak to us through our intuitions and "God, intuition, speaks to us by the way we feel" (*Oprah Winfrey Show*, Apr. 23, 1999).

Simply noting that Winfrey's program became explicitly religious with "Change Your Life TV" does not explain the specific character and appeal of this televised religiosity, however. Beneath the surface variety of topics, experts, and techniques, the underlying themes and messages of the Change Your Life season find their antecedent in nineteenth-century New Thought theology. In *Each Mind a Kingdom* (1999), Beryl Satter argues that the eclectic, loosely organized character of the New Thought movement is what allowed it to "adapt to and influence mainstream American ideas" (6). Emerging during a period of sweeping social and economic change, "New Thought's principles about the creative power of mind … struck early twentieth-century Americans as the wave of the future." Although the movement's institutions and leaders have been relegated to historical footnotes, the "central premise" of New Thought, "the power of thought to alter circumstances," remains "operative in American culture today," according to Satter (ibid.). She finds vestiges of "thought-as-power" in a variety of contemporary venues, including Robert Schuller's "possibility thinking," corporate success seminars, the vast 12-Step universe, and, significantly, *The Oprah Winfrey Show*, whose host "dispenses her New Thought philosophy daily on a show watched by millions" (ibid., 7). In charting the early decades of the New Thought movement and its appeal for social and political reformers, Satter deems it crucial "to understand what the embrace of New Thought reveals not simply about the psychology of individual reformers, but about the underlying beliefs of the broader culture" (ibid., 182). This is also true in considering Winfrey's contemporary appropriation of New Thought principles and the resonance of her enterprise today.

In his study of the history of self-help books in the United States, Steven Starker (1988) describes the literature generated in the late nineteenth and early twentieth centuries by New Thought adherents as noteworthy for the primacy of simple "wish-fulfillment" in its philosophy. It told readers, in effect, to close their eyes and wish very, very hard, and all would be granted. Of course, authors dressed up this simple notion with considerable spiritual and technical paraphernalia, making it seem both theological and scientific to the lay reader. Nevertheless, the essence of New Thought was the fulfilled wish and how to achieve it. While all wishes were possible, those for wealth, health, and power were most frequently addressed in these works. All of this has a rather primitive, magical quality about it. (39)

Despite the century that separates them, New Thought and Winfrey's enterprise have significant affinities. For example, she and her stable of "Change Your Life" experts repeatedly affirmed the power of thought to create reality. Referring to Zukav's *Seat of the Soul,* Winfrey pointed to his claim that "intention is the single most powerful energy in our lives" as the "most important message" of the book: "I mean, I got it so big. . . . this was bing, bing, bing, light bulbs, Indy 500 flags went off in my head" (*Oprah Winfrey Show,* Apr. 23, 1999). In the episode with Breathnach, Winfrey told a panelist that pain and confusion were the result of "living your life by other people's definitions" rather than having "gone inside and asked yourself what do you really want." Such "excavation" was essential, Winfrey said, because "you can have whatever you want." Breathnach agreed the guest's discontent would evaporate if she embraced the idea that she was "a magnificent, fabulous, wise, powerful woman" (*Oprah Winfrey Show,* Oct. 13, 1998). In her initial appearance, Iyanla Vanzant warned a guest she would never marry as long as she believed "good men" were hard to find, because "what you believe, you experience." This, she added, was simply the law of "cause and effect" (*Oprah Winfrey Show,* Sept. 11, 1998). Introducing the first of many appearances by Suze Orman, Winfrey assured viewers they could overcome financial hardship and "have the money you want and deserve" if they would just change the way they think about money. She continued:

How many of you understand now that your thoughts create reality? Does everybody get that? You really do get that? That you have the life you have right now because of everything you thought and then said and then did? You get that? All right. So that also works with money. You have it or you don't have it based upon the way you think about it. (*Oprah Winfrey Show,* Sept. 10, 1998)

In the 1950s, Norman Vincent Peale introduced an important innovation to the mind-cure technology of healing and became "the overwhelmingly popular and influential religious self-help figure of the decade" (Starker 1988, 105). Following in the mind-cure tradition, Peale's *The Power of Positive Thinking* (1952) treated "unhappiness as largely self-manufactured" and prescribed a cure based on "practicing happiness thinking" (106). In Starker's assessment, Peale's work "fell squarely within the mainstream of the New Thought religious movement. All of the basic elements were there: applied religion, determined optimism, visualizations, relaxation, supremacy of the wish, positive affirmations, mental exercises, prayer power, universal vibrations, mind-cure, and so on" (Starker 1988, 107). If the content of Peale's message was recycled nineteenth-century ideas, he breathed new life into it with an innovation in form:

> Beyond simplification, and the requisite engaging anecdotes, he had added the critical element of "technique." Inspiration was supplemented by the nuts and bolts of "howto-ism." Most chapters, therefore, had their Ten Rules, Twelve Steps, Practical Suggestions, Worry-Breaking Formulas, and so on. Every reader emerged with concrete, step-by-step instructions on how to achieve health, wealth and happiness. It is just such specific instruction that has become the hallmark of best-selling self-help work. (ibid., 109)

Such "specific instruction" was also a hallmark of Winfrey's Change Your Life TV. "Remembering Your Spirit" did not just encourage people to meditate—it gave them detailed directions on method and content. In the premiere installment shot at Winfrey's Indiana estate, she described meditating in the bathtub surrounded by prayer books, quotes, poems, and candles, where for fifteen minutes she repeated the words, "O glorious future, my heart is open to you. Come sit in my heart." If viewers followed her example, Winfrey said, "your day will undoubtedly be more focused, more centered. Things tend to fall into line" (*Oprah Winfrey Show*, Sept. 8, 1998). The following week, John Gray insisted that if viewers meditated correctly, "You'll experience peace or you'll experience joy or you'll experience a sense of confidence and power." He also outlined a technique: the way to "speed up" the benefits of meditation was to start "with your hands up in the air, your fingers spread apart" and repeat ten times, "Oh God, my heart is open to you. Come into my heart." Those who "don't have a positive feeling associated with God," he added, could substitute "anything you want to bring into your life" (*Oprah Winfrey Show*, Sept. 16, 1998).

Besides meditation and verbal repetition, another common technique prescribed by Winfrey and her consortium of experts was written exercises. At the beginning of the season she urged the audience to get "a notebook to put your Change Your Life TV homework in" (*Oprah Winfrey Show*, Sept. 23, 1998). Gray offered a technique for "healing anger" by writing a "feeling letter," in which viewers were to progress from conscious anger, to hidden sadness and fear, to their deepest desire, and finally gratitude. For each step, Gray provided specific language and examples. By the end of this exercise, he promised, "anger will go out of your life, you'll feel open and you're ready to move on" (ibid.). Iyanla Vanzant also assigned "homework for the soul," the first of which consisted of "two simple steps." Participants were to write, "Today I accept that I experienced . . . " and then list "the horrible, the good, the bad, the indifferent—all of it—just accept it," Vanzant instructed. The "acceptance" step was to be repeated "every day nine times a day," followed by a second step: "Begin creating what you are willing to have in your life." These "willingness statements" were also to be written nine times. "Go for the stars," Vanzant said, "because you can't have too much" (*Oprah Winfrey Show*, Sept. 11, 1998).

Suze Orman and Sarah Ban Breathnach combined written and verbal techniques. The latter's appearance included directions for creating a "discovery journal." Breathnach also told women in the audience how to turn "self-loathing" into "self-loving": "I want you to look at yourself in the mirror, naked, every day, and I want you to say, 'Blessed am I to live in such a beautiful temple. Blessed am I to live in such a beautiful temple.'" Winfrey endorsed this technique: "If you just do it, just as Sarah has said, what will start to happen, if you say it to yourself enough times, you'll be transformed by the language" (*Oprah Winfrey Show*, Oct. 13, 1998). Orman's "homework"—this time in the realm of financial "healing"—involved creating a "new truth" through written and oral repetition. Most people, she confided, live a lie by telling themselves they will "never get out of debt" or "never have enough." Because "what you think becomes your destiny," viewers needed to "start thinking the truth. And the truth is, you have more than you'll ever need." To create a "new truth," Orman explained, participants were to begin by stating their "money fear" and then fashion their new truth, which should be short, present tense, and "unlimited." They were to write down this new truth twenty-five times a day, then scream it out loud, then look in the mirror and repeat it silently to themselves. "If you can do that," Orman promised, "sooner than later, you'll become your new truth" (*Oprah Winfrey Show*, Sept. 10, 1998).

Although Change Your Life TV epitomized the Oprah "soul brand," it was not greeted with the adulation to which Winfrey was accustomed. In fact, this new inspirational gambit elicited stinging criticism from viewers and the popular press and became the butt of "very unkind skits" on late night TV (Persall 1998). An early volley came on October 12 from Richard Roeper, writing in Winfrey's hometown newspaper, the *Chicago Sun-Times*. Noting her ubiquitous presence in popular culture—the impending release of her film *Beloved*, cover treatments in *Time*, *TV Guide*, and *Vogue*, and numerous interviews that "read more like testimonials than profiles"—Roeper dubbed it "a hurricane of national worship" (Roeper 1998a). Winfrey may have "done a world of good," he said, "but she is not a messenger, nor is she a prophet. She is an entertainer." Roeper suggested that in the show's new season, Winfrey was "really getting goofy" in an "almost frantic quest for spiritual bliss and higher consciousness." Remarking on the "Remembering Your Spirit" segments with Winfrey "surrounded by candles as she welcomes authors and psychobabblers," Roeper concluded, "her obsession with herself is staggering." He also challenged the very premise of the new mission:

You don't improve your life by watching TV—you improve your life by turning off the TV and going back to school, volunteering in the local soup kitchen, coaching a neighborhood team, working hard at controlling your temper. Spending so much time on "me-me-me" is antithetical to true spiritual growth; it's worshipping at a New Age altar. (ibid.)

Other writers followed suit. *New York Post* columnist Thelma Adams announced, "I am so over Oprah" (quoted in Coles 1998). Change Your Life TV, she declared, was "vile.... Springer with a sop of uplift." Adams called for a backlash against "Saint Oprah" with her "sermonizing from high atop a billion dollar bank account. Who couldn't take responsibility for their lives with the help of therapists, personal trainers, private chefs, makeup artists and money managers?" (Adams 1998). TV writer Jeff MacGregor dismissed Change Your Life TV as "devoted to the mind-numbing clichés of personal improvement" (quoted in Garchik 1998). Hal Boedeker, critic for the *Orlando Sentinel,* agreed: "It's therapy as theater. Winfrey is not only going for an Emmy this year, but also the Nobel Peace Prize.... [She] just keeps plugging like a New Age Elmer Gantry" (Boedeker 1998). Writing for the Associated Press, Brian Lowry suggested that "aspiring to 'change people's lives' through a TV show borders on the absurd" (Lowry 1998).

Roeper closed his column with a prediction that if Winfrey continued her on-air "spiritual questing," "I have a feeling all the regular folks watching 'Change Your Life TV' are going to opt for 'Change the Channel TV'" (Roeper 1998a). The following week, he reported on reactions to his critique. Given Winfrey's popularity, Roeper had girded himself for a backlash: "colleagues and readers naturally assumed I'd be assailed with complaints from Oprah's legendarily loyal fans. Some friends in the media even joked (at least I think they were joking) about my career dying in this town because I dared to say something negative about Chicago's first lady" (Roeper 1998b). He was thus stunned to find that of some 300 e-mails and phone calls, "at least 95 percent" were "in sync" with his observations about "Oprah's recent forays into New Age nuttiness." Roeper also noted that most who had contacted him "weren't lifelong Oprah bashers" but "people who admire her talents and have been faithful viewers for years." The response to his column, he suggested, revealed a genuine divide within Winfrey's fan base.

The *Sun-Times* also printed excerpts from twenty-three responses to Roeper, two of which defended Winfrey and the rest strongly negative ("Everyone has opinion" 1998). A few suggested Winfrey's enormous wealth shielded her from the travails faced by ordinary people, making it easy to promote the benefits of "serenity": "What gets me is Oprah constantly preaching how money will never make a person happy.... [This is] a woman who is one of Forbes' highest rated millionaires"; "I am so tired of listening to Oprah one moment telling us she shops only sales, and then bragging about wearing a million dollars worth of jewelry." Others intimated that her ego had grown in proportion to her bank account: "It's so refreshing to read that someone other than myself is sick of Oprah's 'holier than thou' attitude"; "Her pontificating

THE OPRAH BRAND AND THE ENTERPRISING SELF

became too much for me" (ibid.); "I stopped watching her show about two months ago. Just could not stand all this 'I-I-I' business" (Roeper 1998b). Several wondered about the economic motives behind Winfrey's new mission: "I can't help but [note that] Oprah's very public spiritual quest adds mightily to her personal coffers and glory"; "Oprah is no more than a self-promotion machine in a likeable, viewer-friendly package"; "She is a self-absorbed, egotistical, marketing machine" ("Everyone has opinion" 1998). Finally, a number of respondents took issue with the overtly religious tone of Change Your Life TV: "I tuned into her 'New Age' show and when I felt the nausea rising, I turned it off. What makes her think she is some sort of goddess is beyond me"; "I was astonished by her attempts to come off as armchair psychotherapist, relationship expert, and canonized saint"; "I consider myself to be spiritually minded, and I can somewhat relate to what Oprah is experiencing. But I feel uncomfortable with all the emphasis on such a private, individual matter. I'll be watching even less of Oprah this year" (ibid.).

Similar sentiments showed up on AOL's site, Oprah Online, where "disgruntled fans" labeled Winfrey "a female Pat Robertson" and "a preacher bent on having people think the way you do" ("Angry at Oprah" 1998). Critiques of Winfrey and Change Your Life TV were also a focus of a privately created web site, "The Opra-sis," with its stated purpose as "an oasis to take a break from the over-hyped, over-dressed, overly preachy Oprah Winfrey Show" (quoted in Lowney 1999, 140). Further, Winfrey's ratings suggested not all viewers shared her conviction that Change Your Life TV was her best season yet. The *New York Times* reported that the program was losing "nearly a million homes each time a 'Change' show is broadcast" ("Angry at Oprah" 1998). According to *Daily Variety*, the average rating for Change Your Life episodes was 6.0, compared to the show's overall ratings average of 6.2 (Littleton 1998). Even more telling, this represented a 14 percent decline from the previous season, which had garnered a 7.0 average rating, leading *Daily Variety* to speculate that "Winfrey's national audience base is not as rock solid as it once was" (ibid.). In fact, over the past three ratings periods, *The Oprah Winfrey Show* had been beaten by *Jerry Springer*, the poster child of "trash talk TV," and both programs were eclipsed in the November 1998 sweeps by newcomer *Judge Judy* ("How returning shows are faring" 1999).

Winfrey initially dismissed both her critics and the ratings decline. In reference to the "Oprah Online" posts, she declared she would not "throw the baby out with the bathwater because a few people post negative stuff" ("Angry at Oprah" 1998). A few days later she told a reporter that just as "instinct" led her to launch Oprah's Book Club, it had guided her to create Change Your Life TV (Persall 1998). Although she admitted her producers were "now feeling bad, wondering if we're doing the right thing," Winfrey betrayed no such misgivings: "You have to know that you're right and be so steadfast in the knowing that it doesn't matter what other people say." As for the ratings slide, "losing a ratings point doesn't mean anything," she said. "I would have the same ideals even if nobody was watching" (ibid.).

Given the praise and profits showered on Winfrey since she embarked on her first makeover in the mid-1990s, however, the upsurge of criticism was distressing. The decidedly lukewarm critical response to *Beloved* (released on October 16), which Winfrey had predicted would be "my *Schindler's List*," only added to her consternation (Corliss 1998, 75; Waxman 1998). Although she devoted two episodes of her show and a live Q-and-A session on AOL's Oprah Online to promote the film, Winfrey's normally loyal fans failed to follow her to the theaters. When *Beloved* turned out to be a financial bomb as well—its ticket sales dropped 50 percent in the second week and its domestic gross of $23 million was less than half what it cost to make—she fell into a month-long depression ("Autumn flops" 1998; Clemetson 2001, 43). It thus appeared that her "astonishing Midas touch" might be tarnished (Lowry 1998).

Confronted with these disappointments, Winfrey elicited support from Marianne Williamson, who appeared in a pre-taped interview in a December 1998 *Oprah Winfrey Show*. After asking Williamson to define "spirit" (who predictably said it was "love"), Winfrey homed in on the problem of critics who branded them both "New Age." Williamson responded: "Well, I've heard you say, and I know many of us were grateful to you for saying, that you think it's ridiculous to call it New Age because there's nothing new about this. There's something very old about it." Here, Williamson followed her nineteenth-century mind-cure antecedents who had similarly sought to "lend legitimacy to their theory" by arguing that "their techniques were derived from ancient spiritual practices" (Cushman 1995, 126). But if Williamson's appearance was intended to publicly validate Winfrey's spirit quest, behind the scenes she and her producers were unnerved enough by the criticism and ratings slide to put on the brakes. September 1998 had featured eleven Change Your Life episodes, followed by fourteen in October. By November and December, those numbers were three and five, respectively. Meanwhile, celebrity episodes abounded, including appearances by Paul Newman, Julia Roberts, Whitney Houston, and two each for Brad Pitt and Tina Turner. Winfrey, it seems, did care about her ratings and about "what people say." As a *Newsweek* cover story later recounted, feeling "hurt" at being "trashed" in the press and by viewers' complaints that she was "meddling with their religious beliefs," Winfrey "dropped the 'change your life' mantra and toned down the 'Spirit' segments" (Clemetson 2001, 44).

Consolidating the Brand

Although the Change Your Life experiment was an atypical setback for Winfrey—the point at which "the queen of talk finally takes a hit" (Lowry 1998)—fall 1998 was a crucial point in the development of the Oprah brand. On October 12, Winfrey announced she would extend her program through the 2001–2002 season, so as to "continue to enlighten and entertain our millions of viewers around the world"

("Oprah to continue her show" 1998). A week later, just as the latest issue of *Vanity Fair* put Winfrey atop its list of "America's Most Influential Women"—editor Graydon Carter called her "arguably the most influential person in America today" (Gilbert 1998)—she launched Oprah.com to establish her brand in cyberspace. Jointly produced by Harpo and the ABC Internet Group, the web site was promoted as a complement to the Change Your Life campaign where viewers could "access the experts." It was also touted as "an engaging interactive experience," a "strong information resource," and most important, a place for "viewers to expand their relationship with Oprah" ("Change your life—log on with Oprah" 1998).[4]

In November, Geraldine Laybourne, who had headed Nickelodeon at Viacom and run the cable division for Disney/ABC, recruited Winfrey as the newest partner in Oxygen, a cable/Internet network for women that Laybourne planned to launch in January 2000 (McAdams 2000). Other partners included the fabled TV production firm Carsey-Werner-Mandabach, ABC, and America Online.[5] Besides an investment of $20 million—for which she received a 25 percent share—Winfrey would bring to the venture original programming, reruns of her talk show, and Oprah.com, which would be linked to the Oxygen network. For Laybourne, the value of Winfrey's participation was clear: "We can build our brand immediately. There is no source who knows what women want and need more than Oprah" (Melcher 1998).[6]

Laybourne was not the only one looking to cash in on the Oprah brand that fall. Hearst's magazine division president, Cathleen Black, and its *Good Housekeeping* editor, Ellen Levine, had flown to Chicago in October to begin talks with Winfrey about starting a magazine. Contrary to its normal practice, Hearst had not yet conducted focus groups or market research to gauge the prospects for the magazine's success. As Levine told the trade publication *Folio*, "Just taking a look at the success of Oprah Winfrey led us to understand the impact she can have on print. Her viewers are also readers—just take a look at the best-seller list. That was very important to us. For her, the magazine becomes another way to reach people" (D'Orio 1999).

Levine's comment condenses the core characteristics of the Oprah brand: its roots in the success of the book club, its reliance on cross-media synergy, and its aim to capture a specific sector of the market. Winfrey's quest for public legitimacy may have begun with the goal of separating herself from the "trash pack," but that depended on attracting a more "respectable" following. It was her ability to develop a more valuable audience base that made the Oprah brand attractive to advertisers and, by extension, to other corporate media. The building of Brand Oprah—the proliferation of its "core content" through synergistic links across platforms and with other culture industry giants—was thus intimately connected to cultivating a more "upscale" audience commodity. The commercial success of Oprah's Book Club—it was estimated in 1998 that the club was responsible for $160 million in book sales (Rebello 1998)—signaled to Winfrey and potential industry suitors that such a commodity was within reach.

According to Lynette Clemetson, Winfrey's decision to join forces with Oxygen and Hearst resulted from the disappointments of *Beloved* and Change Your Life TV, which had persuaded her to form "partnerships to ease the burden of professional and financial risk" (Clemetson 2001, 43). The attraction of both ventures, moreover, was their resonance with the philosophical and economic priorities of the Oprah brand. When Geraldine Laybourne first approached Winfrey, she described Oxygen as "a women's cable network based on intent and service." As Winfrey told *Fortune's* Patricia Sellers, "I thought, my God, this is my idea exactly," adding that she had already toyed with the possibility of starting her own Oprah Winfrey Network on cable (Sellers 2002, 60). In a *Newsweek* interview, she called Oxygen "an extension of who I am ... creating a network that has the best interest of women at heart—well, that's what I try to do every day. It's such a fit" (Clemetson 1999). Although several publishers—including Time Warner and Condé Nast—had been "spurred by the success" of the book club to pitch Winfrey on the idea of a magazine, she was finally won over by Hearst because, as Cathleen Black said, "We knew we had to engage her in a mission, not just a magazine" (Clemetson 2001, 43, 44). Shortly after the first issue of *O, The Oprah Magazine* hit the stands, Winfrey explained that editor Ellen Kunes had come up with the publication's mission statement: "A personal growth guide for women for the 21st century." For Winfrey, "that was a 'bingo' moment. What I felt was missing [in other magazines] was something that would be beneficial to women, and not just trite magazine speak" (Granatstein 2000).

Equally important was that both Hearst and Oxygen set their sights on the very market targeted by the Oprah brand. In 1998 the *Economist* chided critics who intimated that *Beloved* was a "vanity" project by a figure "uncomfortable being downmarket" who "craves intellectual respectability," pointing out that Winfrey had "been moving upmarket for years" ("Dumbing up" 1998). Along with her legendary influence over her followers, her success at scaling the demographic ladder is precisely what attracted ABC/Disney, Hearst, and Laybourne to seek partnerships with her. Cathleen Black recognized a kindred business spirit in Winfrey—she had been put in charge of Hearst's magazine division in 1996 with a directive to turn the "staid, sleepy publishing giant" into "a dynamic, contemporary publishing company." She did so by finding ways to rid its portfolio of sluggish performers and its magazines of "marginal [i.e., "downmarket"] readers" as well as creating new publications to tap younger, more affluent readerships (Granatstein 1999). An "Oprah magazine" was ideally suited to fulfill all of these goals. Aimed at women ages 18–49, it was "a carefully targeted effort to reach a readership beyond her largely middle-aged and middle-income TV audience" (Brook 2000). Oxygen likewise sought a demographic of 18- to 49-year-old "independent minded, high-achieving women" with programming "designed to fit in with their busy lives" ("Oprah gives TV girl power" 2000). It was especially keen to attract "the educated 35ish crowd," according to the *San Francisco Chronicle* (Rubin 2000). Laybourne touted Oxygen's fusion of "cable television's reach" and "the Internet's depth and flexibility" as a perfect vehicle to help women "fully utilize their tremendous economic power" (Cooper 1998).

From the beginning, then, O, *The Oprah Magazine* was conceived as a means to expand Winfrey's market reach. Publisher Alyce Alston said the magazine would deliver Winfrey an audience "both younger and more affluent than the one that watches her talk show." In exchange, as reported in the *New York Times,* "Hearst gets to use the Oprah Winfrey brand to sell magazines" (Kuczynski 2000b). A writer for the London *Independent* made a similar assessment: "The hope is not just to attract Ms. Winfrey's huge TV audience, but widen it with women who are younger and more affluent, many of whom don't watch Oprah because they are working" (Usborne 2000). Eight months after O's launch, *Newsweek's* Clemetson observed, "With articles on topics like women who rush too much, soul-searching interviews with celebrities like Sidney Poitier and flourishes like pull-out quotes from the likes of Winston Churchill and Deepak Chopra, O is reeling in a whole new breed of Oprah devotees: professionals with little time to watch her show" (Clemetson 2001, 40).

Before it even hit the stands, the magazine was integrated into Winfrey's media empire; it was promoted by Oxygen, which had launched in February 2000, and on *The Oprah Winfrey Show* and Oprah.com, where fans could subscribe online. In fact, of the million readers who had subscribed by O's fourth issue, 210,000 came in through the web site (Kuczynski 2000c). After O's launch, it was fully incorporated into Oprah.com, which also contained a link to Oxygen, including "Oprah Goes Online"—a Harpo-produced program featured on Oxygen's cable network and web site in which Winfrey and best friend Gayle King (designated O's "editor-at-large") learned to navigate the Internet. This cross-platform integration exemplifies what Harpo's Jeff Jacobs called its business plan to "multi-purpose our content" (Sellers 2002, 58). As Winfrey described the TV show–web site–magazine–Oxygen nexus: "One will promote the other" (Kuczynski 2000b).[7] Further, the combined enticements of Oprah.com (with links to the talk show, magazine, and book club), Oxygen's stable of women's sites, and the opportunity to master the Internet alongside Winfrey, were powerful incentives for her audience to spend more time in cyberspace. This, in turn, made Winfrey's audience commodity even more attractive, in that "online women" were "one of the most prized markets in the media industry," a "sort of holy grail to e-commerce aficionados" ("Oprah master class" 2000). As *Variety* commented, "If anyone is going to get women to use the internet, it's going to be Oprah" (Jones 2000).

The content of O obeyed the "multi-purposing" mandate. In line with Harpo's other ventures, Winfrey herself was the "core content." In addition to wielding a heavy hand in the magazine's design, editorial focus, and advertising policies, she adorned every cover, conducted the centerpiece interview, and penned the opening and closing columns ("Let's Talk" and "What I Know for Sure"). The magazine also cannibalized elements of Winfrey's program, web site, and book club. Her favorite quotations, which pepper her on-air conversations and show up on Oprah.com and in the online newsletter to which fans may subscribe, in *O* became perforated pull-outs. The "Oprah's Favorite Books" feature, complete with her favorite quotes from them, includes authors who have been book club picks or otherwise showcased on the program. Books highlighted in the inaugural issue, for example, were Marianne Williamson's *A Return to Love*, Maya Angelou's *I Know Why the Caged Bird Sings*, and *Seat of the Soul* by Gary Zukav. Other familiar faces from *The Oprah Winfrey Show*—Phil McGraw, Suze Orman, Marianne Williamson, and Bob Greene—were drafted as "contributing editors" and/or regular columnists for *O*. Additionally, the magazine included ads for Winfrey's show, book club, and web site. As a BBC writer observed, *O*, which was "heavy on motivational features" and "almost seems to be peddling a soft form of religion," was "definitely a vehicle to promote Winfrey, her world view and her business interests" (Brook 2000).

If *O, The Oprah Magazine* largely duplicated content found in Winfrey's other media platforms—the *Toronto Star* described it as "essentially The Oprah Winfrey Show on paper" ("Uh O!" 2000) and in many respects it resembled the ill-fated Change Your Life TV experiment—this deterred neither readers nor advertisers. Indeed, *O*'s economic performance seemed to defy industry logic. The inaugural issue ran 324 pages, 166 of which were advertising from the likes of Microsoft, Calvin Klein, L'Oreal, Toyota, Revlon, and Hewlett-Packard. So great was the demand that Hearst had to turn away advertisers for the first two issues (Brook 2000). Although the initial plan was to publish *O* every other month in 2005, it went monthly after only two issues, both of which sold out almost immediately "in an industry where obscenely successful magazines sell 50 percent of the copies offered on the newsstand" (Kuczynski 2000c). *USA Today* reported that "one in three who did pick up the inaugural issues decided to become subscribers. Magazine industry watchers say a 33% return is unheard of" (Wilson 2001).

After six issues, *O* had 1.6 million subscriptions and newsstand sales of 1.2 million. A Hearst executive noted that "by comparison, *Martha Stewart Living*, after almost 10 years, has 1.9 million subscribers" (ibid.). Further, those first half-dozen issues contained 905 pages of advertising with revenues of $50.9 million—an accomplishment that left Cathleen Black "absolutely ebullient." Launching *The Oprah Magazine*, she beamed, was "the highlight of my career in publishing. The success of *O* has been a thrill to anybody in magazine publishing today" (ibid.). Advertisers were equally thrilled. New York ad buyer Melissa Pordy said advertisers were "clamoring to be in the magazine" because Winfrey's followers were "so loyal and passionate." What made *O* an especially attractive buy was that it "allows a new audience to be touched by her," and, as Pordy noted, "everything she touches turns to gold" (ibid.).

Meanwhile, *The Oprah Winfrey Show* recaptured its top spot among talk shows in May 2000, aided by a plunge in Jerry Springer's ratings when he toned down his program in response to intensifying criticism (Schlosser 2000). Winfrey's "Midas touch" appeared to have returned, and she capitalized on the momentum with two new self-improvement projects in June 2000: the "Lifestyle Makeovers" series on *The Oprah Winfrey Show* and the first "Personal Growth Summit" tour to promote the new magazine. In late June, Winfrey traveled to 5,000-seat arenas in Detroit, Atlanta, Chicago, and Los Angeles, where attendees—"predominantly white, in their 30s and 40s, and female"—paid $20 to $30 to soak up her patented blend of inspirational quotes, uplifting anecdotes, and motivational prescriptions for self-transformation (Avins 2000). Although, according to a *Los Angeles Times* reporter, Winfrey had been "careful not to flog the magazine or the summit on her TV show" and Hearst's press release said Winfrey saw the tour simply as an "opportunity to practice the personal growth message that's at the magazine's core," the summits were clearly "events staged to garner publicity" (ibid.). Summit attendees filed in to music by Tina Turner and Patti Labelle on the PA system and found on their seats a canvas tote bag sporting the magazine's logo. Inside was a copy of *O* and a nightshirt emblazoned with its logo, a pen from Microsoft and brochure from Ford—both were sponsors of the tour—and a blank notebook in which to jot down Winfrey's words of wisdom. The first summit was so successful—tickets sold out in a few days—that Winfrey would take her personal growth tour on the road again in 2001, 2003, 2005, and 2006.

Lifestyle Makeovers—dubbed by Winfrey "our biggest makeover series ever"—had much in common with Change Your Life TV. It too featured regular episodes, included a team of "makeover experts" offering specific instructions on "how to make over your life from inside out," and closed with a "Remembering Your Spirit" segment.[8] In contrast to the controversial Change Your Life season, however, Lifestyle Makeovers provoked no viewer or press backlash, in part because Winfrey had learned to steer clear of explicitly religious or "New Age" declarations. This time around, for example, "Remembering Your Spirit" featured viewers' accounts of transformative experiences sans candles, prayer, or meditation. Winfrey's strategic partnerships with media giants also helped inoculate her against attacks in the press. Going after a figure whose show was back on top, whose magazine was being hailed as the most successful launch in history, whose business partners included ABC/Disney and Hearst, who had recently received the National Book Foundation's fiftieth anniversary award for her "contribution to books and reading" and made *Time's* list of the 100 most influential Americans of the twentieth century, might come off more as professional envy than legitimate media criticism.

O, The Oprah Magazine not only supplied the missing link in Winfrey's media empire, it vastly fortified the power of the Oprah brand. Alyce Alston pointed out that Hearst's market research showed "Oprah is one of the most trusted brand names, with extraordinary consumer reach" (Feeney 2000). As a *New York Times* reporter observed, the value of Brand Oprah lay in Winfrey's "ability to prompt an almost Pavlovian response in consumers" (Kuczynski 2000a). By the end of the

1990s, according to a report in the business magazine *Success*,[9] Winfrey's influence was "so entrenched, her credibility so unquestioned," that she was "way past merely rich and famous. She's more on the order of, oh, say, ubiquitous. Or peripatetic. Or mega" (Rebello 1998, 64). Her self-described mission had grown equally "mega." Whereas in her first makeover in the mid-1990s Winfrey's goal had been "to uplift, enlighten, encourage and entertain through the medium of television," by the close of the twentieth century it had become "to use television to transform people's lives, to make viewers see themselves differently and to bring happiness and a sense of fulfillment into every home" (Fitch 2000).

From that point—thanks to an "integrated media universe in which all roads lead to Oprah" (Hamilton 1999)—the brand seemed unstoppable. By 2003, when Ellen Rakieten became executive producer, *The Oprah Winfrey Show* was registering "double digit growth in all the key adult women categories" (Albiniak 2003b). Even more promising, the heaviest growth was among the 18–49 demographic and the number of less valuable 50-plus viewers was shrinking. The result of the show's "shift in demographic strength," according to King World executives, was "happier advertisers" (ibid.). Winfrey embarked on her seventeenth season in September 2003 with "the best opening week numbers [7.1 rating] since 1998," and her November sweeps rating was the highest since 1997 ("Oprah, Dr. Phil" 2003; Albiniak 2003a).

In August 2004, after her program had earned its best May sweeps rating in seven years and "its highest performance among key female demos since 1999," Winfrey announced plans to extend the show through the 2010–2011 season, which would mark its twenty-fifth year in syndication (Albiniak 2004). As reported in *Broadcasting and Cable*, the renewal was "great news for . . . stations that flow The Oprah Winfrey Show's massive audience right into their newscasts" (ibid.). Winfrey cast the decision as an opportunity to "grow along with my viewers" and "to use the show as a launching pad to create and develop additional projects" (ibid.). Not only did Winfrey's raw numbers continue to climb, but she was gaining ground among younger, wealthier viewers. In the past two years, both *The Oprah Winfrey Show* and *Dr. Phil* (launched by Harpo in 2002) had increased their share of the "demographic sweet spot"—women ages 18–34 with household incomes over $50,000—by 50 percent. Consequently, both programs were increasingly attractive venues for credit card, car, cosmetics, and cell phone advertisers intent on "chas[ing] after younger, more affluent viewers" (Downey 2004). *The Oprah Winfrey Show* was not just one among many jewels in the Harpo crown—it was the base from which the core content was generated to be multi-purposed elsewhere. Winfrey explained in an *Essence* interview that Stedman Graham had repeatedly urged her to hang onto the program because it was her "power base" (Edwards 2003). It was advice she took to heart. When asked by reporters in 2000 if she planned to forsake the talk show for her new ventures with Oxygen and Hearst, Winfrey replied: "No way. The Oprah Show is the mother lode" (Kuczynski 2000b). The result of Graham's economic reasoning was clear. As *Broadcasting and*

Cable observed, "Oprah is such a profitable enterprise that it rivals the cash flow of a small country" (Albiniak 2004).

By 2005, Brand Oprah appeared to be invincible and the trade press was running out of superlatives with which to describe Winfrey's enterprise. That May, Harpo announced that Oprah.com had "surpassed the 100 million page view milestone" in monthly web site traffic, a 37 percent jump over the previous high three months earlier, and leading online advertisers were flocking to the site ("Oprah.com crosses milestone" 2005). In the November sweeps, *The Oprah Winfrey Show* scored its highest ratings since 1996, the year Oprah's Book Club was born. The program "gave its stations No. 1 finishes among households in 90% of markets, women 18–49 in 97% of markets and women 25–54 in 96%" (Albiniak 2005). As King World's vice president of research stated, "The show just clean swept everything. Its numbers were so much higher than any of its competitors. The show defies all principles of television and the way things work in the television universe today" (ibid.). At that point, Winfrey's audience was "the biggest it has been in 11 years, after climbing steadily for the past three," and its advertising revenue of $208 million was up 16 percent over 2004 (Flamm 2005).

O, The Oprah Magazine was an equally formidable moneymaker. It "defied gravity." It was "outpacing the industry with double-digit growth in ad pages and revenues" and had generated a spinoff with *O at Home* and an annual hardbound compendium of *O* highlights (ibid.). The magazine's fifth-anniversary issue in May 2005 contained more than 200 ad pages, a 10 percent increase over 2004, and its revenues had grown by 15 percent over the past year to $207 million (ibid.). If the talk show was making gains in the younger upscale market, the magazine's performance on that front was stellar. As envisioned from its creation, *O* had "cultivated a considerably younger audience than the TV show," and 70 percent of its readership was employed (ibid.).[10]

Meanwhile, Winfrey's personal growth tour flourished. In its second year in 2001, with stops in Minneapolis, Baltimore, San Francisco, and Raleigh-Durham, the tour was openly sponsored by *The Oprah Magazine* and renamed "Live Your Best Life" after its motto, and expanded to a daylong "seminar." Ticket prices leapt to $185, which included breakfast, lunch, an *O* "goody bag," a solo presentation by Winfrey, and a "workshop" where she was joined by Cheryl Richardson, lead expert from the Lifestyle Makeovers series. Despite the price hike, tickets sold out in less than an hour, and scalpers got as much as $700 per ticket from desperate fans. For the third tour, in 2003 (Seattle, Tampa, St. Louis, and Philadelphia), Winfrey's web site promoted it as an event that "literally brings *O, The Oprah Magazine,* to life" ("Oprah hosts" 2003). This time around, the tour was "presented in association with" Dove, L'Oreal, Toyota, Bali, Dockers, HoMedics, Luna Bar, State Farm, and the Oxygen Network, and attendees were invited to visit a "sponsored interactive area with product samples and demonstrations" (ibid.). Winfrey's growth summits thus became another venue through which advertisers could reap the abundance of the Oprah brand, another way for Harpo and its corporate partners to capitalize on synergistic possibilities across platforms. That year the $185 tickets were snapped up in minutes, and many subsequently surfaced on eBay for up to $800 (Andersen 2003).

This marriage of self-improvement and commerce was fully institutionalized by the 2005 summit in Denver, Washington, D.C., and Dallas. At the first stop, the 5,000 Denver attendees spent some three hours trapped inside the city's convention center at a "trade show masquerading as a 'Personal Growth Center'" before being ushered to the theater for Winfrey's performance (Jefferson and Coffield 2005). Featured at the Growth Center were Toyota, Diet Rite, Maybelline, New Balance, HGTV, State Farm, Dove, HoMedics, and pharmaceutical giant GlaxoSmithKline, from whom *O* reaped "$1.5 million in exhibitor fees and a corollary 76 sponsor ad pages" (Bittar 2005). New Balance, which had introduced a new walking shoe the previous year via the magazine's "Hi Gorgeous" promotional tour, was delighted to participate in the Growth Center to debut its latest shoe model. As a New Balance marketing associate explained, the "local sell-through" on the new footgear had jumped 50 percent after the 2004 event (ibid.). This time, the $185 tickets were gone in minutes and showed up for resale on the Internet for as much as $1,000. When Denver's ABC-TV affiliate announced it had 110 pairs of tickets to sell, the station was flooded with 10,000 requests (Coffield 2005). Although many attendees complained to reporters about being a "captive audience" for *O*'s advertisers and deemed the event "too commercial," they were disinclined to blame Winfrey. "Maybe [the trade show] needed a little better direction," one fan said on leaving the event, "but overall it was worth it. I found God again" (Jefferson and Coffield 2005).

From Brand to Icon and Inspirational Phenomenon

Over the course of two decades, then, the erstwhile talk show queen had transformed herself into "such an incredible brand" she was practically "fail-proof" (Howard 2005). Winfrey had become a brand "four-and-a-half times more valuable than Madonna" (Moran 2002), a "magical pitchwoman" (Grossman 2006) capable of inspiring a "Pavlovian response in consumers" (Kuczynski 2000a). But this was a brand with a soul. Winfrey was not merely "the richest black woman on the planet" but "the ultimate communicator" who had come to teach "the adoring masses how to find their life's purpose" (Edwards 2003). Popular press coverage routinely oscillated between documenting the awesome economic performance of her "cultural and communications empire" ("On the cover" 2001) and paying homage to the putatively noneconomic motives of the "empress of empathy" at its center (Fottrell 2000). *Newsweek*'s 2001 "Age of Oprah" cover story, for example, painted Winfrey as guided by a "spiritual" quest, her show as an "on-air motivational crusade," and her success the result of having "fed people's desire to find meaning in life" (Clemetson 2001, 41). Yet the same issue also identified her as a "tycoon" and "millionaire magnate" perched atop a "multimedia empire" (ibid., 43, 42). Kathryn Lofton captures this duality with her apt description of Winfrey's project as "an ambiguous theism alongside an exuberant consumerism" (Lofton 2006, 616).

This unstable, contradictory union of commercial calculation and spiritualized altruism lies at the heart of the notion of "soul branding," which, as Trysh Travis notes, involves creating an image that evinces "an aura of positive feeling and receptivity" in consumers by addressing their "appetite for higher values" (Travis 2005, 6). A soul brand is especially potent when the values it invokes and projects obscure the economic imperatives behind it. Such is the case with Brand Oprah. Winfrey's repeated assertions that she is not a businesswoman, that she is driven by a "higher good," that each day she tries "to reach out and save other people" (Rebello 1998) and "bring happiness and a sense of fulfillment into every home" (Fitch 2000), constitute the "aura" of the Oprah brand. Because the brand's core content is Winfrey herself, or more accurately, the persona of "Oprah"—every facet of the enterprise must express, reproduce, and validate that aura; hence, the intensely repetitive quality of Winfrey's various endeavors. As David Usborne (2000) notes, "The Winfrey message has remained remarkably focused. To some it may seem preachy and cloying, but it surely has an audience."

Winfrey's fans are not unaware of this fact. An attendee at the Chicago stop of the first Personal Growth Summit remarked of Winfrey, "It's funny, because she basically says the same thing over and over. It's in her book; it's on her show. But when you see her, it makes you feel like you know her" (B. Smith 2000). This sense of personal relationship is precisely what "soul branding" is designed to achieve. Recurring encounters with the brand's essence at once solidify that feeling of familiarity and reinforce Winfrey's aura of "authenticity" through the coincidence of brand message and persona. Through the multipurposing of the core content, each platform helps cement fans' relationship with the brand, renewing the "aura of positive feeling and receptivity" that is central to the strategy of audience building, and thereby guaranteeing the future profitability of the multimedia empire. *Newsweek*'s cover story provides an example of such brand identification in Mary Madden, a 37-year-old suburban mother and homemaker from New York who "watches the talk show religiously," regularly logs on to Oprah.com, buys Oprah-endorsed books, and writes daily in her "gratitude journal." As Madden describes her relationship with Winfrey, "She's giving me the tools to find myself" (Clemetson 2001, 48).

Once again we encounter the centrality of the self in Winfrey's enterprise and the problem of how to think the connection of the citizen-self constituted through the activity of reading, the consumer-self targeted by the Oprah brand, and the spirit-self whose powers are unleashed through the techniques of self-help and mind cure. We might begin to tease out those connections and situate them in relation to the therapeutic ethos and the political-economic priorities of neoliberalism with the help of Nikolas Rose's notion of the "enterprising self." He proposes that neoliberalism is not only a rightward reconstruction of "macroeconomic policy, organizational culture, social welfare, and the responsibilities of citizens" but also a medium for cultivating an "enterprise culture" that "accorded a vital *political* value to a certain image of the human being" (Rose 1998, 150, 151). The concluding chapter explores the parallels between the enchanted, empowered self hailed by Winfrey's enterprise and the enterprising self through which neoliberalism seeks to govern.

CHAPTER

~ 8 ~

The Anxieties of the Enterprising Self and the Limits of Mind Cure in the Age of Oprah

A lot of people see my fame and wealth, but they don't realize that what created it all is a value system that operates in the principle of cause and effect: What you put out comes back. Do the emotional and spiritual work required to develop authentic power ... and you will always be rewarded.

—Oprah Winfrey ("What I know for sure," *O, The Oprah Magazine*, Jan. 2007)

[Winfrey] is the paradigmatic result of her prescriptions; it is her body, her business, her couture closet, her favorite novel, and her latest breakfast marmalade that stand as the ideal demonstrations of the successful enactment of her advice. The message is made manifest in each of her media modes: here's what to do, here's some safe testimony as to the utility of your newly chosen habit, here's where to go to get it done, and here are some smart products to assist and decorate your process of self-realization.

—Kathryn Lofton (2006, 607)

Versions of the same hope are held out: you can change, you can achieve self-mastery, you can control your own destiny, you can truly be autonomous.

—Nikolas Rose (1998, 158)

Oprah Winfrey rang in the 2007 new year from South Africa with the star-studded launch of the Oprah Winfrey Leadership Academy for Girls, a $40 million boarding school located an hour south of Johannesburg on "52 lush acres and spread over 28 buildings" (Samuels 2007). Outfitted in a pink taffeta ball gown, she presided over the opening ceremony alongside the academy's first class of 152 adolescent girls from "deprived backgrounds"—all personally selected because they possessed what she called the "it" quality ("Oprah Winfrey opens school" 2007; "Building a dream" 2007).[1] In addition to providing the girls with state-of-the-art facilities and top-flight instructors, Winfrey plans to teach "leadership" classes by satellite from Chicago and occasionally in person. The most important lesson she hopes to instill in her charges: "that we are responsible for ourselves, that you create your own reality by the way you think and therefore act." As Winfrey stated in her magazine's feature story on the school, she wants the academy students to recognize "you cannot blame apartheid, your parents, your circumstances, because you are not your circumstances. You are your possibilities. If you know that, you can do anything" (Gien 2007, 160, 217).[2]

A month after the school's opening, Winfrey was back in Chicago sharing her excitement about *The Secret*—a DVD and book promising the key to attaining health, wealth, and happiness (*Oprah Winfrey Show*, Feb. 7, 2007). The brainchild of Australian reality TV producer Rhonda Byrne, *The Secret* had been gathering momentum since its March 2006 release, thanks to a "viral marketing" campaign targeting the Internet, New Age bookstores, and New Thought churches (Mastropolo 2006). By year's end it had been featured on *Larry King Live* and *The Ellen Degeneres Show* and the DVD ranked in Amazon's Christmas week top five sellers (Ressner 2006). Given its compatibility with her own mind-cure leanings, it was only a matter of time before *The Secret* caught Winfrey's attention; on February 7, she introduced Byrne and fellow "teachers of 'The Secret'" who, she told the audience, "say you can have it all. And, in fact, you already hold the power to make that happen."

In the opening segment, Byrne revealed "the secret" to be the "law of attraction," described as "the most powerful law in the universe," comparable to the law of gravity, which governs our existence because "we attract into our lives the things that we want ... based on what we're thinking and feeling" (*Oprah Winfrey Show*, Feb. 7, 2007; Salkin 2007). Winfrey found this to be neither a secret nor a revelation, but merely confirmation of what she had long professed. "So what you're saying," she told Byrne, "is that we all ... create our own circumstances by the choices that we make and the choices that we make are fueled by our thoughts. So our thoughts are the most powerful things that we have here on Earth." For Winfrey, the coincidence of nature's laws with her commitment to the power of mind was felicitous. "This is a happy, happy day for me," she beamed. "I've known 'The Secret'—I didn't call it 'The Secret'—for years. And for years on this show, this is what I've been trying to do, is to get people to see it." Just as the Leadership Academy students cannot blame society for their situation, those who embrace the law of attraction must also accept responsibility for their fate. As Winfrey told her audience, "It means that everything that happens to you, good and bad, you are attracting to yourself. It's something that I really have believed in for years, that the energy you put out into the world is always gonna be coming back to you. That's the basic principle" (*Oprah Winfrey Show*, Feb. 7, 2007).[3]

During the show, the various "teachers" counseled the audience to overcome "the tendency to believe in lack, limitation and scarcity" because it stands in the way of the "absolutely unlimited power within us." While a few directives were served up—it is important to "be grateful," for example, to be "conscious" rather than "unconscious" and seek "alignment" of one's thoughts and actions—for the most part *The Secret* boiled down to "the primacy of simple 'wish fulfillment'," or, as the DVD instructs, "Ask, believe, receive" (Starker 1988, 39; Salkin 2007). If the "law of attraction"—like the power of positive thinking of the 1950s and the nineteenth-century mind-cure cosmology that spawned them both—ultimately amounts to the "fulfilled wish and how to achieve it" (Starker 1988, 39), this did not appear to discourage Winfrey's followers. So great was the audience response to *The Secret* that it nearly overwhelmed the Oprah.com web site, which routinely receives 64 million hits per month, persuading Winfrey to add a second installment. In the follow-up show, she was heartened to find that the "law of attraction" had "sort of reached mass appeal" because

> It's what this show is all about, and has been about for 21 years, taking responsibility for your life, knowing that every choice that you've made has led you to where you are right now. Well, the good news is that everybody has the power, no matter where you are in your life, to start changing it today. (*Oprah Winfrey Show*, Feb. 16, 2007)

Uniting these seemingly disparate events—the opening of a school in Africa and the marketing of another "think and grow rich" scheme—is the heady concoction of makeover and magnanimity that defines Oprah Winfrey's technology of healing. Reviewing the premiere issue of *O, The Oprah Magazine*, Richard Roeper quotes a statement by Winfrey featured in an ad for her first Personal Growth Summit—"You only have to believe that you can succeed, that you can be whatever your heart desires, be willing to work for it, and you can have it"—to which he responds:

> Only if you live in Tinkerbell's world. In the real world, of course, there are millions upon millions of people who have tried the believe-desire-work portion of that equation and yet will NEVER have what they want. They will experience an entire life arc without escaping from poverty or despair, without ever finding love or happiness or wealth of material things and-or spirit. (Roeper 2000)

While Roeper is correct about the vast disparity between wish and reality for the large majority of human beings, this has in no way diminished the attraction of Winfrey's "ask, believe, receive" technology of healing or the configuration of self on which it depends. How, then, might we account for the appeal of the notion that the properly formulated wish can become reality?

Anthropologist Maurice Godelier says we should not seek explanations for the power of ideas within the ideas themselves, but look for them instead in "the social relations between humans beings and between human beings and nature" (Godelier 1986, 146). As he argues, "Ideas never contain in themselves all the reasons for their influence and their historical role. Thought alone can never produce those reasons, for this influence derives not simply from what they *are*, but from what they *do*, or better still, from what they *get done* in society" (ibid.). The dominance of an idea in any particular historical moment issues from its "capacity to explain the order or disorder reigning in society" and thereby "facilitate effective action upon the problems connected with the maintenance of this order or with the abolition of this disorder" (ibid.). Making sense of the appeal of mind cure—whether in the present or the past—therefore involves understanding what it gets done. What problems does this technology of healing purport to resolve, for whom is that promised resolution seductive, and why? Such questions lead us back to the historical conditions that have generated "thought as power" (Satter 1999, 7) cosmologies and endowed them with explanatory power.

The decades straddling the turn of the twentieth century, when New Thought took root and flourished, and those leading to the twenty-first, when it enjoyed a broad resurgence, were marked by extensive political-economic change. If the first period witnessed the passage of American capitalism from a "proprietary competitive" to a "corporate industrial" stage (Sklar 1988), whereas the second saw the displacement of Keynesianism by neoliberalism, both were characterized by a centralization and concentration of capital accumulation, escalating economic inequality, and struggle and realignment within and between classes. Importantly, both phases of political-economic restructuring brought growth and expanded opportunities to that sector of the middle class variously called the "professional managerial class" (Ehrenreich and Ehrenreich 1979; Pfeil 1990), "service savants" (Sklar 1988), the "service class" (Lash and Urry 1987), the "upper middle class" (Gilbert 2002), and "new petty/petite bourgeoisie" (Poulantzas 1975; Bourdieu 1984). Situated between labor and capital in the social division of labor and positioned on the mental side of the mental/material divide, this class stratum performs a dual function of reproducing the political relations of power between the capitalist and working classes and reproducing capitalist culture (Ehrenreich and Ehrenreich 1979, 12; Poulantzas 1975, 227–228).

Associated with fields such as law, education, business, science and engineering, medicine, social services, and the media, the professional managerial/new petty bourgeois class fraction strives to maintain and advance its own social power through the valorization of higher education, specialized knowledge, credentialing processes, and so on. Prominent ideological features of this class stratum include its competitive individualism, which reflects the relatively isolated nature of most professional labor, and its affinity for the idea of meritocracy, issuing from a combined fear of slipping down into proletarian territory and longing to ascend to the heights of the bourgeoisie. The professional managerial class is particularly captivated by notions of social promotion and upward social mobility—this it shares with the traditional petty bourgeoisie of small-business owners and artisans—but is even more devoted than the latter to the idea of higher education as the principal means by which to advance. The professional managerial stratum tends to support certain democratic principles, such as the expansion of participation in decision-making and equal opportunities for promotion, but, along with its traditional petty bourgeois counterpart, it is less disposed toward radical structural transformation. That the petty bourgeoisie is more inclined toward "rearranging" the existing political-economic order than challenging its foundations or calling for its replacement, Nicos Poulantzas (1975) argues, "can be summed up by saying that it does not want to break the ladders by which it imagines it can climb" (292).

Not coincidentally, it is predominantly from this professional managerial class fraction that sprang Progressive-era reformers, women's movement leaders, specialists associated with the psychological disciplines, and a majority of the founders, teachers, and followers of the New Thought and mind-cure movements. From the 1890s through the early twentieth century, Beryl Satter notes, "scores of prominent white middle class reformers came to believe that New Thought meditations, as well as hypnotism, telepathy, and other forms of psychic power, were important new tools that could help elevate society" (Satter 1999, 181). Emerging in conditions of sweeping social change, the New Thought movement spoke to its target audience of native-born, urban middle-class Americans about their vital role in a modernizing society, invoked social Darwinism to justify their duty to lead and manage the working class, and reinforced their inclination to view their privileges as the natural result of their own merit, rather than the fruits of an unjust, exploitive system. Given these class origins, the self-help literature associated with New Thought was "a literature of affluence" that "evinced a primary concern with issues of personal expression and growth" rather than focusing on "social evils or needed reforms" (Starker 1988, 39). Indeed, one of the most significant ideological practices of mind cure lay in its ability to fashion itself as a form of liberation as it engaged in constructing a modern self exquisitely attuned to the unfolding corporate capitalist order and accompanying culture of consumption. By promoting a configuration of self that conflated individual freedom, success, and the "accumulation of goods and capital," mind-cure cosmology constituted a powerful means of controlling the very social class to whom it most strongly appealed (Cushman 1995, 132–133).

The unraveling of the Keynesian compromise in the late twentieth century also commenced amid economic crisis, when the shift to a peacetime economy, international oil crisis, and worldwide recession brought to an end the post–World War II boom and launched a new period of stagnant growth, high inflation, deindustrialization, high taxes, rising unemployment, and decline of organized labor. These conditions eroded support for Great Society programs and exacerbated divisions and polarization between "haves" and "have nots," creating an opening for the "divide-and-conquer/unite-and-mobilize" strategies deployed by Reaganism (Reeves and Campbell 1994, 157). Bill Clinton's New Liberalism may have invoked the rhetoric of "empowerment" and "community," but its economic priorities and ideological strategies—rewarding those at the top; shrinking the state; exploiting racial divisions around issues of welfare, crime, and affirmative action to attract white voters; paying homage to "traditional values"—echoed those of its Republican predecessors.[4]

An outstanding feature of the neoliberal era has been the collapse of job security in the United States since the mid-1980s, as "the permanent separation of people from their jobs, abruptly and against their wishes, gradually became standard management practice" (Uchitelle 2006, ix). As Louis Uchitelle documents in *The Disposable American* (2006), between 1984 and 2004, "at least 30 million fulltime workers" were laid off—a figure that does not include "millions more who had been forced into early retirement or had suffered some other form of disguised layoff" (5).[5] By the late 1990s, mass layoffs had become "normal practice, ingrained behavior, just as job security had been twenty-five years earlier" (6). The institutionalization of "flexible" employment and "income volatility" has been central to the transfer of money upward and insecurity downward that has characterized the "new economy" (Henwood 2007; Hacker 2006). Economic uncertainty has been exacerbated by the steady deterioration of the minimum wage after the 1970s, an expanding low-wage workforce that exerts downward pressure on wages at all levels, and proliferating temporary work and low-paying, low-skill jobs (Uchitelle 2006, 143–144, 66–67).[6] Further, although the U.S. economy has grown by 60 percent since the end of the 1970s, that has not translated into a corresponding increase in "good jobs"—ones that pay a decent wage and offer health insurance and a pension plan. In fact, since 1980 "the economy has lost 25 to 30 percent of its capacity to generate good jobs," so that only a quarter of the workforce has such employment today (Schmitt 2005). A crucial consequence of these combined developments, Uchitelle argues, is "a massive shift from a shared, we're-in-it-together way of thinking to a go-it-alone world of personal responsibility" (Uchitelle 2006, x).

Significantly, this period also witnessed a resurgence of what Wade Clark Roof terms "alternative spiritualities," including New Thought and other metaphysical traditions (Roof 1999, 90). Because the New Thought movement from the outset placed "greater emphasis on personal happiness, growth and self-fulfillment," it had always been inclined to "take a positive stance toward economic prosperity and align it with moral and religious practice focused to a great degree on personal interests" (38). As had been true in the previous century, in the 1980s and beyond, mind-cure cosmologies found a hospitable audience among "the educated middle classes," who are also the chief target and constituency of the expanding "spirituality industry" (ibid.), of which Oprah Winfrey's enterprise is a prime example.[7] In contrast to religious traditions that have consoled those at the bottom of society with promises of rewards in the next life, New Thought and its offshoots have attracted the educated middle and upper-middle classes because they "offered peace of mind and emotional tranquility to those already on the way up" (Quebedeaux 1982, quoted in Roof 1999, 140).

Neoliberal restructuring, in contrast, has offered this class stratum economic insecurity and personal anxiety. Corporate downsizing, the expansion of contingent labor, cutbacks in the public sector, and the outsourcing of jobs have had major ramifications for the college-educated middle class, which represents some 30 percent of the U.S. population and is a key target of the Oprah brand (Uchitelle 2006, 66). Whereas a high school education at one time sufficed for most jobs in the United States, by the late 1990s a college degree (or two) had become mandatory for those hoping to secure a spot on the higher rungs of the employment hierarchy. As layoffs spread across white-collar fields and invaded "once-sacrosanct occupations" (ibid., 151), the professional managerial class was simultaneously regaled with promises of the exciting high-tech workplace of the future and warned to beef up its human capital or risk becoming losers in the "new economy." Even as it became imperative to accrue the education and skills necessary to join the ranks of the "symbolic analysts" or "knowledge workers" (see Reich 1991), the downsizing of federal and state governments since the early 1980s had driven the cost of higher education beyond many Americans' reach.[8] Significant numbers of the professional middle-class cadre were also discovering they had more skills than their jobs demanded as the number of college graduates outpaced that of jobs requiring a degree (Uchitelle 2006, 66). At the same time, the professional managerial ranks were undergoing further stratification into an "haute expertoisie" (e.g., partners in major corporate law and accounting firms) at the top, followed by "small business people," the "lesser specialists in technical support, education and human services," and, at the bottom, an "apprentice class" of "graduate students, research assistants, interns and the like" (Brint 1994, 206).

From the 1980s on, then, as a limited subset of occupations and the education and credentials necessary to attain them were becoming the "key to prosperity in an increasingly polarized economy," competition for these scarce species of cultural capital grew increasingly fierce (P. Smith 1997, 245). In the face of this "intensified system of reward and punishment," economic anxiety marched "up the social ladder" (Henwood 2006, 1). Paeans to the "new economy" notwithstanding, real economic growth under neoliberalism has lagged well behind the growth of the rate of returns to capital, a disparity made possible through a "massive upward redistribution of income" (Baker 2007, 4; "Growth bypasses all but wealthiest" 2006).[9] Having reduced government's function to facilitating this upward transfer of wealth, while thwarting its ability to provide infrastructural support for collective life, neoliberal restructuring has left us to stand alone before the rigid indifference of the market. Meanwhile, neoliberal ideology asserts the absolute determinism of natural economic laws while insisting we are also absolutely free to create our own destinies.

This is the context in which Oprah Winfrey has attained the status of inspirational phenomenon and ubiquitous soul brand. Her enterprise can be understood as an ensemble of ideological practices that help legitimize a world of growing inequality and shrinking possibilities by promoting and embodying a configuration of self compatible with that world. Proclaiming individuals' ability to become whatever their minds can conjure, Winfrey appeals to the upscale, middle-class "sweet spot" that is the prime real estate of her target market by tapping into and flattering its petty bourgeois values. At the same time, by instructing the lower ranks of her following to adopt those values as their own, citing her own success as proof the prescription works, and scorning anyone who refuses it, her "personal responsibility" nostrum helps bind "broader social strata to the growing prosperity of the few, really or fictitiously" (Dumenil and Levy 2002, 45). That is, the ideological practice of Winfrey's enterprise prescribes and universalizes the values of the petty bourgeoisie—which is mind cure's original architect, strongest advocate, and principal beneficiary, the core target of the Oprah brand, and the ideological home of Winfrey herself.[10]

That ideological labor was readily displayed in Winfrey's Leadership Academy project and in her promotion of *The Secret*. Although the launch of her namesake school won the international media attention such spectacles are designed to elicit, it was not entirely of the laudatory tenor Winfrey expected. Indeed, she quickly found herself having to justify spending $40 million on a sumptuous, exclusive[11] school for a few hundred girls in a country with one of the highest unemployment rates in the world (36–42 percent), where some 45 percent of the population lives on less than $2 a day, nearly 20 percent of those aged fifteen and older are infected with HIV/AIDS, and the average life expectancy is forty-seven years (Kingdon and Knight 2005; World Bank Group 2006; Population Reference Bureau 2006; United Nations Development Programme 2007).[12] The *Boston Globe* reported that the school was under attack from international aid groups in the United States and "leaders of grass-roots organizations" in Africa. Critics reproached Winfrey for spending "so much for so few," for failing to ask local communities to identify their own development needs, and for fostering an "atmosphere of privilege" that divides the school's students from their communities (Donnelly 2007). By way of contrast to Winfrey's multimillion-dollar investment, for $80,000 the Catholic AIDS Action program provided meals, school uniforms, and after-school programs for 1,500 orphans and vulnerable children in northeast South Africa in 2006; and the Rwanda Women Community Development Network, with an annual budget of $300,000, supported forty grass-roots groups that care for 50,000 orphans (ibid.). The South African government, whose own adoption of neoliberal economic policies led to levying fees for school attendance that has put basic education beyond reach for millions of poor children (Hjort and Ramadiro 2004; see also Bond 2004; Ngonyama 2007), initially planned to partner with Winfrey in building the school but got cold feet amid mounting criticism of the facility's opulence. As a government school official told *Newsweek*, albeit anonymously to avoid offending Winfrey, "The country is obviously poor, and so few children have a chance at education. It is hard not to see that many feel that what Ms. Winfrey is doing is too much" (Samuels 2007).

Winfrey's response to the criticism was reminiscent of her reaction to condemnations of Change Your Life TV—a combination of dismissal and defensive explanation. At the school's January launch, where reporters questioned her about the project's "excesses"—among its amenities are a yoga studio, a beauty parlor, two theaters, "fireplaces in every building and white duvets for each bed"—Winfrey conceded that "many" in South Africa "feel that I'm going overboard," but added, "This is what I want to do" (Donnelly 2007). In a statement prepared for the *Boston Globe*, she described the school as "a symbol of leadership for all of Africa" and defended the price tag: "I wanted these girls to have the best—the best campus, the best curriculum, and of course, the best opportunities" (Statement 2007). In fact, Winfrey oversaw every aspect of the school's design and construction, down to personally selecting the bedding, dishes, even the doorknobs. So too with the girls' clothing and shoes. As presented in her magazine and prime-time special, "Building a Dream," the school is akin to a grand makeover project that extends to the students themselves, who are to be transformed first into Winfrey's "dream girls" and then into South Africa's future "leaders" through her largesse. Or, more to the point, the girls are to become replications of their patron, who compared looking at their faces to "looking into the face of myself" and who decided to spare no expense in creating "everything in this school that I would have wanted for myself" (Gien 2007, 158, 156). Providing beautiful surroundings for the academy's students, Winfrey insisted to critics, would not only "bring out the beauty" of the fortunate few she would groom for leadership but also inspire "girls and boys all over Africa" ("Statement from Oprah Winfrey" 2007).

Interestingly, Winfrey's justification of her lavish investment in poor children in South Africa has been coupled with her critique of poor children in the United States. In a *Newsweek* interview, for example, Winfrey said she chose to build her school in South Africa rather than in impoverished U.S. communities because American youth fail to value the educational opportunities they have. She continued,

> I became so frustrated with visiting inner-city schools that I just stopped going. The sense that you need to learn just isn't there. If you ask the kids what they want or need they will say an iPod or some sneakers. In South Africa, they don't ask for money or toys. They ask for uniforms so they can go to school. (Samuels 2007)

She also portrayed the Leadership Academy as a corrective to previous mistaken efforts to help poor Americans. In her "What I Know For Sure" column in the January 2007 issue of *O, The Oprah Magazine*, Winfrey wrote of her decision to halt a "mentorship program for teenage girls living in the [Chicago] Cabrini-Green housing projects" because "I was able to work with them only once a week, which wasn't enough time to instill values in girls whose upbringing wasn't aligned with my teaching." Ditto for her "misguided idea of moving families out of the projects and into new homes." As Winfrey put it, "Trying to show people how to build successful lives was overwhelming—I had taken for granted that they understood what it means to go to work, be on time, and make sure their children go to school and do their homework. So I failed with that idea, but I learned something invaluable: In order to make meaningful changes, you have to transform the way people think" (Winfrey 2007, 218; also Edmonds 2006).

Winfrey displayed similar sentiments in April 2006, when she devoted two episodes of her show to "the disastrous consequences of America's failing high school
education system" (two-part Oprah's Special Report, 2006). Days later, in Baltimore
to deliver the keynote address at a fundraiser for a private school, she called that city's
public school system "an atrocity" and "a crime to the children" ("Oprah sounds off"
2006). Although many of said children also hailed from "deprived backgrounds,"
they did not warrant Winfrey's support. As she told a local broadcaster, who asked
if she planned to give money to Baltimore public schools, "What I've learned from
my philanthropic giving is that unless you can create sustainable change, then it's a
waste, you might as well pee on it" (ibid.; also Rodricks 2006). The implication of
this uncharacteristically crude response is that Baltimore's schools are beyond hope,
a waste of good money. Unspoken, but also implied, is that the students themselves
are incapable of "sustainable change"—and hence unworthy of resources—because
the desire to learn "just isn't there."[13]

This reduction of material structural constraints to personal deficiencies also
figured in her show's handling of *The Secret*. In the second installment, for example,
Clarissa, a young single parent in the studio audience, described being summarily fired
from her job and worrying about her toddler's future, to which Winfrey remarked,
"any time you get fired, you should say thank you," because "it obviously means you're
not supposed to be there" (*Oprah Winfrey Show*, Feb. 16, 2007). Clarissa was featured
because her story validated Winfrey's mind-cure message. Although she had initially
been very angry with her boss, Clarissa explained that watching the previous week's
"Secret" episode made her realize the problem "wasn't him, it was me. He was right.
I was negative. It wasn't his fault." Winfrey affirmed this diagnosis and invited the
young mother to read the letter she had since written her former boss, in which she
thanked him for firing her and credited *The Oprah Winfrey Show* for supplying her
with "key words" such as "forgiveness and gratitude." Significantly, Clarissa framed
her loss of employment as freedom to go back to school, thus demonstrating her fitness for induction into the ranks of the educated middle class. Indeed, so well did
her tale of personal responsibility illustrate the principles of *The Secret*—and of petty
bourgeois values—that it was saved for the episode's closing segment.

As neoliberal restructuring has eroded public buffers against the vagaries of the
market and undermined the "structure of solidarity" on which the welfare state was
based, autonomous individuals like Clarissa must fend for themselves in a Hobbesian
universe, armed only with their entrepreneurial spirit and positive thoughts (Van Der
Pijl 2006, 28). In such a milieu of scarcity and competition, Kees Van Der Pijl argues,
the "only aspiration meaningfully entertained is that of individual improvement, placing each and every citizen in the position where he or she must ask, 'How will I achieve
this? What are my chances?'" (ibid., 30). Here we find the link between the "enchanted
self" exalted by Winfrey and the "enterprising self" championed by neoliberalism. The
former takes responsibility for her life and creates her own circumstances by thinking

positive thoughts and making good choices. The latter "makes an enterprise of its life, seeks to maximize its own human capital, projects itself a future, and shapes itself in order to become what it wishes to be" (Rose 1998, 154).

The appeal of the enchanted/enterprising self—which simultaneously accounts for and naturalizes social inequality—is intimately bound up with the fortunes of Winfrey's upscale target audience faced with the demands of the neoliberal order. It reassures the "haves" (i.e., the "symbolic analysts" residing in the professional mana-gerial sector of the middle class) that any benefits they have reaped from the "new economy" result from their positive attitudes and behavior, while absolving them of responsibility for the plight of their less affluent fellows. Conversely, as Nikolas Rose observes, the "have nots" can be "problematized in terms of their lack of enterprise, which epitomizes their weaknesses and their failings" (Rose 1998, 154). And because those weaknesses are posited as entirely self-induced, such irresponsible individuals deserve neither public assistance nor private empathy. Winfrey's brand of mind cure also acknowledges and tries to assuage the economic anxieties of her petty bour-geois followers in this "new gilded age" by promising to help them finesse the brute facticity of market logic so as to avert failure and secure abundance (Uchitelle 2007, 1).[14] Her multiple media outlets are filled with special techniques for harnessing the mind's natural powers, providing an edge to those struggling for a foothold in the professional/managerial ranks. Through this conflation of material and spiritual abundance, Winfrey's mind-cure mission not only supports, it helps sanctify the mu-tually reinforcing ideas of a self-ordering market and a self-interested human nature. Indeed, Kathryn Lofton writes that Winfrey's media products "serve as paradigmatic profiles in the spiritual practice of capitalism" (Lofton 2006, 599).

Fredric Jameson argues that the "power of a mass cultural artifact" resides in its "twin capacity to perform an urgent ideological function at the same time that it provides the vehicle for the investment of a desperate Utopian fantasy" (Hardt and Weeks 2000, 145). The "ideological function" of Winfrey's "ask-believe-receive" cosmology consists in positing a natural economic order operating independently of human intervention, while also insisting that individuals are absolutely free, hence absolutely responsible for whatever exigencies the market throws their way. This contradiction becomes the basis upon which Winfrey's enterprise summons powerful "utopian fantasies." At one moment, she holds out the possibility of evading both the absolute determination of the market and the absolute responsibility of the individual by means of the magnanimous intervention of a divine/charismatic figure (the persona of Oprah) who will make one's "wildest dreams" come true. At another, she offers the key to discovering and harnessing the laws that drive individual behavior (i.e., the "law of attraction") so as to engage in a makeover to bring oneself into accord with the market's own laws (the endless instruction dispensed by Brand Oprah). At the same time, both fantasies disclose subterranean longings to transcend both the absolute power of the market and the absolutely free individual—which condemn us to atomism and solitary struggle for survival—and thereby restore social connectedness.

This "management of desire" constitutes the ideological work of mass cultural forms, which must represent "social and political anxieties and fantasies" in order to manage them with "imaginary resolutions" that preserve the "optical illusion of social harmony" (ibid., 138). Winfrey's empowerment project, like mind-cure cosmologies generally, offers a vision of social harmony composed of millions of separate, self-interested individuals busily accumulating social capital and thinking their way to health, wealth, and happiness so as to "live their best lives." Such "enterprising" individuals are at once ideal neoliberal subjects adapting their lives to market logic and ideal targets of the Oprah brand's fusion of "inner awakening with capitalist pragmatism" (Lofton 2006, 599). In her study of self-help culture, Micki McGee (2005) identifies in Winfrey's "Lifestyle Makeover" series a "labor of displacement" that turns "women's shortage of time and money" into a purely personal issue independent of "social, political, and economic realities" (107). Citing the series' use of the term *revolutionary*, McGee argues that the "work of avoiding politics" is achieved "by adopting the notion of revolution to the most depoliticized possibilities: revolution is alive and well just as long as it's a revolution from within that stays within: as long as it's a revolution of the spirit, or a plea for help" (ibid.). As I have argued throughout this book, recourse to the "most depoliticized possibilities" is one of the most reliable ideological moves in Winfrey's repertoire. Rather than conceiving this simply as a way of avoiding politics, I propose that it epitomizes the neoliberal project, in that neoliberalism's defining political practice is precisely that of depoliticization.

One way to understand the past three decades, according to Anthony Russo, is as an "exhaustion of previous visions of politics and a paramount de-politicization" arising from a crisis in the multiparty systems of Western democratic states (Russo 2006, 675). Such political systems are premised on parties representing specific constituencies and engaging in interparty rivalry, which fosters wider public debate and democratic participation. With the globalization of the neoliberal political-economic order, Wang Hui contends, the "character and representative nature" of parties in the United States and Europe have become "increasingly muddled" and their values "increasingly indeterminate within a broad macro-economic consensus" (Wang 2006a, 32). In such a scenario, "real democratic politics disappears" and the party system is "transformed from a kind of public sphere into an apparatus for ensuring national stability" (ibid.). This process of depoliticization constitutes a "crisis in party politics" reflecting a broader "crisis of democracy in the world today" (Wang 2006b, 686).

In the United States, that crisis has materialized in the erosion of meaningful philosophical and policy differences between and within the Republican and Democratic parties. Since the late 1970s, both parties have been eager to identify government as the cause and the market as the solution to nearly every societal problem. Both have embraced the idea of the "spontaneously self-ordering market" and view its "unlimited expansion" into all spheres of social existence as "an apolitical, 'natural' process" (Wang 2006a, 38). The ideology of the self-driven market has a particularly strong depoliticizing effect because it encourages people to see themselves as individual consumers rather than as interdependent citizens, which pulls the political process itself into the logic of the market. And, as political parties increasingly rely on marketing techniques and branding strategies to disguise the diminishing differences between their actual policies, they have helped undermine the public's "ability to engage in deep political reflection" (Wang 2006b, 690).

Winfrey's endorsement of Barack Obama is of a piece with this depoliticizing impulse. Noting that she does not consider herself political, Winfrey interviewed the newly elected Illinois senator for her magazine in 2004 precisely because he represented for her "something beyond and above politics" ("Oprah's cut" 2004). Two years later she told Larry King she would stump for Obama if he sought the presidency because "he says all the things I would want to say for this country" if "I were ever gonna run myself." Those "things" were upbeat, vague, and apolitical—much like her own mission—as she cited his "sense of hope and optimism for this country and what is possible for the United States" and "commitment and concern for the rest of the nation" (Fornek 2006).[15] It is hard not to observe certain commonalities between the pair. Like Winfrey, Obama has been described as having "transcended race" and has attracted white support in part by keeping a measured distance from black activism and political critique associated with the civil rights movement (Klein 2006; Beinart 2007; Hart 2007; Mac Farquhar 2007; Silverstein 2007). *Chicago Sun-Times* columnist Laura Washington noted approvingly that Obama had followed Winfrey's example in becoming "the first African-American [presidential] contender with serious crossover appeal." She credited the senator's rejection of "race appeals" that "turn off voters," the fact that he hails neither from "the South, or the ghetto," that he "didn't march" for civil rights, and that he attended "Hah-vaard" as key in overcoming the deficiencies of the "black political establishment" and winning the backing of the "black bourgeoisie" and "white liberal wealth" (Washington 2006). Writing in *The Nation*, Patricia Williams (2007) described the "Double O's" as "an arresting team [and] brilliant speakers, easy with large audiences" whose "particular form of raced celebrity enshrines the notion of American mobility."

What is striking about much of the popular press coverage of Obama is the emphasis on style over substance. Detailed examination of political issues and policy proposals take a back seat to considerations of the candidate's "charisma," "eloquence," and "mesmerizing ability to connect with people," exhibiting a degree of fawning found in much of the media treatment of Winfrey (Sirota 2006, 21; see also Street 2007; Klein 2006; Beinart 2007). It is this lack of substance that characterizes depoliticized politics. *Harper's* and the *Nation* in 2006 asked writers to put some flesh on this skeleton and find out why and how a candidate who routinely declares himself a "progressive" was igniting passionate fans across the political spectrum (Mac Farquhar

2007). Both reporters concluded that operating inside a party that had been moving to the right for a quarter-century, and in a political system that "has become thoroughly dominated by the corporate perspective" (Silverstein 2006), Barack Obama had learned to master "the art of the possible within the system" (Sirota 2006, 22) by honing a "remarkable ability to convince you that his positions are motivated purely by principles, not tactical considerations," even as he was "fighting only for those changes that fit within the existing boundaries of what's considered mainstream Washington" (ibid., 23). As corporate money has grown central to electoral success in the 1980s and 1990s, politicians of both major parties have learned well how to dance to the tune of those who foot their massive campaign bills. One lobbyist confided anonymously to *Harper's* that "big donors would not be helping out Obama if they didn't see him as a 'player'" (Silverstein 2006, 11).

Proving oneself a valuable player to big donors is a quality Obama shares with a chief rival in the presidential race: Hillary Rodham Clinton (Sirota 2006; Silverstein 2006; Hart 2007; Reed 2007). Like her husband, Clinton is an archetypical New Liberal, part of the Democratic Leadership Council's leadership team, and chair of its "American Dream Initiative," which is devoted to strengthening the middle class, "the core of America's greatness" (Clinton 2006). Though not a card-carrying member of the DLC, Obama was on its list of "rising new stars" and "Democrats to watch" in 2003; he is mentioned in some twenty articles on the organization's web site (www.dlc.org); and he energetically supported former DLC-chair Senator Joseph Lieberman's independent race against Ned Lamont, the 2006 Democratic primary winner. His chief economic adviser, Austan Goolsbee, was named the senior economist for the DLC and its think tank, the Progressive Policy Institute, and both men "favor achieving Democratic goals through market-oriented policies" (Leonhardt 2007; "Austan Goolsbee joins" 2006). As David Leonhardt (2008) observes in the *New York Times,* Obama and Clinton "occupy roughly the same place on the ideological spectrum" as "middle-of-the-road Democrats." Resemblances are evident even to Winfrey, who made it clear to Larry King that supporting Obama "does not mean that I am against Hillary.... I have not one negative thing to say about Hillary Clinton" (Daunt 2007). As David Sirota concluded in his piece for the *Nation,* "Beltway publications and think tanks have heaped praise on Obama and want him to run for President ... because he has shown a rare ability to mix charisma and deference to the establishment" (Sirota 2006, 23). Oprah Winfrey commands this same combination of attributes, which may be why she has showered not only praise but also her considerable influence and wealth on the man she calls "my favorite guy" (Bellandi 2007). Whether, the "Oprah effect" extends to influencing the outcome of a presidential race remains to be seen, but there are already signs of backlash from her audience. Having fashioned herself as apart from and above partisan politics in general and the politics of race in particular, Winfrey's decision to endorse a black Democrat has generated fissures in her following. After she appeared with Obama in Iowa and South Carolina, fans lashed out on the Oprah.com message boards, many of them charging Winfrey with being racist and vowing to stop watching her program (e.g., "Stop the tour with Obama" 2007; also Mastony 2007).

The retreat of representative political organizations and public spaces within which to engage fellow citizens that characterizes the triumph of neoliberalism has reinforced people's sense of vanishing social solidarity in the face of a "go-it-alone world of personal responsibility" (Uchitelle 2006, x). Oprah Winfrey has risen to fame and fortune in an era marked by sustained political and ideological struggles to replace structures of social solidarity with that "go-it-alone world," the result of which has been a relentless advance of economic inequality. A conspicuous beneficiary of that campaign, she has played an important role in promoting, validating, and exporting it through her extensive media empire. Thus, during an era when people's actual power over their lives has declined while the power of capital has expanded, Winfrey ascended to the position of cultural icon of mainstream America by telling us we can do anything we put our minds to.

As structures of solidarity wither, Van Der Pijl (2006) argues, "Religion gravitates back to centre-stage as a consolation prize" (28). I propose that mind-cure cosmologies, like that on which Winfrey stakes her claim as modern-day prophet, can be understood as one such consolation. The ideological power of Winfrey's enterprise issues from the antithetical demands of the two central premises of bourgeois thought: the absolute freedom of the individual, and the total determination of human existence by the inhuman laws of the market. Her mind-cure project responds to those irreconcilable premises by simultaneously spiritualizing the existing political-economic order and promising her followers the "secret" to being exempted from its heartlessness. While her enormous wealth attests to the appeal of that message, the fact that it must be ceaselessly repeated across myriad platforms and settings also betrays ideological fissures, some of which surfaced in the wave of criticism surrounding her Leadership Academy and her endorsement of *The Secret* (e.g., Birkenhead 2007; Donnelly 2007; Langley 2007; Robinson 2007; Samuels 2007; Bornstein 2007; Deggans 2007; Dowd 2007; McGee 2007).[16] That is, Winfrey says "the same thing over and over" precisely because the symbolic resolutions offered by mind-cure technologies of healing cannot resolve in reality the determinate social conditions to which they are a particular response.

It is through the affirmation of the enchanted enterprising self and the celebration of consumption that neoliberalism, mind-cure cosmologies, and Oprah Winfrey's enterprise have exerted their depoliticizing power. The outcome of that process is neither finished nor guaranteed, however. As Fredric Jameson points out, for popular cultural artifacts to carry out their ideological work, they must present, if only in distorted or indirect ways, "our deepest fantasies about the nature of social life, both as we live it now and as we feel in our bones it ought rather to be lived" (Hardt and Weeks 2000, 146). It is here that we might begin to counter the depoliticizing thrust of the privatized, psychologized Age of Oprah, with its fetishization of personal responsibility, fatuous recipes for aesthetic self-invention, and abandonment of any notion of public responsibility. Perhaps a first step toward a process of repoliticization—which would aim to reinvigorate political values, reactivate political spaces, and revive political discussion and debate—is with two assertions: first, that while the economic order does indeed exert objective determinations upon human activities and relations, it is itself the product of those actions and relations, and hence open to being humanly changed; and second, that contrary to what Winfrey "knows for sure," we are all responsible for each other.

Oprah Winfrey Show *Episodes Cited*

September 26, 1986 "Women: Life in the '80s"
October 3, 1986 "Runaway Mothers"
October 29, 1986 "Adult Children of Alcoholics"
November 17, 1986 "Pros and Cons of Welfare"
December 2, 1986 "Women Who Love Too Much"
December 3, 1986 "Homeless People"
January 14, 1987 "Male Chauvinism"
June 12, 1987 "Obsessive Love"
July 17, 1987 "How Mom's Working Affects the Kids"
September 7, 1987 "Unemployment"
October 12, 1987 "America's Poor"
March 14, 1988 "Old-fashioned Women"
January 4, 1989 "How to Leave a Dependent Spouse"
March 22, 1989 "Three Generations of Underclass"
June 20, 1990 "Self-help Addicts"
June 20, 1990 Special: "In the Name of Self-esteem"
September 5, 1990 "Childhood Wounds Seminar"
March 13, 1991 "Child Victims of Crime"
April 17, 1991 "Codependency Conspiracy"
June 18, 1991 "Angry Taxpayers/Angry Tenants: The Public Housing
    Controversy"
January 23, 1992 "How to Cope in Bad Economic Times"
February 4, 1992 "My Life Is Driving Me Crazy"
June 24, 1992 "Understanding 'A Return to Love'"
November 20, 1992 "Set Free to Kill Again"
September 29, 1993 "Five Sisters with 500 Grudges"
January 14, 1994 "Moral Dilemmas: What Would You Do?"
January 19, 1994 "I Kicked Welfare, You Can Too"
February 15, 1994 "Random Acts of Kindness"
April 6, 1994 "The Power of Prayer"
April 22, 1994 "Love Letters to Your Parents"

July 6, 1994 "There Are Angels Around Us"
August 17, 1994 "How to Live Your Dreams"
August 22, 1994 "Only Good News"
September 12, 1994 "Are Talk Shows Bad? Part 1"
September 13, 1994 "Are Talk Shows Bad? Part 2"
September 19, 1994 "Thank You Day"
October 3, 1994 "Violent Children: Detroit, Part 1"
October 4, 1994 "Violent Children: Detroit, Part 2"
December 14, 1994 "Marianne Williamson"
April 11, 1995 "Is Affirmative Action Outdated?"
April 19, 1995 "Should Welfare Pay for Her Kids?"
October 18, 1996 "Newborn Quintuplets Come Home"
January 22, 1997 "Debbie Reynolds and Albert Brooks"
February 28, 1997 "'3rd Rock from the Sun'"
April 8, 1997 "Selena's Family"
May 9, 1997 "Salute to Mothers"
September 22, 1997 "Oprah's Book Club Anniversary Party"
October 17, 1997 "Should You Let Your Daughter Diet?"
October 27, 1997 "Oprah's Book Club Goes to Louisiana"
September 8, 1998 "Season Premiere"
September 9, 1998 "John Gray"
September 10, 1998 "Suze Orman"
September 11, 1998 "Iyanla"
September 16, 1998 "Personal Success with John Gray"
September 23, 1998 "Personal Success with John Gray"
October 7, 1998 "Personal Success with John Gray"
October 13, 1998 "Finding Your Authentic Self"
December 13, 1998 "Angel Network Kindness Chain"
April 23, 1999 "Letters to Gary Zukav"
September 18, 2000 "Lifestyle Makeovers: The Energy of Money"
October 30, 2000 "Lifestyle Makeovers: What Do You Need to Surrender?"
September 26, 2001 "What Really Matters Now?"
September 27, 2001 "Americans Take Action"
June 22, 2004 "Bill Clinton and Oprah: The Interview"
April 21, 2006 "Class in America"
February 7, 2007 "'The Secret'"
February 16, 2007 "One Week Later: The Huge Reaction to 'The Secret'"

Notes

Notes to Preface

1. As described in the *Times*, the eleven-part series, which ran from May 15 to June 12, 2005, examines "the role of social class in America today. A team of reporters spent more than a year exploring ways that class—defined as a combination of income, education, wealth and occupation—influences destiny in a society that likes to think of itself as a land of unbounded opportunity" (Scott and Leonhardt 2005).

2. All figures are taken from Mediamark 2003.

Note to Chapter 1

1. In both appearances, Winfrey said her intention was to get behind the "wall" of sound bites to "reveal the real man" so her viewers could determine "who feels like the right candidate" ("Vice President Al Gore," *Oprah Winfrey Show*, Sept. 11, 2000; "Presidential Candidate George W. Bush," *Oprah Winfrey Show*, Sept. 19, 2000).

Notes to Chapter 2

1. Donahue billed his program as the talk show "for women who think" (Katz 1996b).

2. A sampling of scholarly works on talk shows that address their therapeutic dimensions includes Shattuc (1997), Cloud (1998), Dovey (2000), Gamson (1998), Masciarotte (1991), Lowney (1999), Abt and Mustazza (1997), Andersen (1995), Epstein and Steinberg (1998), and Illouz (2003). An assessment of these programs from the perspective of the psychology profession is found in Heaton and Wilson (1995).

3. White (1992) argues that television in general is permeated with "therapeutic discourse" (34) in forms as diverse as religious programming, home shopping channels, and prime-time entertainment. Reeves and Campbell (1994) propose that journalism has incorporated a therapeutic perspective in its coverage of social problems. Cloud (1998) contends that therapeutic rhetoric has become a predominant contemporary means of framing and managing a broad range of public issues, including labor strife, international relations, and race and gender inequality. Carlone (2001) considers the incorporation of therapeutic assumptions and strategies by business management

theory for purposes of increasing worker productivity. And self-help literature, long a staple of American life and now one of the fastest growing arms of the publishing industry, is founded on therapeutic premises with its prescriptions for dealing with problems ranging from physical health to relationships to work difficulties (Starker 1988; Simonds 1992; Grodin, 1995).

4. Various strands of what came to be termed "mass society" theory, for example, have their roots in this period, including Emile Durkheim's account of individual "anomie" as a product of the transition from a "mechanical" to "organic" form of social organization, Ferdinand Tonnies's lament over the dissolution of gemeinschaft (community) into gesellschaft (society), and Max Weber's critique of rationalization and the development of the "iron cage" of bureaucracy.

5. According to Scull, psychiatry's legitimacy rested on its embrace of an organic definition of mental disturbance. Locating the cause of emotional distress in physical pathology brought psychiatry into line with the "reigning models of the somatic machine that characterize the medical mainstream" and served as the basis of "psychiatrists' jurisdiction over the insane, their expertise as medical specialists, and popular acceptance (however grudging) of that expertise" (Scull 1989, 22).

6. The mental hygienist movement was itself an outgrowth of the medical establishment's incorporation of elements of mind cure by means of the Emmanuel movement (Caplan 1998, 146–148).

7. Second-wave feminists such as Betty Friedan (1963), Kate Millett (1970), and Phyllis Chesler (1972) also launched attacks on Freud's view of women, with the latter exploring in detail "how Freud focused on negative traits produced by the male oppression of women, such as helplessness and self-destructiveness, and then attributed them to the inherent nature of women" (Breggin 1991, 340). Rachel Hare-Mustin reiterated this critique of Freudian theory for privileging male development and designating women as biologically inferior (Hare-Mustin 1983, 594). And Jeffrey Masson's *Freud: The Assault on Truth* (1984), which met with virulent opposition from the psychoanalytic establishment, outlined how Freud denied his own clinical findings of extensive sexual abuse of young women and girls—and thus betrayed his own patients—to win professional acceptance.

8. This growth of the recovery movement continued into the 1990s. Jones (1990, 16) claims that in 1990, 15 million Americans were attending 500,000 recovery groups, while Rapping contends that by 1996, there were at least 500 different AA-style fellowships (Rapping 1996, 67).

9. The ascendance of this new phase of "biopsychiatry" was significantly aided by the creation of a growing arsenal of drugs designed to treat an ever-expanding range of newly labeled mental diseases and disorders. Two of the most publicized of these drugs—both introduced in the 1980s—were the antidepressant Prozac (manufactured by Eli Lilly) and the psychostimulant Ritalin (produced by Ciba-Geigy). The phenomenal growth of prescriptions for these drugs attests to the mental health industry's success in defining people's suffering in strictly organic terms. Thanks to the friendly relationship between Eli Lilly and then–Vice President Dan Quayle, the Federal Drug Administration's approval process for Prozac was shortened by several years and the drug went on the market in January 1988 (Breggin 1991, 181). By 1994, one million prescriptions per month were being written for the antidepressant—the majority for women (ibid., 3). The use of psychostimulants on children (primarily boys) to treat the "disorder" of "hyperactivity" also escalated in the 1980s and 1990s. In the late 1980s it was

estimated that 500,000 to one million school children were taking Ritalin (Breggin 1991, 304) and the National Institute of Mental Health suggested that one in ten boys in the United States were afflicted with some form of hyperactive disorder (ibid.). Both drugs became prominent weapons in the campaign to counteract behaviors purportedly caused by the "dysfunctional family," and both were topics on *The Oprah Winfrey Show* in the late 1980s and early 1990s. The long-standing partnership between the state and the mental health industry proceeded apace as President George H. W. Bush signed a congressional resolution in 1990 declaring it the first year of the "Decade of the Brain." Twelve years later, George W. Bush established the New Freedom Commission on Mental Health to conduct a "comprehensive study of the United States mental health delivery system" (Lenzer 2004). In 2003 the commission issued its recommendations, calling for "comprehensive mental health screening" of the entire U.S. population, starting with public school children, which would be linked to "state-of-the-art treatments" using "specific medications for specific conditions" (ibid.). Among those state-of-the-art medications is Zyprexa, an antipsychotic manufactured by Eli Lilly and the company's top-selling drug, with 70 percent of its sales paid for by government agencies such as Medicare and Medicaid. It is perhaps no coincidence that George Bush Sr. was a member of Lilly's board of directors, that Bush Jr. appointed the pharmaceutical giant's chief executive officer to the Homeland Security Council, or that in 2000, Lilly "made $1.6 million in political contributions, 82 percent of which went to Bush and the Republican Party" (ibid.).

Notes to Chapter 3

1. In Henwood's estimation, Carter's support for "military expansion, balanced budgets, and lowered expectations" makes him "something of a proto-DLC figure," referring to the Democratic Leadership Council's agenda to move the Democratic Party to the right (Henwood 1997, 162). Bill Clinton was an early member of the DLC and served as its chair in 1990–1991.

2. The Reagan administration created "the largest sustained peacetime [military] buildup in U.S. history." Between 1980 and 1985, military spending increased 39 percent and the national defense budget grew 53 percent (Ferguson and Rogers 1986, 124).

3. William Rusher anticipated this alliance in his 1975 book, *The Making of the New Majority Party*, wherein he argued that the United States was best conceived as divided between "producers" and "nonproducers." In the former category, Ehrenreich notes, he placed "blue-collar people who make things, plus the capitalists who generously and thoughtfully pay them to do so." In the latter were grouped the poor and a "New Class" of professionals (Ehrenreich 1989, 165–166).

Notes to Chapter 4

1. Winfrey's descriptions are taken directly from *Women Who Love Too Much*.

2. Faludi (1991) documents the battle fought and lost by female American Psychological Association members to prevent this "disorder" from being included in the *DSM*.

3. Di Leonardo (1999) explores and critiques this fetishization of "women's culture."

4. Helen Deutsch, a student of Freud, was one of the first psychotherapists to label women as masochistic, narcissistic, and passive by nature (see Caplan 1985, 18).

Notes to Chapter 5

1. During the February program, Winfrey distributed 1,000 copies of Williamson's book to the studio audience.

2. My thanks to Rick Angell, who was raised in the Christian Science tradition, for his insights into how adherents of the mind-cure varieties of religious belief view their relationship to the material world.

3. James Nolan also notes the conflation of therapeutic and political discourse in the 1992 presidential race: "The therapeutic rhetoric employed by Clinton and other candidates in the 1992 debates points to a fundamental change in the nature of political discourse" (Nolan 1998, 275).

4. According to Rick Perlstein, the DLC's think tank was "built on the model of the Heritage Foundation," and DLC director Al From and its president, Will Marshall, even "consulted Heritage's director, Ed Feulner, for advice" (Perlstein 2005, 6).

5. Early neoliberal Democrats in Congress included Gephardt, Wirth, Gore, Paul Tsongas, Bill Bradley, Dukakis, and Gary Hart, and Governors Dick Lamm (CO), James Hunt (NC), Bruce Babbitt (AZ), and Jerry Brown (CA).

6. Timothy Brennan proposes that 1975 to 1980 constituted a "transitional moment" in U.S. political history "best characterized as the fusing of right and left positions" that is most evident in their shared visions of "the state as an arena of innate corruption to which no claims for redress can or should be made" (Brennan 2006, ix). Both major parties thereby adopted "the neoliberal doctrine defining freedom as freedom from the state" (ibid., 11).

7. Putnam's thesis has come under considerable scrutiny and critique. For examples, see Samuelson 1996; Levi 1996; Fine 2001.

8. Clinton's economic vision and loyalties were clear. Two years into his first term, the *New York Times* observed that Clinton had "done more for the Fortune 500 than virtually any other President in this century" by "making trade the No. 1 priority," pushing through the North American Free Trade Agreement "over the objections of labor," and opening economic relations with Vietnam (Sanger 1995).

9. Putnam was invited to meet with the president at Camp David in late 1994; Clinton incorporated Putnam's ideas in the 1995 State of the Union Address; Putnam was among several people Clinton consulted prior to the 1996 Democratic National Convention regarding his nomination acceptance speech and campaign platform; and Putnam is cited specifically in Clinton's 1996 platform, which was published as *Between Hope and History: Meeting America's Challenges for the 21st Century* (Clinton 1996b, 115–116).

10. During Clinton's tenure, Arkansas's composite "green index," which assessed air and water quality, energy use, toxic waste risks, environmentally related health indicators, and state environmental spending and regulatory policies, was ranked forty-eight among the fifty states (Henwood 1997, 164, 174).

11. DLC executive director Al From rewrote a section of the speech at Clinton's request (Baer 2000, 237–238).

Notes to Chapter 6

1. Although this episode gave the appearance of a spontaneous response to Clinton's speech, it was clearly a planned event, in that the panelists would have been notified and invited in advance of the previous evening's broadcast press conference.

2. For an early vivid example of hostility toward social welfare linked to race, see Perlstein (2001, 130–133).

3. According to Reed (1999d, 180), the term "underclass" had been around since 1980 but "caught fire in popular and academic circles after Ken Auletta canonized it" in his 1982 book, *The Underclass.*

4. Davis (2002) notes the failure of the Reagan-Bush "war on drugs," which "imposed crushing costs upon cities" and whose chief effect, according to a *Los Angeles Times* editorial, was to "devastate minority communities without significantly impairing narcotics distribution" (250).

5. Star Parker was indeed touting welfare reform at the behest of the Republican Party and would become a featured speaker at the GOP's 1996 convention. She subsequently joined Project 21, a black conservative organization funded by the right-wing National Center for Public Policy Research (Parker 1999).

6. Dellamarie was correct. As Bartlett and Steele note in *America: Who Really Pays the Taxes* (1992), 73 percent of federal taxes in the 1990s were collected from individuals, compared to 15 percent collected from corporations. In the 1940s those shares were 43 percent and 33 percent, and in the 1960s, 57 percent and 27 percent (140; cited in Collins and Yeskel 2000, 101).

7. Winfrey also hosted a special program titled *In the Name of Self-Esteem,* which aired on ABC on June 20, 1990.

8. The $22,000 annual income in 1996 of the single mother deemed FBL's most notable "success story" was slightly less than the 1997 median annual earnings of $22,378 among black women. This figure should be compared to the 1997 median incomes of white women ($25,726), black men ($26,844), and white men ($35,741), which reflects the existence of structural income inequities based on gender and race (Costello and Stone 2001, 274).

9. According to Brown, a key reason behind the end of Families for a Better Life was that the "program's managers were found to have used nearly all the money for personnel and administrative budget expenses, a public relations fiasco Winfrey could not abide" (Brown 2002, 244).

10. Chris Rock, who was described in a *Vanity Fair* profile as someone who has "sometimes been labeled a voice of young black conservatism," has, like Toni Morrison, labeled Clinton "the first black president" (Brown 2002, 239).

11. Democratic liberals referred to the DLC in its early stages as the "southern white boy caucus." Jesse Jackson called the DLC leadership "Dixiecrats" and "Mason-Dixoncrats" (Baer 2000, 82, 185).

12. In fact, Clinton appeared in Macomb County on March 12, 1992—two days after Super Tuesday. To an audience of white "Reagan Democrats," Clinton talked about "middle-class effort and middle-class values" (Greenberg 1996a, 219). In contrast, at a black church in Detroit the following day, his theme was "responsibility." Clinton "warned his listeners not to be 'misled by politicians who come here asking for your votes and pretending that we can do something for you if you don't do things for yourselves,'" and he said his promise was "a chance to give you the opportunity to assume responsibility that every American should assume for his or her own life" (ibid., 222).

13. Despite the racial coding attached to welfare, black civil rights organizations have "consistently fought for universal social policies that would benefit all poor Americans" in conjunction with a campaign to end racial discrimination (Manza 2000; Hamilton and Hamilton 1997; Brown 1999).

14. Winfrey's association with Williams dates to the late 1980s when he and Graham were coworkers and friends at the African American–owned public relations firm B&C Associates of North Carolina. Williams handled the PR account of the Oprah Winfrey Charitable Giving Foundation and also managed publicity for Maya Angelou, who became a fast friend of Winfrey. In 1991 Graham and Williams launched their own public relations company, the Graham Williams Group. Thanks to Williams's political connections, the firm quickly acquired "an array of well-paying corporate clients," along with Angelou, who moved her account to the duo's new venture (Curry 2005). Although Graham would eventually sell his share of the firm and open his own public relations outfit in Chicago, he continued to be involved in political activities with Williams. In 1996 the two attended a "power dinner" aboard the yacht of unsuccessful Republican presidential candidate Steve Forbes; among the other guests were former British prime minister Margaret Thatcher, Senator Strom Thurmond, former Reagan defense secretary Casper Weinberger, and Ed Feulner, president of the Heritage Foundation ("Names and faces" 1996, C3). In 2003 the Graham Williams Group sponsored a "soiree" to honor the George W. Bush administration's black appointees—a gathering timed to coincide with and counter the Congressional Black Caucus Foundation's annual convention, which, Williams told the *Washington Times*, would be "a 'bash Bush' event." The *Times* identified "Oprah Winfrey boyfriend Stedman Graham" as Williams's partner (S. Miller 2003). Although Winfrey does not publicize her relationship with Williams—Mair suggests she is cautious about revealing her conservative views because it might "alienate many of her black and liberal white fans" (Mair 1994/1998, 180)—he has been a guest on her program, joined Winfrey and Graham for the 1998 New York premiere of her film *Beloved* (which he praised lavishly in his column), and his personal papers collection at the University of South Carolina contains two photographs "inscribed to Williams by Oprah Winfrey" (Williams 2005; Williams 1998; Armstrong Williams papers 2001).

15. Armstrong Williams owes his rise to the self-described status of "multimedia wonder" to his two "mentors": the late Senator Strom Thurmond, for whom Williams worked after college as a staff aide, and Clarence Thomas, whom he served as "confidential assistant" when Thomas headed the Equal Employment Opportunity Commission under Reagan (Williams 2005). Williams made his debut as a "media personality" in 1991 during the Clarence Thomas/Anita Hill hearings. As "chief architect of Thomas' media strategy," his columns defending his boss

and attacking Hill appeared in newspapers across the nation (Armstrong Williams papers 2001; Williams 2005). In his syndicated radio and TV programs (*The Right Side with Armstrong Williams*), his syndicated newspaper column, his commentator slot on the American Black Forum cable program, and his regular appearances on FOX, CNN, MSNBC, BET, and NPR, Williams extols the "virtues of the right wing of the Republican Party" and sings the praises of the free market, "Christian living," and "individual accountability" (Mitchell 2005; O'Brien 2005). With equal vigor, he denounces the black civil rights establishment, the welfare state, affirmative action, and blacks who "focus on victimization and 'blame whitey'" (Mair 1994/1998 121).

16. Williams's practice may be at odds with what he preaches. In 1997, Stephen Lee Gregory, a former employee of Graham Williams Group, filed a $200,000 sexual harassment suit against Williams and the firm. Two years later, Gregory, Williams, and Stedman Graham signed a consent decree to dismiss the case "with prejudice," which suggests the matter was settled out of court ("Case Against Armstrong Williams" 1999; Byrne 2005). In 2004 Williams made national news when it was revealed he received $240,000 from the U.S. Department of Education to promote President Bush's No Child Left Behind law on his TV program and in his syndicated column. Williams publicly conceded he had "exercised bad judgment" but refused to return the money, saying it "would be ludicrous because they bought advertising and they got it." Following the revelations of Williams's wrongdoing, his syndicator, Tribune Media Services, summarily cancelled his column. Black Entertainment Television and "America's Black Forum" also cut ties with Williams (Mitchell 2005; Hamburger 2005; Lewis 2005).

17. Winfrey was the 1993 recipient of the annual Horatio Alger Award ("Oprah Winfrey to receive the Horatio Alger Award" 1993).

18. Zinn (1990) makes a parallel argument about the economic basis of urban poverty and its effect on black families in the 1980s (371–375).

19. Examples of conservative guest experts featured on Winfrey's program are blacks Juan Williams, Armstrong Williams, Stanley Crouch, Larry Elder, Na'im Akbar, and John Williams, and whites Frederick Lynch and Lawrence Mead.

20. This intersection of race and class—and the role of the latter in fostering division—is seen in a Pew Research Center survey that found 37 percent of African American respondents agreed that "blacks today can no longer be thought of as a single race" because of a growing divide between middle-class and poor blacks (Pew Research Center 2007). The inclination to interpret this divide largely in terms of the need for improvement of the values, ethics, and behavior of poor African Americans is illustrated in a *New York Times* op-ed piece by Henry Louis Gates, Jr. (Gates 2007a).

Notes to Chapter 7

1. Winfrey terminated her book club six months after a much-publicized confrontation when Jonathan Franzen had expressed ambivalence about his novel, *The Corrections*, being chosen as an "Oprah book." Winfrey subsequently dropped his book and withdrew his invitation to appear on her show. Some analysts have suggested Winfrey's decision to halt the club was a response to the Franzen affair. As Kathleen Rooney writes, "Owing in no

small part to this highly publicized challenge [by Franzen] to her cultural authority, Winfrey seemed to have come to the conclusion that the club was just no longer worth it if it meant being exposed to such derision" (2005, 171).

2. Gary Zukav, a Harvard graduate and former Green Beret who served in Vietnam, is the co-founder (with his "spiritual partner" Linda Francis) of Genesis: The Foundation of the Universal Human, which offers retreats and programs. He teaches that "'authentic power' comes from humanity's evolution from five-sensory beings into multisensory beings aligned with the 'mother ship' of their souls." Zukav also borrows from Hinduism's concepts of karma and reincarnation (Taylor 2002).

3. Iyanla Vanzant identifies herself as a "priestess" of the Yoruba religion, which originates in West Africa and is based on nature workshop and ancestor reverence. The religion, brought to the Americas by African slaves, took hold in Brazil and Cuba. Vanzant is also founder of Inner Visions Worldwide (Taylor 2002).

4. Inaugural areas of Oprah.com included *The Oprah Winfrey Show*, Be On the Show, Oprah's Book Club, Oprah's Angel Network, Oprah's Health and Fitness, Remembering Your Spirit, Pix and Clips (of "choice moments" of the show), and Computer School, where novices could become computer and Internet literate.

5. Paul Allen of Microsoft would later become a partner in Oxygen.

6. By 2002, Winfrey was less enthusiastic about Oxygen, which was struggling to find an audience. In particular she regretted handing over the rights to reruns of her program, which, she stated in a *Fortune* interview in April 2002, was "not just a commodity.... It's my soul, it's who I am" (Sellers 2002, 61). Later that year, she made a deal to reclaim those rerun rights in exchange for providing Oxygen with a primetime series, *Oprah After the Show*, which features Winfrey chatting with her studio audience for thirty minutes following the taping of her talk show. Laybourne touted the new program as a way for "women who work during the day" to "be able to see Oprah in primetime" (Moss 2002).

7. Because of Winfrey's financial interest in Oxygen, Hearst lost out on the chance to link the magazine to the cable site (Women.com) and cable network (Lifetime) in which it owned interest. Black said Hearst was "happy to give up the advantages of cooperating with its own television and Internet operations because of the power of Oprah's appeal" (Rose 2000, B1).

8. Besides lead expert Cheryl Richardson, whose book *Take Time for Your Life* was the inspiration for the Lifestyle Makeovers season, other featured experts in the series were Debbie Ford, author of *The Dark Side of the Light Chasers*, who instructed viewers on how to uncover their "shadow beliefs," and Suze Orman, who once again helped Winfrey's audience understand how "self-worth determines [one's] net worth" (*Oprah Winfrey Show*, Sept. 18, 2000).

9. As stated in its web site, *Success* is "The only business magazine designed to inspire and guide motivated business people to lead truly successful lives" (About Success 2007).

10. According to market research data from 2003, 70 percent of *O* readers were 18–49, compared to 50 percent of *Oprah Winfrey Show* viewers. Some 70 percent of the magazine's audience was employed (full and/or part-time) and 68 percent had attended or graduate college, while the corresponding numbers for the show's audience were 50 percent in both categories (Mediamark 2003).

Notes to Chapter 8

1. In attendance were a roster of A-list celebrities and members of what *Essence* magazine called "Black royalty," including Nelson Mandela, who had suggested to Winfrey that she donate money to support education in South Africa; his wife, Graca Machel; Winfrey's father, Vernon; Sidney Poitier; Cicely Tyson; Quincy Jones; Andrew Young; Spike Lee; Tina Turner; and Chris Rock (Taylor and Burns 2007).

2. Winfrey also plans to build a house for herself on the campus so as to be involved in the students' lives (Gien 2007, 217).

3. The effect of Winfrey's endorsement was predictable. As McGee notes, weekly sales of *The Secret* went "from 18,000 to 101,000 copies in the week after the first *Oprah* show endorsing the book and to a staggering 190,000 copies the week after the second program aired" (McGee 2007, 5). By late August the book had been atop the *New York Times* best-seller list for thirty-one weeks ("Advice, how-to" 2007).

4. The parallels between Reaganism and Clintonism are well documented. See Meeropol 1998; Klinkner 1999; Schell 1999; Miroff 2000; Diane Harvey 2000; Pollin 2000; Roediger 2002; and Perlstein 2005.

5. Taking into account both groups, a more realistic estimate would find 7 to 8 percent of full-time U.S. workers "had been laid off annually on average" from 1984 to 2004 (Uchitelle 2006, 5).

6. According to Uchitelle, 70 percent of the "ten occupations expected to grow the fastest" in 2002–2012 pay less than $13.25 an hour (Uchitelle 2006, 67).

7. Like their Progressive-era New Thought forbearers, contemporary adherents of mind cure tend to envision their spiritual practices of self-healing as a means of resolving social and environmental problems. Monica Emerich explores this dynamic in her study of "healthy living media," which target an elite market with the message that "one can heal the self as a way to heal the world, through commodified practices on the mind, body and spirit" (Emerich 2006, iii).

8. By 2005, the average income of college graduates was 48 percent higher than for those with a high school diploma, and those with postgraduate degrees earned 59 to 72 percent more than high school graduates. These percentages are calculated from data on "earnings by education" supplied in the *New York Times Magazine*, which states its source as the U.S. Census Bureau (Tough 2007, 54). According to Lowenstein (2007), "only about a third of the [U.S.] population graduates from college" (14).

9. Since 1980 the overall growth in GDP (gross domestic product) has averaged 3.1 percent a year, compared to a 3.7 percent annual growth rate in the years from 1945 to 1980. In the period from 1980 to 2005, the richest 5 percent of U.S. families saw their share of national income grow by more than 33 percent while the share of the poorest fifth of Americans decreased by more than 25 percent (Baker 2007, 4). Further examples of that widening gap are provided by *New York Times* columnist Bob Herbert: "Chief executives at California's largest 100 companies took home a collective $1.1 billion in 2004, an increase of nearly 20 percent over the previous year," versus "the 2.9 percent raise that the average California worker saw last year." Thanks to the tax cuts under George W. Bush, "the 400 taxpayers with the highest incomes—a minimum of $87 million in 2000, the last year for which the government will release such data—now pay

income, Medicare and Social Security taxes amounting to virtually the same percentage of their incomes as people making $50,000 to $75,000. Those earning more than $10 million a year now pay a lesser share of their income in these taxes than those making $100,000 to $200,000" (Herbert 2005d). The Economic Policy Institute reported that despite gains in productivity since 2000, wages for most people had been flat or falling, with the fruits of the growth "increasingly flowing to the top" ("Growth bypasses all but wealthiest" 2006).

10. In his study of Winfrey's genealogy, Henry Louis Gates, Jr., discovered that a decade after the end of slavery, her great-grandfather Constantine Winfrey had bartered cotton he picked on his own time for 80 acres of Mississippi farmland (Gates 2007a, 2007b). The impulse toward proprietorship was thus well established in her family's history. Although popular media accounts of Winfrey typically focus on her early childhood living in poverty in rural Mississippi under the care of her maternal grandmother, she spent a substantial portion of her youth—from age fourteen to twenty-two—living with her father and stepmother in a lower-middle-class area of Nashville. There she was schooled in traditional petty bourgeois values of self-discipline and hard work by her father, who owned a barber shop, and her stepmother, a strict churchgoing woman who made Winfrey read and report on ten books a month and dress and behave like "a lady." Mair writes that in Winfrey's "own assessment, if she hadn't moved back with her father and stepmother, today she would be a poor, unwed mother, just another failed statistic on the urban landscape" (Mair 1994/1998, 24). Both parents also insisted she earn top grades to be eligible for college (ibid., 27). Despite her vast wealth, Winfrey has retained a petty bourgeois orientation. Like her father, she started her own business to be her own boss. She runs Harpo with a high degree of personal involvement in every aspect of its extensive holdings and refuses to take the company public because it would mean relinquishing that control (Sellers 2002). Throughout its history, *The Oprah Winfrey Show* has regularly aired episodes featuring individuals who have realized their dreams and/or built their fortune by starting their own businesses. Winfrey's vision of herself as a self-made woman, her view of education and entrepreneurship as the chief gateways to success, and her insistence that upward mobility is available to anyone who puts her mind to it exemplify her core petty bourgeois values.

11. More than 3,000 girls applied for the 152 spots, a 4 percent acceptance rate, compared to a 9 percent acceptance at Harvard University (Samuels 2007).

12. According to the UN's human development index, South Africa ranks 121 of 176 countries, with an annual per capita income of $11,192; the United States ranks eighth, with a per capita income of $39,676 (United Nations Development Programme 2006).

13. For an analysis of Baltimore's public school system that considers the historical and political-economic forces that have made it one of the most racially and class-segregated in the nation, see Orr (1998), Kane (2004), and Dillon (2007).

14. One sign of the extent of that anxiety is the formation of United Professionals, a nonprofit organization launched in 2007 by writer Barbara Ehrenreich to support "unemployed, under-employed and anxiously employed" Americans (Merritt 2007).

15. Internet sites were soon offering "Oprah Obama '08" paraphernalia—further cementing the pair's identification (Page 2006).

16. Criticism of the Leadership Academy was transformed into scandal in October 2007, when allegations of abuse of some of the students by a staff member surfaced. Winfrey, along with Gayle King and child psychologist Dr. Bruce Perry flew to South Africa to investigate.

She fired the headmistress and hired U.S. investigators to look into the charges, which led to the arrest of a dorm matron on thirteen counts of indecent assault. As this book went to press, the case was scheduled for a December court date (Makapela 2007; "Oprah takes action on abuse case" 2007; Rudolph 2007).

References

"About success." 2007. http://successmagazine.com/about_us.php/ (accessed June 11, 2007).

Abramovitz, M., and A. Withorn. 1999. "Playing by the rules: welfare reform and the new authoritarian state." In *Without justice for all,* ed. A. Reed, 151–173. Boulder, CO: Westview Press.

Abt, V., and L. Mustazza. 1997. *Coming after Oprah.* Bowling Green, OH: Bowling Green State University Press.

Abt, V., and M. Seesholtz. 1994. "The shameless world of Phil, Sally, and Oprah: television talk shows and the deconstructing of society." *Journal of Popular Culture* 28:171–191.

Adalian, J. 2006. "Oprah's real adventure." *Daily Variety* (December 15): 1–2.

Adams, T. 1998. "Let the Oprah backlash begin." *New York Post* (October 19): 39.

Adkins, J. I., Jr. 1994. "Self-help should be focus into the 21st century." *Chicago Tribune* (February 9): 14.

Adler, B., ed. 1997. *The uncommon wisdom of Oprah Winfrey.* Secaucus, NJ: Birch Lane Press.

"Advice, how-to, and miscellaneous." 2007. *New York Times Book Review* (August 26): 24.

"Africans in America: episode 1419, Stedman Graham." 1998. University of North Carolina TV, http://www.unctv.org/bif/transcripts/1998/bif1419.html/ (accessed July 4, 2005).

Albe, J. 1996. "Rising to the welfare challenge." *New Orleans Times-Picayune* (October 8): B6.

Albiniak, P. 2003a. "November loves syndication." *Broadcasting and Cable* (December 15): 22.

———. 2003b. "Oprah wears its age well." *Broadcasting and Cable* (January 20): 47.

———. 2004. "Oprah is on a roll." *Broadcasting and Cable* (August 9): 2.

———. 2005. "Good old Oprah: her numbers are improving." *Broadcasting and Cable* (January 24): 52.

Allen, H. 1993. "A new phrase at the White House: Michael Lerner preaches 'the politics of meaning'—whatever that is—and the first lady is listening." *Washington Post* (June 9): D1.

Andersen, R. 1995. *Consumer culture and TV programming.* Boulder, CO: Westview Press.

Anderson, Peggy. 2003. "Oprah doesn't disappoint Seattle fans." *Seattle Times* (May 31), http://seattletimes.nwsource.com/ (accessed September 18, 2004).

Anderson, Porter. 2001. "Prayer service: 'we shall not be moved.'" *CNN.com* (September 23), http://archives.cnn.com/2001/US/09/23/vic/yankee.service.report/index.html/ (accessed May 1, 2007).

Angelou, M. 1989. "Oprah Winfrey." *Ms.* (January/February): 88.

"Angry at Oprah." 1998. *New York Times* (October 11): Sec. 6, 19.

"Applications of self-help love." 1992. *Maclean's* (April 6): 45.

Archerd, A. 2003. "Oprah's AIDS speech draws Clinton, Mandela." *Variety.com* (November 24), http://www.variety.com/index.asp?layout=print_story&articleid=VR1117896232& categoryid=2/ (accessed January 18, 2004).

"Armstrong Williams papers, 1987–2000." (2001). University of South Carolina Library, Manuscripts Division, http://www.sc.edu/library/socar/uscs/2001/williams.html/ (accessed July 4, 2005).

Ashanti, K. 2006. "Oprah expands empire: media maven inks $55 million deal with XM Radio." *Black Enterprise* (June): 41.

Auletta, K. 1982. *The underclass.* New York: Random House.

"Austan Goolsbee joins DLC and PPI as senior economist." 2006. Democratic Leadership Council web site (June 19), http://www.dlc.org/ndol_ci.cfm?contentid=253912& skaid=858subid=108 (accessed August 9, 2007).

"Autumn flops. *Beloved* it's not." 1998. *The Economist* (November 21): 86.

Avins, M. 2000. "Flocking to the church of Oprah." *Los Angeles Times* (June 25): Southern California Living, Sec. E1, 3, http://lexis-nexis.com/.

Baer, K. S. 2000. *Reinventing Democrats.* Lawrence: University Press of Kansas.

———. 2004. "Children of Bill." *American Prospect Online* (April 28), http://www.prospect. org/web/printfriendly-view?id=7658/ (accessed July 11, 2004).

Baker, B. 2004. "Women and the Democratic party." In *Dime's worth of difference,* ed. A. Cockburn and J. St. Clair, 61–71. Petrolia, CA: CounterPunch.

Baker, D. 2007. *The United States since 1980.* Cambridge, UK: Cambridge University Press.

Ball, K. 1996. "Spirit moves Bill, Hil." *New York Daily News* (June 26): 6.

Balz, D., and D. S. Broder. 1991. "Democrats argue over quota clause: meeting to reshape party image opens." *Washington Post* (May 7): A8.

Barnes, J. A., and R. E. Cohen. 1994. "Seeking the center." *National Journal* (November 12): 2622–2624.

Barrett, P. M. 1993. "Peeling back the labels; through their Republican affiliations, two African-Americans defy political pigeonholing." *Seattle Times* (January 17): J1.

Bartlett, D. L., and J. B. Steele. 1992. *America: what went wrong?* Kansas City: Andrews and McMeel.

Beard, G. 1881. *American nervousness: its causes and consequences.* New York: G. P. Putnam's Sons.

Beason, T. 2003a. "Oprah's coming to town, and tickets have topped $800." *Seattle Times* (May 8): A1.

———. 2003b. "2,600 fans live it up with Oprah Winfrey." *Seattle Times* (June 21), http:// seattletimes.nwsource.com/ (accessed September 18, 2004).

Beatty, M. 1987. *Co-dependent no more.* Center City, MN: Hazelden.

Beatty, S. G. 1995. "Campaign will urge sponsors to clean up some talk shows." *Wall Street Journal* (December 7): B6.

Beinart, P. 2007. "Black like me." *New Republic* (February 5): 6.

Belcher, W. 2003. "The church of Oprah." *Tampa Tribune* (June 20): Baylife, 1.

Bellandi, D. 2007. "Oprah Winfrey to host fundraiser for Obama." *Chicago Sun-Times online,* http://www.suntimes.com/news/metro/472156,oprah071707.article (accessed August 12, 2007).

Benjamin, J. 1988. *The bonds of love.* New York: Pantheon.

Bennet, J. 1997a. "Clinton, in 2 speeches, urges racial healing." *New York Times* (July 18): A20.

———. 1997b. "Clinton plans moves aimed to improve nation's race relations." *New York Times* (June 5): A22.

———. 1998a. "Clinton, at race forum, is confronted on affirmative action." *New York Times* (July 9): A23.

———. 1998b. "President confesses 'I sinned.'" *Portland Oregonian* (September 12): A1.

Bennett, W. J. 1996a. "In civilized society, shame has its place." *Los Angeles Times* (January 26): B9.

———. 1996b. "Television's destructive power." *Washington Post* (February 29): A23.

Berg, B. 1986. *The crisis of the working mother.* New York: Summit Books.

Berke, R. L. 1994. "Moderate Democrats' poll sends the president a warning." *New York Times* (November 18): A30.

Berman, L. 1996. "Oprah's blessed sellers." *Detroit News* (November 25): B1.

Berman, M. 2002. "Familiar faces flickering: daytime talk lineup is changing." *Mediaweek* (March 18), http://lexis-nexis.com/.

Birkenhead, P. 2007. "Oprah's ugly secret." *Salon.com,* http://www.salon.com/mwt/feature/2007/03/05/the_secret/index_np.html (accessed September 2, 2007).

Bittar, C. 2005. "Oprah tour touts 'live your best life.'" *Brandweek* 46 (11): 38.

"Blacks picket Winfrey show in white county." 1987. *Chicago Tribune* (February 10): 4.

"Blacks play biggest role in Clinton inauguration." 1993. *Jet* (February 8): 44–48, 51–58.

Bluestone, B., and T. Ghilarducci. 1996. "Rewarding work: feasible antipovery policy." *American Prospect* (May–June): 40–46.

Bly, N. 1993. *Oprah! Up close and down home.* New York: Kensington Publishing.

Boedeker, H. 1998. "Not content with the Emmy, Oprah reaches for the Nobel." *Salt Lake Tribune* (September 21): B5.

Boldt, D. 1995. "Investing in human bonds." *Philadelphia Inquirer* (January 31): B1.

Bond, P. 2004. "From racial to class apartheid, South Africa's frustrating decade of freedom." *Monthly Review* (March): 45–59.

Bornstein, L. 2007. "Does she inspire or exploit?" *Denver Rocky Mountain News* (February 7): Spotlight, 2.

Braden, C. S. 1963. *Spirits in rebellion: the rise and development of new thought.* Dallas: Southern Methodist University Press.

Braun, S. 1997. "The Oprah seal of approval." *Los Angeles Times* (March 9): 8.

Braxton, G. 1996. "New talk shows try to come clean." *Los Angeles Times* (January 22): F1.

Brecher, J., and T. Costello. 1994. *Global village or global pillage.* Boston: South End Press.

Breggin, P. 1991. *Toxic psychiatry.* New York: St. Martin's Press.

Bremner, C. 1992. "Haunted by the underclass." *Times* (London) (May 8): N.p., http://proquest.umi.com/.

Brennan, T. 2006. *Wars of position.* New York: Columbia University Press.

Brenner, R. 2006. "Structure vs. conjuncture: the 2006 elections and the rightward shift." *New Left Review* 43 (January–February): 33–59.

Brinkley, A. 2006. "Clear and present dangers." *New York Times Book Review* (March 19): 1, 10–11.

Brint, S. 1994. *In an age of experts: the changing role of professionals in politics and public life.* Princeton, NJ: Princeton University Press.

Broder, D. S. 1990. "Hill liberals launch Democratic coalition: U.S. doesn't need 2 GOPs, manifesto says." *Washington Post* (May 14): A20.

————. 1992. "Clinton finds biracial support for criticism of rap singer." *Washington Post* (June 16): A7.

Brodsky, A. M., and R. T. Hare-Mustin, eds. 1980. *Women and psychotherapy.* New York: Guilford Press.

Brook, T. 2000. "Oprah goes under cover." *BBC News Online* (April 18), http://news/bbc.co.uk/1/hi/special_report/1999/03/99/tom_brook/717757.stm/ (accessed January 18, 2004).

Brooks, D. 2005. "The savior of the right." *New York Times* (October 23): 12.

"'Brotherhood march' aftermarch." 1987. *Houston Chronicle* (February 12): 9.

Brown, E. 2002. *The condemnation of Little B.* Boston: Beacon Press.

Brown, L. 1994. "Oprah to help welfare families." *Austin* (TX) *American Statesman* (September 15): B15.

Brown, M. K. 1999a. "Race in the American welfare state: the ambiguities of 'universalistic' social policy since the New Deal." In *Without justice for all,* ed. A. Reed, 93–122. Boulder, CO: Westview Press.

————. 1999b. *Race, Money, and the American Welfare State.* Ithaca, NY: Cornell University Press.

————, et al., eds. 2003. *Whitewashing race: the myth of a color-blind society.* Berkeley: University of California Press.

Brownmiller, S. 1993. *Against our will: men, women and rape.* New York: Fawcett Columbine.

Brownstein, R. 1992. "After the riots: the search for answers." *Los Angeles Times* (May 9): 2.

"Building a dream: the Oprah Winfrey Leadership Academy." 2007. Harpo Productions. O. Winfrey & K. Davis, executive producers. Aired on ABC television, February 26, 2007.

Burnell, B. 2000. "The Clintons and gender politics." In *The Postmodern presidency,* ed. S. Schier, 238–254. Pittsburgh: University of Pittsburgh Press.

Burton, L. 1992. *What's a smart woman like you doing at home?* Vienna, VA: Mothers at Home.

"Bush kisses Oprah and tells all." 2000. *BBC Online* (September 20), http://news.bbc.co.uk/1/hi/in_depth/americas/2000/us_elections/election_news/933511.stm/ (accessed April 2, 2004).

Butterfield, F. 2004. "Despite drop in crime, an increase in inmates." *New York Times* (November 8): A14.

Byrne, J. 2005. "Armstrong Williams lashed out at NAACP for sex harassment after settling harassment suit himself." *Raw Story* (January 10), http://www.bluelemur.com/index.php?p=536/ (accessed July 4, 2005).

Cady, H. E. 1894. *Lessons in truth.* Lee's Summit, MO: Unity Press.

Callinicos, A. 2001. *Against the third way.* Cambridge, UK: Polity Press.

Calmes, J. 1998. "Fast friends: Clinton's best allies are the liberals he spurned in the past." *Wall Street Journal* (October 9): A1.

Cameron, J. 1989. "Simply ... Oprah!" *Cosmopolitan* (February): 212–214.

Campbell, C., and B. Rockman, eds. 2000. *The Clinton legacy.* New York: Seven Bridges Press.

Canellos, P. 1997. "Popular Winfrey looks beyond TV." *Boston Globe* (May 29): A1.

Caplan, E. 1998. *Mind games: American culture and the birth of psychotherapy.* Berkeley: University of California Press.

Caplan, P. 1985. *The myth of women's masochism.* New York: Dutton.

Caragonne, A. 2000. "Tikkun seeks to create alternative road map to peace." *San Antonio Express-News* (July 3): 7B.

Carbaugh, D. 1988. *Talking American: cultural discourses on Donahue.* Norwood, NJ: Ablex.

Carlone, D. 2001. "The use of self-help business discourse in the contemporary organization: implications for workplace subjectivity." Unpublished thesis. Boulder: University of Colorado.

Carlson, P. 2000. "O is for Oprah, oozing oodles of optimism." *Washington Post* (April 25): C1.

Carmichael, S., and C. Hamilton. 1968. *Black power.* London: Jonathan Cape.

Carpignano, P., R. Andersen, S. Aronowitz, and W. Difazio. 1991. "Chatter in the age of electronic reproduction: talk television and the 'public mind.'" *Social Text* 25/26: 33–55.

Carr, D. 2006. "Oprahness trumps truthiness." *New York Times* (January 30): C1, 5.

Carter, B. 1995. "The media business: television." *New York Times* (March 20): D7.

"Case against Armstrong Williams dismissed." 1999. *Chicago Independent Bulletin* (February 11): 6.

Cashin, S. 2004. *The failures of integration.* New York: Public Affairs.

Chandler, A. 1977. *The visible hand: the managerial revolution in American business.* Cambridge, MA: Belknap Press.

"Change your life. Log on with Oprah." 1998. *Businesswire.com* (October 19), http://www.businesswire.com/ (accessed June 12, 2006).

Chesler, P. 1972. *Women and madness.* Garden City, NY: Doubleday.

———. 1986. *Mothers on trial: the battle for children and custody.* New York: McGraw-Hill.

Clemetson, L. 1999. "Talk show: 'Oxygen gives me that voice.'" *Newsweek* (November 15): 64.

———. 2001. "Oprah on Oprah." *Newsweek* (January 8): 38–48.

Clifford, T. 1992. "Bush in Los Angeles shocked by destruction, he calls for faith in the family." *Newsday* (May 8): 5.

Clinton, B. 1992. "'Put people first' to end urban strife, Clinton says." *Los Angeles Times* (May 26): 5.

———. 1995a. 1995 State of the Union Address (January 24), http://www.washingtonpost.com/wp-srv/politics/special/states/docs/sou95.htm/.

———. 1995b. "Excerpts from the news conference with President Clinton." *New York Times* (April 19): B8.

———. 1996a. 1996 State of the Union Address (January 23), http://www.washingtonpost.com/wp-srv/politics/special/states/docs/sou96.htm/.

———. 1996b. *Between hope and history.* New York: Random House.

———. 2004. *My life.* New York: Knopf.

———, and A. Gore. 1992. *Putting people first.* New York: Times Books.

Clinton, H. R. 1996. *It takes a village.* New York: Simon and Schuster.

———. 2003. *Living history.* New York: Simon and Schuster.

———. 2006. "Fulfilling the American dream." *Blueprint Magazine* (October), http://www.dlc.org/ndol_ci.cfm?kaid=137&subid=900111&contentid=254078 (accessed August 15, 2007).

Cloud, D. 1996. "Hegemony or concordance? The rhetoric of tokenism in Oprah Winfrey's rags-to-riches biography." *Critical Studies in Mass Communication* 13: 115–137.

———. 1998. *Control and consolation in American culture and politics: rhetoric of therapy.* Thousand Oaks, CA: Sage Publications.

Cloward, R. A., and F. F. Piven. 1993. "A class analysis of welfare." *Monthly Review* (February): 25–31.

Cockburn, A., and J. St. Clair. 2004. "War on the poor." In *Dime's worth of difference*, eds. A. Cockburn and J. St. Clair, 45–60. Petrolia, CA: CounterPunch.

Coffield, D. 2005. "Oprah: the must-have ticket." *Denver Post* (April 28): A1.

Cohen, R. 1992a. "Racist rappings of Sister Souljah." *Washington Post* (May 15): A25.

———. 1992b. "The rap on Jesse Jackson." *Washington Post* (June 23): A21.

———. 1992c. "Sister Souljah: Clinton's gumption." *Washington Post* (June 16): A21.

———. 1999. "Clinton's true legacy." *Washington Post* (October 8): A29.

Coleman, J. J. 2000. "Clinton and the party system in historical perspective." In *The postmodern presidency*, ed. S. Schier, 145–166. Pittsburgh: University of Pittsburgh Press.

Coleman, J. S. 1990. *Foundations of social theory*. Cambridge, MA: Harvard University Press.

Coles, J. 1998. "Discord is struck by Oprah." *Times* (London) (October 24): 15.

Colford, P. D. 1996. "A push from Oprah goes a long way." *Los Angeles Times* (October 31): Life & Style, 3.

Collins, C., and F. Yeskel. 2000. *Economic apartheid in America*. New York: New Press.

"Column for rent: White House pays black columnist $240,000 in propaganda." 2005. *Take Pride! Community Magazine* (January 24–30): 1.

Conley, D. 2001. "The black-white wealth gap." *Nation* (March 26): 20–22.

Connolly, C., and R. E. Pierre. 1998. "Clinton's strongest constituency: to African Americans, president's record outweighs personal problems." *Washington Post* (September 17): A1.

Coontz, S. 1992. *The way we never were: American families and the nostalgia trap*. New York: Basic Books.

Cooper, J. 1998. "Oprah takes a hit of Oxygen." *Mediaweek* (November 30): 8.

Corliss, R. 1998. "Bewitching *Beloved*." *Time* (October 5): 75–77.

Costello, C. B., and A. J. Stone. 2001. *The American woman 2001–2002*. New York: W. W. Norton.

Coyle, K., and D. Grodin. 1993. "Self-help books and the construction of reading: readers and reading in textual representation." *Text and Performance Quarterly* 13: 61–78.

Crain, R. 1995. "'50s quiz show fate looms for talk shows." *Advertising Age* (March 27): 12.

Crosbie, L. 2000. "Getting Oprah critical mass." *Toronto Star* (November 19): Entertainment, http://web.lexis-nexis.com/.

Cruse, J. 1989. *Painful affairs: looking for love through addiction and co-dependency*. Deerfield Beach, FL: Health Communications.

Curiel, J. 2000. "Fighting spirit: Tikkun magazine's Michael Lerner, moving beyond 'politics of meaning,' calls for radical transformation." *San Francisco Chronicle* (December 12): E1.

Curry, S. 2005. "UPN leads field for NAACP Awards." *Television Week* (February 21): 14–16.

Cushman, P. 1995. *Constructing the self, constructing America: a cultural history of psychotherapy*. Boston: Addison-Wesley.

Dahlgren, P. 1995. *Television and the public sphere*. London: Sage Publications.

Daley, D. 1996. "Lieberman asks local TV execs to take out the talk show trash." *States News Service* (January 22).

Daunt, T. 2007. "Winfrey, Obama just the ticket." *Los Angeles Times online* (July 18), http://www.latimes.com/news/politics/la-et-cause18jul18,1,5049839.story (accessed August 18, 2007).

Davidson, C. 1986. *Revolution and the word: the rise of the novel in America*. New York: Oxford University Press.

———, ed. 1989. *Reading in America*. Baltimore, MD: Johns Hopkins University Press.

Davidson, O. G. 1996. *Broken heartland: the rise of America's rural ghetto*. Iowa City: University of Iowa Press.

Davis, M. 1986. *Prisoners of the American dream*. London: Verso.

———. 1990. *City of quartz*. London: Verso.

———. 1992. "Urban America sees its future: in L.A., burning all illusions." *Nation* (June): 743–746.

———. 2002. *Dead cities*. New York: New Press.

———. 2007. "The Democrats after November." *New Left Review* 43 (January/February): 5–31.

Dean, M. 1995. "A black-and-right view of life, Armstrong Williams has found his voice." *Washington Times* (February 16): C10.

Decker, J. L. 2006. "Saint Oprah." *MFS Modern Fiction Studies* 52 (1): 169–178.

DeFrancisco, V. L. 1995. "Helping ourselves: an introduction." *Women's Studies in Communication* 18 (2): 107–110.

Deggans, E. 2003. "Oprah's followers get into the spirit." *St. Petersburg* (FL) *Times* (June 21): 1A.

———. 2007. "Dishing on O and her dough." *St. Petersburg* (FL) *Times* (January 21): 1P.

"Demand for change grows nationally for better high schools: 'Oprah' to report on American schools in crisis on April 11th and 12th." 2006. *PR Newswire* (April 11), http://proquest. umi.com/pqdweb?did=1050918741&sid=5&Fmt=3&clientid=56281&RQT=309& VName=PQD.

Democratic Leadership Council. 2001. "New Democrat credo" (January 1), http://www. dlc.org/ndol_ci.cfm?kaid=86&subid=194&contentid=3775/ (accessed October 13, 2005).

Denning, M. 1987. *Mechanic accents*. London: Verso.

DeParle, J. 2005. "Liberal hopes ebb in post-storm poverty debate." *New York Times* (October 11): A1.

Devroy, A. 1994. "Clinton revs up, steers to the center: DLC speech reveals new attempt to reach out to middle class." *Washington Post* (December 8): A1.

De Witt, K. 1995. "Dial 1-800-MY GURU." *New York Times* (December 5): Sec. 4, 2.

Diehl, B. 2000. "O, happy day. Oprah to launch new magazine." *ABCNews.com* (April 17), http://www.abcnews.go.com/sections/entertainment/DailyNews/oprahmag000417. html/ (accessed April 18, 2000).

di Leonardo, M. 1999. "'Why can't they be like our grandparents?' and other racial fairy tales." In *Without justice for all*, ed. A. Reed, 29–64. Boulder, CO: Westview Press.

Dillon, Naomi. 2005. "The loss of diversity." *American School Board Journal: December 2005 Special Report*, http://www.asbj.com/specialreports/1205SpecialReports/S2.html (accessed June 22, 2007).

Dionne, E. J., Jr. 1995. "The speech the people heard." *Washington Post* (January 31): A15.

———, and M. Schwartz. 1992. "Clinton issues plea for racial harmony." *Washington Post* (May 3): A28.

Disch, R. 1973. *The future of literacy*. Englewood Cliffs, NJ: Prentice-Hall.

Dizon, K. 2003. "Oprah urges finding your passion, acting on greater purpose." *Seattle Post-Intelligencer* (June 2): D1.

Donahue, D. 2001. "Live your best life, with Oprah." *USA Today* (July 2): D1.

Donald, M. 2000. "Analyze this." *Dallas Observer* (April 13), http://www.lexis-nexis.com/.

Donnelly, J. 2007. "Outside Oprah's school, a growing frustration: critics in Africa urge wider impact." *Boston Globe* (January 20), http://www.boston.com/news/world/africa/articles/2007/01/20/outside_oprahs_schhol_a_growing_frustration?mode=PF/ (accessed January 30, 2007).

D'Orio, W. 1999. "Creating Oprah: the magazine." *Folio* (September 1), http://www.lexis-nexis.com/.

Dovey, J. 2000. *Freakshow: first person media and factual television.* London: Pluto Press.

Dowd, M. 2007. "A giant doom magnet." *New York Times* (February 17): A15.

———, and F. Rich. 1992. "Democrats in New York—garden diary; I'm in therapy, you're in therapy." *New York Times* (July 15): A7.

Downey, K. 2004. "Talk gets younger, richer crowd." *Broadcast and Cable* (December 6): 30.

Dreazen, Y. J. 2000. "U.S. racial wealth gap remains huge—despite booming economy, disparities didn't alter in the course of the 1990s." *Wall Street Journal* (March 14): A2.

Dreier, P. 1998. "There's no racial justice without economic justice." *Social Policy* 29 (2) (Winter): 41–49.

Dreifus, C. 2005. "A sociologist confronts 'the messy stuff' of race, genes, and disease." *New York Times* (October 18): D2.

Drew, E. 2004. *On the edge: the Clinton presidency.* New York: Simon and Schuster.

Duckett Cain, J. 2000. "Iyanla's gift." *Essence* (January), http://www.lexis-nexis.com/.

Duffy, M. 1993. "Urging the boss to lighten up." *Time* (May 10): 32–33.

"Dumbing up." 1998. *The Economist* (October 17), http://www.lexis-nexis.com/.

Dumenil, G., and D. Levy. 2002. "The nature and contradictions of neoliberalism." In *Socialist register 2002*, eds. L. Panitch and C. Leys, 43–71. London: Merlin Press.

———. 2004. "Neoliberal income trends: wealth, class, and ownership in the USA." *New Left Review* 30 (November/December): 105–133.

Dyer, R. 1988. "White." *Screen* 29 (4): 44–65.

Dziemianowicz, J., and Z. Kasha. 1995. "The Oprah you don't know." *McCall's* (August): 72–74, 76.

Eagleton, T. 1996. *Literary theory.* Minneapolis: University of Minnesota Press.

Ebben, M. 1995. "Off the shelf salvation: a feminist critique of self-help." *Women's Studies in Communication* 18 (2): 111–122.

Eckholm, E. 2006. "Plight deepens for black men, study warns." *New York Times* (March 20): A1, 18.

Edmonds, P. 2006. "This time I won't fail." *USA Weekend* (December 15–17): 6–7.

Edsall, T. B. 1992a. "Black leaders view Clinton strategy with mix of pragmatism, optimism." *Washington Post* (October 28): A16.

———. 1992b. "Clinton stuns Rainbow Coalition: candidate criticizes rap singer's message." *Washington Post* (June 14): A1.

———. 1992c. "Democrats scramble to win black support: Wilder's withdrawal may allow party to begin resolving racial tensions before convention." *Washington Post* (January 10): A4.

———. 1992d. "What Clinton won." *New York Review of Books* (December 3): 43.

———. 1993. "The special interest gambit: how Clinton is changing the Democratic discourse." *Washington Post* (January 3): C1.

———. 1996. "New electoral challenges in a changing landscape: for black candidates, test is biracial support." *Washington Post* (July 18): A16.

———. 2000. "Voting conflict reopens racial split among Democrats." *Washington Post* (November 29): A29.

———, and M. D. Edsall. 1991. *Chain reaction: the impact of race, rights, and taxes on American politics*. New York: W. W. Norton.

Edwards, A. 2003. "50 women who are shaping our world: the O factor." *Essence* (October): 175, http://www.lexis-nexis.com/.

Edwards, E. 1995. "Oprah Winfrey admits drug use: during taping, TV host confesses she smoked cocaine." *Washington Post* (January 13): A1.

Ehrenreich, B. 1989. *Fear of falling*. New York: Pantheon Books.

———, and J. Ehrenreich. 1979. "The professional-managerial class." In *Between labor and capital*, ed. P. Walker, 5–45. Boston: South End Press.

———, and D. English. 1978. *For her own good: 150 years of experts' advice to women*. Garden City, NY: Anchor Press.

Elder, L. 2004. "When liberals play the race card." *World Net Daily* (November 25), http://www.worldnetdaily.com/news/article/asp?ARTICLE_ID=41647/ (accessed December 27, 2004).

Ellison, M. 2000. "Portrait: they bowl alone.... Harvard professor Robert Putnam has boiled down America's social woes to one simple analogy: they don't go to bowling leagues anymore." *Guardian* (London) (June 6): 4.

Ellwood, D. 1988. *Poor support: poverty in the American family*. New York: Basic Books.

Elmasry, F. 2007. "Oprah uses power of media to change lives." *VOA News* (January 29), http://www.voanews.com/english/Americanlife/2007-01-26-voa42.cfm?renderforprint=1/ (accessed February 1, 2007).

Emerich, M. 2006. "The spirituality of sustainability: healing the self to heal the world through healthy living media." Unpublished thesis. Boulder: University of Colorado.

"End near for fed-up Oprah?" 1999. *Mr. Showbiz* (February 9), http://www.movies.com/.

Entman, R. M., and A. Rojecki. 2000. *The black image in the white mind: media and race in America*. Chicago: University of Chicago Press.

Epstein, D., and D. L. Steinberg. 1998. "'American dreamin': discoursing liberally on the *Oprah Winfrey Show*." *Women's Studies International Forum* 21 (1): 77–94.

Etzioni, A. 1993. "Is Bill Clinton a communitarian?" *National Civic Review* (Summer): 221–225.

"Everybody's talking!" 1992. *First* (November 30): 30–37.

"Everyone has opinion about Oprah." 1998. *Chicago Sun-Times* (October 19): 30.

"Facts and Figures: African Americans." *The State of Working America*. Washington, DC: Economic Policy Institute, http://www.stateofworkingamerica.org/news/SWA06Facts-African-Americans.pdf (accessed August 31, 2007).

Faludi, S. 1991. *Backlash: the undeclared war against American women*. New York: Crown.

Farley, C. J. 1998. "Queen of all media." *Time* (October 5): 82–84.

Farr, C. K. 2005. *Reading Oprah*. Albany: State University of New York Press.

Feder, R. 2001. "'Chicago Matters' coup: Oprah a season opener." *Chicago Sun-Times* (February 20): 51.

Feeney, M. K. 2000. "New territory for the Oprah Winfrey empire." *Los Angeles Times* (April 17): E3.

Feldman, L. 1996. "Clinton dons rosy Reagan mantle." *Christian Science Monitor* (January 23): 1.

Ferguson, R. 1998. *Representing "race": ideology, identity, and the media*. London: Arnold.

Ferguson, T., and J. Rogers. 1986. *Right turn: the decline of the Democrats and the future of American politics*. New York: Hill and Wang.

Findley, P. 2006a. "Oprah offers words of hope, inspiration: 2-hour show mixes humor with religion." *Charleston* (SC) *Post and Courier* (February 26): B3.

———. 2006b. "Ticket rush leaves Oprah fans disappointed." *Charleston* (SC) *Post and Courier* (February 2): N.p.

Fine, B. 2001. *Social capital versus social theory*. London: Routledge.

Fineman, H. 1993. "The new age president." *Newsweek* (January 23): 22.

Finkle, J. 2004. "King makes Oprah new talk czar: her first effort is expected in 2006." *Broadcasting and Cable* (December 13): 10.

Firstman, R. 1989. "Oprah power." *Newsday* (November 1): Sec. 2, 4.

Fisher, P. 1989. "Oprah's theme: only the strong survive, thousands jam meeting on women." *Newsday* (February 26): 19.

Fitch, J. M. 2000. "Oprah Winfrey, 46." *Chicago Sun-Times* (October 31): 6.

Flamm, M. 2005. "The Oprah factor." *Crain's New York Business* (April 25): 1.

"Forbes magazine's ranking of the 400 richest Americans." 2004. *Denver Rocky Mountain News* (September 24), http://www.rockymountainnews.com/drmn/business/article/ (accessed October 6, 2004).

Ford, G., and P. Gamble. 2002. "America's black rightwing forum: the grotesque devolution of a black news program." *Black Commentator* (December 12), http://www.blackcommentator. com/ (accessed May 4, 2007).

Fornek, S. 2006. "If Obama runs, I'll campaign for him, Winfrey says." *Chicago Sun-Times* (September 28): 3.

Fottrell, Q. 2000. "The Cult of Oprah Inc." *Irish Times Weekend Magazine* (August 5): 61, http://www.lexis-nexis.com/.

Foucault, M. 1965/1988. *Madness and civilization*. New York: Vintage Books.

———. 1977. *Discipline and punish*. New York: Pantheon Books.

Frank, T. 2000. *One market under God: extreme capitalism, market populism, and the end of economic democracy*. New York: Doubleday.

———. 2004. *What's the matter with Kansas?* New York: Metropolitan Books.

Freeman, M. 1992. "Talk shows flourish during May sweeps." *Broadcasting and Cable* (June 15): 11.

Freud, S. 1964. *The future of an illusion*. Trans. W. D. Robson-Scott. Garden City, NY: Doubleday Books.

Freund, C. P. 1993. "Getting his heads together." *Washington Post* (February 7): C5.

Friedan, B. 1963. *The feminine mystique*. New York: W. W. Norton.

Fritsch, L. 2004. "Thank you, Bill Cosby, for saying the right thing at the right time." *Project 21 New Visions Commentary*, http://www.nationalcenter.org/P21NVFritschCosby904. html/ (accessed July 8, 2005).

Frolick, J. 1995. "'Coarsening' of U.S. culture is major issue again." *Cleveland Plain Dealer* (June 11): 18A.

Fromm, E. 1947. *Man for himself*. New York: Rinehart.

Fuller, R. C. 1982. *Mesmerism and the American cure of souls*. Philadelphia: University of Pennsylvania Press.

Gaddis, J. L. 2004. "The last empire, for now." *New York Times Book Review* (July 25): 11.

Gaines, P. 1995. "Oprah's confession tumbled out." *Washington Post* (January 13): B1.

Gallup, G., Jr. 1992. "Oprah is America's number one talk show host." *Gallup Poll Monthly* (April): 43–54.

Galston, W., and E. C. Kamarck. 1989. *The politics of evasion.* Washington, DC: Progressive Policy Institute.

Gamson, J. 1996. "Pathology on parade." *Denver Rocky Mountain News* (January 14): 71A.

———. 1998. *Freaks talk back.* Chicago: University of Chicago Press.

Garchik, L. 1998. "The Oprah backlash." *San Francisco Chronicle* (October 29): E10.

Gardiner, J. K. 1992. "Psychoanalysis and feminism: an American humanist's view." *Signs* 17 (2) (Winter): 436–466.

Garrett, L. 1998. "Oprah gets spiritual." *Publishers Weekly* (September 14): 34.

Garvey, M. 1995. "The first lady charms the second city." *Washington Post* (May 17): C01.

Gates, D. 1997. "She speaks volumes." *Newsweek* (Winter 1997, Special Edition): 76.

Gates, H. L., Jr. 2007a. "Forty acres and a gap in wealth." *New York Times* (November 18): Sec. Week in Review, 14.

———. 2007b. *Finding Oprah's roots; finding your own.* New York: Crown Publishers.

Gellene, D. 1995. "Company town: big advertisers pull spots from some talk shows." *Los Angeles Times* (November 14): D7.

Gemin, J. 1997. "Manufacturing codependency: self-help as discursive formation." *Critical Studies in Mass Communication* 14: 249–266.

Geoghegan, T. 2006. "How pink slips hurt more than workers." *New York Times* (March 29): B6.

Gersch, B. 1999. "Class in daytime talk television." *Peace Review* 11 (2): 275–281.

Gien, P. 2007. "Building a dream." *O, The Oprah Magazine* (January): 154–160, 217.

Gilbert, M. 1998. "Oprah tops 'most influential' list." *Milwaukee Journal Sentinel* (October 19): 2.

Gilder, G. 1973. *Sexual suicide.* New York: Quadrangle Books.

———. 1986. *Men and marriage.* Gretna, LA: Pelican Publishing.

Gilens, M. 1996. "'Race coding' and white opposition to welfare." *American Political Science Review* 90 (3) (September): 593–604.

———. 1999. *Why Americans hate welfare: race, media, and the politics of antipoverty policy.* Chicago: University of Chicago Press.

Gillette, F., and L. Neyfakh. 2007. "Oprah cranks up the Obama machine." *New York Observer* (August 13), http://www.observer.com/2007/oprah-cranks-obama-machine (accessed August 17, 2007).

Givhan, R. 2007. "In Oprah's South African school, girls will get a beautiful education." *Washington Post* (January 5): C1.

Godelier, M. 1986. *The mental and the material.* London: Verso.

Golab, A. 1994. "Oprah's offer triggers 20,000 cries for help." *Chicago Sun-Times* (September 16): 4.

Goldman, D. 1995. "The group life." *Adweek* (April 3): N.p., http://www.lexis-nexis.com/.

Goldman, L., and Blakeley, K. 2007. "The 20 richest women in entertainment." *Forbes.com.* http://www.forbes.com/2007/01/17/richest-women-entertainment-tech-media-cz_lg_richwomen07_0118womenstars_lander.html. (accessed December 26, 2007).

Goodman, E. 1995. "Shock of talk-show murder is it didn't happen sooner." *Minneapolis Star-Tribune* (March 16): 21A.

———. 2007. "Black women torn between race, gender." *Columbia* (MO) *Daily Tribune* (May 24), http://proquest.umi.com/pqdweb?did=1276620391&sid=1&Fmt=3&clientid=56281&RQT=309&VName=PD (accessed August 12, 2007).

Goodman, F. 1991. "Madonna and Oprah: the companies they keep." *Working Women* (December): 52–55, 84.

Gorski, E. 2003. "The un-churches." *Denver Post* (December 21): A1.

Gorov, L. 1997. "Faith: Marianne Williamson is full of it." *Mother Jones* (November/ December), http://www.motherjones.com/mothre_jones/ND97/gorov.html/ (accessed December 31, 2002).

Gowan, P. 1999. *The global gamble.* London: Verso.

———, L. Panitch, and M. Shaw. 2001. The state, globalisation, and the new imperialism: a roundtable discussion. *Historical Materialism* 9: 3–38.

Graff, H. 1979. *The literacy myth.* New York: Academic Press.

———. 1995. *The labyrinths of literacy.* Pittsburgh: University of Pittsburgh Press.

Graham, R. 1996. "Oprah lit." *Boston Globe* (December 6): C1.

Graham, S. 1997. *You can make it happen: a 9-step plan for success.* New York: Simon and Schuster.

———. 2000. *Teens can make it happen: nine steps to success.* New York: Simon and Schuster.

Graham Williams Group. 2005. http://www.sourcewatch.org/index.php?title=Graham_ Williams_Group/ (accessed July 4, 2005).

Granatstein, L. 1999. "Expanding Hearst's castle." *Mediaweek* (September 6): 45–49.

———. 2000. "Oprah explores a new frontier." *Chicago Sun-Times* (April 16): 14.

———, and J. Cooper. 1999. "Hearst empire expands." *Mediaweek* (July 12): 5.

Grant, T. 1988. *Being a woman.* New York: Random House.

Gray, H. 1989. "Television, black Americans, and the American dream. *Critical Studies in Mass Communication* 6: 376–386.

Gray, K. A. 2004. "Clinton and black Americans." In *Dime's worth of difference,* eds. A. Cockburn and J. St. Clair, 93–100. Petrolia, CA: CounterPunch.

Green, J. 2000. "Ford, Microsoft, Prudential hit the road with Oprah in bid for 'growth.'" *Brandweek* (June 5): 59.

Greenberg, A., and S. B. Greenberg. 2000. "Adding values." *American Prospect Online* (August 1), http://prospect.org/web/printfriendly-view.ww?id=5446/ (accessed July 5, 2004).

Greenberg, S. B. 1995. "After the Republican surge." *American Prospect Online* (September 1), http://www/prospect.org/web/printfriendly-view.ww?id=4986/ (accessed July 5, 2004).

———. 1996a. *Middle class dreams.* New Haven, CT: Yale University Press.

———. 1996b. "Private heroism and public purpose." *American Prospect Online* (September 1), http://www.prospect.org/web/printfriendly-view.ww?id=4891/ (accessed July 5, 2004).

———. 1997a. "Democratic possibilities: a family-centered politics." *American Prospect Online* (November 1), http://www.prospect.org/web/printfriendly-view.ww?id=4762/ (accessed July 5, 2004).

———. 1997b. "The mythology of centrism." *American Prospect Online* (September 1), http:// www.prospect.org/web/printfriendly-view?id=4785/ (accessed July 5, 2004).

———. 2005. "How we found—and lost—a majority: 1991." *American Prospect* 16 (6): 27.

———, and A. Greenberg. 2004. "Contesting values." *American Prospect Online* (March 1), http://www/prospect.org/web/printfriendly-view.ww?id=7247/ (accessed July 5, 2004).

Greenspan, M. 1983. *A new approach to women and therapy.* New York: McGraw-Hill.

Grimm, M. 2006. "The real story of O." *Brandweek* (February 6): 17.

Grindstaff, L. 2002. *The money shot: trash, class, and the making of TV talk shows.* Chicago: University of Chicago Press.

Grodin, D. 1995. "Women reading self-help: themes of separation and connection." *Women's Studies in Communication* 18 (2): 123–134..

Grossman, B. 2006. "Talk of the town: first-run chat, game, and court shows post major gains." *Broadcasting and Cable* (February 6): 11.

"The group life." 1995. *Adweek* (April 3), http://www.lexis-nexis.com/.

"Growth bypasses all but wealthiest few." 2006. *The State of Working America*, http://www. stateofworkingamerica.org/news/SWApr-final.pdf (accessed August 31, 2007).

Gumbel, A. 2006. "The cult of Oprah." *London Independent* (October 28): 44.

Gumpert, G., and S. Fish. 1990. *Talking to strangers*. Norwood, NJ: Ablex.

Guth, J. L. 2000. "Clinton, impeachment, and the culture wars." In *The postmodern presidency*, ed. S. Schier, 203–222. Pittsburgh: University of Pittsburgh Press.

Haag, L. I. 1993. "Oprah Winfrey: The construction of intimacy in the talk show setting." *Journal of Popular Culture* 26 (4): 115–121.

Habermas, J. 1989. *The structural transformation of the public sphere*. Cambridge, MA: MIT Press.

Hacker, A. 1993. "The blacks and Clinton." *New York Review of Books* (January 28): 12–15.

Hacker, J. S. 2006. *The great risk shift*. Oxford, UK: Oxford University Press.

Hale, J. F. 1995. "The making of the New Democrats." *Political Science Quarterly* 110 (2) (Summer): 207–233.

Hall, Jane. 1996a. "At the end of a long run, Phil Donahue looks back." *Los Angeles Times* (May 3): F3, 28.

———. 1996b. "Did Donahue's genre become his nemesis?" *Los Angeles Times* (January 19): F4.

Hall, Julie. 2003. "A very civic servant: he is known as Tony Blair's community renewal guru." *Guardian* (London) (October 1): 6.

Hall, M. 2003. "The 'Oprahfication' of literacy: reading 'Oprah's Book Club.'" *College English* 65 (6): 646–667.

Halliday, J., and C. Atkinson. 2004. "Pontiac gets major mileage out of $8 million 'Oprah' deal." *Advertising Age* (September 20): 12.

Halperin, M. 2007. "Why Oprah won't help Obama." *Time Online*. http://www.time.com/ politics/article/o,8599,1687526,00.html. (accessed December 11, 2007).

Hamburger, T. 2005. "The nation: White House curbs probe of commentator's hiring." *Los Angeles Times* (April 15): A13.

Hamilton, D. C., and C. V. Hamilton. 1997. *The dual agenda: race and social welfare policies of civil rights organizations*. New York: Columbia University Press.

Hamilton, K. 1999. "Oprah's going glossy." *Newsweek* (July 19): 43.

Hamilton, R. A. 1996. "Connecticut Q&A: Senator Joseph Lieberman; what, he asks, are the children viewing?" *New York Times* (January 28): Sec. 13, CN 3.

Hardt, M., and K. Weeks, eds. 2000. *The Jameson reader*. Oxford, UK: Basil Blackwell.

Hardy, T. 1992. "After L.A. riots, key concept is 'empowerment.'" *Chicago Tribune* (May 17): 1.

Hare-Mustin, R. 1983. "An appraisal of the relationship between women and psychotherapy." *American Psychologist* (May): 593–601.

———. 1987. "The problem of gender in family therapy theory." *Family Process* 26 (1) (March): 15–27.

———, and J. Marecek, eds. 1990. *Making a difference: psychology and the construction of gender*. New Haven, CT: Yale University Press.

"Harpo launches 17th season of *The Oprah Winfrey Show* and debuts Paramount Domestic Television's *Dr. Phil.*" 2002. Oprah.com (September 17), http://www.oprah.com/about_press_newseason.jhtml/ (accessed September 25, 2003).

Harrison, B. G. 1989. "The importance of being Oprah." *New York Times Magazine* (June 11): 28, 30, 46–47, 54, 130, 134, 136.

Hart, P. 2007. "Obamamania: how loving Barack Obama helps pundits love themselves." *Extra!* (March/April), http://www.fair.org/index.php?page=3094 (accessed August 18, 2007).

Hartmann, H. 1958. *Ego psychology and the problem of adaptation.* New York: International Universities Press.

Harvey, David. 1989. *The condition of postmodernity.* Oxford, UK: Basil Blackwell.

———. 2005. *A brief history of neoliberalism.* Oxford, UK: Oxford University Press.

Harvey, Diane H. 2000. "The public's view of Clinton." In *The postmodern presidency,* ed. S. Schier, 124–142. Pittsburgh: University of Pittsburgh Press.

Harwood, J. 1998. "GOP's new campaign themes copied from Clinton playbook." *Wall Street Journal* (October 18): A8.

Heaton, J. A., and N. L. Wilson. 1995. *Tuning in trouble: talk TV's destructive impact on mental health.* San Francisco: Jossey-Bass Publishers.

Heffernan, N. 2000. *Capital, class, and technology in contemporary American culture.* Sterling, VA: Pluto Press.

Heffernan, V. 2006. "Ms. Winfrey takes a guest to the televised woodshed." *New York Times* (January 27): A13.

Heinze, D. (n.d.) "Pedagogy of the talk show hosts and hostesses." *NEA Higher Education Journal,* 19–30.

Henwood, D. 1997. "Clinton's liberalism: no model for the left." In *Socialist register 1997,* ed. L. Panitch, 159–175. London: Merlin Press.

———. 2003. *After the new economy.* New York: New Press.

———. 2004. "Hostile takeover?" *Left Business Observer* (107) (April 23): 3, 7.

———. 2007. "LBO at 20." *Left Business Observer* (114) (January), http://www.leftbusinessobserver.com/LBOAt20.html (accessed August 24, 2007).

Herbert, B. 2005a. "Blood on their hands." *New York Times* (September 29): A35.

———. 2005b. "Good grief." *New York Times* (September 19): A25.

———. 2005c. "Voters' remorse on Bush." *New York Times* (September 22): A31.

———. 2005d. "The mobility myth." *New York Times* (June 6): A19.

Herman, Edward., and R. Rothstein. 1995. "Clinton's not-so-good deeds." *American Prospect Online* (March 21), http://www.prospect.org/web/printfriendly-view?id=5035/ (accessed July 11, 2004).

Herman, Ellen. 1995. *The romance of American psychology.* Berkeley: University of California Press.

"Hillary has a new guru." 1994. *Albany* (NY) *Times Union* (December 20): A2.

Hjort, L., and B. Ramadiro. 2004. "A long walk to nowhere—ten years of democracy in South Africa." *AIDC, Alternative Information and Development Centre,* http://www.aidc.org.za/?q=node/view/585 (accessed July 2, 2007).

Hohenberg, J. 1997. *Reelecting Bill Clinton.* Syracuse, NY: Syracuse University Press.

Holahan, J. 2000. "Here's an epiphany: Oprah is overdoing it." *Lancaster* (PA) *New Era* (June 14): B1.

Hollandsworth, S. 1999. "Phillip McGraw: the psychology of self-help." *Texas Monthly* (September): 42.

Holmstrom, D. 1998. "Book clubs give people something to talk about." *Christian Science Monitor* (January 2): 10.

Holt, P. 1997a. "Oprah speaks and books sell." *San Francisco Chronicle* (May 11): Sunday Review 2.

———. 1997b. "The spiritual side of U.S. politics: Williamson urges rethinking of roles." *San Francisco Chronicle* (October 14): B1.

Hopfensperger, J. 1993. "Sociologist traces roots of poverty." *Minneapolis Star-Tribune* (November 19): 7B.

Horton, D., and R. R. Wohl. 1976. "Mass communication as para-social interaction: observations on intimacy at a distance." In *Drama in life: the uses of communication in society*, eds. J. E. Combs and M. Mansfield, 212–228. New York: Hastings House.

"How returning shows are faring in the 1998–1999 TV season." 1999. *Mediaweek* (January 18), http://www.lexis-nexis.com/.

"How to make anti-poverty policies popular." 1991. *The Economist* (April 27): 23–24.

Howard, J. L. 2005. "The 'Oh' factor: cynics aside, Winfrey's empire stretches far beyond her popular TV talk show. But do some fans take their adoration too far?" *Denver Post* (April 24): L1.

Huntington, S. P. 1985. "The visions of the Democratic party." *Public Interest* 79 (Spring): 63–78.

Huyssen, A. 1986. *After the great divide*. London: Macmillan.

Ifill, G. 1992a. "Clinton aims to phase out welfare by training." *Portland Oregonian* (September 10): A14.

———. 1992b. "Clinton bid for support by blacks successful." *Portland Oregonian* (March 7): E6.

———. 1993. "Unlikely battle pits Clinton against unions." *New York Times* (November 9): 11A.

Ihejirika, M. 1995. "7 star in Oprah's pilot: charity plan gives families a chance." *Chicago Sun-Times* (September 15): 14.

Illouz, E. 2003. *Oprah Winfrey and the glamour of misery*. New York: Columbia University Press.

"Investing in human bonds." 1995. *Philadelphia Inquirer* (January 31): B1.

Irvine, L. 1999. *Codependent forevermore*. Chicago: University of Chicago Press.

Ives, N. 2006. "Most readers say Oprah has escaped brand damage." *Advertising Age* (February 6): 4.

Jacoby, R. 1975. *Social amnesia*. Boston: Beacon Press.

James, C. 1996. "Harnessing TV's power to the power of the page." *New York Times* (November 21): C15.

———. 2004. "Online book clubs as Lit 101 fun." *New York Times* (March 12): B25, 34.

James, W. 1902. *The varieties of religious experience*. New York: Longmans.

Jameson, F. 1981. *The political unconscious*. Ithaca, NY: Cornell University Press.

Janofsky, M. 1995. "The march on Washington." *New York Times* (October 16): B6.

Jefferson, E. A., and D. Coffield. 2005. "TV host tunes in 5,000 fans." *Denver Post* (May 1): 1A, 10A.

Jencks, C. 1992. *Rethinking social policy: race, poverty, and the urban underclass*. New York: Basic Books.

———. 2004. "Our unequal democracy." *American Prospect Online* (June 7), http://www.prospect.org/web/printfriendly-view.ww?id=7748/ (accessed July 11, 2004).

Jhally, S., and J. Lewis. 1992. *Enlightened racism*. Boulder, CO: Westview Press.

Jicha, T. 1993. "Winfrey is a standout in tale of inner city." *St. Louis Post-Dispatch* (November 27): 8D.

———. 2004. "President Oprah, anyone?" *South Florida Sun-Sentinel* (June 19), http://www.sun-sentinel.com/features/lifestyle/sfl-tv26tjjun19,0,1922713.column?soll=sfla-/ (accessed July 8, 2004).

"John Kerry—ask Oprah Winfrey to be vice president." 2004. http://www.petitiononline.com/MS1692ms/petition.html/ (accessed December 4, 2004).

Johnson, M. 1997. "Oprah Winfrey: a life in books." *Life* (September): 47–48, 53–56, 60.

Johnson, Pamela. 1985. "Fine tuning!" *Essence* (July): 46.

Johnson, Peter, and A. Bash. 1995. "Winfrey casts no bad light on daytime talk shows." *USA Today* (October 30): 3D.

Johnson, S. 1996. "The end of an earful? Trashy TV talk shows are being scrapped faster than you can say 'my mother is a hooker.'" *Chicago Tribune* (January 15): Tempo 1.

Jones, J. 2007. "Beyond books: Oprah Winfrey's seal of approval goes presidential." *New York Times* (May 7): C6.

Jones, L. 2000. "Has Oprah found the perfect pitch?" *London Independent* (January 30): 1, 2.

Jones, Margaret. 1989. "'Convergence' at the bookstore." *Publishers Weekly* (November 3): 32–34.

———. 1990. "The rage for recovery." *Publishers Weekly* (November 23): 16–24.

Jones, Mary Lynn F. 2003. "Vote Oprah." *American Prospect Online* (January 21), http://www.prospect.org/web/printfriendly-view.ww?id=971/ (accessed June 17, 2004).

Jones, T. 1999. "Oprah now is a brand unto herself, celebrity conglomerate." *Columbus* (OH) *Dispatch* (August 1): 1H.

———. 2000. "The irony of Oprah Winfrey." *Ottawa Citizen* (April 18): G1.

Jordan, R. A. 1985. "Blacks split on Democrat move to woo back whites." *Houston Chronicle* (March 11): 9.

Jubera, D. 1995. "TV preview: *The Oprah Winfrey Show*." *Atlanta Journal-Constitution* (October 30): 1D.

Judd, D. R. 1999. "Symbolic politics and urban policies: why African Americans got so little from the Democrats." In *Without justice for all,* ed. A. Reed Jr., 123–150. Boulder, CO: Westview Press.

Judis, J. B. 2002. "Is the third way finished?" *American Prospect Online* (July 1), http://www/prospect.org/web/printfriendly-view?id=6338/ (accessed July 11, 2004).

———, and J. Faux. 1995. "Not just the economy, stupid." *American Prospect Online* (June 23), http://www.prospect.org/web/printfriendly-view?id=5002/ (accessed July 11, 2004).

Jurkowitz, M. 2000a. "Oprah seeks new audience via magazine." *Denver Post* (April 13): 5F.

———. 2000b. "The media: Oprah delivers her message in a magazine." *Boston Globe* (April 13): D1.

Kakutani, M. 1995. "When fluidity replaces maturity." *New York Times* (March 20): C11.

Kaminer, W. 1990. *A fearful freedom: women's flight from equality.* Reading, MA: Addison-Wesley.

———. 1992a. *"I'm dysfunctional, you're dysfunctional."* Reading, MA: Addison-Wesley.

———. 1992b. "Oprah dependency." *Image* (June 28): 14–15.

Kane, G. 2004. "50 years later, gaps separate the races in our schools." *Baltimoresun.com* (May 12), http://www.baltimoresun.com/news/local/bal-md.kane12may12,0,5312940.column (accessed June 22, 2007).

Kantrowitz, B. 2005. "When women lead." *Newsweek* (October 24): 46–49.

Kaplan, A. G., and L. Yasinski. 1980. "Psychodynamic perspectives." In *Women and psycho-therapy,* eds. A. Brodsky and R. Hare-Mustin, 121–215. New York: Guilford Press.

Katz, I. 1996a. "New York stories: Oprah's new TV tie-in." *Guardian* (London) (December 19): T8.

———. 1996b. "'Salacious' chat show pioneer out-talked by new generation." *London Guardian* (January 19): A12.

Katz, S. J., and A. Liu. 1991. *The codependency conspiracy.* N.p.: Replica Books.

Kaus, M. 1994. "They blew it." *New Republic* (December 5): 14, 16, 18–19.

Kaus, R. M. 1981. "Reaganism with a human face." *New Republic* (November 25): 29–36.

Keeler, J. K. 2000. "The power of 'O.'" *St. Petersburg* (FL) *Times* (April 23): 1F.

Keller, J. 1992. "'Broken hearts' a helpful sequel on child abuse." *Columbus Dispatch* (December 1): 8E.

Kellner, D. 2003. *Media spectacle.* New York: Routledge.

Kendall, D. 2005. *Framing class.* Lanham, MD: Rowman and Littlefield Publishers.

Kennedy, D. 1994. "Oprah act two." *Entertainment Weekly* (September 9): 20–28.

Kennedy, R. 1999. "Is he a soul man? On black support for Clinton." *American Prospect Online* (March 1), http://www.prospect.org/web/printfriendly-view.ww?id=4544/ (accessed July 11, 2004).

Kest, K. 1995. "What Oprah really wants." *Redbook* (August): 74–77, 116.

Kiefer, F. 1999. "The Clinton presidency's feminine mystique: from tears to town meetings, Clinton's style has resonated with many." *Christian Science Monitor* (June 7): 2.

Kiernan, L. 1996. "Oprah's bold plan to confront poverty put on hold." *Denver Post* (September 8): 12A.

Kim, C. J. 2000. "Clinton's race initiative: recasting the American dilemma." *Polity* 33 (2) (Winter): N.p.

———. 2002. "Managing the racial breach: Clinton, black-white polarization, and the race initiative." *Political Science Quarterly* 117 (1): 55–79.

King, L. 1995. "Oprah Winfrey, January 4, 1995." In *The best of Larry King Live,* 366–378. Atlanta: Turner Publishing.

Kingdon, G., and J. Knight. 2005. "Unemployment, race, and poverty in South Africa." Global Poverty Research Group, http://www.gprg.org/themes/t2-inc-ineq-poor/unem/unem-pov.htm (accessed July 2, 2007).

Kinsella, B. 1997. "The Oprah effect: how TV's premier talk show host put books over the top." *Publishers Weekly* (January 20): 276.

Kirkpatrick, D. D. 2005. "TV host says U.S. paid him to back policy." *New York Times* (January 8): A1, A10.

Kirksite, L. 1982. *Men first, last, and always.* Reno, NV: Kirk Publishing.

Klein, J. 2006. "The fresh face." *Time* (October 23): 44–49.

Klein, K. 2007. "Self-help gone nutty." *Los Angeles Times* (February 13), http://www.latimes.com/ (accessed February 17, 2007).

Klein, N. 2000. *No logo.* New York: Picador.

Klinkner, P. A. 1999. "Bill Clinton and the politics of the new liberalism." In *Without justice for all,* ed. A. Reed, Jr., 11–28. Boulder, CO: Westview Press.

Knickerbocker, B. 1999. "Many Americans use scandal to reexamine their views of morality." *Christian Science Monitor* (February 12): 1.

Knowles, L. L., and K. Prewitt. 1969. *Institutional racism in America.* Englewood Cliffs, NJ: Prentice-Hall.

Koinange, J. 2006. "Oprah's school: pandemonium and shouts of 'viva!'" *CNN.com* (August 26), http://www.cnn.com/2006/WORLD/africa/08/26/btsc.koinange/index.html/ (accessed February 17, 2007).

Kolko, J. 1988. *Restructuring the world economy.* New York: Pantheon.

Kornblut, A. E. 2005. "Third journalist was paid to promote Bush policies." *New York Times* (January 29): A13.

Kotz, D. 2003. "Neoliberalism and the U.S. economic expansion of the 1990s." *Monthly Review* 54 (11) (April): 15–32.

Kovel, J. 1980. "The American mental health industry." In *Critical psychiatry: the politics of mental health,* ed. D. Ingleby, 72–101. New York: Pantheon.

Kramer, M. 1992a. "The brains behind Clinton." *Time* (May 4): 45.

———. 1992b. "Two ways to play the politics of race." *Time* (May 18): 35–36.

Krasner, D. 2004. "Review of *Oprah Winfrey and the glamour of misery* by Eva Illouz." *African American Review* 38 (3): 539–541.

Krestan, J., and C. Bepko. 1991. "Codependency: the social reconstruction of female experience." In *Feminism and addiction,* ed. C. Bepko, 49–66. New York: Haworth Press.

Krugman, P. 2004. "No surrender." *New York Times* (November 5): A27.

———. 2005. "Tragedy in black and white." *New York Times* (September 19): A25.

———. 2006. "The big disconnect." *New York Times* (September 6): A19.

Kubasik, B. 1994. "Expect softer Oprah show with hard producer gone." *Minneapolis Star-Tribune* (June 6): 6E.

Kuczynski, A. 2000a. "Oprah, coast to coast." *New York Times* (October 2): C1.

———. 2000b. "Winfrey breaks new ground with magazine." *New York Times* (April 3): C1.

———. 2000c. "Winfrey's O a reassuring hit." *Cleveland* (OH) *Plain Dealer* (October 3): 2C.

Kupcinet, I. 1996. "Kup's column." *Chicago Sun-Times* (August 28): 60.

Kurtz, H. 1995a. "Morality guru takes on talk TV: daytime confessionals are William Bennett's new targets." *Washington Post* (October 26): CO1.

———. 1995b. "'Trash TV' ads play no favorites: GOP donors among Bill Bennett's targets." *Washington Post* (December 7): D1.

La Franco, R. 1995. "'Piranha is good.'" With J. McHugh. *Forbes 400* (October 16): 66, 68.

Lague, L. 1994. "The white tie house: celebs fete Japan's emperor and empress at the Clintons' first state dinner." *People Weekly* (June 27): 58.

Lamb, L. 1989. "Talk show angst." *Utne Reader* (September/October): 30.

Langley, W. 2007. "The next time you watch a politician's lip quivering on TV, remember: it's all Oprah's fault." *London Sunday Telegraph* (January 7): 25.

Larsen, E. 1983. *Basics of co-dependency.* Brooklyn Park, MN: E. Larsen Enterprises.

Larson, M. 2004. "Cable TV: Oxygen finding its way." *Mediaweek.com* (March 22), http://www.lexis-nexis.com/.

Latham, L. M. 2000. "O no! Oprah produces a deeply flawed magazine for the deeply flawed." *Salon* (May 25), http://www.salon.com/mwt/feature/2000/05/25/oprah/print.html/ (accessed June 5, 2005).

Lawrence, J. 1995. "Expert on hot topic of poverty is out in cold during current welfare debate." *Fort Lauderdale* (FL) *Sun Sentinel* (September 26): 17A.

Leach, W. 1993. *Land of desire.* New York: Pantheon.

Lears, T. J. J. 1981. *No place of grace.* New York: Pantheon.

Lebowitz, F. 1996. "Talk show host." *Time* (June 17): 65.

Lebowitz, M. 2004. "Ideology and economic development." *Monthly Review* 56 (1) (May): 14–24.

Legette, W. M. 1999. "The crisis of the black male: a new ideology in black politics." In *Without justice for all*, ed. A. Reed, Jr., 291–326. Boulder, CO: Westview Press.

Lehmann, C. 1998. "It's class, stupid." *In These Times* (October 18): 24–27.

———. 2001. "Literati: the Oprah wars." *American Prospect Online* (December 3), http://www.prospect.org/web/printfriendly-view.ww?id=6031/ (accessed June 17, 2004).

———. 2002. "Oprah's book fatigue." *Slate* (April 10), http://slate.msn.com/toolbar.aspx?action=print&id=2064224/ (accessed June 26, 2003).

Lenzer, J. 2004. "Bush plans to screen whole U.S. population for mental illness." *BMJ* (June 19): 1458.

Leonhardt, D. 2007. "Assessing the advisers in the '08 race." *New York Times* (April 18): C1.

———. 2008. "Democrats: more than health care." *New York Times* (January 2): C1–2.

Lerner, H. G. 1990. "Problems for profit?" *Women's Review of Books* (April): 15–16.

Lerner, M. 1993. "Hillary's politics, my meaning: what are these ideas everyone seems afraid of?" *Washington Post* (June 13): Outlook C1.

Levi, M. 1996. "Social and unsocial capital: a review essay of Robert Putnam's *Making democracy work*." *Politics and Society* 24 (1) (March): 45–55.

Levine, R. M. 1993. "I feel your pain." *Mother Jones* (July/August): N.p.

Lewis, M. M. 2005. "Armstrong Williams: 'I'm coming back stronger than ever.'" *BlackAmericaWeb.com* (February 21), http://www.blackamericaweb.com/site.aspx/bawnews/williams222/ (accessed July 7, 2005).

Lichtman, R. 1982. *The production of desire.* New York: Free Press.

Lipman, L. 1996. "States to distribute public assistance to the poor." *Palm Beach Post* (August 23): 1A.

Lippman, L. 1997. "The Oprah canon." *Baltimore Sun* (June 18): 1E.

Lipsitz, G.1998. *Possessive investment in whiteness.* Philadelphia: Temple University Press.

Littleton, C. 1998. "'Change' hasn't hindered but hasn't helped 'Oprah.'" *Daily Variety* (November 12): 6.

Livingston, S., and P. Lunt. 1994. *Talk on television.* New York: Routledge.

Lofton, K. 2006. "Practicing Oprah; or, the prescriptive compulsion of a spiritual capitalism." *Journal of Popular Culture* 39 (4): 599–621.

Long, M. 1988. "Paradise tossed." *Omni* (April): 36–39, 42, 96, 98–102, 106, 108.

Lorando, M. 1994. "Oprah focuses on the light side." *Minneapolis Star-Tribune* (November 8): 1E.

lotus7. 2002. "Your favorite Oprah moment." Post 380 (January 5), http://www.oprah.com/.

Lowe, J. 1998. *Oprah Winfrey speaks.* New York: John Wiley and Sons.

Lowenstein, R. 2007. "The inequality conundrum." *New York Times Magazine* (June 10): 11–12, 14.

Lowney, K. S. 1999. *Baring our souls: TV talk shows and the religion of recovery.* New York: Aldine De Gruyter.

Lowry, B. 1998. "The queen of talk finally takes a hit." *Bergen County* (NJ) *Record* (November 15): Y2.

Loynd, R. 1993. "'No children' role takes Oprah to projects." *Los Angeles Times* (November 27): F15.

Lu, C. 2001. "Oprah tour draws throngs." *Chicago Tribune* (July 4): 8.

Lynch, F. R. 2001. "The end of bias? Or the beginning of preferences?" (July 26), http://adversity.net/FRAMES/Editorials/42_The_end_of_bias.htm/ (accessed December 27, 2004).

MacArthur, M. 1997. "Is talking about racism in America 'presidential Oprah'?" *American Politics Journal* (December 17), http://www.americanpolitics.com/121797_ClintPressConf.html/ (accessed January 18, 2004).

Macek, S. 2006. *Urban nightmares: the media, the right, and the moral panic over the city.* Minneapolis: University of Minnesota Press.

MacFarquhar, L. 2007. "The conciliator. Where is Barack Obama coming from?" *NewYorker.com.* http://www.newyorker.com/reporting/2007/05/07/070507fa_fact_macfarq. (accessed December 17, 2007).

Madrick, J. 2002. *Why economies grow.* New York: Basic Books.

Maio, E. 1998. "CEOs must manage brands for value." *Brandweek* (May 18), http://www.findarticles.com/ (accessed May 12, 2004).

Mair, G. 1994/1998. *Oprah Winfrey: the real story.* Secaucus, NJ: Carol Publishing.

Makapela, L. 2007. "South Africa: Oprah promises to restore dignity in school." (November 6). http://allafrica.com/stories/200711060286.html (accessed November 18, 2007).

Manga, J. E. 2003. *Talking trash: the cultural politics of daytime TV talk shows.* New York: New York University Press.

Manning, C. 2000. "Review of *Each Mind a Kingdom: American Women, Sexual Purity, and the New Thought Movement* by Beryl Satter." *Journal for the Scientific Study of Religion* 39 (3): 390–391.

Manza, J. 2000. "Race and the underdevelopment of the American welfare state." *Theory and Society* 29: 819–832.

Marable, M. 1983. *How capitalism underdeveloped black America.* Boston: South End Press.

Marchand, R. 1985. *Advertising the American dream.* Berkeley: University of California Press.

Marks, A. 1995. "Talk television goes on trial." *Christian Science Monitor* (October 11): 12.

———. 2007. "Obama and the 'Oprah Effect.'" *Christian Science Monitor Online* (December 10). http://www.csmonitor.com/2007/1210/p01s03-uspo.html (accessed December 11, 2007).

Marver, K. 2001. "Oprah Winfrey and her self-help saviors: making the new age normal." *Christian Research Journal Online,* http://www.equip.org/store/topical.asp?Keyword=oprah&x=0&y=0&Div=Keyword/ (accessed June 6, 2006).

Masciarotte, G. 1991. "C'mon girl: Oprah Winfrey and the discourse of feminine talk." *Genders* 11 (Fall): 81–110.

Massey, D. S. 2003. "The race case." *American Prospect Online* (March 1), http://www.prospect.org/web/printfriendly-view.ww?id=6714/ (accessed December 18, 2004).

Masson, J. M. 1984. *The assault on truth.* New York: Farrar, Straus and Giroux.

Mastony, C. 2007. "Oprah's gamble." *Chicago Tribune Online* (December 13). http://www.chicagotribune.com/features/lifestyle/chi-1213oprahbacklashdec13,0,85399.story?page=1 (accessed December 13, 2007).

Mastropolo, F. 2006. "'The secret' to success?" *ABC News* (November 26), http://abcnews.gocom/Health/print?id-2681640/ (accessed February 19, 2007).

Matteo, S., ed. 1993. *American women in the nineties.* Boston: Northeastern University Press.

Max, D. T. 1999. "The Oprah effect." *New York Times Magazine* (December 26): 37–41.

———. 2000. "How Oprah makes books worth watching." *Ottawa Citizen* (January 7): A13.

May, C. D. 1994. "The politics of meaning: writer's inspirational philosophy has found sympathetic ear in White House." *Denver Rocky Mountain News* (October 23): 89A.

May, E. T. 1988. *Homeward bound.* New York: Basic Books.

McAdams, D. D. 2000. "Counting down to Oxygen." *Broadcasting and Cable* (January 17): 132.

McDougal, D. 1990. "Once upon a time, there was a man who had a great idea for an afternoon talk show." *Los Angeles Times* (January 28): Calendar 8.

McGee, M. 2005. *Self-help, inc.* Oxford, UK: Oxford University Press.

———. 2007. "*The Secret*'s success." *Nation* (June 4): 4–6.

McGilvray, M. 2000. "All talk and no books, please." *Times* (London) (December 22), http://www.lexis-nexis.com/.

McKee, S. C., and D. R. Shaw. 2003. "Suburban voting in presidential elections." *Presidential Studies Quarterly* 33 (1): 125–144.

McKee, V. 1995. "Beware couch potatoes." *Guardian* (London) (September 25): 1.

McNett, G. 1999. "Reaching to the converted." *Salon* (November 12), http://www.salon.com/books/feature/1999/11/12/oprahcon/.

McNichol, T. 1993. "The new co-dependent covenant: sure, he'll lead—but can Clinton heal your inner Democrat?" *Washington Post* (February 28): C1.

McRoberts, F. 1994a. "Oprah's offer strikes responsive chord." *Bergen County* (NJ) *Record* (September 20): D11.

———. 1994b. "Oprah Winfrey commits $6 million for CHA families." *Chicago Tribune* (September 14): 3.

McSmith, A. 2001. "No 10 gets to grips with the theory of the lonely bowler." *London Daily Telegraph* (March 9): 10.

Mead, L. 1986. *Beyond entitlement.* New York: Basic Books.

"Media makers: Armstrong Williams." 2005. The History Makers, http://www.thehistorymakers.com/biography/biography.asp?bioindex=634&category=mediaMakers/ (accessed July 7, 2005).

Mediamark Research Inc. 2003. *Oprah Winfrey Show* and *O: The Oprah Magazine* (Fall).

Meeropol, M. 1998. *Surrender: how the Clinton administration completed the Reagan revolution.* Ann Arbor: University of Michigan Press.

Mehegan, D. 2003. "Oprah, book clubs help readers find their 'Eden.'" *Boston Globe* (July 3): D1.

Melcher, R. 1998. "What women really want?" *Business Week* (December 7): 50.

Mellencamp, P. 1990. *High anxiety.* Bloomington: Indiana University Press.

Memmott, C. 2007. "'Secret' attracts plenty of attention." *USA Today* (February 14), http://usatoday.com/life.books.news/2007-02-14-the-secret_x.htm/ (accessed February 19, 2007).

Merritt, J. 2007. "White-collar organizer: union workers have their locals. But in these scary times, who speaks for the anxious affluent?" *Cnnmoney.com* (May 24), http://money.c(accessednn.com/magazines/moneymag/moneymag_archive/2007/06/01/100033972/index.htm (accessed August 15, 2007).

Mertes, T. 2004. "A Republican proletariat." *New Left Review* 30 (November/December): 37–47.

Michaels, W. B. 2004. "Diversity's false solace." *New York Times Magazine* (April 11): 12–13.

Mifflin, L. 1995. "Falling ratings threaten all except top talk shows." *New York Times* (December 20): C11, 20.

———. 1996. "Phil Donahue announces retirement from TV." *New York Times* (January 18): A19.

Miles, R. 1989. *Racism.* New York: Routledge.

Miller, J. 1990. *My holding us up is holding me back.* N.p.: Health Communications.

Miller, M. C. 1988. *Boxed in.* Evanston, IL: Northwestern University Press.

Miller, S. 2003. "Republicans to honor black senior officials." *Washington Times* (September 16), http://www.washtimes.com/national/20030916-125737-4544r.htm/ (accessed January 1, 2006).

Millett, K. 1970. *Sexual politics.* New York: Doubleday.

Millman, J. 2000a. "Airheads." *Salon* (February 22), http://www.salon.com/ent/col/mill/2000/02/22/oxygen/ (accessed March 5, 2001).

———. 2000b. "The road to the White House goes through Oprah." *Salon* (September 25), http://www.salon.com/ent/col/mill/2000/09/25/oprah/print.html/.

Millman, N. 1992. "Winfrey's fiancé talks up a sports show." *Chicago Tribune* (December 6): 1.

Mills, C. W. 1994. "Under class under standings." *Ethics* 104 (July): 855–881.

Mills, D. 1993. "The vision thing: new age guru looks to heal what ails us." *Washington Post* (July 7): C1.

Miroff, B. 2000. "Courting the public: Bill Clinton's postmodern education." In *The postmodern presidency,* ed. S. Schier, 106–123. Pittsburgh: University of Pittsburgh Press.

Mitchell, A. 2000. "Full of banter, Bush takes on 'Oprah' circuit." *New York Times* (September 20): A1.

Mitchell, M. 2005. "Armstrong Williams didn't give U.S. what it paid for." *Chicago Sun-Times* (January 16): 14.

Moore, M. 2004. "Draft Oprah for president." http://www.michaelmoore.com/books-films/dudewheresmycountry/draftoprah/index/php/ (accessed July 8, 2004).

Moore, T. S. 1994. "How *The Oprah Winfrey Show* helps people live better lives." *Jet* (April 18): 56.

Moran, C. 2002. "She's still talking the talk." *Times* (London) (April 3): 2.

Morrison, T. 1998. "The talk of the town." *New Yorker* (October 5): 31–32.

Mosle, S. 1988. "Grand new Oprah." *Savvy* (August): 20.

Moss, L. 2002. "Oxygen gets Oprah's post-show show." *Multichannel News* (June 17): 42.

Moynihan, D. P. 1965. *The Negro family: the case for national action.* Washington, DC: Government Publication Office.

Mulkern, A. C. 2004. "Risks of Prozac revisited." *Denver Post* (September 12): 1A, 6A.

Munson, W. 1993. *All talk: the talkshow in media culture.* Philadelphia: Temple University Press.

Murray, C. A. 1984. *Losing ground: American social policy, 1950–1980.* New York: Basic Books.

"NAACP opposes welfare reform proposals." 1995. *Afro-American Red Star* (September 30): B5.

"Names and Faces." 1996. *Washington Post* (August 8): C3.

"NATPE2000: 1999–00 syndicated programming scorecard." 2000. *Mediaweek* (January 17), http://www.lexis-nexis.com/.

Neal, T. M., and T. B. Edsall. 1998. "Democrats fear loss of black loyalty: to survive in key states, party battles discontent." *Washington Post* (August 3): A1.

Nelson, M. Z. 2002. "Dispensing a gospel of health and happiness." *The Christian Century* (September 25–October 8), http://www.marciaznelson.com/articles7.htm/ (accessed December 4, 2004).

"New politics turns on meaning of life." 1992. *St. Louis Post-Dispatch* (July 16): 3C.

Ngonyama, P. 2007. "Far from free education." *Amandla,* http://www.amandlapublishers. com/Site/Education.pdf (accessed July 2, 2007).

Nichols, B. 1996. "From moderate Democrats, liberal praise for Clinton." *USA Today* (December 12): 4A.

———, and J. Lee. 1998. "Dems try last-minute push to boost black votes." *USA Today* (November 2): 9A.

Nichols, J. 2004. "Reagan's politics of passion." *Nation* (June 7), http://www/thenation. com/docprint/mhtml?I=20040621&s=nicholsreagan/.

"No gurus at the White House." 1995. *Albany* (NY) *Times Union* (January 27): A2.

Nolan, J. L., Jr. 1998. *The therapeutic state.* New York: New York University Press.

Norwood, R. 1985. *Women who love too much.* Los Angeles: J. P. Tarcher.

Novak, M. 1987. *The new consensus on family and welfare: a community of self-reliance.* Washington, DC: American Enterprise Institute for Public Policy Research.

Noveck, J. 2007. "Can Oprah's blessing boost Obama?" *SFGate.com* (November 27). http:// www.sfgate.com/cgi-bin/article.cgi?f=/n/a/2007/11/27/politics/p135908S26.DTL (accessed December 6, 2007).

O'Brien, T. L. 2005. "Spinning frenzy: P.R.'s bad press." *New York Times* (February 13): Sec. 3, 1.

O'Hara, D. 2000. "Overnight success." *Chicago Sun-Times* (May 14): Real Life 5.

Ohmann, R. 1985. "Literacy, technology, and monopoly capital." *College English* 47 (7): 675–689.

"On the cover." 2001. *Newsweek* (January 8): 3.

"Open letter asks her to pick new novels for TV book club." 2005. *MSNBC.com,* http://msnbc. com/id/76000721/ (accessed October 22, 2005).

"Oprah admits she 'misused' TV." 1999. *BBC News Online* (February 23), http://news/bbc. co/uk/1/hi/entertainment/284931.stm/ (accessed January 18, 2004).

"Oprah begins 13th season with 'renewed mission.'" 1998. *Jet* (September 21): 65.

"Oprah: a brand new car—for everybody!" 2004. *CNN.com* (September 13), http://www.cnn. com/2004/SHOWBIZ/TV/09/13/people.oprahs.surprise.ap/index.html/ (accessed September 13, 2004).

"Oprah to continue her show through year 2002." 1998. *Jet* (October 12): 61.

"'Oprah,' 'Dr. Phil' see strong syndie starts." 2003. *Broadcasting and Cable* (October 1): 18.

"Oprah gets first Bob Hope humanitarian award." 2002. http://www.emmys.com/ primetime/2002/awards/oprah.html/ (accessed January 8, 2003).

"Oprah gets Oxygen: gains full distribution in Chicago." 2004. Oprah.com (April 30), http://www.oprah.com/about/press/about_press_distribution.jhtml/ (accessed June 24, 2006).

"Oprah gets two-month progress report from African school." 2007. ABC News (February 26), http://www.abcnews.go.com/GMA/print?id=2904581/ (accessed February 27, 2007).

"Oprah gives TV girl power." 2000. *BBC News Online* (February 3), http://wwwnews.bbc. co/uk/1/hi/entertainment/629368.stm/ (accessed January 18, 2004).

"Oprah hosts Live Your Best Life Tour 2003: a four-city, interactive, day-long seminar." 2003. Oprah.com (March 18), http://www.oprah.com/about/press/releases/2003/ about_press_lybl.jhtml/ (accessed January 1, 2007).

"Oprah master class." 2000. *Guardian* (London) (January 31): 60.

"Oprah for president." 2000. http://www.dreamagic.com/oprah/ (accessed January 18, 2004).

"Oprah for president? She'll always say 'never.'" 2003. *Salt Lake Deseret News* (June 2): A2.

"Oprah sets the standard." 2004. *USA Today* (September 17): 12a.

"Oprah show is good to go until '11 season." 2004. *Daily Variety* (August 6): 4.

"Oprah signs new contract through 2003–2004 season." 2000. *Atlanta Journal-Constitution* (November 3): 5E, http://www.lexis-nexis.com/.

"Oprah sounds off on Baltimore's education climate." 2006. wbaltv.com (April 11), http://www.wbaltv.com/news/8627555/detail.html?subid=10100681 (accessed June 22, 2007).

"Oprah takes action on abuse case." 2007. *BBC News,* http://www.news.bbc.co.uk/2/hi/africa/7079327.stm (accessed November 18, 2007).

"Oprah and Tom, at peace." 2004. *New York Times* (October 14): B2.

"Oprah under attack." 1998. *New Orleans Times-Picayune* (October 20): A13.

"Oprah Winfrey." 2002. *Business Week* (January 14): 56.

"Oprah Winfrey helps 100 poor families to a better life." 1994. *New York Amsterdam News* (September 24): 28.

"Oprah Winfrey inducted into TV hall of fame." 1994. *Jet* (October 17): 8.

"Oprah Winfrey opens school for girls in South Africa." 2007. *CNN.com* (January 2), http://www.cnn.com/2007/WORLD/africa/01/02/oprah.school.ap/index.html/ (accessed January 30, 2007).

"Oprah Winfrey, Philadelphia's 2003 recipient of the Marian Anderson Award." 2003. http://www.marianandersonaward.org/oprahWinfrey.html/ (accessed January 18, 2004).

"Oprah Winfrey to receive the Horatio Alger Award." 1993. *Jet* (February 1): 52.

"Oprah Winfrey reigns supreme." 2004. *Broadcasting and Cable* (December 20): 9.

"Oprah Winfrey reveals the real reason why she stayed on TV." 1997. *Jet* (November 24): 58–61.

Oprah Winfrey Show. (N. d.) http://www.nytix.com?TV_Shows/OprahWinfrey/oprahwinfrey.html/ (accessed December 4, 2004).

"Oprah Winfrey signs with King World Productions for a new three-year contract to continue as host and producer of *The Oprah Winfrey Show* through 2010–2011." 2004. Oprah.com (August 5), http://www.oprah.com/about/press/about_press_2010renew.jhtml/ (accessed September 14, 2004).

"Oprah Winfrey tells why blacks who bash blacks tick her off." 1990. *Jet* (September 17): 60–62.

"Oprah Winfrey's biography." 2007. Oprah.com, http://www.oprah.com/about/press/about_press_bio.jhtml/ (accessed December 26, 2007).

"Oprah.com crosses milestone of 100 million monthly page views." 2005. Oprah.com (June 6), http://www.2.oprah.com/about/press/releases/200506/press_releases_20050606.jhtml/ (accessed January 1, 2007).

Oprah.com "Facts." 2006 (March). http://www2.oprah.com/about/press/about_press_comfaq.jhtml/.

"Oprah-di, Oprah-da, life goes on." 1999. *Newsweek* (February 22): 10.

"Oprah's book club returns to living writers." 2005. *ABC News,* http://abcnews.go.com/Entertainment/print?id=1152480/ (accessed October 22, 2005).

"Oprah's cut with Barack Obama." 2004. *O, The Oprah Magazine* online (November 2004), http://www.oprah.com/omagazine/200411/omag_200411_ocut.jhtml (accessed August 6, 2007).

"Oprah's difficult welfare lesson." 1996. *Tampa Tribune* (September 18): 8.

"Oprah's Personal Growth Summits." 2000. *O, The Oprah Magazine* (May): 179.

"Oprah's show on GA march bars blacks; protest called." 1987. *Chicago Sun-Times* (February 9): 5.

"Oprah's special report: American schools in crisis." 2006. http://www.oprah.com/about/press/releases/200604/press_releases_20060404 (accessed May 29, 2007).

"Oprah's welfare idea hits hard realities." 1996. *Tacoma* (WA) *News Tribune* (September 17): A10.

Orr, M. 1998. "Jobs or education: how racial politics in Baltimore thwarted education reform." http://www.children.smartlibrary.org/NewInterface/segment.cfm?segment=2134 (accessed June 22, 2007).

Ouroussoff, N. 2004. "An earnest building for a complex president." *New York Times* (November 25): B1, B7.

Ott, B. 1997. "After Oprah." *Booklist* 94 (1) (September 1): 64–65.

Page, C. 1987. "The Forsyth saga comes to TV." *Chicago Tribune* (February 15): 3.

———. 1993. "Black churches can inspire families to community revival." *Chicago Tribune* (October 13): 23.

———. 1995. "With tabloid TV hosts dishing out tons of unbelievable garbage, can they actually be shamed into raising the standards of their programs?" *Chicago Tribune* (October 29): 21C.

———. 2006. "Oprah and the leadership gap." *Buffalo News* (October 3): A9.

Park, D. W. 2005. "Review of *Oprah Winfrey and the glamour of misery* by Eva Illouz." *Journal of Communication* 55 (4): 874–875.

Parker, S. 1999. "Let's put some spirit into government aid." *Project 21 New Visions Commentary,* http://www.nationalcenter.org/P21NVParkerFaith999.html/ (accessed July 8, 2005).

Patterson, J. T. 1994. *America's struggle against poverty, 1900–1994.* Cambridge, MA: Harvard University Press.

Pattison, R. 1982. *On literacy.* New York: Oxford University Press.

Peale, N. V. 1952. *The power of positive thinking.* New York: Prentice-Hall.

Peck, J. 1994. "Talk about racism: framing a popular discourse of race on Oprah Winfrey." *Cultural Critique* (Spring): 89–126.

———. 1995. "TV talk shows as therapeutic discourse: the ideological labor of the televised talking cure." *Communication Theory* 5 (1) (February): 58–81.

———. 1996. "No place like home: the family, the baby boom, and the crisis of the public sphere in *Wild Palms.*" *American Studies* 37 (2) (Fall): 1–25.

Peele, S. 1975. *Love and addiction.* With A. Brodsky. New York: Taplinger Publishing.

———. 1985. *The meaning of addiction.* San Francisco: Jossey-Bass Publishers.

———. 1989. *Diseasing of America.* Lexington, MA: Lexington Books.

Perelberg, R. J., and A. C. Miller, eds. 1990. *Gender and power in families.* London: Tavistock Routledge.

Perlstein, R. 2005. "Party cannibals." *Nation* (February 7): 5–6.

Persall, S. 1998. "Oprah's inner voice." *St. Petersburg* (FL) *Times* (October 13): Floridian 1D.

Peterson, J. 1997. "Clinton urges end to racism in America." *Denver Post* (June 15): 1A, 16A.

Pew Research Center. 2007. "Blacks see growing values gap between poor and middle class" (November 13), http://pwesocialtrends.org/pubs/700/black-public-opinion (accessed November 18, 2007).

Philips, C. 1992. "'I do not advocate ... murdering'; 'raptivist' Sister Souljah disputes Clinton charge." *Los Angeles Times* (June 17): F1.

Phillips, K. 1992. "A new politics of race could move nation left." *Los Angeles Times* (May 10): M1.

Pitney, J., Jr. 2000. "Clinton and the Republican Party." In *The postmodern presidency*, ed. S. E. Schier, 167–182. Pittsburgh: University of Pittsburgh Press.

Piven, F. F., and B. Ehrenreich. 2005. "The truth about welfare reform." In *Telling the truth: socialist register 2006*, eds. L. Panitch and C. Leys, 78–92. London: Merlin Press.

Plott, M. 1987. "Oprah's 'Live from Forsyth County' was stroke of programming genius." *Atlanta Journal-Constitution* (February 10): B1.

Pollin, R. 2000. "Anatomy of Clintonomics." *New Left Review* (3) (May–June): 17–46.

———. 2003. *Contours of descent.* London: Verso.

———, and A. Cockburn. 1991. "The world, the free market, and the left." *Nation* (February 25): 224–236.

Poniewozik, J. 1998. "Oprah Winfrey, journalist?" *Salon* (October 27), http://www.salon.com/media/poni/1998/10/27poni.html/.

Population Reference Bureau. 2006. South Africa, statistics. http://www.prb.org/Countries/SouthAfrica.aspx (accessed July 2, 2007).

Porter, K. 1989. *Poverty in rural America.* Washington, DC: Center on Budget and Policy Priorities.

Poulantzas, N. 1975. *Classes in contemporary capitalism.* London: New Left Books.

Powell, B. 1997. "President asked to view economics of race issue." *Denver Post* (June 15): 16A.

Powers, W. F. 1995. "The lane less traveled: can a nation of individuals give community a sporting chance?" *Washington Post* (February 3): D1.

"President Clinton signs the National Child Protection Act." 1993. *New York Times* (December 21), http://www.vachss.com/mission/president.html/ (accessed January 18, 2004).

"'President Oprah' hits the web." 1999. *BBC News Online* (October 6), http://news.bbc.co.uk/1/hi/entertainment/466767.stm/ (accessed April 2, 2004).

"President steps up anti-crime drive." 1993. *New York Times* (December 21): A24.

Priest, P. J. 1995a. *Public intimacies.* Cresskill, NJ: Hampton Press.

———. 1995b. "Staunch the raunch: must talk TV be filthy to be fun?" *Washington Post* (November 19): C1.

Pringle, C. 1996. "Welfare reform." *Los Angeles Daily News* (August 25): V1.

Pugh, C. 2000. "O-some, or O-verkill? Fans, the curious are buying Oprah Winfrey's new magazine." *Houston Chronicle* (April 22): 7.

Putnam, R. D. 1996. "The strange disappearance of civic America." *American Prospect Online* (December 1), http://www.prospect.org/web/printfriendly-view.ww?id=4972/ (accessed September 20, 2004).

———. 2000. *Bowling alone.* New York: Simon and Schuster.

———. 2002. "Bowling together." *American Prospect Online* (February 11), http://www.prospect.org/web/printfriendly-view.ww?id=6114/ (accessed September 20, 2004).

Quebedeaux, R. 1982. *By what authority: the rise of personality cults in American Christianity.* San Francisco: Harper and Row.

"Queen Oprah." 1997. *Wall Street Journal* (September 17): A22.

Radway, J. 1984. *Reading the romance.* Chapel Hill: University of North Carolina Press.

———. 1997. *A feeling for books.* Chapel Hill: University of North Carolina Press.

Randolph, L. B. 1993a. "Black America's biggest inaugural bash." *Ebony* (March): 116.

————. 1993b. "Oprah opens up about her weight, her wedding, and why she withheld the book." *Ebony* (October): 130, http://web.lexis-nexis.com/.

Rapping, E. 1996. *The culture of recovery.* Boston: Beacon Press.

"Reading with Oprah." 1996. *Christian Science Monitor* (December 12): 20.

Rebello, S. 1998. "Oprah Winfrey: connecting with 20 million 'customers' a day." *Success* (May): 64–66.

Reed, A., Jr. 1999a. "Introduction: the new liberal orthodoxy on race and inequality." In *Without justice for all,* ed. A. Reed Jr., 1–10. Boulder, CO: Westview Press.

————. 1999b. *Stirrings in the jug: black politics in the post-segregation era.* Minneapolis: University of Minnesota Press.

————. 1999c. "Where the idea of 'race' came from." *Labor Standard* 6, http://biblioline. nisc.com/.

————. 2002. "America becoming—what exactly? Social policy research as the fruit of Bill Clinton's race initiative." *New Politics* 8 (4) (Winter), http://biblioline.nisc.com/.

————. 2004. "Color codes." *Dissent Magazine* (Summer), http://biblioline.nisc.com/.

————. 2007. "Interview." *Behind the News with Doug Henwood* (June 7). Podcast, http://shout. lbo-talk.org/lbo/RadioArchive/2007/07_06_07.mp3.

————, ed. 1999d. *Without justice for all: the new liberalism and our retreat from racial equality.* Boulder, CO: Westview Press.

Reeves, J., and R. Campbell. 1994. *Cracked coverage.* Durham, NC: Duke University Press.

Reich, R. 1988. *Tales of a new America.* New York: Vintage Books.

————. 1991. *The work of nations.* New York: A. A. Knopf.

————. 1999. "We are all third wayers now." *American Prospect Online* (March 1), http://www. prospect.org/web/printfriendly-view.ww?id=4538/ (accessed July 11, 2004).

————. 2000. "Working principles." *American Prospect Online* (June 19), http://www.prospect. org/web/printfriendly-view?id-4452/ (accessed July 11, 2004).

Remnick, D. 1996. "Mr. Wilson's neighborhood." *New Yorker* (April 29–May 6): 96–102.

"Republicans and the president." 1994. *Washington Post* (January 28): A22.

Ressner, J. 2006. "The secret of success." *Time* (December 28), http://www.time.com/time/ printout/0,8816,1573136,00.html/ (accessed February 19, 2007).

Rice, C. 2006. "Oprah Winfrey: telling America's story." *Time* (May 8): 65.

Richman, A. 1987. "Oprah." *People Weekly* (January 12): 52–55, 58.

Rieff, P. 1966. *The triumph of the therapeutic.* London: Chatto and Windus.

Riessman, C. K. 1983. "Women and medicalization: a new perspective." *Social Policy* 4 (1) (Summer): 3–18.

Rivkin, J. 1990. "Recovery stores: a sense of mission. *Publishers Weekly* (November 23): 26–28.

Robertson, N. 1988. "Donahue vs. Winfrey: a clash of talk titans." *New York Times* (February 1): C30.

Robinson, E. 2007. "Despite her generosity, Oprah misses the mark." *Gary* (IN) *Post-Tribune* (January 11): B11.

Robinson, J. 1993. "Marianne Williamson: a new age oracle comes down to earth." *Boston Globe* (May 20): Living 55.

Robinson, S. 1996. "Clinton displays little enthusiasm for 'building bridge to 21st century.'" *Ottawa Citizen* (December 7): A10.

Rodricks, D. 2006. "Listen up, Oprah: there are other ways to help city kids." *Baltimore Sun* (April 13), http://find/galegroup.com/itx/start.do?prodld=ITOF, Gale document number CJ144442614 (accessed February 12, 2007).

Roediger, D. 2002. *Colored white.* Berkeley: University of California Press.

Roeper, R. 1998a. "'Deepak Oprah's' inner journey is an ego trip." *Chicago Sun-Times* (October 12): 11.

———. 1998b. "Surprising response to column critical of talk show diva." *Chicago Sun-Times* (October 19): 31.

———. 2000. "O, what an ego trip." *Chicago Sun-Times* (April 30): 11.

Rollins, E. J. 1992. "Craven post-riot act shows 'Slick Willie' lacks convictions." *Seattle Times* (May 13): A15.

Roof, W. C. 1993. *A generation of seekers.* New York: HarperCollins.

———. 1999. *The spiritual marketplace.* Princeton, NJ: Princeton University Press.

Rooney, K. 2005. *Reading with Oprah.* Fayetteville: University of Arkansas Press.

Rose, M. 2000. "In Oprah's empire, rivals are partners." *Wall Street Journal* (April 3): B1, B12.

Rose, N. 1998. *Inventing our selves.* Cambridge, UK: Cambridge University Press.

———. 1999. "Inventiveness in politics." *Economy and Society* 28 (3) (August): 467–493.

Rosenberg, H. 1987. "Oprah's sweep through Georgia." *Los Angeles Times* (February 16): Calendar 1.

Rosenthal, P. 1994. "Ratings soar as Ricki Lake adjusts to fame." *Minneapolis Star-Tribune* (November 24): 24E.

———. 2003. "Her authentic self tells Oprah to stay on till '08." *Chicago Sun-Times* (May 7): 69.

Ross, S. 1996. "Experts disagree on the impact of new welfare law." *St. Louis Post-Dispatch* (August 26): 12.

Rothenberg, R. 1984. *The neoliberals.* New York: Simon and Schuster.

Rothstein, E. 2004. "Political self-celebration in a library guise." *New York Times* (November 25): B1, B7.

Rubin, S. 2000. "Oxygen—a new cable channel aimed at women—gets ready for lift-off." *San Francisco Chronicle* (January 26): B1.

Rubinstein, L. 1987. "Oprah! Thriving on faith." *McCalls* (August): 137–138.

Rudolph, I. "The truth behind Oprah's school scandal." *TV Guide* (November 9), http://www.tvguide.com/news/oprah-winfrey-scandal/071109-04 (accessed November 18, 2007).

Russo, A. 2006. "How to translate 'Cultural Revolution.'" *Inter-Asia Cultural Studies* 7 (4): 673–682.

Russo, N., ed. 1985. *A woman's mental health agenda.* Washington, DC: American Psychological Association.

Ryan, J. 1996. "Losing yourself on Oprah." *San Francisco Chronicle* (April 21): 10.

Salkin, A. 2007. "Shaking riches out of the cosmos." *New York Times* (February 25), http://www.nytimes.com/2007/02/25/fashion/25attration.html/ (accessed February 26, 2007).

Salvino, D. 1989. "Ideologies of race and literacy in antebellum America." In *Reading in America,* ed. C. Davidson, 140–158. Baltimore: Johns Hopkins University Press.

Sampson, E. E. 1981. "Cognitive psychology as ideology." *American Psychologist* 36: 730–743.

Samuels, A. 2007. "Oprah Winfrey's lavish South African school." *Newsweek* (January 8), http://www.msnbc.msn.com/id/16396343/site/newsweek/print/1/displaymode/1098/ (accessed January 30, 2007).

Samuelson, R. J. 1996. "'Bowling alone' is bunk." *Washington Post* (April 10): A19.

Sanger, D. E. 1995. "Fault lines. The big one: Washington's political earthquake; seismic shift in the parties reflects view on business." *New York Times* (September 24): Sec. 4, 1.

Sapiro, V., and D. T. Canon. 2000. "Race, gender, and the Clinton presidency." In *The Clinton legacy,* eds. C. Campbell and B. Rockman, 169–199. New York: Chatham House Publishers.

Sarason, S. B. 1981. "An asocial psychology and a misdirected clinical psychology." *American Psychologist* 36: 826–836.

Satter, B. 1999. *Each mind a kingdom: American women, sexual purity, and the New Thought movement, 1875–1920.* Berkeley: University of California Press.

Sawicki, J. 1991. *Disciplining Foucault: feminism, power, and the body.* New York: Routledge.

Schaef, A. W. 1987. *When society becomes an addict.* San Francisco: Harper and Row.

Schaeffer, T. E. 1997. "Boycott Oprah's book club to protect literary variety." *Houston Chronicle* (September 22): A23.

Schell, J. 1999. "Master of all he surveys." (Review.) *Nation* (June 21): 25.

Schier, S. E., ed. 2000. *The postmodern presidency: Bill Clinton's legacy in U.S. politics.* Pittsburgh: University of Pittsburgh Press.

Schlesinger, A., Jr. 1986a. "Election aftermath: money and meaning." *Wall Street Journal* (November 18): 1.

———. 1986b. "For Democrats, me-too Reaganism will spell disaster." *New York Times* (July 6): E13.

Schlosser, J. 2000. "Tough spring for 'Springer.'" *Broadcasting and Cable* (May 1): 71.

Schmitt, J. 2005. *How good is the economy at creating good jobs?* Washington, DC: Center for Economic and Policy Research, http://www.cepr.net/documents/publications/labor_markets_2005_10.pdf (accessed August 28, 2007).

Schneider, W. 1998a. "No modesty please, we're the DLC." *National Journal* 30 (50) (December 12): 2962.

———. 1998b. "To the 'new rich,' Bill's OK." *National Journal* 30 (46) (November 14): 2746.

Schorow, S. 1994. "Tattle tales, unauthorized Oprah bio tells all—there's just not much to tell." *Boston Herald* (October 20): 45.

Schorr, D. 1993. "Behind the 'politics of meaning.'" *Christian Science Monitor* (June 21): 18.

Schwartz, A. 1996. "Will Oprah save the book?" *Washington Post* (December 15): C7.

Scott, J., and D. Leonhardt. 2005. "Class in America: shadowy lines that still divide." *New York Times* (May 15), http://proquest.umi.com/pqdweb?did=839712251&sid=3&Fmt=3&clientid=56281&RQT=309&VName=PQD (accessed August 7, 2007).

Scull, A. 1989. *Social order/mental disorder.* Berkeley: University of California Press.

Seelye, K. Q. 2007. "The Oprah party wants you." *New York Times* (December 2): Sunday Styles, 1, 9.

Sellers, P. 2002. "The business of being Oprah." *Fortune* (April 1): 50–54, 58, 60–61, 64.

———, A. Harrington, and M. Shanley. 2003. "The fifty most powerful women in American business." *Fortune* (October 13): 103.

Shattuc, J. 1997. *The talking cure.* New York: Routledge.

Sherrill, M. 1993. "Hillary Clinton's inner politics." *Washington Post* (May 16): D1.

Sherrill, R. 1998. "Preachers to power." *Nation* (July 13): 11–14.

"A shining star named Oprah." 1994. *Chicago Sun-Times* (September 15): 29.

Showalter, E. 1987. *A female malady.* London: Virago.

Shribman, D. M. 1998. "Past Clinton, on middle road." *Boston Globe* (September 22): A3.

Siegel, F. 1991. "Waiting for Lefty." *Dissent* (Spring): 175–180.

Siegel, L. 2006. "The strange genius of Oprah." *New Republic Online* (June 12), http://www. tnr.com/doc.mhtml?i=20060612&s=siegel1206/ (accessed July 2, 2007).

Silverstein, K. 2006. "Barack Obama, inc." *Harper's Magazine* (November): 31–40.

Simonds, W. 1992. *Women and self-help culture.* New Brunswick, NJ: Rutgers University Press.

Sinker, R. P. 1997. "My case of Oprah envy: she's got America reading—and critics weeping." *Washington Post* (April 6): Outlook C1.

Sirota, D. 2006. "Mr. Obama goes to Washington." *Nation* (June 26): 20–23.

Skinner, D. 2000a. "George W. Bush gets the Oprah gig right, all the way down to the tears." *Salon* (September 20), http://www.salon.com/politics/feature/2000/09/20/oprah/print. html/ (accessed March 2, 2001).

———. 2000b. "Gore's soft sell on 'Oprah.'" *Salon* (September 12), http://www.salon/com/ politics.feature/2000/09/12/oprah/index/html?sid-979149/ (accessed June 16, 2004).

Sklar, M. 1988. *The corporate reconstruction of American capitalism, 1890–1916.* Cambridge, UK: Cambridge University Press.

Sloven, J. 1991. "Codependent or empathically responsive? In *Feminism and addiction,* ed. C. Bepko, 195–210. New York: Haworth Press.

Smalley, S. 2002. "All she needs is a miracle." *Newsweek* (September): 10.

Smith, B. 2000. "Oprah inspires a large turnout; growth summit hits Chicago." *Chicago Sun-Times* (June 27): 1.

Smith, J. 1997. "The ideology of 'family and community': New Labour abandons the welfare state." In *Socialist register 1997,* ed. L. Panitch, 176–196. London: Merlin Press.

Smith, L. 1995. "Oprah exhales." *Good Housekeeping* (October): 120, 185–187, 192.

Smith, P. 1997. *Millennial dreams.* London: Verso.

Smith, P. H. 1999. "'Self-help,' black conservatives, and the reemergence of black privatism." In *Without justice for all,* ed. A. Reed, Jr., 257–290. Boulder, CO: Westview Press.

Smith, R. 1999. "Toward a more perfect union: beyond old liberalism and neoliberalism." In *Without justice for all,* ed. A. Reed, Jr., 327–352. Boulder, CO: Westview Press.

Smith, R. C. 1986. "She once trashed her apartment to make a point." *TV Guide* (August 30): 30–31.

Smokler, K. 2002. "The lesson of Oprah's book club." Alternet (April 12), http://www. alternet.org/print.html?StoryID=12806/ (accessed April 12, 2002).

Smoron, P. 2000. "All the Oprah you could want." *Chicago Sun-Times* (April 18): 6.

Soltow, L., and E. Stevens. 1981. *The rise of literacy and common school in the United States.* Chicago: University of Chicago Press.

Southwell, D. 2000. "Oprah offers more than talk; Roosevelt students hear spiritual speech." *Chicago Sun-Times* (May 22): 3.

Span, P. 1996. "The retiring titan of talk." *Washington Post* (May 3): D2.

Squire, C. 1994. "Empowering women? *The Oprah Winfrey Show.*" *Feminism and Psychology* 4 (1): 63–79.

Stacey, J. 1990a. *Brave new families.* New York: Basic Books.

———. 1990b. "Sexism by a subtler name?" In *Women, class, and the feminist imagination,* eds. K. V. Hansen and I. J. Philipson, 338–355. Philadelphia: Temple University Press.

Stack, P. F. 2002. "Spirit guide: Oprah turns rituals into a 'religion.'" *Salt Lake Tribune* (November 2): A1.

Stanfield, R. L. 1992. "Rethinking federalism." *National Journal* (October 3): 2255–2257.

Stanley, A. 2005a. "Oh, Oprah, 20 years of talk, causes, and self-improvement." *New York Times* (November 15): B1, B7.

————. 2005b. "Oprah, no diva she, accepts an apology from Hermes." *New York Times* (September 20): C22.

Starker, S. 1986. "Promises and prescriptions: self-help books in mental health and medicine." *American Journal of Health Promotion* 1 (2) (Fall): 19–24, 68.

————. 1988. *Oracle at the supermarket: the American preoccupation with self-help books.* New Brunswick, NJ: Transaction Publishers.

"Statement from Oprah Winfrey." 2007. *Boston Globe Online* (January 20), http://www.boston. com/news/world/africa/articles/2007/01/20/statement_from_oprah_winfrey?mode=PF (accessed January 30, 2007).

Steinhorn, L., and B. Diggs-Brown. 1999. *By the color of our skin.* New York: Dutton.

Stevens, M. 1996. "Cold reality of welfare reform." *Chicago Sun-Times* (August 28): 45.

Steyn, M. 1998. "Comic Oprah." *National Review* (March 23): 30–33.

Stieglitz, J. E. 2003. "Bush's tax plan—the dangers." *New York Review of Books* (March 13): 13–15.

Stodghill, R. 1998. "Daring to go there." *Time* (October 5): 80–82.

"Stop the tour with Obama. *Oprah.com Message Boards.* http://www.oprah.com/community/ thread/10292?tstart=0&start=0. (accessed January 2, 2008).

Strauss, R. 1995. "Why is everybody talking?" *Los Angeles Times* (October 1): California 4.

Street, P. 2005. "The full blown 'Oprah effect': reflections on color, class, and new age racism." *Black Commentator* (February 24), http://www.blackcommentator.com/ (accessed July 20, 2005).

————. 2007. "The Obama illusion." *Z Magazine Online* (February), http://zmagsite.zmag. org/Feb2007/streetpr0207.html (accessed August 18, 2007).

Streitfield, D. 1997. "Frappucino and fiction to go? Starbuck's plans to sell Oprah's book club selections." *Washington Post* (May 28): C1.

Striphas, T. 2003. "A dialectic with the everyday: communication and cultural politics on Oprah Winfrey's book club." *Critical Studies in Media Communication* 20 (3) (September): 295–316.

"Study finds gap in wages and housing costs." 2004. *New York Times* (December 12): A12.

Subby, R. 1990. *Healing the family within.* Deerfield Beach, FL: Health Communications.

Sub-Saharan Africa. Regional fact sheet from the world development indicators. 2007. World Bank, http://siteresources.worldbank.org/DATASTATISTICS/Resources/ssa_wdi.pdf (accessed July 2, 2007).

"Survey: mental illness strikes 48% of U.S. population." 1994. *Minneapolis Star-Tribune* (January 14): 1A, 15A.

Suskind, R. 2004. "Without a doubt." *New York Times Magazine* (October 17): 44–51, 64, 102, 106.

Sweeney, A. 2000. "Winfrey honored, lends her name to research fund." *Chicago Sun-Times* (October 30): 9.

Sweet, L. 2007. "It's party time!" *Chicago Sun-Times online,* http://www.suntimes.com/news/ sweet/472624,CST-NWS-sweetob18.article (accessed August 12, 2007).

"Syndication watch." 2000. *Broadcasting and Cable* (October 2): 25.

"Syndication wrap-up." 2000a. *Broadcasting and Cable* (May 1): 71.

————. 2000b. *Broadcasting and Cable* (May 22): 35.

Tabb, W. 2003. "After neoliberalism?" *Monthly Review* 55 (2) (June): 25–33.

"Take a deep breath, Oxygen is here." 2000. *Guardian* (London) (January 31): 9.

Tallen, B. S. 1990. "Co-dependency: a feminist critique." *Sojourner: The Women's Forum* (January): 20–21.

Taraborrelli, J. R. 1997. "The change that has made Oprah so happy." *Redbook* (May): 94.

Tatalovich, R., and J. Frendreis. 2000. "Clinton, class, and economic policy." In *The postmodern presidency*, ed. S. Schier, 41–59. Pittsburgh: University of Pittsburgh Press.

Taylor, L. 2002. "The church of O." *Christianity Today* (April 1): 38–46.

Taylor, S. L., and K. Burns. 2007. "Oprah opens school for girls in South Africa." *Essence* (January 2), http://www.essence.com/essence/print/0,14882,1573448,00.html/ (accessed February 20, 2007).

Teepen, T. 1995. "Democrats cower from welfare fight." *Austin* (TX) *American Statesman* (September 29): A15.

"Television." 1991. *Ebony* (August): 50, 52.

"Television notes." 2002. *St. Louis Post-Dispatch* (February 21): TV E6.

Thompson, B. 2005. "Oprah's imprint on one man's memoir." *Washington Post* (September 24): C1.

Thorn, P. 2002. "The world of literature still turns without Oprah." *Denver Rocky Mountain News* (April 20): 3E.

Tillotson, K. 2001. "Oprah's 'girlfriend' talk inspires, beguiles." *Minneapolis Star-Tribune* (June 18): 5B.

Toner, R. 2004a. "Kerry message begins leaning toward center." *New York Times* (June 25): A1, A18.

———. 2004b. "Southern Democrats decline is eroding the political center." *New York Times* (November 15): A1, A14.

———. 2005. "Democrats are advised to broaden appeal." *New York Times* (October 7): A22.

Torpey-Kemph, A. 1998. "Media notes: news of the market." *Mediaweek* (September 28), http://www.lexis-nexis.com/.

Tough, P. 2007. "The class-consciousness raiser." *New York Times Magazine* (June 10): 52–56.

Travis, T. 2005. "Rationalization and re-enchantment in Oprah's Book Club. Unpublished manuscript.

———. 2007. "It will change the world if everybody reads this book: new thought religion in Oprah's book club." *American Quarterly* 59 (3) (September): 1017–1041.

Treacher, A., and G. Baruch. 1980. "Towards a critical history of the psychiatric profession." In *Critical psychiatry*, ed. D. Ingleby, 120–149. New York: Pantheon.

Trebbe, A. 1989. "Oprah's guy moves to Chicago." *USA Today* (September 27): 2D.

Trine, R. W. 1897. *In tune with the infinite*. New York: Crowell.

Turkle, S. 1980. "French anti-psychiatry." In *Critical psychiatry*, ed. D. Ingleby, 150–183. New York: Pantheon.

"TV news and notes: Oprah signs new contract through 2003–2004 season." 2000. *Atlanta Journal-Constitution* (November 3): 5E.

"TV short." 1998. *St. Petersburg Times* (October 21): Floridian 5D.

"Twenty and O." 2005. *People* (November 28): 248–250, 252.

Tyson, J. L. 1995. "Welfare and the rural poor." *Christian Science Monitor* (April 25): 3.

Uchitelle, L. 2004. "Layoff rate at 8.7%, highest since 80s." *New York Times* (August 2): C2.

———. 2005. "For blacks, a dream in decline." *New York Times* (October 23): Sec. 4, 1, 3.

———. 2006. *The disposable American: layoffs and their consequences*. New York: Alfred A. Knopf.

————. 2007. "The richest of the rich, proud of a new gilded age." *New York Times* (July 15): 1, 18–19.

"Uh O! Self-help us all." 2000. *Toronto Star* (April 22), http://www.lexis-nexis.com/.

Ulrich, C. W. 2006. "The Oprah effect: the $1.4 billion woman influences pop culture, creates stars, and drives entire industries." *Essence* (October): 190.

United Nations Development Programme. 2006. "Beyond scarcity: power, poverty, and the global water crisis. South Africa." http://hdr.undp.org/hdr2006/statistics/countries/data_sheets/cty_ds_ZAF.html (accessed August 1, 2007).

United States Census Bureau. 2003. "Weighted average poverty threshholds for nonfarm families, by size, 1959–2002." *Annual Statistical Supplement, 2003.* Table 3.E1, p. 3.10. http://www.ssa.gov/policy/docs/statcomps/supplement/2003/3e.pdf/ (accessed January 29, 2005).

United States Department of Health and Human Services. 2005. "Prior HHS poverty guidelines and federal register references" (January 4), http://aspe.hhs.gov/poverty/figures-fed-reg.shtml/ (accessed January 29, 2005).

Usborne, D. 2000. "Seen the show, watched the movie? Now read the magazine. It's what the US has been waiting for: the gospel according to Oprah." *Independent* (London) (April 18): 8.

VandenBos, G., P. DeLeon, and C. Belar. 1991. "How many psychological practitioners are needed? It's too early to know." *Professional Psychology: Research and Practice* 22 (6): 441–448.

Van Der Pijl, K. 2006. "A Lockean Europe?" *New Left Review* (January–February): 9–37.

Vidal, G. 2004. "State of the Union, 2004." *Nation* (September 13), http://www.thenation.com/doc/20040913/vidal/ (accessed September 17, 2005).

Waldron, R. 1987. *Oprah!* New York: St. Martin's Press.

Walsh, S. 2000. "Oxygen loses some of its air." *Industry Standard* (August 21), http://lexis-nexis.com/.

Wang, H. 2006a. "Depoliticized politics from east to west." *New Left Review* 41 (September–October): 29–45.

————. 2006b. "Depoliticized politics, multiple components of hegemony, and the eclipse of the sixties." *Inter-Asia Cultural Studies* 7 (4): 682–700.

Wapnick, K. 1989. *A talk given on* A Course in Miracles. Roscoe, NY: Foundation for a Course in Miracles.

Ward, B. 2000. "Oh no: all Oprah, all the time." *Ottawa Citizen* (April 29): Style E10.

Warner, M. 1990. *The letters of the republic.* Cambridge, MA: Harvard University Press.

Wartzman, R., and H. Stout. 1995. "Clinton asks Congress to pass welfare reform by July." *Wall Street Journal* (April 20): 6.

Washington, L. 2007. "Black pols see Obama as threat to their clout." *Chicago Sun-Times* (January 29): 35.

Wavell, S. 2002. "All he wants is a hugs-and-kisses economy." *Times* (London) (January 6), http://www.lexis-nexis.com/.

Waxman, S. 1998. "'Beloved' is a tough sell; filmgoers favor light fare over story of slavery." *Washington Post* (November 11): D1..

Weaver, R. K., R. Y. Shapiro, and L. R. Jacobs. 1995. "The polls—trends: welfare." *Public Opinion Quarterly* (59): 606–627.

Wegscheider-Cruse, S. 1984. *Co-dependency: an emerging issue.* Pompano Beach, FL: Health Communications.

Weitzman, L. J. 1985. *The divorce revolution.* New York: Free Press.

"Welfare and punishment in the Bush era." 2001. *Social Justice* 28 (1) (Spring): 1–2.

"Welfare watershed." 1996. *Cleveland Plain Dealer* (August 1): 10B.

White, M. 1992. *Tele-advising: therapeutic discourse in American television.* Chapel Hill: University of North Carolina Press.

"White House race takes a feminine feel: from 'Oprah' to 'Regis,' candidates court women, who may make up 61 percent of undecided voters." 2000. *Christian Science Monitor* (September 25): 3.

"Who will be on the cover of Oprah's magazine next?" 2000. *Toronto Star* (October 16): Entertainment section. http://www.lexis-nexis.com/.

Wicker, T. 1981. "Democrats in search of ideas." *New York Times Magazine* (January 25): 30–31, 34, 38–41.

Wieseltier, L. 1993. "Total quality meaning: notes toward a definition of Clintonism." *New Republic* (July 19): 16–18.

Will, G. 1996. "Surrendering his way to strength." *Washington Post* (January 25): A25.

Williams, A. 1995. *Beyond blame.* New York: Free Press.

———. 1998. "Oprah's slavery film is for all viewers." *USA Today* (October 16): 15A.

———. 2005. "Armstrong Williams Biography." http://armstrongwilliams.com/ (accessed July 7, 2005).

Williams, B. 1999. "The great family fraud of postwar America." In *Without justice for all,* ed. A. Reed, Jr., 65–89. Boulder, CO: Westview Press.

Williams, J. B. 1995. "Review of *Rethinking Social Policy* by C. Jencks." *Perspectives on Political Science* 24 (4) (Fall): 219.

Williams, M. E. 1999a. "She's all chat." *Salon* (May 4), http://www.salon.com/people/be/1999/05/04/oprah/index.html/ (accessed March 2, 2001).

———. 1999b. "Silence the snobs!" *Salon* (November 12), http://www.salon.com/books/feature/1999/11/12/oprahpro/ (accessed March 5, 2001).

Williams, P. 2007. "The Audacity of Oprah." *Nation Online* (December 24). http://www.thenation.com/doc/20071224/williams. (accessed December 22, 2007).

Williams, Raymond. 1977. *Marxism and literature.* Oxford, UK: Oxford University Press.

Williams, Richard. 1986. *They stole it, but you must return it.* Rochester, NY: HEMA Publications.

Williamson, M. 1992. *A return to love.* New York: HarperCollins.

———. 1995. *Illuminata.* New York: Riverhead Trade.

———. 1997. *The healing of America.* New York: Simon and Schuster.

———. 2002. "Rising to the call: remembering 9/11." Renaissance Alliance (September 11), http://renaissancealliance.org/imagine/Healing/remeb911.htm/ (accessed December 31, 2002).

Wills, G. 2004. "The day the enlightenment went out." *New York Times* (November 4), http://www.nytimes.com/2004/11/04/opinion/04wills.html/ (accessed November 6, 2004).

Wilson, C. 2001. "O sister, where art thou? Buying 'O' Winfrey's touch sparks nearly overnight success for magazine." *USA Today* (January 18): 10D.

Wilson, W. J. 1987. *The truly disadvantaged.* Chicago: University of Chicago Press.

Winfrey, O. 2000. "Inner revolution." *Zukav.com* (January 15), http://www/zukav.com/frames/guest_20000115.htm/ (accessed March 5, 2001).

———. 2007. "What I know for sure." *O, The Oprah Magazine* (January): 218.

"Winfrey-aided poverty effort is in trouble." 1996. *Peoria* (IL) *Journal Star* (August 28): A11.

"Winfrey opens African school." 2007. *Chicago Tribune* (January 3), http://www.chicagotribune.com/news/nationworld/chi-0701030052jan03,1,316315,print.story?coll=chi-newsnationworld-hed&ctrack=1&cset=true/ (accessed February 20, 2007).

"Winfrey's spiritual entourage." 2000. *Chicago Sun-Times* (April 18): 6.

"Winning the presidency." 2004. *San Jose* (CA) *Mercury News* (October 24): 20A.

Withorn, A. 1996. "'Why do they hate me so much?' A history of welfare and its abandonment in the United States." *American Journal of Orthopsychiatry* 66 (4) (October): 496–509.

Woititz, J. G. 1983. *Adult children of alcoholics.* Pompano Beach, FL: Health Communications.

Wolffe, R. 2007. "Can Obama's substance match his style?" *MSNBC.com Newsweek online* (May 7), http://www.msnbc.com/id/18367799/site/newsweek/page/0/ (accessed August 19, 2007).

Wood, L.A. 1988. "Self-help bying trends." *Publishers Weekly* (October 14): 33.

Wood, L. 1998. "Voices of 30-plus exclaim: can we talk?" *Advertising Age* (October 14): S6–7.

Word of Mouth. 2005. "Letter to Oprah Winfrey," http://wordofmouthwriters.org (accessed May 1, 2005).

Wright, Sharon D. 2000. "Clinton and racial politics." In *The postmodern presidency*, ed. S. Schier, 223–237. Pittsburgh: University of Pittsburgh Press.

Wyatt, E. 2005. "Oprah's book club reopening to writers who'll sit and chat." *New York Times* (September 23): A1.

———. 2006. "Live on 'Oprah,' a memoirist is kicked out of the book club." *New York Times* (January 27): A1, A13.

Wypijewski, J. 2004. "The instructive history of Jackson's rainbow." In *Dime's worth of difference*, eds. A. Cockburn and J. St. Clair, 73–92. Petrolia, CA: CounterPunch.

Zavarzadeh, M. 1991. *Seeing films politically.* Albany: State University of New York Press.

Zeleny, J. 2007. "Oprah Winfrey hits campaign trail to boost Obama." *New York Times* (December 9): 31.

Zinn, M. B. 1990. "Minority families in crisis." In *Women, class, and the feminist imagination*, eds. K. V. Hansen and I. J. Philipson, 363–379. Philadelphia: Temple University Press.

Index

MEDIA&POWER

Media and Power
David L. Paletz, Series Editor
Duke University

Paradigm Publishers is proud to announce a new book series that publishes work uniting media studies with studies of power.

In keeping with Paradigm's mission, the series is innovative and original. It features books that challenge, even transcend, conventional disciplinary boundaries, construing both media and power in the broadest possible terms. At the same time, books in the series are designed to fit into several different types of college courses: in political science, public policy, communication, journalism, media, history, film, sociology, anthropology, and cultural studies.

Intended for the scholarly, text, and trade markets, the series should attract authors and inspire and provoke readers. Series editor David L. Paletz is Professor of Political Science and Director of the Film/Video/Digital Program at Duke University, and former editor of *Political Communication*. He is known for his research on media and power and his encouragement of original work from others.

About the Author

Janice Peck is Associate Professor at the University of Colorado in the School of Journalism and Mass Communication. Her research and teaching focus on contemporary and historical intersections of media, culture, and politics. Peck is the author of a book on religious television titled, *The Gods of Televangelism* (1993), and has published on media theory, television and the family, cultural studies, TV talk shows, Oprah's Book Club, advertising, and representations of race in media. She is currently working on a study of the political implications of the rise of "social entrepreneurship" and celebrity-driven philanthropy. Peck has worked as a journalist, editor, and free-lance writer for newspapers, magazines, and radio.